The New Handbook of Children's Rights

The New Handbook of Children's Rights provides up-to-date information on a topic of increasing importance across a range of disciplines and practices. It covers:

- the debate concerning children's rights and developments in rights provision over the last twenty years
- the impact of recent British legislation on children's rights in key areas such as education, social and welfare services and criminal justice
- the key provisions of the UN Convention on the Rights of the Child and Human Rights Act and their implications for children and young people
- recent policy proposals and initiatives in the British setting intended to establish and promote rights for children and young people
- the rights claims of particular groups of children, for example children who are carers or children who are disabled
- children's claims for particular rights such as the right to space, to sex education and citizenship
- the ways in which the voices of children and young people are or might be articulated more clearly in policy debates and other arenas
- issues and developments in Australia, Belgium, Scandinavia and China

The New Handbook of Children's Rights offers a comprehensive and radical appraisal of the field which will be invaluable to students and professionals alike.

Bob Franklin works in the Department of Sociological Studies at the University of Sheffield.

The New Handbook of Children's Rights

Comparative policy and practice

Edited by Bob Franklin

London and New York

First published 2002
by Routledge
11 New Fetter Lane, London EC4P 4EE

Simultaneously published in the USA and Canada
by Routledge
29 West 35th Street, New York, NY 10001

Routledge is an imprint of the Taylor & Francis Group

Typeset in Times by Taylor & Francis Books Ltd
Printed and bound in Great Britain by The Cromwell Press,
Trowbridge, Wiltshire

British Library Cataloguing in Publication Data
A catalogue record for this book is available from the British Library

Library of Congress Cataloging in Publication Data
The new handbook of children's rights : comparative policy and
practice / edited by Bob Franklin. [2nd ed.]
Includes bibliographical references and index.
1. Children–Legal status, laws, etc.–Great Britain. I. Franklin, Bob.
II. Handbook of children's rights.

KD735 .N487   2001
323.3'52–dc21   2001031754

ISBN 0–415–25035–8 (hbk)
ISBN 0–415–25036–6 (pbk)

This book is dedicated to Annie Franklin: a formidable advocate of children's rights

Contents

Contributors

Priscilla Alderson is Professor of Childhood Studies at the Social Science Research Unit, Institute of Education, University of London. Publications include *Young Children's Rights: Exploring Beliefs, Principles and Practice* (2000), *Listening to Children: Children, Social Research and Ethics* (1995) and *Children's Consent to Surgery* (1993).

Jo Aldridge is a Senior Research Associate in the Young Carers Research Group, Department of Social Sciences, Loughborough University.

Monica Barry has been a Research Fellow at the University of Stirling's Social Work Research Centre since 1994, although between 1999 and 2000 she was employed by Save the Children to investigate the views and experiences of young people looked after in Scotland.

Saul Becker is Director of the Young Carers Research Group and a Senior Lecturer in Social Policy, Department of Social Sciences, Loughborough University.

Lesley Campbell is National Children's Officer at Mencap.

Mano Candappa is a Research Officer at the Thomas Coram Research Unit, Institute of Education, University of London. Her main research interests are in children and childhood, socially marginalised groups, and research methodology. Recent publications include, *Why Do They Have to Fight? Refugee Children's Stories from Bosnia, Kurdistan, Somalia and Sri Lanka* (1998) with Jill Rutter and "Building a new life: the role of the school in supporting refugee children", *Multicultural Teaching* (2000).

Vicki Coppock is Senior Lecturer in Social Policy and Social Work at Edge Hill College, Ormskirk, Lancashire. She has extensive professional experience as a mental health social worker in both child and adult mental health settings. She is co-author of *The Illusions of "Post-Feminism": New Women, Old Myths* (with Deena Haydon and Ingrid Richter) (1995); a major contributor to *"Childhood" in "Crisis"?* (Scraton, P. ed.) (1997);

and co-author of *Critical Perspectives on Mental Health* (with John Hopton) (2000).

Judith Ennew is a member of the Centre for Family Research at the University of Cambridge and Visiting Fellow in the Anthropology Department of Goldsmith's College, University of London. Since 1979, she has been an activist and researcher on children's rights, specialising in street and working children. Besides academic articles on this and related topics, she is the author of *Street and Working Children: A Guide to Planning*, which has been widely translated and was published in a second English edition by Save the Children UK in 2000.

Malfrid Grude Flekkøy is a clinical psychologist. She was Norwegian Ombudsman for Children 1981–9. She has also been a Senior Fellow, UNICEF, International Child Development Centre. Publications include *A Voice for Children. Speaking out as their Ombudsman* (1991), *A Framework for Children's Participation* (1999), *The Participation Rights of the Child: Rights and Responsibilities in Family and Society* (1998).

Jane Fortin is Reader in Law at King's College London. She writes widely on issues relating to child and family law and is joint editor of the *Child and Family Law Quarterly*. Her special interest in children's rights led her to write a book entitled *Children's Rights and the Developing Law* (1998) and various articles considering the implications of the Human Rights Act 1998 for children and their families.

Bob Franklin teaches and writes about media, communications and social policy in the Department of Sociological Studies at the University of Sheffield. He is the editor of *Journalism Studies*. Publications include *Social Policy, the Media and Misrepresentation* (1999), *Hard Pressed: National Newspaper Reporting of Social Services* (1998) and *The Rights of Children* (1986).

Michael Freeman is Professor of English Law, University College London. He is author of *The Rights and Wrongs of Children*, *The Moral Status of Children* (1997), and editor of the *International Journal of Children's Rights*.

Deena Haydon is a Principal Officer for Research and Development at Barnardos and a Research Fellow at the Centre for Studies in Crime and Social Justice at Edge Hill University College. Formerly a primary school teacher and Senior Lecturer in Education and Childhood Studies, she is a co-author of *The Illusions of "Post-Feminism": New Women, Old Myths*, (1995), *Getting Personal* (1996) and *Citizenship and Personal, Social and Health Education* (2000) schemes for Key Stage 2; and a contributor to *"Childhood" in "Crisis"?* (1997).

Tina Hyder is a Development Officer in Save the Children's Centre for Young Children's Rights. Tina worked in and managed community nurseries in London for more than twelve years. Since joining Save the Children she has written articles and publications on a range of issues concerning equality and children's rights. She is co-author of *It Hurts You Inside: Children Talking About Smacking* (Save the Children and the National Children's Bureau) and *Refugee Children in the Early Years: Issues for Policy Makers and Providers* (Refugee Council and Save the Children).

Tony Jeffs teaches in the Community and Youth Work Studies Unit, Department of Sociology and Social Policy at the University of Durham. He is an editor of *Youth and Policy*.

Perpetua Kirby is a freelance researcher and visiting research fellow at the Social Science Research Centre, South Bank University. Previously she was a Research Adviser at Save the Children and undertook research at the Universities of Manchester and Staffordshire. She works predominantly with children and young people, and much of her work focuses on participatory practice. Perpetua has recently authored a manual on participatory research with young people, published by the Joseph Rowntree Foundation, entitled *Involving Young Researchers: How to Enable Young People to Design and Conduct Research* (1999).

Gerison Lansdown is a freelance writer and researcher in the field of children's rights. She was the founder director of the Children's Rights Development Unit, now the Children's Rights Alliance for England, established to promote implementation of the UN Convention on the Rights of the Child. She has published and lectured widely on the subject of children's rights, both nationally and internationally. She is on the executive boards of Liberty, the Children's Discovery Centre in east London and the UK Committee for UNICEF. She works as a consultant for UNICEF's Innocenti Research Centre in Florence.

Virginia Morrow is Senior Research Fellow at the Gender Institute at the London School of Economics. She has conducted research into English secondary school children's involvement in work (broadly defined); carried out a study of children's conceptualisations of "family", funded by Joseph Rowntree Foundation, and published as *Understanding Families: Children's Perspectives* (1998).

John Muncie is Senior Lecturer in Criminology and Social Policy at the Open University. He has published widely and extensively in criminology, youth studies and youth justice. His most recent publications include: *Youth and Crime: A Critical Introduction* (1999), *The Problem of Crime* (2001), *Controlling Crime* (2001) and *Criminological Perspectives* (1996).

Peter Newell is Co-ordinator of EPOCH – End Physical Punishment of Children and of EPOCH-WORLDWIDE, an informal network of over 70 organisations in 40 states campaigning to end all corporal punishment of children. He chairs the Council of the Children's Rights Alliance for England and is Adviser to the European Network of Ombudspeople for Children (ENOC).

Moira Rayner is Director of the Office of the Children's Rights Commissioner for London. Previously she chaired the Board of the National Children's and Youth Law Centre in Sydney, NSW; was a Hearings Commissioner of the Australian Human Rights and Equal Opportunity Commission, Commissioner for Equal Opportunity for Victoria, and Chair of the Western Australian Law Reform Commission. Her publications include *The A–Z of Children's Rights* (2002), *The Women's Power Pocketbook*, with Joan Kirner (2001), *Resilient Children and Young People*, with Meg Montague (1999), *Rooting Democracy: Growing the Society We Want* (1997) and *The Commonwealth's Role in Preventing Child Abuse* (1995).

Jeremy Roche is based at the School of Health and Social Welfare at the Open University. He has written widely on children's rights and the law and is co-editor (with Stanley Tucker) of *Youth in Society* (1997) and (with Pam Foley and Stanley Tucker) *Children in Society* (2001).

Carole Scott is a sixth form teacher and tutor in a large city boys' comprehensive school and coordinator for gifted and talented students in the sixth form (Key Stage 5).

Ankie Vandekerckhove is Children's Rights Commissioner for the Flemish Community in Belgium. She also chairs the European Network of Ombudspersons for Children (ENOC).

Andy West has been a museum curator, youth worker, counsellor and advice worker and university lecturer. Research has included facilitating children's and young people's own research in Britain and Bangladesh. He has worked for short periods in Bangladesh, Thailand and Vietnam, and for two years as a child welfare adviser in China. Publications include a range of book chapters and journal articles on children, young people, and on material culture and ethnographic museum collections.

Stephanie Williams chairs the charity Children's Express, which she set up in the UK in 1995. A journalist and editor, she has written extensively on architecture and environment for numerous titles, ranging from *Apollo* and the *Architectural Review* to *The Sunday Times*, *The Independent*, *Wall Street Journal*, *New Statesman* and *The South China Morning Post*. She is the author of *Hongkong Bank* (1989) and *Docklands*, (1990, 1993) and is currently working on a book based in Siberia during the Russian Civil War.

Children's rights

An introduction

Bob Franklin

Twelve days into the new Bush administration, the leader of the American delegation to the UN General Assembly Special Session on Children launched a "blistering attack" on children's economic, welfare and cultural rights. Ambassador Southwick suggested that "the human rights based approach, while laudable in its objectives, poses significant problems" (CRIN, 2 February 2001). Turning specifically to the UN Convention on the Rights of the Child, Southwick stated that "The United States does not accept obligations based on it nor do we accept that it is the best or only framework for developing programmes and policies to benefit children" (ibid.). Given these sentiments, it is perhaps unsurprising that America together with Somalia remain the only two countries in the world which have failed to ratify the Convention. The Ambassador's uncompromising rejection of the Convention highlights the fragility of any policy consensus to resolve the problems confronting children and young people in the emerging global economy and society. But these problems are considerable and growing. Children's most basic rights to drinking water, food, shelter and even the right to life are being denied on a scale which is alarming.

A quarter of the world's children live in poverty. Childhood and poverty go together. In poorer countries such as Angola, which the UN claims is the worst place in the world to be a child, children under 15 constitute 48 per cent of the population. Globally, an estimated 120 million children aged 5–14 work full time while a further 130 million work part time. More than 130 million of the 625 million children of primary school age in developing countries have no access to basic education. 183 million of the world's children weigh less than they should for their age, 158 million children under 5 are malnourished, 800 million lack access to health services and, in the poorest countries, preventable diseases such as diarrhoea kill 2 million children every year (UNICEF, 1998).

Children, moreover, face very different futures. Globalisation seems increasingly to create a dualistic world characterised by divergence rather than any convergence in children's material circumstances. While

Americans spend $5 billions each year on special diets to lower their calorie consumption ... the world's poorest 400 million people are so under-nourished they are likely to suffer stunted growth, mental retardation or death. As water from a single spring in France is bottled and shipped to the prosperous around the world, 1.9 billion people drink and bathe in water contaminated with deadly parasites and pathogens ... In 1988 the world's nations devoted $1 trillion – $200 for each person on the planet – to the means of warfare, but failed to scrape together the $5 per child it would have cost to eradicate the diseases that killed 14 millions that year.

(Durning, 1992: 37)

In Sub-Saharan Africa, 173 in every 1,000 children born die before their fifth birthday: in the rich northern countries the equivalent figure is six per 1,000 (UNICEF, 2000).

More parochially, evidence from the UK sounds appropriately cautionary notes warning against undue optimism concerning the circumstances of children and young people. A "Manifesto", signed by 50 children's charities and published by NSPCC, Barnardos and the Child Poverty Action Group, revealed that while children and young people under 18 constitute one-quarter of the population (approximately 15 million people) "their rights and well being are rarely given the priority they deserve" (NSPCC, 2000: 3). The problems children confront are acute. One in three children in the UK lives in poverty and this figure has doubled since 1979 (Bradshaw, 2000: 2). Twenty-six per cent of recorded rape victims are children, 4,000 children are placed on child protection registers each year, and more than 40,000 children a year are killed or injured in road accidents. The litany of childhood suffering is considerable. Twenty per cent of children and adolescents in the UK suffer some form of mental health problem, 75 per cent of looked after children leave school without any formal qualifications, African-Caribbean children are six times more likely to be excluded from school than other children, half of all disabled children and their families live in unsuitable accommodation, one in five 16–25-year-olds experiences homelessness, while young people leaving local authority care are a staggering 50 times more likely to spend time in prison, 60 times more likely to be homeless and 88 times more likely to be involved in drug use than their peers (NSPCC, 2000: 7–23). Children and young people in the UK do not, of course, enjoy the right to vote.

These figures are shocking as well as shaming and illustrate clearly that progress towards securing social, welfare and participation rights for children and young people has tended to be faltering and uneven rather than strident. The ambitions of the UN Convention have not been fully realised or translated into commonplace entitlements for children in the UK despite the government's ratification of the Convention a decade ago. But there have been significant developments in children's rights since *The Handbook of Children's Rights*, a precursor of the present volume, was published in 1995.

Children's rights: a brief progress report

Recent progress concerning children's rights in the UK can be grouped under five broad headings.

Intellectually, the discussion of children's rights has achieved a degree of respectability. Instead of being dismissed as "utopian nonsense" or mere "political correctness" the idea that children possess rights which adults should respect and help to promote now informs aspects of government policy and legislation, the policy of voluntary sector and charitable organisations as well as the practice of welfare professionals. In part this recently achieved respectability reflects a growing scholarly interest in the study of childhood, children and society. A burgeoning literature in this field has helped to popularise the emergence of a "new paradigm" concerning children and childhood (James and Prout, 1997, and Foley, Roche and Tucker, 2001). But the paradigm is not as "new" as is often claimed since the key assumptions which inform it have been influenced substantively by the work of early children's rights advocates such as John Holt (1975) and Richard Farson (1978): in turn, these assumptions have helped to shape the writings of more recent scholars such as Eugeen Verhellen (1999).

First, childhood is judged to be a social rather than a biological construct. Consequently childhood does not assume a universal form in all societies but differs reflecting particular class, gender, ethnic and other cultural relations. It follows that there are many, rather than a single, childhood(s) (Campbell, chapter 11; Candappa, chapter 13; Franklin, chapter 1; Haydon, chapter 10; Rayner, chapter 21 and West, chapter 20).

Second, children's social relationships are worthy of study, not merely as the construction of adults, but as the outcome of children who actively help to shape their own and others' social lives as well as the societies of which they are members (see Alderson, chapter 8; Aldridge and Becker, chapter 12; Barry, chapter 14; Morrow, chapter 9; Newell, chapter 23; Williams, chapter 15; and Hyder, chapter 19).

Third, ethnography provides a useful methodological approach to the study of childhood. It provides greater opportunities for children's participation and creates possibilities for a more direct voice for children in research than alternative research frameworks (Barry, chapter 14; Ennew, chapter 24 and Kirby, chapter 16). The emergence of this new paradigm has influenced scholarly theorising about children and childhood and has undoubtedly helped to shape popular opinion thereby securing a greater legitimacy for rights advocacy.

Politically, children's rights have become contested territory for mainstream political parties. The Liberal Democrats' election manifesto for 2001 retained the party's commitment to reducing the age of suffrage to 16.

Undoubtedly the most significant political development for children's rights has been the election of more "children friendly" Labour governments in 1997 and again in 2001. The government has raised family incomes by introducing a national minimum wage and through policies such as the working families tax credit. An estimated 1.5 million children have been lifted from poverty between 1998 and 2000 (CPAG, 2001). The establishment of a Cabinet Committee on Children and Young People's Services, and a Children and Young People's Unit in the Department for Education and Skills (DfES), with a remit to develop a cross-departmental approach to policy as well as administering the Children Fund (with £450 million to help to alleviate child poverty and social exclusion), offer further testament to government commitments to children. The introduction of the National Childcare Strategy and Quality Protects (with its strong recommendation that local authorities appoint a Children's Rights Officer for looked after children), combined with the establishment of the Social Exclusion Unit and a number of community initiatives such as Sure Start (designed to help pre-school children), have increased assistance to children and their families, especially in severely disadvantaged areas. The guidelines for the government's national childcare strategy, moreover, require childcare partnerships to state how they have sought and responded to very young children's views on their day care and education settings.

But any review of the Labour government's record must include brickbats alongside bouquets. Labour has reduced the number of children in poverty in recent years but the figures remain substantial for a country which ranks among the seven most industrialised nations in the world. Young people under the age of 22, moreover, are exempted from the adult minimum wage of £4.10. The centralisation of education, the imposition of national curricula and league tables and the privatising of certain aspects of education, are unlikely to promote children's participation rights or provide them with a voice in the running of their schools (Jeffs, chapter 2). Perhaps most significantly, New Labour's election promise to be "tough on crime and tough on the causes of crime", has regressed into a populist and authoritarian series of measures, such as curfews and electronic tagging. The Home Office, moreover, has fed a tabloid frenzy and encouraged public perceptions of young people as unruly, out of control and requiring policies which stress containment (Franklin, chapter 1; Muncie, chapter 4).

Legally, the paternalistic notion that the "best interests of the child" must be protected has increasingly come to be supplemented by the principle that children have a right to express their views and have their wishes taken into account in legal decisions which concern them. The Children Act 1989 carefully straddles the divide between protectionist (paternalist) and participatory rights. Its guiding principle is that "the child's welfare is paramount" but the legislation also supports the principle that, where possible and appropriate, the "ascertainable wishes and feelings of the child concerned" should inform decisions (Children Act, 1989: Section 1 (3) (a)). In truth the judiciary continue to interpret this latter requirement conservatively falling back on paternalistic assumptions of children's incompetence (see Roche, chapter 3 and Freeman, chapter 5).

The most significant legal development regarding children's rights is the incorporation of the European Convention on Human Rights into English domestic law in 1998 (The Human Rights Act) but this has been only fully operational since 2 October 2000. Some lawyers have interpreted the new Act as the most significant event in the history of English law: others have dismissed it as a "damp squib" (see Fortin, chapter 6; Freeman, chapter 5; Jeffs, chapter 2 and Muncie, chapter 4). The new system will empower children to apply to the domestic courts if they believe a government or public agency has infringed their rights as specified in the European Convention. If the court agrees with them, the government must put matters right through a "fast track" parliamentary procedure to bring the legislation in conformity with the Convention (Human Rights Act, 1998: Section 4(2), 10, Sch. 2 cited in chapter 6).

Institutionally, the development of organisations such as End Physical Punishment of Children (EPOCH) along with the appointment of more than fifty Children's Rights Officers in different local authorities offers testament to the growing commitment to children's rights (see Newell, chapter 23). The last decade has also witnessed a considerable growth in the number of ombudsmen or Children's Rights Commissioners. In Europe for example, there are commissioners in Austria, Belgium, Denmark, France, Hungary, Iceland, Norway, Portugal, Russian Federation, Spain and Sweden while proposals are being developed in Germany, Ireland, Latvia, Poland and Switzerland. Beyond Europe there are similar offices in Australia, Canada, Costa Rica, Guatemala, New Zealand, Philippines and South Africa (see Lansdown, chapter 17; Grude Flekkøy, chapter 25). The Belgian Children's Commissioner for the Flemish community reflects on the prospects for her new office, as well as some of the difficulties experienced in the early years of its operation in chapter 22 (Vandekerckhove).

In the UK, the recommendations of the Waterhouse report have been influential in creating a Children's Commissioner for Wales. In England in April 2000, the office of Children's Rights Commissioner for England was established on a three-year footing. Its brief is to promote respect for children's views and to represent children's perspectives on all aspects of London government. In 1999, a Children's Rights Commissioner was established in Oxfordshire to help ensure that the policy and practice of local services is informed by children's rights principles and to increase children's involvement in local government (see Lansdown, chapter 17).

A further development has been the emergence of a number of institutions to enhance citizenship in the local arena (Willow, 1997). Such developments reflect the UN Convention's emphasis (Article 12) on children's right to participate, but also the fact that children and young people are the major users of local government services such as schools, libraries, sport and leisure facilities, education, parks and public transport. Youth Councils and Youth Forums have been the typical institutional expression of this desire to increase young people's local involvement. Youth Councillors are usually elected by students attending schools in the local area. The Council then elects its own Chair, decides its own agenda, meets quarterly and feeds back decisions into the main City Council. (Geddes and Rust, 2000: 46–48). Such experiments in local democracy are inevitably open to criticisms of tokenism, but may yet offer a better education in citizenship than is promised in the government's Curriculum for Citizenship (see Scott, chapter 18).

Internationally, the UN Convention on the Rights of the Child has established a near global consensus (American and Somalian objections notwithstanding) concerning the minimum necessary rights for children: rights to provision, protection and participation - the 3 "Ps". The significance of the Convention reflects this widespread acceptance by the very disparate groups which constitute what might be termed the children's rights movement. In the UK this includes such diverse bodies as A Voice for the Child In Care, Barnardos, CPAG, NCH Action for Children, the Woodcraft Folk and the Youth Council for Northern Ireland. The Convention has become effectively a manifesto for that movement (Franklin and Franklin, 1996: 102–105). Its centrality to discussions of children's rights is underscored by the fact that virtually every contributor to this volume mentions the Convention and measures the value and success of their work with children and young people by the yardsticks the Convention provides. But it is important not to mistake the word for the deed. The significance of the Convention has grown substantially in recent years but Freeman regrets that initial support for the convention was "half hearted, a number of reservations were entered and no legislative or other changes were introduced to promote compliance". Subsequently, the government's attitude to the Convention is still one of "smug self-satisfaction". The UK's Second Report to the UN Committee creates the illusion that a child's experience of living in England is akin to "Nirvana" (see Freeman, chapter 5). Ignorance of the Convention moreover continues to be widespread among teachers, welfare practitioners and significantly among children themselves (Alderson, 1999).

It should be clear from these initial observations that recent progress in achieving rights for children continues in the rather uneven fashion which has always characterised developments. But progress has also been structured by important landmarks across the last century. It was 1889 before cruelty to children became a criminal offence in Britain, some sixty years after similar legislation outlawed cruelty to animals. It was 25 years later that Eglantyne Jebb and her Save the Children Fund International Union drafted the Geneva Convention. In 1959, the United Nations issued its first Declaration of the Rights of Children announcing young people's entitlements to adequate nutrition, free education and medical care, as well as rights against exploitation and discriminatory practices. The 1980s were characterised by an increasing interest and concern with children's moral and political status, as well as their social and welfare needs. 1989 witnessed the signing of a redrafted, but considerably strengthened, Convention on the Rights of the Child. Thirty years after the original Declaration and four years after International Youth Year, the Convention marked the tenth anniversary of the UN International Year of the Child. In the early 1990s, individual nation signatories began to report to the UN on their progress in implementing the Convention. In the late 1990s the British government enacted the Human Rights Act incorporating the European Convention on Human Rights into English law. The Act became operational in October 2000. Consequently, it seems an appropriate time to reassess some of the central arguments concerning children's rights and to take stock of the achievements of recent years in securing and promoting rights for children.

The New Handbook of Children's Rights: the book in outline

The publication of *The New Handbook of Children's Rights* is timely given the growing interest in children's rights among the general public, policy-makers, governments, social and welfare practitioners and academics. Since 1995, when the first *Handbook of Children's Rights* was published the major children's charities have assumed a commitment to children's rights which has come to enjoy the status of almost a guiding principle informing much of the policy and practice within a growing number of voluntary sector organisations working with children.

The New Handbook has fourteen new chapters by sixteen additional contributors and differs from its predecessor in a number of other ways. First, it has been updated to include recent developments such as the Human Rights Act. Second, it foregrounds new issues which have achieved prominence in children's rights debate across the last five years. The chapter exploring children's rights to public space (chapter 9) for example, examines the growing exclusion of children from the public sphere as a consequence of government policy (curfews), environmental concerns (increased traffic flows/planners' neglect of play space provision) and parents' changing attitudes towards children's autonomy of movement (increased fears around "stranger danger"). Other new chapters focus on children's rights to sex education in the context of the debate around "Section 28" (chapter 10), issues around rights for children who are refugees (chapter 13), as well as children's rights concerns emerging from the increasing tendency to "medicalise" children's oppositional behaviour (chapter 7).

Third, *The New Handbook* places a stronger emphasis on practitioner concerns with a greater number of chapters focused on project work with children and young people. The chapters reviewing the early years of operation of the Flemish Children's Commissioner (chapter 22) and the work of Save the Children's Young Children's Rights Centre (Chapter 19) are obvious examples here.

Finally, there is a new part titled "Listening to Children and Young People's Voices", devoted to chapters which articulate children and young people's concerns (chapter 14, the views of young people in care): chapters which explore new mechanisms for protecting children and young people's interests (chapter 17, Children's Rights Commissioners and chapter 18, citizenship education); as well as a chapter which details innovatory ways of involving children and young people as active researchers investigating issues concerning children (chapter 16).

The New Handbook of Children's Rights has six broad objectives. First, to examine and assess the various strands in the debate concerning children's rights and review developments in rights provision in the UK throughout the 1980s and 1990s. Second, to evaluate the impact of recent British legislation on children's rights in key areas such as education, social and welfare services and criminal justice, as well as looking at some of the key provisions of the UN Convention and the Human Rights Act. Third, to examine recent policy proposals and initiatives in the British setting intended to establish and promote rights for children and young people (e.g. a Children's Commissioner for London). Fourth, to consider the rights claims of particular groups of children – for example children who are carers or children who are disabled – as well as children's claims for particular rights such as the right to enjoy and occupy public space, to sex education and citizenship. Fifth, to consider the various ways in which the voices of children and young people are, or might be, articulated more clearly in policy debates and other arenas. Finally, to offer a comparative perspective on children's rights by exploring issues and developments in Australia, Belgium, Scandinavia and China, by considering the specific rights claims of street children and by examining the claims of children everywhere to have their rights to physical integrity respected.

The New Handbook brings together contributions from academics and researchers, social and welfare practitioners working in both the voluntary and statutory sectors, lawyers, educationalists, child psychologists, teachers and professionals working in pressure groups promoting children's rights in specific spheres. Some chapters consider the divergent responses of governments, the voluntary sector and other agencies to young people's rights claims by exploring and assessing the policies designed to meet them, or restrict them. Other chapters describe innovative ways of working with children and young people which are based upon respect for their rights and an ambition to extend and promote them.

In the opening part Bob Franklin explores some of the complexities inherent in the terms "children" and "rights" and argues that persistently negative media representations of children as either "victims" or "villains" has generated a climate of public opinion which is less congenial to discussions of children's rights. Part II explores the changing legal framework for children's rights. Tony Jeffs draws on the writings of Godwin and contemporary radicals to argue that the educational system must be "free from state control" if children and young people are to win "autonomy over the content and pace of their education" (chapter 2). Jeremy Roche examines case law on the Children Act 1989 and argues that the promotion of children's rights requires "a shift in adult thinking and practice concerning children" rather than "amendments to the Children Act, though some useful amendments could be made" (chapter 3). John Muncie explores the extent to which children's rights are present in welfare-based systems of youth justice (Scotland) or systems based on the principle of "just deserts" (England and Wales). He suggests that the "new youth justice" can uphold little more than a rhetorical commitment to children's rights (chapter 4). Michael Freeman considers the prospect for improving English law in the light of the first decade following ratification of the UN Convention. He concludes that the UN Convention should be incorporated into English law so that a "breach of a provision of the Convention should be an infringement of English law with all the implications this would have" (chapter 5). Jane Fortin considers the possible implications of the Human Rights Act 1998 for extending children's rights. She argues that some of its provisions might "be used very effectively to promote children's rights" but suggests that the wording of others "provides little obvious encouragement to view children as independent individuals, separate from their parents". She warns against parents and adults using the Act to "promote their own rights at children's expense" (chapter 6).

Part III considers particular cases where children's rights are a matter for concern. Vicki Coppock discusses the ways in which parents and professionals define the oppositional behaviour of children and young people as "illness" and prescribe drugs such as Ritalin to "treat" such behaviour. Attention Deficit (Hyperactivity) Disorder forms the case study example for her wider argument (chapter 7). Drawing on research conducted across a decade, Priscilla Alderson's concern is to establish at what age children can begin to express views which have due weight in health matters and when they are able to give legally valid consent (chapter 8). Virginia Morrow explores the exclusion of children from public spaces from children's perspectives (chapter 9), while Deena Haydon details the history of successive governments' policies on sex education and proposes the adoption of a rights-based agenda for sex education policy and practice (chapter 10). Lesley Campbell examines disabled children's rights to life, protection, information and education and argues that "securing the rights of disabled children would bring home rights for all children" (chapter 11). Jo Aldridge and Saul Becker focus on the rights of children who are carers and trace the social and political changes that have affected their lives and the lives of their families (chapter 12) while Mano Candappa examines refugee children's entitlements to basic human rights and sets them against the realities and experiences of young refugees in the UK (chapter 13).

Part IV considers a number of ways in which children and young people's voices might be included in policy debates to help shape decision-making. Monica Barry details the opinions of young people about growing up in care as well as their experiences of family life prior to being taken into care (chapter 14), while Stephanie Williams outlines the experiences of young people who work in the news agency Children's Express, whose two-fold mission is "to give young people a voice" and "to get their views into arenas where they can actually influence policy makers and opinion formers" (chapter 15). Perpetua Kirby considers the different ways in which children and young people can be involved as researchers and how that involvement can challenge the power imbalances in youth research (chapter 16). Gerison Lansdown traces the recent history of attempts to establish Children's Commissioners in the UK (chapter 17). Carole Scott critiques government plans to introduce a national curriculum for citizenship education (chapter 18) while Tina Hyder sets out the work of Save the Children's Centre for Young Children's Rights which attempts to "act as a bridge between theory and practice in the realisation of rights for young children by developing, testing and advocating the use of approaches that will enable adults to listen to even the youngest children" (chapter 19).

The final part of the book provides comparative case studies of children's rights in different national settings. Andy West looks at children's rights in China, which has 20 per cent of the world's children and where diversity and difference are defining characteristics. His "thumbnail sketch" looks at the impact of gender, disability and the one-child-policy on children (chapter 20). Moira Rayner suggests that for some children Australia is a "lucky country" in which to live. For others, particularly children who are Aboriginal or Torres Strait Islander, the luck changes. Since 1993, when Australia ratified the UN Convention on the Rights of the Child, real human rights abuses have been revealed and left without redress (chapter 21). Ankie Vandekerckhove details the lessons learned and the genuine progress achieved for children's rights in the early years of operation of the Commissioner for Children's Rights in Belgium (chapter 22), while Peter Newell charts the global progress towards respecting children's rights not to be hit and looks particularly closely at developments in the UK since the election of the Labour government in 1997 (chapter 23). Judith Ennew argues that street children are excluded from Western definitions of what it means to be a child. Childhood takes place "inside": inside society, inside families, inside a private dwelling. In this sense street children are society's ultimate outsiders. This Westernised notion of children, moreover, has been globalised despite its inappropriateness in many settings (chapter 24). Finally, Malfrid Grude Flekkøy analyses the history of the ombudsman concept in Scandinavia (especially Norway) and considers recent developments in establishing further offices in different national and international settings (chapter 25).

Across all chapters, the intention is to offer a radical appraisal of recent developments in children's rights and, thereby, to promote and support them.

References

Alderson, P. (1999) "Civil Rights in Schools: The Implications for Youth and Policy" *Youth and Policy* no. 64, pp. 56–71

Bradshaw, J. (2000) *Poverty: The Outcomes for Children* Children 5–16 Research Briefing No. 18 July, ESRC, London

CPAG (2001) *An End In Sight? Tackling Child Poverty in the UK* London: Child Poverty Action Group

CRIN (Children's Rights Information Network) (2001) *On The Record Your Link to the UN General Assembly Special Session on the Child* Volume 14, Issue 5, 2 February

Durning, A. (1992) "Life on the Brink" in G. W. Albee, L. Bond and T. V. Cook Monsey (eds) *Improving Children's Lives: Global Perspectives on Prevention* London: Sage, pp. 37–49

Farson, R. (1978) *Birthrights* London: Penguin

Foley, P., Roche, J. and Tucker, S. (2001) *Children in Society: Contemporary Theory, Policy and Practice* London: Palgrave in association with the Open University

Franklin, A. and Franklin, B. (1996) "Growing Pains: The Developing Children's Rights Movement in the UK" in J. Pilchar and S. Wagg *Thatcher's Children? Politics, Childhood and Society in the 1980s and 1990s* London: Falmer Press, pp. 94–114

Geddes, M. and Rust, M. (2000) "Catching Them Young: Local Initiatives to Involve Young People in Local Government and Local Democracy" *Youth and Policy* no. 69 Autumn, pp. 42–62

Holt, J (1975) *Escape From Childhood* London: Penguin

James, A. and Prout, A (1997) *Constructing and Reconstructing Childhood: Contemporary Issues in the Sociological Study of Childhood* London: The Falmer Press

NSPCC (2000) *Our Children Their Future: A Manifesto* London: NSPCC. Available at *www.nspcc.org.uk*

UNICEF (1998) *The State of the World's Children* New York: UNICEF

—— (2000) *The State of the World's Children* New York: UNICEF

Verhellen, E. (ed.) (1999) *Understanding Children's Rights* Ghent: University of Ghent

Willow, C. (1997) *Hear! Hear! Promoting Children and Young People's Democratic Participation in Local Government* London: Local Government Information Unit

Part I

Children's rights

An overview

1 Children's rights and media wrongs

Changing representations of children and the developing rights agenda

Bob Franklin

The issue of children's rights achieved an untypical prominence in the British press during the last week of August 2000. Newspapers reported the public controversy prompted when parents refused consent for an operation to separate their child Mary from her Siamese twin Jodie. Their decision was taken to protect Mary's right to life, although medical evidence suggested this would result in the death of both twins. The parents' decision was eventually overturned in the High Court. A chorus of sensational headlines addressed an ethically and legally complex issue. "One Twin Must Die" declared the *Mirror* (26 August 2000) while the *Daily Mail* headlined "Why I Must Order Twin Baby To Die – Judge's heartbreaking decision to separate Siamese sisters" (26 August 2000). The broadsheets offered scarcely more measured judgements with the front page of the *Guardian* claiming "Twins Must Have Fatal Surgery" (26 August 2000), while *The Times* headed its coverage "Life And Death Decision For Siamese Twins" (26 August 2000).

Other less dramatic stories sustained the media focus on children's rights. The *Guardian*, for example, reported that children conceived by artificial insemination after their father's death were to enjoy a new right to have their father's name on their birth certificate ("Rights For Babies on Fatherless Status", *Guardian*, 26 August 2000). A local paper in Bradford reported the Council's decision to evict the parents of children who upset neighbours by playing football in the street. The front page headline of Bradford's *Telegraph and Argus* explored the significant issue of the lack of adequate play provision for children in urban environments: "A Red Card For Soccer In Street – Parents of football gangs warned 'You face eviction'" (*Telegraph and Argus*, 26 August 2000).

Such examples illustrate four typical characteristics of discussions of rights, especially children's rights. First, the discussion of rights – including questions addressing the competencies necessary to possess them and identifying which claims might properly be considered as rights – has proved perennially contentious. Second, the rights of different individuals may conflict, even in those cases where the claims of all parties are judged legitimate. In the examples above the claims of both Mary and Jodie to the right to life and children's right to play can be set against council tenants' rights to live without "disturbance" and "nuisance". Third, the state is often cast in a contradictory role in rights discourse. On the one hand, the state provides safeguards and protection for individual rights and is often the arbiter in disputes between competing rights claims. On the other, history reveals the state to be the major culprit in matters of rights violation, too frequently eager to encroach on individuals' freedoms (Beetham, 1995). Fourth, rights claims express a considerable range and diversity encompassing the most significant right to life alongside a child's right to play.

There is a fifth feature of rights which is noteworthy and arises from the local newspaper report about the ban on street football. When an *elected* authority is called upon to adjudicate between the conflicting rights claims of two parties (in this case the rights of children to play and the rights of residents to freedom from nuisance and protection of property), that authority is more likely (I would argue, is inherently disposed) to favour the claims of those who possess full citizen rights and are able – at some future date – to hold that body electorally accountable for its decision. Authorities (exemplified here by the local state) are electorally irresponsible to children who, by virtue simply of their age, are denied rights of citizenship.

A concern to address some of these issues informs the twin ambitions for this chapter. First, I intend to outline the substantive themes in the debate between advocates and opponents of rights for children. Second, I wish to argue that the 1990s have witnessed radical shifts in public perceptions of children and childhood, reflecting a growing tendency for news media to report children in ways which are negative and damaging to their interests. Two prominent, but oppositional, images of children can be identified in media accounts. According to the first, children are passive, vulnerable and in need of adult protection (Davis and Bourhill, 1997; Holland, 1992): according to the second, children are unruly and "out of control" (Lumley, 1998; Muncie, 1999; West, 1999). In short, children are increasingly represented as "victims" or "villains". These images of children have proved influential in shaping public opinion and government policy and created a political climate which is less conducive to the achievement of certain rights, especially participation rights. The "quiet revolution" in children's rights, which some observers believe has occurred, has been accompanied by a noisy counterblast from the media (Van Bueren, 1996: 27).

But I need to begin by clarifying some of the ambiguities and complexities in the phrase "children's rights" in order to contextualise the discussions of later chapters.

Children's rights: definitions

What is a child?

Societies tend to divide their members' life cycle into the two broad age states of childhood and adulthood. The transition between them is typically

associated with the acquisition of distinctive rights, privileges and obligations. Most societies celebrate the achievement of maturity to confirm the
significance of this *rite de passage*. In Britain, the age of 18 signals the age
of majority, when individuals formally become adult, although this age
boundary creates a number of anomalies. It means, for example, that a nurse
or a soldier on active service, or even a parent with two children of her own,
may still be defined as "a child" for legal purposes.

In truth, definitions of children, as well as the varied childhoods which
children experience, are social constructs shaped by a range of social, historical and cultural factors. Being a child is not a universal experience of any
fixed duration, but is differently constructed expressing the divergent gender,
class, ethnic or historical locations of particular individuals at particular
moments in the development of their societies. Consequently, the sociological study of childhood is more accurately a study of "childhoods" in which
the universality of the biological immaturity of children is differently shaped,
interpreted and understood by distinctive societies and cultures (James, Jenks
and Prout, 1998). Understood in this way, childhood becomes a social institution which the "new paradigm" for the sociology of childhood understands
as "a negotiated set of social relationships within which the early years of
human life are constituted" (James and Prout, 1997: 2). This suggestion that
distinctive histories, as well as cultures, construct different worlds of childhood is reflected in the titles of a growing scholarly literature concerned to
explore, for example, *Growing Up In Ancient Egypt* (Rosalind and Janssen,
1990), *Childhood In The Middle Ages* (Shahar, 1990) and *The Victorian Town
Child* (Horn, 1997). Other titles such as *Shaping Childhood* (Cox, 1996),
Constructing and Reconstructing Childhood (James and Prout, 1997) and
Contesting Childhood (Wyness, 2000) signal the influence of sociological
factors in both the "experience" and "observation" of childhood (Mayall,
1994), while *The Erosion of Childhood* (Rose, 1991) and *The Disappearance of
Childhood* (Postman, 1983) again identify the shifting, if not transitory, character of childhood. Gittins is undoubtedly correct to challenge the tendency
to identify "one child, one childhood" (Gittins, 1998: 3).

The modern conception of childhood, which in Europe dates from the
sixteenth century and stresses the innocence, frailty and dependence of children, forcefully ejected children from the worlds of work, sexuality and
politics – in which previously they were active participants – and designated
the classroom as the major focus for their lives (Plumb, 1972: 153; Aries,
1962: 329; Laslett, 1965: 105; Holt, 1975: 21). Children were no longer
allowed to earn money or to decide how to spend their time; they were
forced into dependency on adults and obliged to study or play (Pinchbeck
and Hewitt, 1973). These significant structural shifts in children's lives have
been accompanied by new "mythologies" which represent childhood as a
"golden age" in which children, untroubled by the "adult" concerns of work
and economic life, are free to enjoy themselves. Adult platitudes routinely
attempt to persuade children that childhood years are the "best years of

their lives". Cute and contented, but dependent on adults and denied autonomy in important decisions concerning their lives, children are encouraged to be "seen and not heard". John Holt argues that this understanding of childhood is most aptly represented by the metaphor of a walled garden in which children "being small and weak are protected from the harshness of the outside world until they become strong and clever enough to cope with it" (Holt, 1975: 22). Interestingly, English is the only language which uses the word "nursery" to describe a place where both plants and children are nurtured (Franklin, 1986: 9). But the "golden age" mythology is difficult to sustain when confronted by the reality of many children's experiences, which reflect their powerlessness in relation to adults and their subordinate location in the social institutions of the family and school. The opening lines of Frank McCourt's novel *Angela's Ashes* recall, with much good humour but little sentimentality, the challenges of his own childhood:

> When I look back on my own childhood I wonder how I survived at all. It was, of course, a miserable childhood. ... Worse than the miserable childhood is the miserable Irish Childhood, and worse yet is the miserable Irish Catholic childhood. People everywhere brag and whimper about the woes of their early years, but nothing can compare with the Irish version: the poverty; the shiftless loquacious alcoholic father; the pious defeated mother moaning by the fire; pompous priests; bullying schoolmasters; the English and the terrible things they did to us for eight hundred years. Above all – we were wet. ... The rain dampened the city ... and drove us into the church – our refuge, our strength, our only dry place. ... Limerick gained a reputation for piety, but we knew it was only the rain.
>
> (McCourt, 1997: 1–2)

The suggestion that childhood is a "golden age" is difficult to sustain in the face of such an onslaught of childhood recollections.

Two other factors underscore the complexity and diversity of the modern notion of childhood. First, the experiences of children in other countries can radically subvert the mythologised and modern understanding of childhood and point to a potentially arbitrary and inconsistent relativism (Ennew, 1986). Ennew, for example, argues that the conception of childhood which stresses domesticity and dependency is largely a Western definition which places certain children – especially street children – "outside" childhood. The place for childhood to take place, she argues is "inside"; "inside society, inside a family, inside a private dwelling". Consequently street children are society's "ultimate outlaws" placed "outside childhood" (see chapter 24). In Britain too, children's experiences illustrate the tensions which can exist between the realities of childhood and its socially constructed image. Child carers, for example, are not *dependent* but *depended upon*; perhaps even to toilet an incontinent or profoundly ill parent (see chapter 12). Similarly, children who have been in care may have found that their previous "family life offered little protection" but "vice versa" required them to "protect their parents" (see chapter 14).

Second, while precise definition is evidently problematic and elusive, a sense and circumstance of powerlessness seems central to the experience of childhood. It is important to recall that the term "child" was used initially to describe anyone of low status, without regard for their age (Hoyles, 1979: 25). Being a child continues to express more about power relationships than chronology, although the two are intimately intertwined. Children's powerlessness reflects their limited access to economic resources, their exclusion from political participation and the corresponding cultural image of childhood as a state of weakness, dependency and incompetence. Definitions of a "child" and "childhood" entail more than a specification of an age of majority; they articulate a particular society's values and attitudes towards children. These adult perceptions and values are typically disdaining and ageist (Franklin and Franklin, 1990).

Rights

The definition of rights is perhaps less problematic, although it has not always been so. In the early 1970s, for example, children's rights were described as "a slogan in search of a definition" (Rodham, 1973: 487), but across the subsequent three decades an expansive academic literature focused on children's rights, in tandem with a growing awareness of the UN Convention on the Rights of the Child, has mapped out a good deal of the rights terrain.

The greater part of the academic discussion of children's rights has been conceptual in character and concerned to: establish the legitimacy of children's claims for rights (Alderson, 2000; Franklin, 1995; Freeman, 1985; Harris, 1996); to construct elaborate classificatory schemes for children's rights (Hart, 1992; Rogers and Wrightsman, 1978; Wald, 1979); or to examine children's competence to make decisions (Hutchby and Moran-Ellis, 1998; Mortier, 1999). More radical studies have explored the possibilities for extending children's political rights (Children's Rights Alliance for England, 2000; Franklin, 1986 and 1992; Harris, 1984; and Holt, 1975) or attempted to develop a political economy of ageism (Franklin and Franklin, 1990). Inevitably some scholars work has argued against children's claims to certain rights (Purdy, 1994; Scarre, 1980). Others have explored a range of possible institutional mechanisms for implementing children's rights, including a children's ombudsman (Flekkøy, 1991; Verhellen and Spiesschaert, 1989), a children's commissioner (Newell, 2000), conventions on rights for children (Saporiti, 1998; Verhellen, 1999) and children's rights officers and self-advocacy groups such as Article 12 in the UK (Franklin and Franklin, 1996). There is also a growing literature examining the ways in which charitable and voluntary organisations can incorporate their commitment to children's rights in the practice of welfare professionals who work with children (Cuninghame, 1999).

The UN Convention on the Rights of the Child has also substantially increased public awareness of children's rights. The Convention, which has attracted an unprecedented number of signatory countries to ratify its principles (only Somalia and the US are not signatories), embraces a comprehensive set of civil, economic, social and cultural rights which it argues the global community of children should enjoy as a minimum.

The 54 Articles of the UN Convention embrace a wide range of rights which are grouped under three broad categories and labelled the "three Ps"; rights to provision, protection and participation (Wringe, 1995: 19). These include the most basic right to life, the right to adequate health care, food, clean water, shelter and education (provision), rights to protection against sexual abuse, neglect and exploitation (protection) and rights to privacy and freedom of association, expression and thought (participation). Alderson identifies four features of the rights embodied in the convention. First, rights are "limited" and relate to obligations which may not always be met. Parents, for example, may be subject to legal redress for abusing a child but not for failing to love that child. Second, rights are "aspirational" since their realisation will reflect available resources. Consequently a country which is struggling to ensure that all children are fed may not be able to meet claims for educational and welfare rights. Third, rights are "conditional" rather than absolute and will be influenced by the "capacities of the child", the character of national law and other factors. Finally, rights are "shared" and acknowledge that everyone enjoys an equal claim to the same rights. In this sense convention rights are "our" rights not "my" rights (Alderson, 2000: 23).

Three Articles in the Convention have assumed a particular significance. Article 2 affirms the principle of non-discrimination and demands the Convention's provisions apply to all children without regard to "race, colour, sex, language, religion, political or other opinion, national, ethnic or social origin, property, disability, birth or other status". Article 3 affirms the principle that "in all actions concerning children ... the best interests of the child shall be a primary consideration". Article 12 "assures to the child who is capable of forming his or her own views, the right to express those views freely in all matters affecting the child, the views of the child being given due weight in accordance with the age and maturity of the child" (see chapter 5). This is a very mixed bag in terms of the variety and range of rights which are being claimed, the problems inherent in enforcing those claims, the financial and material resources necessary to meet them and the social, political and economic consequences of granting them.

Some of this complexity which rights discussions entail can be resolved by keeping two broad distinctions in mind: between legal and moral rights and welfare and liberty rights.

The distinction between legal and moral rights is easy to establish. A legal right is an entitlement which is acknowledged and enforced by an existing law in a specific state or polity; i.e. legal rights are context specific. They are actual rights which children possess. A moral right (sometimes referred to as a human right or a natural right), however, enjoys no legal endorsement (Feinberg, 1973: 84). A moral or human right is a claim for a right which it is believed children, indeed all human beings, should possess by virtue of their common humanity. The claim to a moral right does not depend on the legal arrangements of particular states, but is a universal entitlement of human beings, without regard to their claims as citizens to legal rights. Children's right to education is a legal right in the UK since every child has a statutory entitlement to be educated to the age of 16. But children's right to vote at the age of 16 is not guaranteed by law. It is a moral claim for an additional right and signals the need to reform existing legal entitlements. Recognition of the legitimacy of such moral claims often serves as the catalyst for changes to legal entitlements (Ekman Ladd, 1996).

The distinction between welfare and liberty rights corresponds to Rogers and Wrightsman's early division of rights into the "nurturance" versus "self determination orientations" (Rogers and Wrightsman, 1978: 61). These two kinds of rights can conflict and are at the centre of much of the controversy which surrounds discussions of children's rights. Welfare rights prioritise the provision for children's welfare needs and the protection of children even if this involves restricting children's choices and behaviour. In brief, welfare rights may be paternalist. Liberty rights focus on children's rights to self-determination. On this account, children should enjoy greater freedom and rights in decision-making even when this involves the right to choose what is not in their best interests (Eekelaar, 1994: 42).

Welfare and liberty rights are, of course, very different kinds of rights both in terms of the type of claims which rights holders are making as well as the "qualifications" necessary to exercise them. The possession of welfare rights – to education, health, shelter and a minimum standard of living – require only that the right holder possesses "*interests* which can be preserved, protected and promoted" (Archard, 1993: 65). But claims for liberty rights – to participate in decision-making, to vote – require that the right holder "must be capable of making and exercising choices" (Archard, 1993: 65). Children's claims to protection rights have rarely been contested. Their claims for liberty rights invariably are.

Children's rights: the debate

Children in all societies are denied basic human rights which, as adults, we take for granted. Among the most significant is children's right to make decisions about their affairs. This denial of rights is evident in the public realm of children's involvement in education and the care arrangements of the state, as well as the private realm of the family. The latter is significant since conventions cannot enforce rights within the family: it is virtually impossible to police what goes on behind closed doors. Children's exclusion from decision-making ranges from relatively unimportant matters such as decisions about what to eat, which clothes to wear or what time to go to bed, to more significant concerns about the right to a voice in shaping the curriculum at school and the right to vote.

This exclusion of children from decision-making is an uncontentious matter of fact. What is up for debate is whether it can be justified. In democratic societies, however, the burden of proof should rest with those who wish to deny children – or any other group – rights that are the common property of others. But advocates of exclusion have rarely argued a sustained and cogent case. Too frequently they have offered irrational and ill-considered prejudice masquerading as "common sense". Few have accepted Bertrand Russell's suggestion that "no political theory is adequate unless it is applicable to children as well as to men and women" (Russell, 1971: 100). When reasoned argument has supplanted "common sense" the case has two related strands.

First, it is alleged that children are not rational and seem incapable of making reasoned and informed decisions. Rights to autonomy in decision-making grow with maturity. Locke stated the matter unequivocally. "We are born free as we are born rational" he claimed, "not that we have actually the exercise of either; age that brings one brings with it the other too" (Locke, 1964: 326). Second, children lack any wisdom based on experience and consequently they are prone to making mistakes. By denying children the right to participate and make decisions for themselves, society's motives are allegedly benign, seeking only to protect children from the harmful consequences of their own incompetence.

A succession of distinguished philosophers have endorsed this disparaging assessment of children's capacities across two millennia. Aristotle's claim that children's "deliberative faculty" is "immature" (Aristotle, 1959: 1260A), for example, finds support in Kant's suggestion that a child must reach the age of 10 before "reason appears" (Kant, 1930: 250) while Mill presents "mere children" as "incapable of being acted upon by rational consideration of distant motives" (Mill, 1910: 139). D. H. Lawrence in a rare essay on education eschews any semblance of measured judgement and articulates the classic paternalist case based on presumptions of childhood irrationality. "We've got to educate our children", he argues, "which means we've got to decide for them; day after day, year after year, we've got to go on deciding for our children. It's not the slightest use asking little Jimmy 'What would you like dear?' because little Jimmy doesn't know. And if he thinks he knows, its only because as a rule he's got some fatal little idea into his head" (Lawrence, 1919).

Feminist philosopher Judith Hughes argues that these assessments are self-serving, partisan, and little more than elaborate, albeit unconscious, rationales reflecting and articulating the interests of socially powerful groups: invariably adult men. Consequently children have been consigned philosophically to that category of "not men" which includes "women, animals, madmen, foreigners, slaves, patients and imbeciles ... in contrast with which male philosophers have defined and valued themselves" (Hughes, 1996: 15). Hughes identifies important links between the denial of citizenship to women and the current exclusion of children, but also offers a counsel of caution. To suggest that the arguments which have excluded women – which have subsequently been shown to be false – are similar to those deployed to exclude children, must not ignore the evident differences between members of the "not men" group and do not offer "a proof" that the argument "about a child is false". "But", she concludes, "it should make us very suspicious" (Hughes 1996: 17).

Child libertarians are certainly very suspicious, if not sceptical, about the paternalist case concerning the alleged irrationality of children and object on a number of grounds.

First, they suggest that children do reveal a competence for rational thought and do make informed decisions (Hutchby and Moran-Ellis, 1998: 8; Mortier, 1999: 85). These include decisions about which television programmes to watch or which football teams to support, as well as more important issues such as dealing with a bully at school or an abusing parent at home. Even very young children have proved themselves to be competent decision-makers. Miller's study of nursery children, for example, observed how children were "making decisions all the time". These children were also adept at negotiation and conciliation when conflicts occurred: "they talked about what happened, how they felt and what they might do next that would be fair to everyone. ... We watched as children as young as two years old planned, negotiated and co-operated with each other" (Miller, 1999: 71). Alderson's research, moreover, reveals children's capacity to make even the most important life and death (literally) decisions about their treatment for serious medical conditions. And on occasion their ability to decide when treatment should be terminated (Alderson, 1993 and chapter 8). These studies reveal children possess a greater competence for decision-making than is typically acknowledged by adults. Comparative social policy research offers further supportive evidence for such a claim. In the Nordic countries, where legislation such as the Finnish Child Custody and Rights of Access Act 1983 and the Norwegian Childrens Act 1981 acknowledges children's competencies and offers a more democratic involvement in decision-making, this has not "placed children at risk by allowing them greater autonomy over their own lives" (Lansdown, 1995: 22–23). On the contrary, it has illustrated children's capacity for decision-making without any of the harmful consequences which paternalists predict.

The continuing exclusion of children, in the face of the evidence that these and other studies provide, is testament to the persuasive impact of sustained representations of children as irrational and incompetent on the public consciousness. The self-serving rhetoric of philosophers, identified by Hughes, has leaked from the academy into the public sphere where it has helped to shape public perceptions and aspects of "common sense". The end

result of this process is that "the child has been historically de-intellectu-
alised" (Mortier, 1999: 89). Mortier, moreover, criticises the contemporary
understanding of competence by asserting the "inherently normative character of competency judgements". There is, he argues "no neutral way of
defining competence" (Mortier, 1999: 86–87). Jaffe concurs but suggests
further that this social construction of competence signals that it cannot be
understood in the abstract but must be assessed as it is displayed and
evidenced in concrete settings (Jaffe and Rey Wicky, 1998: 51).

Second, the argument which suggests that children are likely to make
mistaken choices, because they lack experience of decision-making, rests on
tautology and a confusion. The tautology is evident. If children are not
allowed to make decisions because they have no experience of decision-
making, how do they ever get started? This is catch 22. "Even children, after
a certain point, had better not be 'treated as children'", Feinberg remarks,
"else they will never acquire the outlook and capability of responsible
adults" (Feinberg, 1980: 110).

The confusion in the argument is also clear. It does not follow that children should not make decisions simply because they might make the wrong
ones. It is important not to confuse the right to do something with doing the
right thing. As Dworkin argues, we often accept that adults have the right to
do something which is wrong for them (Dworkin, 1977: 188). Smoking
tobacco offers an obvious example: excessive drinking of alcohol another.

Third, there is nothing wrong with making mistakes; it constitutes a near
universal pastime. On the contrary, mistakes provide key opportunities for
learning which children and adults should be encouraged to grasp. My old
school motto "Discimus faciendo" (which I never imagined I might find
useful) translates from the Latin as "We learn by doing" and captures some
of the importance of that pedagogic sentiment. Why not allow children, like
adults, the possibility of learning from their mistakes and growing in knowledge and experience as a consequence?

Fourth, adults are not skilled decision-makers but since *they* are not
excluded from making decisions on this ground, it is important to avoid
double standards. A brief scan of modern history reveals a catalogue of
adult blunders and the extent of human fallibility. War, inequality, famine,
the burning of witches, nuclear weapons, apartheid and environmental
pollution are some of the fruits of rational adult deliberation. Mortier's
suggestion that "there are few reasons to boast about the practical rationality of adults" risks allegations of understatement (Mortier, 1999: 87).
Indeed it is difficult to imagine that children might match the extraordinary
incompetence of the adult record and consequently to deny children the
right to make mistakes would be hypocritical since it is a right which adults
have exercised extensively.

Fifth, allocating rights according to an age principle is incoherent and
arbitrary, with different age requirements for adult rights applying in
different spheres of activity. Anomalies abound. In the UK, for example, a

child is sexually an adult at 16 but is not politically an adult until 18. These boundaries, moreover, are constantly shifting. The age of political suffrage was lowered from 21 to 18 in 1969, while the age of homosexual consent was reduced from 21 to 18 in 1994: and in 2000 the government made a further reduction to 16. Occasionally, the injustices and inconsistencies of such age limits are brought home with great force. The death of a 17-year-old soldier in the Gulf War offers a harrowing example. Old enough to be a soldier but not old enough to vote for or against the war.

Sixth, rights should be allocated according to competence and not age. Paternalists agree. They do not wish to exclude children from decision-making because they are children (merely another tautology) but because they are judged to lack competence in certain key and relevant respects. The argument about age ultimately regresses to an argument about competence. But if paternalists apply their argument consistently, their principled concern to allocate rights in accordance with competence excludes everyone who lacks the relevant competence and obliges them to confront the uncomfortable fact that this would lead to the exclusion of adults as well as children. There are subsidiary, but not insignificant, difficulties which arise from formulating the problem of inclusion around competence. What might serve as criteria of competence for participation, how might we test for them and who would decide whether particular individuals met those criteria? Such questions are especially significant in the context of the suggestions of philosophers cited above that there are no neutral definitions of competence (Mortier, 1999: 87).

Seventh, the denial of participation rights to children is unfair because children can do nothing to change or ameliorate the conditions which exclude them. If the grounds for exclusion were ignorance or lack of education, then the ignorant might endeavour to become wise and uneducated people might be motivated to read and learn. But young people cannot prematurely grow to the age of majority even if foolish enough to entertain such an ambition. Nor is the allegation of inequity met by the suggestion that the denial is temporary since children eventually become adults and acquire the appropriate status and rights. The argument here rests on a confusion between particular children and children as a social group. An individual child matures to adulthood, but this does not alter the status of children as a social group. Thirteen million people in the UK are denied the right to participate in making decisions about important matters in their lives (Children's Rights Alliance for England, 2000).

Finally, to define everyone under 18 years of age as a child, or more accurately as a "non-adult", obscures the inherent diversity of childhood and attempts to impose a homogeneity upon children which the plurality of their intellectual and emotional needs, skills, competencies and achievements undermines. Consequently, the period between birth and adulthood is usually divided into four distinct periods: infancy, childhood, adolescence and early adulthood with different needs, rights and responsibilities being judged appropriate for different age groups. This definition of all children less than 18 years as "non adult", or in Hughes phrase "not men", is strategic. It allows opponents of children's rights to ridicule their claims for additional rights by comparing like with unlike and explains the cheap jibe, "Whatever next, votes for 6-year-olds?", a comment intended to undermine the legitimate claim for votes for 16-year-olds. It seems improbable that a 16-year-old might enjoy greater empathy with a 6-year-old than a near age mate of 19 years, but it is the 6-year-old and 16-year-old who are children. But children, of course, are not a homogeneous group with uniform needs. Disabled children, children who are carers, children who are looked after and children who are refugees have particular needs which must be met and may confront particular difficulties in achieving their rights (see chapters 11, 12 and 13).

In summary the argument for denying participation rights to children on the grounds that they are not rational and lack experience has been strongly contested by libertarians. Opponents of children's rights have offered three additional arguments.

First, drawing on the writings of the German philosopher Kant, they have argued that children are not entitled to participation rights because they are incapable of what Kant called "self maintenance"; what might now be described as self-sufficiency. Kant believed that "children ... attain majority and become masters of themselves ... by ... attaining to the capability of self maintenance' (Kant, 1887: 118). But the criterion of self-maintenance fails to distinguish adults from children and merely distinguishes those who are capable of self-maintenance from those who are not. It might, for example, be used to justify excluding disabled adults or sick and older people, as well as people who are unemployed, from participating in decision-making since each of these groups might be judged incapable of self-maintenance. It is, however, a dubious moral claim to suggest that anyone who lacks self-sufficiency understood in these terms should be subject to the intervention of others in their affairs and denied autonomy rights.

A second argument connects rights and responsibilities and suggests that those who wish to claim and exercise rights must be willing and capable of assuming the related responsibilities. Since children are presumed incapable of shouldering responsibilities for certain matters, they are necessarily excluded from the possession of certain rights. The presumption informing the argument is that rights and responsibilities are "two sides of the same coin – that the exercise of rights must be matched by the exercise of responsibility within the same person" (Lansdown, 1995: 29). The argument presents a rather hybrid variant of what philosophers call the principle of the correlativity of rights and duties (Ekman Ladd, 1996: 4). But the argument fails for two reasons. First, there are rights without corresponding duties. It might be claimed, for example, that a foetus has certain rights – including the most significant right to life – but it makes no sense to ask what duties might be a precondition for claiming these rights. Second, as

Lansdown suggests, while the correlativity principle argues that if rights are to be meaningful there must be a corresponding duty, it does not imply the same person must exercise both rights and responsibilities (Ekman Ladd, 1996: 4). Consequently while children have a right to protection, Lansdown argues that "the responsibility for ensuring that protection rests with, first, the parents and in the event of their inability or unwillingness, with the state" (Lansdown, 1995: 29). Similarly, children have a right to education but they can only exercise that right if government locally and nationally assumes responsibility for its provision.

A third argument is based on what might be termed "future oriented consent" or what Archard calls the "caretaker argument" (Archard, 1993: 51–57). The argument suggests that a parent (or some other rational adult) has a right to restrict a child's freedom and to make decisions in a child's best interest, guided by the principle that the child must eventually come to acknowledge the correctness of the decision made on their behalf. A child, for example, may be reluctant to attend school, but education is essential if that child is to develop into a rational and autonomous adult. A parent is therefore entitled to override the child's current wishes to guarantee their future independence. It is precisely because the caretaker argument places such a high value on individual autonomy and critical rationality in decision-making that intervention in children's affairs is judged permissible. As Archard notes, "the caretaker thesis thinks self determination too important to be left to children" (Archard, 1993: 52).

Dworkin suggests that these parental interventions constitute "a wager by the parent on the child's subsequent recognition of the wisdom of restrictions. There is an emphasis on … what the child will come to welcome, rather than on what he does welcome" (Dworkin, 1977: 119). This is no mean trick. As Archard observes, the caretaker must not only choose what the child would choose if competent to make the choice autonomously, but also have regard for the interests of the adult which the child will become. "The caretaker", Archard claims, "chooses for the child in the person of the adult which the child is not yet but will eventually be" (Archard, 1993: 53).

There are two difficulties here. The first is merely a logical problem: if the justification for the intervention depends on future consent, there is no way of judging at the time of the intervention whether it is desirable, appropriate and in the child's best interests. The more serious objection is that the intervention by the adult might generate "self justifying" rather than "future oriented" consent. The consent of the child at some future date may simply be a product of the very process of intervention.

Rawls offers an illustrative example which undermines the legitimacy of future oriented consent. "Imagine two persons", Rawls says, "in full possession of their reason and who will affirm very different religious or philosophical beliefs, and suppose that there is some psychological process that will convert each to the other's view, despite the fact that the process is imposed upon them against their wishes. In due course, let us suppose both will come to accept conscientiously their new beliefs. We are still not permitted to submit them to this treatment" (Rawls, 1972: 249). The benchmark of successful brainwashing, of course, is that the person violated in this way is happy and confirmed in their new beliefs. If Freud was correct to suggest that the child is father to the man, then on this account the man may be substantially fashioned by the caretaker and the caretaker argument may amount to little more than a vicious circle of self-justifying adult intervention in children's lives.

Libertarians like Holt have little time for caretakers. They argue that children possess the competencies necessary to make decisions about important matters in their lives and should be allowed to participate in making them. But the political climate for discussing children's rights has altered significantly across the 1990s; and for the worse. In part, this less congenial mood reflects changing media representations of children and young people.

Children's rights: "victims", "villains" and disempowering discourses

Media representations of children have promoted two contradictory images of children as either passive, dependent, vulnerable and in need of protection or, alternatively, as anti-social, deviant, irresponsible and in need of firm social control. In media accounts, children have become "victims" or "villains". Gittins, for example, argues that while images of children may vary "there are certain recurring and central themes: dependency, victimisation/helplessness, loss, nostalgia, innocence" (Gittins, 1998: 111). By contrast, Marina Warner in her Reith lectures in 1994 notes that "the child has never before been seen as such a menacing enemy as today. Never before have children been so saturated with all the projected power of monstrousness to excite repulsion – and even terror. ... We call children 'little devils', 'little monsters', 'little beasts' " (Warner, 1994: 43).

These two apparently contradictory images of children have coexisted in literature since the Enlightenment: the location identified by Aries as the birthplace of the modern conception of the child (Aries, 1962). Blake's *Songs of Innocence and Experience*, for example, offer eulogies to the innocence of childhood, while Heinrich Hoffman's tale of *Struwwelpeter* features "Cruel Frederick": "A horrid wicked boy was he; He caught the flies the poor little things, And then tore off their tiny wings" (Petley, 1999: 89). A rhyme reminiscent of the *Daily Telegraph's* claim (and probably equally fictitious) that "one of James Bulger's killers pulled the heads off live baby pigeons" (*Daily Telegraph*, 25 November 1995: 21).

Both images of children continue to inform public perceptions. Journalist Sean French, for example, argues that "most of us have vestiges of the Romantic idea of the child as innocent and naturally good, and we get occasional glimpses of it when they are in a nice mood and playing well together. But the world of *Lord of The Flies* is never all that far away" (French, 1997:

14). These representations of children, moreover, are increasing prevalent in popular and political discourses and are deployed strategically in policy debates. "Never before", Allsopp suggests, "have children and images of childhood had such symbolic force in adult debate. Their pictures are like banners carried into war in a struggle over how best to order our social and economic relations" (Allsopp, 1997: 122).

These varying constructions of children, however, are adult products, reflecting a particular "adult gaze" and designed to serve adult purposes. They are simply "alternative placements that the adult world creates ... into which children are located at different times and different circumstances" (Stainton Rogers and Stainton Rogers, 1992: 192). Both are unhelpful to children's claims for rights. Adults construct the children they need. They "present children as victims out of a protective instinct ... it justifies not taking them seriously ... newspapers show children as small vulnerable members of society" and "say they're not responsible enough to need any sort of stake in society" (Children's Express, 1998: 7). Media representations of children as villains are similarly damaging and have proved influential in shaping public opinion and government policy, especially in the run up to recent general elections: "villains" are undeserving of increased participation or liberty rights.

Across the 1990s a growing moral panic about children was exacerbated by, but also helped to shape, dramatic shifts in media representations of children and young people. The image of the child as a victim requiring protection – so prevalent at the end of the 1980s – has been replaced by an image of the child as a villain from which society needs protection via an increasingly authoritarian policy agenda (Franklin, 1996). I have argued elsewhere that media reporting influences policy by a process described as "legislation by tabloid" (Franklin and Lavery, 1989: 28) and consequently I wish to suggest here that these changing media representations have impacted on policies and prospects for children. The high ideals of the Children Act have given way to discussions of curfews, boot camps and electronic tagging.

From victims to villains: changing media representations of children

The influence of media reporting on policy-making was evident in certain aspects of the Children Act 1989. The Act represented a significant legislative statement of children's rights. It embodied the principle that "the best interests of the child" should be central in determining outcomes for children but acknowledged that decisions concerning children should, where appropriate, take into account the "wishes of the child" (see Roche, chapter 3). Regrettably, the impetus behind the Children Act was provided not only by a reassessment of children's competencies, but by the extensive press coverage of a succession of tragedies involving the deaths of young children following sustained physical abuse by their parents or carers. The Act was also shaped by press reporting of what the media dubbed the "Cleveland

Affair": "The Scandal The Daily Mail First Brought To The Nation's Attention" (*Daily Mail*, 23 June 1987). In their coverage of the deaths of Jasmine Beckford, Kimberley Carlile, Tyra Henry and the unravelling of the Cleveland story, the media played a crucial role in generating a public mood of concern which triggered a policy response from politicians.

The prominent contemporary image of children in press coverage was that of childhood innocence or, more accurately, violated childhood innocence: enter the child as "victim". The widely canvassed press concern was that children were at considerable risk of abuse from two sources. First, children required greater protection from their parents who, press reports revealed, were subjecting them to physical and sexual abuse in far greater numbers than society had previously realised. Headlines such as "Child Sexual Abuse Unit Finds 183 Cases In A Year" (*Guardian*, 17 May 1988), "Teeth Marks on Little Jason" (*Daily Express*, 18 November 1987), "The Growing Shame of Child Sex Abuse in City" (*Yorkshire Post*, 4 July 1989) and "Child Abuse: Astounding Figures Reveal Hidden Scandal" (*Telegraph and Argus*, 12 May 1989), heightened public awareness and anxieties about the extent and severity of child abuse and signalled children's need for increased rights to protection.

Second, press coverage of Cleveland highlighted the social services systems' abuse of children and their families. News media denounced social workers as sinister characters, the over-zealous representatives of an unduly interventionist state, who were too eager to intervene in the private realm of the family in ways which denied children autonomy. Social workers were "authoritarian bureaucrats" (*The Times*, 17 June 1987) and "abusers of authority" (*Daily Mail*, 7 July 1988), while social services were "merely another organisation with the initials SS" (*Guardian*, 30 June 1987). One conclusion emerging from this press attack on social workers was that children needed enhanced rights and increased opportunities to participate in decision-making about their family life.

The Children Act 1989 attempted to provide both protection and participation rights for children by constructing a new rights equilibrium between the competing claims of children, parents and the state. It offered children protection in accordance with their best interests but also offered them a new autonomy in decision-making based on a benign assessment of their competencies. Children's voices needed to be heard and taken seriously if problems of physical and sexual abuse were to be resolved. The Children Act undoubtedly spoke to children's qualities and strengths but equally certainly the Act's provisions reflected the circumstances of its birth: in many respects it was the child of Cleveland. In many respects it was a product of the moral panic about child abuse in which the media heightened public anxieties and prompted calls for legislative action (Franklin and Parton, 1991: 29–30).

These media images of childhood innocence, of children as victims requiring adult protection, have been sustained across the 1990s. They were particularly evident, for example, in press coverage of events at Dunblane.

The *Glasgow Herald's* front-page headline announced the "Slaughter of the Innocents" (14 March 1996). The *Sun* designed a masthead logo which featured on all pages of Dunblane coverage, picturing parents comforting a child and with the message "Massacre of the Little Ones" (14 March 1996). In much the same way, the *News of The World's* campaign during July and August 2000 to name and shame paedophiles represented children as "innocents" and "potential victims" who are "at risk". But the prevalent and foregrounded image of children in media reporting during the 1990s has been different.

Exit the victim, enter the villain

Three features of press coverage have been notable across the last decade. First, since 1990, news media reporting of children and young people has become almost wholly focused on crime. In press reports children have become one-dimensional. They have been represented as young offenders, muggers, ram raiders, drug abusers, rapists and even murderers. The prominent media image of children and young people is one which alleges they are beyond the control of the police, the courts, the criminal justice system and the communities in which they live. A selection of phrases taken from recently published newspapers signals the disparaging and demonising language used to describe children. They are "Boy Yobs" (*Sheffield Star*, 21 December 2000), "evil" (*Daily Express*, 26 March 1998), "Gang rapists" (*Daily Mail*, 9 May 1999), "psychos" and "gun nuts" (*Sun*, 27 March 1998), "baby faced killers" (*The Times*, 26 March 1998), "Robbers and black-mailers" (*Daily Mail*, 16 May 1997), "Child Yobs" (*Sheffield Star*, 1 June 2000), "Truants, street robbers and burglars" (*Guardian*, 2 January 1998), "drug dealers" (*Guardian*, 4 December 1997), "nasty little thugs" (*Guardian*, 17 April 1998) and "arsonists" (*Daily Mail*, 25 November 1997). Contemporary children are in Polly Toynbee's words "The Children From Hell" (*Guardian*, 14 April 2000), a "demographic crime bomb" (*Guardian*, 21 November 1996) who have created "a discipline crisis in our schools" (*Guardian*, 29 October 1996), "plague local residents" (*Sheffield Star*, 1 June 2000) and are poised to unleash "A Rule Of Terror" (*Daily Mail*, 9 May 1997). Little wonder that one observer's tongue-in-cheek attempt at a parodic and alliterative headline reads "Enter the Persistent Pre-Pubescent Predators from Purgatory" (Pitts, 1995: 6).

Second, *children* rather than *adolescents* have featured as the *dramatis personae* of press reports. Newspapers, of course, have traditionally suggested that young people pose a challenge, if not a threat, to society's basic values and stability (Pearson, 1983). A succession of moral panics since the 1950s have demonised the youth subcultures of Teddy boys, mods and rockers, punks and new age travellers as deviant, while early research on portrayals of adolescents in British media revealed that it was young people's involvement in crime which journalists found most newsworthy

(Murdock, Porteus and Colston, 1980: 325). But recent press reports have featured ever-younger children. This journalistic trend was exemplified in the *Sun's* "Exclusive" about "Britain's Youngest Mum", headlined "Sex At 11, Mum At 12 – A Story To Shock Britain" (*Sun*, 4 July 1997) and "CAGED – Monster, 13, No One Wants" (*Sheffield Star*, 21 December 2000). The *Daily Mail's* story about five young boys (one aged 9 and the others aged 10), who gang raped a 9-year-old girl in the school, followed a similar pattern (*Daily Mail*, 9 May 1997). The message is clear. There are not only more offenders, but they are younger.

Finally, newspaper coverage, especially tabloid reporting which displays an editorial style intended to shock, has generalised the "evil" which allegedly characterises *some* children to include *all* children. This has been especially notable in the reporting of children following press coverage of the death of James Bulger in 1993 and constitutes a significant change in the representation of children and childhood.

Adverse media reporting of children and young people began with coverage of what the press described as "the urban riots" in Bristol and a number of northern cities including the Meadowell estate in Tyneside in 1991. The events offered television journalists opportunities for their favourite type of coverage: a "strong picture led story". Successive nightly news broadcasts presented images of young people driving through the estate at high speed in stolen cars chased by trained police pursuit drivers seemingly unable to catch them. Such images were highly symbolic and seemed to underscore a growing public belief that young offenders were beyond the reach and control (literally) of the police, the courts and the criminal justice system.

Throughout the 1990s, media reports fed the panic. A significant feature of coverage was the tendency to identify and scapegoat individual children. The *Guardian 2* supplement (23 April 1996), for example, featured a full page colour picture of a young school boy (with school tie suitably awry) head-lined "Boys Will Be Boys Or *Is* He The Worst Pupil In Britain?" Interestingly, the opening line of the story conflates the two prominent representations of children as victim or villain. "Is he the schoolboy from hell" the reporter asks "or a muddled and misunderstood 13 year old boy going home sniffling to his pet rabbit after a weird and lonely day of 'special treatment' at his local comprehensive" (*Guardian 2*, 23 April 1996: 1–3).

Reports of criminal justice lacked such equivocation as young people were branded as "super criminals" or, in another overused phrase, a "one boy crime wave". The tabloids dubbed one young person "Rat Boy": a nick-name earned because he evaded arrest by hiding and living in a ventilation shaft. On 7 October 1993, the *Daily Express* headlined with evident approval, "Rat Boy Is Put Behind Bars As Minister Acts". The story revealed that the 14-year-old boy had 55 offences on his criminal record and had absconded from local authority homes on 37 occasions. (*Daily Express*, 7 October 1993). By 1993, the popular media had identified children and young people as the "enemy" in the "battle against rampaging youth and spiralling crime": the *Daily Express* headline announced that parents were "Living With The Enemy" (30 October 1993).

Occasionally, the enthusiasm of journalists for extrapolating statistical trends prompts a bizarre mathematics of criminology and stokes public anxieties. In a story headlined "Young Offenders Rampant Say Police", the *Guardian* reported claims by Northumbria Police that "58 youngsters – mostly 15 or younger – are officially responsible for 1079 crimes in Newcastle upon Tyne last year" and were "arrested on 883 occasions. They include one boy arrested 37 times in a year, who was a thief and a burglar at 11 and another thought to have committed at least 300 crimes. He has been arrested 64 times in 3 years. ... But on the assumption that the 58 have committed an average of 7.8 crimes for every arrest ... they could have been responsible for a staggering 6,500 crimes last year" (*Guardian*, 12 November 1996: 6). Such projections are certainly staggering but barely credible.

The *Daily Star* published a story about an 11-year-old offender, which seemed to capture the growing press and public concern. "We've gone too soft" the newspaper claimed. "Children are supposed to be little innocents not crooks in short trousers. But much of Britain is now facing a truly frightening explosion of kiddie crime ... too many kids are turning into hardened hoods almost as soon as they've climbed out of their prams" (*Daily Star*, 30 November 1992). Hyperbole was not restricted to tabloids with *The Times* reporting that "juvenile arson" was "on the increase" and costing £500 millions each year (10 September 1992), while the *Guardian* identified truanting school pupils as being responsible for "a wave of street crime" (2 January 1998).

But it was the apprehension and trial of Jon Venables and Bobby Thompson for the murder of James Bulger in 1993 which was to prove the crucial watershed in press reporting of children. Reporting triggered three interconnected consequences. First, the earlier romanticised social construct of children as innocent "angels" was challenged, toppled and reconstructed in more sinister guise. In press coverage children become "devils" and villains (Franklin, 1996: 20). Second, reporting of the Bulger case provided additional impetus to the existing media generated moral panic about children and crime (Franklin and Petley, 1996: 142). Finally, the Bulger case seemed to legitimise the increasingly authoritarian criminal justice polices of successive governments (Muncie, 1999: 177; Haydon and Scraton, 2000: 447).

On 25 November 1993 the front page of the *Daily Star* featured pictures of two smiling young boys; the photos were captioned "Killer Bobby Thompson – Boy A' and 'Killer Jon Venables – Boy B'". The headline below the photographs queried, "How do you feel now you little bastards?" The Bulger case witnessed the abandonment of the "normal" requirements for objectivity in reporting in favour of hysterical, populist and vindictive editorialising which vilified Venables and Thompson as "monsters", "freaks", "animals" or simply as "evil". Tabloid headlines became alarming and bigoted rants which obscured rather than clarified events.

The press took its cue from Justice Moreland's summary observation that "the killing of James Bulger was an act of unparalleled evil and barbarity" (Morrison, 1997: 228). *Today* alleged the two boys were an "evil team" and that their friendship represented the "chemistry of evil" (*Today*, 25 November 1993: 4), while the *Daily Mail* published a 16-page supplement titled "The Evil and The Innocent" (*Daily Mail*, 25 November 1993). The demonising of the two boys was exemplified by a *Telegraph* report which alleged that Thompson's nickname was Damien – a reference to the series of *Omen* films – and recalled that Venables was born on Friday the 13th. The *Sun* announced that "the devil himself could not have made a better job of raising two fiends" (*Sun*, 25 November 1993: 28) while the *Daily Star* claimed "The Devil went shopping in Merseyside that afternoon" (*Daily Star*, 25 November 1993).

This "demonising" of Thompson and Venables by the British press was so relentless that one observer was prompted to describe it as "the kind of outbreak of moral condemnation that is usually reserved for the enemy in times of war" (King, 1995: 8). But journalists moved beyond their attack on the two boys to more generalised assertions about the nature of *all* children. In denouncing Thompson and Venables as "evil", the press began to reshape the public understanding of childhood itself; the age of childhood innocence was over. The *Daily Mail* dismissed as "sentimental" and "relatively modern" the "view that children are born innocent" (*Daily Mail*, 25 November 1993). *The Times* in full editorial flight announced its opposition to "the belief prevalent since the Victorian era, that childhood is a time of innocence". It declared with an unwarranted uncertainty that "childhood has a darker side which past societies perhaps understood better than our own" (*The Times*, 25 November 1993). Blake Morrison expressed the transition from innocence to evil with moving eloquence.

> Some deaths are emblematic, tipping the scales, and little James's death ... seemed like the murder of hope. If child-killings are the worst killings, then a child child-killing must be worst than worst, a new superlative in horror. In that spring of cold fear, it was as if there'd been a breach in nature: the tides frozen; stars nailed to the sky; the moon weeping from sight. Those nameless boys had killed not just a child but the idea of childhood ... No good could grow from the earth. Ten-year-olds were looked at with a new suspicion, and toddlers kept on tight reins.
>
> (Morrison, 1997: 21)

It became clear that the extent and character of press coverage of the Bulger case signalled a phenomenon with a significance which extended beyond the tragic death of an individual child. The immediate policy response was

"Back to Basics", an authoritarian and punitive policy summarised by John Major's injunction that we "should understand a little less and condemn a little more". Major believed "it was time to get back to basics ... to self discipline and respect for law; to consideration for others; to acting responsibility for yourself and your family and not shuffling it off on the state" (*The Times*, 9 October 1993). The immediate consequence was to "establish a set of controls upon children's activities" (Jenks, 1996: 133). "Truancy Watch" offered an immediate example. The then Education Minister John Patten claimed truancy "had become too serious for schools to deal with alone and parents did not always fulfil their moral and legal duties. Adults who saw children hanging around in shopping centres, travelling alone on buses or trains, playing in parks or renting videos, should contact the authorities" (*Independent*, 23 November 1993). The imprint of the events in the Bulger case is more than a little evident in shaping these remarks. The public mood following Bulger also provided a pretext for a number of criminal justice initiatives "including the building of 170 further places in secure units for 12–16-year-old offenders" (Young, 1996: 126). Major's commitment to "respect for the law" is clearly reflected in such policies. As he observed, "better the guilty behind bars than the innocent penned in at home" (*The Times*, 9 October 1993: 8). In the wake of Bulger, politicians were keen to address public anxieties by the promise of ever tougher and more repressive legislation to police what appeared to be a generation of children and young people who were "out of control".

During the mid 1990s education, as much as criminal justice, became an arena for media allegations that children were "out of control". An *Express* headline "Expelled By School At The Age Of Four" told of a boy expelled after thirteen days for hitting other children; his father confessed that "he can be wicked just like any other kid". But the *Express* was quick to point out that this was not a record. Another child had been "kicked out on day one and was in police custody later that day" (*Daily Express*, 23 October 1993). But it was the murder of head teacher Philip Lawrence – who was stabbed at the gates of his school while trying to protect a child who was being bullied – which gave the press a story with almost the same emotive impact and political salience as the Bulger story.

On 21 October 1996, Lawrence's widow Frances wrote an article in *The Times* in which she identified a breakdown of communities and suggested a number of proposals to restore community and civic values. There should be: school lessons in citizenship for young people; a ban on the sale of combat knives; a reduction in portrayals of violence on television; an emphasis in teaching on effort, earnestness and excellence; and a restoration of family values. In brief, a repackaged "Back to Basics". The article struck a chord with politicians and the public and discussion of the issues dominated the news agenda for the following week. In the run up to a general election, rival politicians seemed eager to "bid up" the policy response to the threat posed by young people in ever more authoritarian directions. Some journalists acknowledged the close connection between public anxiety about law and order, media coverage of Frances Lawrence's "manifesto" and politicians' commitments to particular policies. The front page lead of the *Guardian* on 22 October 1996 claimed "The Conservatives, Labour and Liberal Democrats began a stampede yesterday to claim they were closest to the moral agenda for the regeneration of Britain set out by the widow of Philip Lawrence".

Coverage of the Lawrence case created a news agenda for other education stories which otherwise might not have enjoyed media attention (Lumley, 1998: 1). The day after Frances Lawrence's article in *The Times*, the Ridings school in Halifax achieved considerable news prominence. Teachers were balloting for strike action because they wished to see 60 students (one tenth of the school) excluded to restore order in the classroom. Teachers alleged that discipline within the school had collapsed: "from the start of the school day, everyday, teachers at the Ridings school face disruption" (*Guardian*, 29 October 1996: 1). Teachers were being physically assaulted (three teachers had been attacked in a single day), verbal abuse of teachers was common-place ("They are regularly told where to go in no uncertain terms"), cans of urine were allegedly thrown at teachers and one teacher was stoned by a group of boys as he tried to rescue a young female student who was being attacked by a group of her peers (*Guardian*, 29 October 1996). Tabloid accounts displayed a predictable love of hyperbole and lack of measure. The *Sun*, for example, published a story about a young woman teacher "sexually assaulted by a boy of 14" under the headline "Sex Attack on Sobbing Miss Shuts Hell School" (1 November 1996). The "shameful attack happened as thugs already banned from the school rampaged through the classrooms reducing teachers to tears".

A week later, the chaos seemed to be endemic and spreading. A new school featured in headlines. The head teacher of Manton junior school in Nottinghamshire announced that he was closing the school indefinitely because he was unable to guarantee the safety of the 200 children at the school now that Matthew Wilson, a 13-year-old previously excluded from the school for violent behaviour, was returning. Even the liberal-minded *Guardian* announced that "the discipline crisis in schools took another twist yesterday" with the closure of a school "in a row over a ten year old pupil accused of assaulting other pupils" (*Guardian*, 29 October 1996: 1). Calls for the reinstatement of corporal punishment came from the then Secretary of State for Education, Gillian Shepherd (*Guardian*, 30 October 1996: 1) and *Sun* columnist and erstwhile politician Norman Tebbit (*Sun*, 1 November 1996). An editorial in the Sun lamented the passing of "the days when a few strokes of the cane could deal a short, sharp, shock to any pupil who stepped out of line" (*Sun*, 30 October 1996: 6).

This barrage of adverse media coverage of children during the 1990s has undoubtedly challenged prevailing assumptions about children and child-hood. The innocent "victims" of the 1980s who required the protection from abusive adults offered by the provisions of the Children Act are hardly recognisable among the current media images of children. Seemingly inevitable policy consequences follow from such images and perceptions.

Protecting society from the villains

Such anxieties have triggered populist and authoritarian policy responses from the two major parties, which stress the management and containment of young people, despite a plethora of research studies and official advice which illustrate the futility of such measures (Cavadino and Dignan, 1997). The consequences for children's rights have been considerable. The 1991 Criminal Justice Act, with its commitment to community alternatives to custodial offences and the three "D's" of diversion, decriminalisation and decarceration, was superseded by the Criminal Justice and Public Order Act 1994 which offered an increasingly punitive penal policy. The Act offered the new secure training order for 12–14-year-olds, longer-term detention and electronic tagging. Calls for harsher measures to deal with child and youth crime reached a crescendo at the Conservative party conference in October 1993 where Michael Howard announced his "27 point crime-busting package" of measures which constituted the "biggest crackdown on crime ever mounted in Britain" (*Daily Express*, 7 October 1993). Howard promised "young lawbreakers will find punishments less soft. There will be 'sin bins' for 12 to 14 year olds and longer sentences for 15 year olds. Punishments in the community for under 17 year olds will be made tougher" (*Express*, 7 October 1993). The public clamour for action to control young people was irresistible for politicians: a classic case of legislation by tabloid. "We must get on", Howard claimed, "pass the legislation and take these young thugs off the street" (*Daily Express*, 7 October 1993). Two years later a headline in *The Times* announced "Howard Plans 'House of Pain' Regimes For Young Offenders" (6 February 1995).

Measures to deal with children and young people who are "out of control" have also been central to the New Labour project. In the run up to the 1997 general election, the party's intention to be "tough on crime and tough on the causes of crime" became a widely known soundbite underscoring the emphasis which the party placed on issues of youth crime and criminal justice. Being "soft" on young offenders has never been a vote winning strategy for UK politicians. In government, New Labour, and particularly Home Secretary Jack Straw, have sustained the considerable policy impetus signalled in opposition. In September 1997 Straw published a consultation document announcing the "biggest crack down on young criminals for 50 years" which was intended to "break the excuses culture that has developed, where a young offender seeks to excuse their behaviour" (*Guardian*, 26 September 1997). Straw claimed the proposed measures were intended to be "extremely tough" (*Guardian*, 22 September 1997). Nothing less would satisfy public opinion nurtured by the tabloid headlines of the 1990s.

The Crime and Disorder Act 1998 delivered a predictable list of populist measures for controlling children and young people to an anxious public. These included: anti-social behaviour orders to tackle harassment by children over 10; parenting orders; child safety orders; curfews; the abolition of *Doli Incapax*; final warnings for young offenders with reparations for victims; electronic tagging; fast track punishments and a shift away from the welfare role of the youth justice system to emphasise the major aim which is to prevent children offending.

In September 2000, Straw returned to "a popular theme for Home secretaries facing a party conference – cracking down on teenage tearaways" (*Guardian*, 25 September 2000: 6). At a cost of £45 millions over the next three years, 2,500 "hardcore young criminals" will be kept under "24 hours a day, seven days a week" surveillance in the community "where this is necessary". The technology of containment is remarkable and includes "electronic tagging, voice verification, tracking by probation and social work staff and policing": some young people will be issued with pagers (Straw quoted in the *Guardian*, 25 September 2000). A spokesperson for the National Association of Probation Officers doubted the effectiveness of such surveillance in reducing crime without measures to tackle poverty, social exclusion and the disadvantage that "cause offending". But the *Guardian's* home affairs editor makes an obvious point. A major purpose of the statement and its timing is "to blunt the Conservative's political attack on his [Straw's] record in the run up to an election in the face of rising crime figures" – i.e. in the context of a continuing moral panic about youth offending and crime. In January 2001 with a general election predicted for May, Straw announced the introduction of a new Criminal Justice and Police Bill designed to "tackle yobs". The Bill which promised "the most sweeping extension of police powers since Michael Howard's infamous 1994 Criminal Justice and Public Order Act" included among its proposals the extension of child curfew schemes to 15-year-olds (*Guardian*, 20 January 2001: 1).

This continuing emphasis on containment and control in criminal justice policy reflects persistent media representations and shifting public perceptions of children and young people. In press headlines children have been identified and denounced as "villains". In sharp contrast, at the beginning of the 1990s in the wake of widely publicised inquiries into the deaths of a number of young children at the hands of their parents, as well as events at Cleveland, children were victims and society was shaping policies designed to protect them. At the turn of the new millennium, society is designing policies to protect the community from unruly, criminal and anti-social children. The sensational, partisan and dramatic media reporting of certain incidents concerning children (especially the Bulger case) has provided much of the impetus behind these cultural and policy shifts. There is a discernible irony here when the UN Convention suggests that the prime function of the media should be "to disseminate information and material of social and cultural benefit to the child ... especially [materials] aimed at the promotion of his or her social, spiritual and moral well being" (Article 17). But it is difficult to read headlines which describe children as "Yobs", "Gang Rapists", "Evil", "Murderers" or "The Children From Hell" and conclude that these are "beneficial to the child". Regrettably, a new public mood about children is evident. It is a mood which is increasingly receptive to authoritarian policies targeted at children. It is a mood which is much less receptive to the discussion of children's rights.

References

Alderson, P. (2000) *Young Children's Rights*, Jessica Kingsley/Save the Children
—— (1993) *Children's Consent to Surgery*, Open University Press, Buckingham
Allsopp, M. (1997) "A Triptych For Our Times" *Index on Censorship* vol. 26, no. 2, pp. 122–130
Archard, D. (1993) *Children; Rights and Childhood*, Routledge, London
Aries, P. (1962) *Centuries of Childhood*, Jonathan Cape, London
Aristotle (1959) *Politics*, Everyman, Dent, London
Beetham, D. (1995) "Human Rights In The Study Of Politics" in D. Beetham (ed.) *Politics and Human Rights*, a special issue of *Political Studies* vol. 43, pp. 41–61
Cavadino, P. and Dignan, J. (1997) *The Penal System*, Sage, London
Children's Express (1998) *Kids These Days*, Children's Express, London
Children's Rights Alliance for England (2000) *The Real Democratic Deficit: Why 16 and 17 year olds should be allowed to vote*, Children's Rights Alliance for England, London
Cox, R. (1996) *Shaping Childhood*, Routledge, London
Cuninghame, C. (1999) *Realising Children's Rights*, Save the Children, London
Davis, H. and Bourhill, M. (1997) " 'Crisis': The Demonization of Children and Young People" in P. Scraton (ed.) *"Childhood" in "Crisis"*, University College London Press, London
Dworkin, R. (1977) *Taking Rights Seriously*, Duckworth, London
Eekelaar, J. (1994) "The Interests of the Child and the Child's Wishes; the role of dynamic self determination" *International Journal of Law and the Family* vol. 8
Ekman Ladd, R. (1996) *Children's Rights Revisioned: Philosophical Readings*, Wadsworth Publishing, Belmont, USA
Ennew, J. (1986) *The Sexual Exploitation of Children*, Polity Press, Cambridge
Farson, R. (1977) "Birthrights" in B. Gross and R. Gross (eds) *The Children's Rights Movement*, USA
Feinberg, J. (1980) "Legal paternalism" *Rights, Justice and the Bounds of Liberty: Essays in Social Philosophy*, Princeton University Press, USA
—— (1973) *Social Philosophy*, Prentice Hall, USA
Flekkøy, M. (1991) *A Voice For Children; Speaking Out As Their Ombudsman*, UNICEF/Kingsley
Franklin, B. (1996) "From Little Angels To Little Devils: Changing Media Representations of Children and Childhood" *Community Care* 24 October, pp. 20–21
—— (1995) "The Case For Children's Rights: A Progress Report" in B. Franklin (ed.) *The Handbook of Children's Rights: Comparative Policy and Practice*, Routledge, London, pp. 3–25
—— (1992) "Votes for Children" *Childright* April, no. 85, pp. 10–15

—— (1989) "Children's Rights: Developments and Prospects" *Children and Society* vol. 3, pp. 50–67

—— (ed.) (1986) *The Rights of Children*, Blackwells, Oxford

Franklin, B. and Parton, N. (1991) "Media Reporting of Social Work; a framework for analysis" in B. Franklin and N. Parton (eds) *Social Work, the Media and Public Relations*, Routledge, London

Franklin, A. and Franklin, B. (1996) "Growing Pains: The Developing Children's Rights Movement in the UK" in S. Wagg and J. Pilchar (eds) *Thatcher's Children: Politics, childhood and society in the 1980s and 1990s*, Falmer Press, London, pp. 94–114

—— (1990) "Age and Power. A Political Economy of Ageism" in T. Jeffs and M. Smith (eds) *Youth Work in a Divided Society*, Macmillan, pp. 1–28

Franklin, B. and Lavery, G. (1989) "Legislation by Tabloid? Social Work, The Press and the Law", *Community Care*, 24 March, pp. 23–28

Franklin, B. and Petley, J. (1996) "Killing the Age of Innocence: Newspaper reporting of the death of James Bulger" in S. Wagg and J. Pilchar (eds) *Thatcher's Children: Politics, childhood and society in the 1980s and 1990s*, Falmer Press, London, pp. 134–154

Freeman, M.D.A. (1985) *The Rights and the Wrongs of Children*, Pinter

French, S. (1997) "The Devil's Seed" *Guardian* 21 May, pp. 14–15

Gittins, D. (1998) *The Child in Question*, Macmillan Press, London

Harris, J. (1996) "Liberating Children" in M. Leahy and D. Cohn-Sherbrok (eds) *The Liberation Debate – Rights at Issue*, Routledge, London

—— (1984) "The Political Status Of Children" in K. Graham (ed.) *Contemporary Political Philosophy: Radical Studies*, Cambridge University Press, pp. 35–59

Hart, R. (1992) *Children's Participation from Tokenism to Citizenship*, Innocenti Essays No. 4, UNICEF, London

Haydon, D. and Scraton, P. (2000) " 'Condemn A Little More And Understand A Little Less' The Political Context and Rights Implications of the Domestic and European Rulings in the Venables Thompson Case" *Journal of Law and Society*, vol. 27, no. 3, pp. 416–448

Holland, P. (1992) *What Is A Child? Popular Images of Childhood*, Virago Press, London

Holt, J. (1975) *Escape From Childhood*, Penguin, London

Horn, P. (1997) *The Victorian Town Child*, Sutton Publishing, Gloucestershire

Hoyles, M. (1979) *Changing Childhood*, Writers and Readers, London

Hoyles, M. and Evans, P. (1989) *The Politics of Childhood*, Journeyman, London

Hughes, J. (1996) "The Philosopher's Child" in R. Ekman Ladd (ed.) *Children's Rights Revisioned: Philosophical Readings*, Wadsworth, Belmont, USA, pp. 15–20

Hutchby, I. and Moran-Ellis, J. (1998) "Situating Children's Social Competence" in I. Hutchby and J. Moran-Ellis (eds) *Children and Social Competence: Arenas of Action*, Falmer Press, London, pp. 7–27

Jaffe, P. and Rey Wicky, H. (1998) "Children's Competence" in A. Saporiti (ed.) *Exploring Children's Rights*, Franco Angeli, Milan, pp. 51–63

James, A. and Prout, A. (1997) *Constructing and Reconstructing Childhood: Contemporary issues in the sociological study of childhood*, Falmer Press, London

James, A. Jenks, C. and Prout, A. (1998) *Theorising Childhood*, Polity Press, Oxford

Jenks, C. (1996) *Childhood*, Routledge, London

Kant, I. (1930) *Lectures on Ethics*, Methuen, London

—— (1887) *The Philosophy of Law*, T. and T. Clark, London

King, M. (1995) "The James Bulger Murder Trial: Moral Dilemmas and Social Solutions", *The International Journal of Children's Rights*, vol. 3, pp. 1–21

Lansdown, G. (1995) *Taking Part: Children's Participation in Decision Making*, London, IPPR

Laslett, P. (1965) *The World We Have Lost*, Methuen, London

Lawrence, D.H. (1919) *An Essay on Education*, cited in P. Jenkins (1993) *Children's Rights*, Longman, Harlow, p. 43

Locke, J. (1964) *Two Treatises of Government*, P. Laslett (ed.) Cambridge University Press

Lumley, K. (1998) " 'Teeny Thugs in Blair's Sights': Media Portrayals of Children in Education and their Policy Implications" in *Youth and Policy* no. 61, Autumn, pp. 1–12

Mayall, B. (1994) *Children's Childhoods: Observed and Experienced*, Falmer Press, London

McCourt, F. (1997) *Angela's Ashes: A Memoir of A Childhood*, HarperCollins, London

Mill, J. S. (1969) *Utilitarianism*, M. Warnock (ed.), Fontana, London

—— (1910) *On Liberty*, Everyman, Dent, London

Miller, J. (1999) "Young Children as Decision Makers" in C. Cuninghame (ed.) *Realising Rights*, Save the Children, London, pp. 71–76

Morrison, B. (1997) *As If*, Granta Books, London

Mortier, F. (1999) "Rationality and Competence to Decide in Children" in *Understanding Children's Rights*, E. Verhellen (ed.), University of Ghent, Ghent, pp. 79–100

Muncie, J. (1999) "Exorcising Demons: Media, Politics and Criminal Justice" in B. Franklin (ed.) *Social Policy, the Media and Misrepresentation*, Routledge, London, pp. 174–190

Murdock, G., Porteous, S. and Colston, H. (1980) "How Adolescents are Reported in the Press", *Journal of Adolescence*, no. 3, pp. 322–339

Newell, P. (2000) *Taking Children Seriously: A Proposal For A Children's Rights Commissioner*, Calouste Gulbenkian Foundation, London

Pearson, G. (1983) *Hooligan: A History of Respectable Fears*, Macmillan, Basingstoke

Petley, J. (1999) "The Monstrous Child" in M. Aaron (ed.) *The Body's Perilous Pleasures. Dangerous desires and contemporary culture*, Edinburgh University Press, Edinburgh, pp. 87–107

Pinchbeck, I. and Hewitt, M. (1973) *Children in English Society*, 2 vols, Routledge and Kegan Paul, London

Pitts, J. (1995) "Youth Crime" in Polly Neate (ed.) *Scare in the Community: Britain in a Moral Panic*, Community Care, London, p. 6

Plumb, J. H. (1972) *In The Light of History*, Penguin, London

Postman, N. (1983) *The Disappearance of Childhood*, W.H. Allen, London

Purdy, L. (1994) "Why Children Should Not have Equal Rights" in *International Journal of Children's Rights*

Rawls, J. (1972) *A Theory of Justice*, Oxford University Press, Oxford

Rodham, H. (1973) "Children Under the Law" *Harvard Educational Review* vol. 43, pp. 479–493

Rogers, C.M. and Wrightsman, L.S. (1978) "Attitudes Towards Children's Rights: Nurturance or Self Determination" *Journal of Social Issues* vol. 34, no. 2

Rosalind, M. and Janssen, Jac. J. (1990) *Growing Up In Ancient Egypt*, Rubicon Press, London

Rose, L. (1991) *The Erosion of Childhood. Child oppression in Britain 1860–1918*, Routledge, London

Russell, B. (1971) *Principles of Social Reconstruction*, Allen and Unwin, London

Saporiti, A. (ed.) (1999) *Exploring Children's Rights*, Franco Angeli, Milan

Scarre, G. (1980) "Children and Paternalism" *Philosophy* vol. 55

Shahar, S. (1990) *Childhood In The Middle Ages*, Routledge, London

Stainton Rogers, R. and Stainton Rogers, W. (1992) *Stories of Childhood*, Harvester Wheatsheaf, London

Van Bueren, G. (1996) *Children in Charge: The Child's Right To A Fair Hearing*, Jessica Kingsley, London, pp. 27–38

Verhellen, E. (1999) *Understanding Children's Rights*, Ghent: University of Ghent Press

Verhellen, E. and Spiesschaert, F. (eds) (1989) *Ombudswork for Children*, Amersfoort, Leuven

Wald, M. (1979) "Children's Rights; A Framework For Analysis" *University of California Davis Law Review* vol. 12, pp. 255–282

Warner, M. (1994) *Six Myths of Our Time: Managing Monsters*, Vintage, London

West, A. (1999) "They Make Us Out to be Monsters: Images of children and young people in care" in B. Franklin, *Social Policy, the Media and Misrepresentation*, Routledge, pp. 253–269

Worsfold, V. (1974) "A Philosophical justification For Children's Rights" *Harvard Educational Review* vol. 44, pp. 142–157

Wringe, C. (1995) "Children's Welfare Rights: A Philosopher's View" in M. John (ed.) *Children in Our Charge: The Child's Right To Resources*, Jessica Kingsley, London, pp. 19–23

Wyness, M. (2000) *Contesting Childhood*, Falmer Press, London

Young, A. (1996) *Imagining Crime: Textual Outlaws and Criminal Conversations*, Sage, London

Part II

Children's rights

The changing legal framework

2 Schooling, education and children's rights

Tony Jeffs

Tangible progress has been achieved regarding young people's rights within school settings since the 1980s (see Jeffs, 1995). First corporal punishment has been eradicated. So significant has been the shift that teachers who caned and slapped with impunity a decade ago now face automatic suspension if accused and dismissal if guilty. Britain, the last European country to outlaw corporal punishment, did so not because public opinion desired or politicians willed it but because the European Court of Human Rights insisted on it. Reluctant acceptance of the decision by politicians, teacher unions and the public reflects a widespread belief that hitting children is acceptable and Europe wrong to meddle. Consequently regulations are now imposed on schoolteachers that neither the majority of politicians nor the public apply to themselves. Consequently, humbug and hypocrisy surround the issue of violence against children. The previous Secretary of State for Education, for example, who enforced the regulations "de-frocking" teachers who use violence, unapologetically boasts in an interview "I smacked my children and it worked" before proceeding to argue that parents, nannies and childminders (but not teachers struggling to control a class rather than an individual child) must retain the right to smack because it is often "the only way of getting the message across" (Wheen, 2000: 7). By "message" he presumably means the need for obedience rather than the superiority of violence over negotiation or persuasion? He is not alone in advocating this tactic. The current Prime Minister, ex-Leader of the Opposition and Archbishop of Canterbury all advocate violence against children, everywhere except in the school. Even the Prince of Wales offers very public support to a teacher accused of unlawfully slapping a child (Henry, 2000). Fortunately European legislation currently prevents politicians putting the clock back. However the two main parties are determined to avoid being classified as "soft" and therefore support childminders' right to smack (Hackett, 2001).

Second, the protection of scholars from random violence and bullying within the school environment has become a public issue. The scale of the problem is difficult to calibrate though it appears that at all levels there exists an unparalleled determination to address this issue. Legal action from victims, the backwash from pupil suicides, court cases involving perpetrators and the courage of victims publicising their plight have all contributed to the promotion of policies supporting victims and the curtailing of the frequency of incidents. Coupled with the elimination of corporal punishment these policies will help to ensure most schools become far less violent and physically threatening.

Third, as with other policy areas discussed in this volume (see chapters 5 and 6), the Human Rights Act (1998) will secure beneficial changes relating to school students' rights. The Act will force change, although how and where is difficult to predict. The HRA makes it unlawful for public authorities, local education authorities (LEAs) and schools alike to behave in ways incompatible with the European Convention on Human Rights, unless they can demonstrate they acted according to the provision of primary legislation (such as another Act of Parliament). Courts and tribunals dealing with exclusions and appeals on the allocation of school places are similarly obliged to take account of Convention Rights and the case law of the European Court of Human Rights. The British government accepted Article 2 on the right to education that states:

> No person shall be denied the right to education. In exercise of any functions which it assumes in relation to education and to teaching, the state shall respect the right of parents to ensure such education and teaching in conformity with their own religious and philosophical convictions.

Acceptance was subject to a reservation that the government would comply only "so far as it is compatible with the provision of efficient instruction and training and the avoidance of unreasonable expenditure" (Home Office, 2000: 37). Clearly what is "unreasonable expenditure" along with other matters will be tested in law. We can expect, for example, cases relating to LEAs' failure to offer adequate educational provision for excluded and disabled students seeking entry to "mainstream schools". The outcome of test cases is unpredictable but it seems likely that the capacity of schools to exclude and to enforce regulations regarding such matters as uniforms and codes of dress will be curtailed. Many illiberal and archaic practices may be swept aside. As a result, schools may come to resemble those operating elsewhere in Europe in matters of discipline and social norms. Unquestionably the HRA will wreak havoc upon certain practices within the school system that have remained virtually unaltered since Victorian times. School uniforms offer an obvious example. Almost a third of LEAs provide no help towards their cost, while the majority that does have failed to ensure grants keep pace with inflation: average grants cover only half the cost of the cheapest outfit (Henry, 2001). Most schools however insist on uniforms and suspend or exclude those who fail to comply. When tested in court, schools' right to deny those unable or unwilling to match arbitrary dress codes will go. The government's reaction is predictable when faced with the choice of meeting the cost of uniforms for those who can't afford them or allowing their use to fade away.

Fourth despite the government's June 2000 decision to sideline plans for a parliamentary bill extending the remit of disability rights legislation to cover schools and colleges and to update the law in relation to educational special needs, reforms can be expected. Campaigners will not achieve all they want but they are pushing against an open door given the government's position stated in 1997:

> We want to see more pupils with SEN included in mainstream primary and secondary schools. We support the United Nations Education, Scientific and Cultural Organisation (UNESCO) Salamanca World Statement on Special Needs Education 1994. This calls on governments to adopt the principles of inclusive education enrolling all children in mainstream schools. ... This implies a progressive extension of the capacity of mainstream schools to provide for children with a wide range of needs.
>
> (DfEE, 1997: 44)

Reform is urgently needed especially to prevent schools labelling those likely to perform badly in tests as "special needs". For students this ploy both stigmatises and restricts seriously their subsequent educational options. Schools, notably the "successful" with more applicants than places, are rejecting those with special needs or who they judge to be "less likely to make the grade". As one LEA report explained they "fear it will affect their standing in league tables" (Walker, 2000: 1). However reluctant the government is to spend money, it will have no choice but to bribe schools with grants and top-up funding to take these students. This will occur primarily because exclusion on such grounds, once legally challenged, will probably not be allowed to continue and because the alternatives of home tuition and special units are more expensive.

Finally the appointment of a Children's Commissioner in Wales has certainly hastened the creation of a similar post in England. Initially his function was to promote the rights and welfare of looked-after young people and those using regulated services such as day care, childminding and boarding schools. Political pressure within the Welsh Assembly led to an extension of the remit giving the Commissioner powers to investigate wider concerns and complaints; to ensure young people's opinions are considered regarding legislation and decisions that collectively affect them; to review advocacy and complaint procedures; and allocates the capacity and resources to sustain recurrent face-to-face contact with young people. Currently Wales and ten other European Union states have Children's Commissioners, based on the Children's Ombudsman model launched in

Norway two decades ago (Flekkøy, 1991; see also chapters 17, 22 and 25). All have powers to intervene in matters "educational". Britain promised it will "watch with interest" developments in Wales (Willow, 2001). Undoubtedly advocates such as Newell (2000) will press the case for a similar appointment in England; almost certainly they will succeed, sooner rather than later.

Is it churlish to classify these advances as insignificant? Especially when, alongside the burgeoning of locally based children's rights services, 40 in 1999 and over 100 by December 2000 (Gledhill, 2001), they promise to ameliorate many of the restrictions that young people encounter in schools. Securing these reforms will satisfy many but in key respects they are superficial because they fail to address two fundamental questions – the right of students to influence the curriculum and the retention of compulsory attendance.

The big question

The rise of mass education, largely funded by taxation, during the eighteenth and nineteenth centuries provoked fierce opposition. Predictably, Gradgrind employers and pinchfist members of the "superior" classes objected, resenting the loss of cheap, malleable labour and the "tax burden". However the widespread opposition amongst radicals and educated members of the working class is less predictable. Their objections were neither the by-product of miserliness nor ignorance. After all, many of these made prodigious sacrifices to secure educational opportunities for themselves and others. They found time for education despite 80-plus-hour working weeks and meagre holidays. They supported societies and clubs, libraries, Sunday schools, circulating libraries and lectures from paltry wages. They nevertheless rejected state interference – why?

Godwin articulated the reasons for their distrust, outlining three prime objections to state control. First it would "expend its energies in the support of prejudice" and focus on teaching what is known rather than the inquisitiveness to discover what is not. Second rather than "incite men to act for themselves" it would endeavour "to retain them in a state of perpetual pupillage". Third governments and churches would use it to "strengthen its hand and perpetuate its institutions" (1976: 44). Godwin, perhaps the first modern advocate of children's rights, was convinced liberty and freedom, for young and old, demanded an educational system free from state control, in which young people had autonomy over the content and pace of their education, allowing them to "go first, and the master to follow" (Godwin, 1797 quoted Ward, 1991: 45).

Working-class radicals retained deep-seated antagonism to state involvement in education, even while campaigning for universal suffrage, proclaiming

Bowed down and oppressed as we already are, we manage to keep alive the principles and spirit of liberty; but if ever knavery and hypocrisy succeed in establishing this centralizing, state-moulding, knowledge-forcing scheme in England, so assuredly will the people degenerate into passive submission to injustice, and their spirit sink into the pestilential calm of despotism.

(Lovett and Collins, 1840: 74)

They secured the vote, but their stance on education failed to secure the administrative and funding structure they desired: arrangements akin to those adopted in Denmark during this period largely through the efforts of N.F.S. Grundtvig. This entrusted central government with responsibility for funding education via direct taxation but delegated management (including control of the curriculum) to autonomous groups of teachers, parents and students (Davies, 1931: Koch, 1952: Jeffs, 1999). Grundtvig concluded, after a visit to England in 1843, that Denmark must never adopt this model which was creating a "dismal" society transforming people into "mere accessories, mere appendices to machines" (quoted Davies, 1931: 34). His followers were so determined to retain independent "free" schools, they issued an ulti-matum to the Danish government that they would rather close their schools than accept the yoke of centralised control. Their victory produced a system which Davies and Kirkpatrick found still "characterised by a dialogue culture" (2000: 16), one where democratic practices flourish alongside levels of achievement that put our system to shame (De la Cour, 1988). In Britain autonomous working-class education was destroyed by a combination of blatant oppression, poverty and governmental funding of "safe" alterna-tives. While state schools and colleges were rigorously inspected and straight-jacketed, private schools, and "Ivy League" universities operated without interference. The Victorian Code, like today's National Curriculum, was never imposed on the private schools despite large-scale subsidies via grants and tax breaks. As Lovett and Collins predicted we acquired an entrenched two-tier configuration protecting and sustaining inequality and injustice, devoid of a "dialogue culture".

Nowadays the views of Godwin and the Chartists evoke scant sympathy even among the "left leaning". Activists and academics alike overwhelm-ingly perceive "progress" as emanating from heightened state involvement, not reduced levels of intervention. Children's rights advocates today charac-teristically clamour for more legislation to "protect" young people, but rarely for its removal. Yet I am no longer inclined to disregard those pioneers – individuals who fought state control believing it would curtail the freedom of the majority; destroy for many the love of learning; and require the imposition of sanctions that would annihilate the individuality and integrity of teacher and student alike; who feared the extension of child-hood because it encouraged immaturity and prevented young people being "educated as if they were one day to be men" (Godwin, 1797: 112).

A place for children

Lovett and Collins' antipathy towards a "centralizing, state-moulding, knowledge-forcing scheme" (1840: 74) would surely be reinforced if they surveyed the current school system. Over the last two decades Whitehall has appropriated control from LEAs, communities and teachers for itself. Taking the right to: decide via the National Curriculum what is taught; seize control of schools from locally elected councils and transfer them to private companies; implement Education Action Zones run by individuals appointed the Education Secretary or an emergency educational service likewise comprising ministerial appointees. Such regulatory powers mock local democracy, forcing electors to pay for services which they do not control. These encourage cronyism and will inevitably trigger corruption. In Leeds, for example, in what was described as a "populist move", management of the schools was transferred to a joint venture company run by the local football club chairman. An individual who, without embarrassment, admits he knows nothing about education. His Board, also selected by the Education Secretary, comprises two councillors and two representatives of a private education company. This unaccountable troupe, prior to taking over, distributed consultancy contracts worth over £600,000 (Wainwright, 2000).

Within classrooms this regime produces ever more standardisation. First the government tells teachers what to teach, then how to teach it. The National Curriculum is assembled by hand-picked committees, chosen by the Education Secretary, who can alter, amend or reject their suggestions. What started out as a concept based on guidelines has degenerated into farce as politicians find themselves unable to resist the temptation to manage by diktat. The result is lunacy such as national lists of words scholars must learn to spell by a given age (600 in year 6) and a junior minister, without an A-level to her name let alone a science one, ordering science teachers to use English, not international spellings, for scientific terms (Smithers and Robinson, 2000; *Birmingham Post*, 2000). Teacher compliance is enforced by regulated tests; competitive league tables based on them; by linking pay and promotion to test scores; and vindictive inspections which keep LEAs, heads and teachers "on message" by threatening those failing to comply with the approved norms relating to teaching methods, discipline codes and curricula with dismissal, humiliation or, in the case of LEAs, loss of control. The resulting structure deliberately sets student against student, teacher against teacher, school against school, LEA against LEA, manufacturing far more losers than winners. The defining climate of fear works solely for the benefit of politicians and mandarins seeking to impose their order and writ. Inevitably a desiccating air of failure pervades the system.

Any debate regarding children's rights within the context of education must start by recognising this situation. Current arrangements ensure that many young people receive a sub-standard education from teachers who neither enjoy teaching nor wish to remain within the profession. Research evidence indicates as many as a third of current teachers would leave if they could find alternative employment. Among those who do leave almost half accepted lower paid jobs because they were so desperate to escape a profession where "initiative and resourcefulness are banned" (Ross, Hutchings and Menter, 2001: 9). Anecdotal evidence is equally unsettling. One trainee informed the author how during teaching practice in three schools no teachers encouraged him to join the profession. All expressed amazement that an accountant could possibly wish to be a teacher. So low has teacher status plummeted that, apart from two years, since 1980 university B.Ed. and postgraduate places have gone begging despite a lowering of entry qualifications and expensive advertising campaigns (Smithers and Robinson, 2000). Young people are not stupid. Their own experiences of school tell them teaching has become for too many a miserable, dispiriting occupation devoid of the opportunities for creative intellectual endeavour that once compensated for long hours and poor remuneration. No other career has more opportunities to recruit its next generation. That it is incapable of doing so is a damming indictment of our present system.

As the intellectual quality of teachers declines we will rapidly enter, if we have not already, a downward spiral. Culturally and intellectually deficient teachers (along with the lazy and exhausted) welcome pre-packaged lessons and prepared scripts, as they eradicate the requirement to think through content and delivery. They are not alone. Managements also like ready-wrapped lessons. First they help ensure students receive the inputs to pass "tests" and make comparative assessment of staff easier. Second they allow institutions to operate with increasingly casualised workforces; in 1999–2000 approximately half the vacancies were filled by temporary contracts (Woodward, 2001). Like fast food outlets, they allow schools to serve up what can be delivered by low-grade, high-turnover labour. Existing and potential teachers with significant cultural and intellectual capital inevitably recoil from such menial work, unless they have no alternative. Students cannot opt out, unless their parents can pay for it.

Our young people find their education dominated by the need to prepare for and sit an endless diet of tests. Education is reduced to the pursuit of test scores and qualifications. Although this trend is encountered elsewhere it may be more intrusive here. Certainly some countries, such as New Zealand and France, manage without national tests until students reach their mid teens. Currently the treadmill of testing commences from day one and grinds on until closure:

- Age 4 or 5: Baseline Assessment that must be undertaken within seven weeks of starting primary school. This covers basic speaking and listening, reading, writing, mathematics and personal and social development;
- Age 7: Key Stage 1 tests in reading and maths;

- Age 8: Optional Tests in English and maths available from the Qualifications and Curriculum Authority;
- Age 9: Optional Tests in maths and English from QCA. In 2001 "world class" tests to enable comparison with the educational performance of other industrialised nations will be introduced for the "top" 10 per cent of students;
- Age 10: Optional Tests in maths and English from QCA;
- Age 11: Key Stage 2 externally marked tests in English and maths signal the end of primary schooling;
- Age 11: many young people are obliged to sit tests prior to entry into secondary schools. They are used to grade and "select" applicants;
- Age 12: tests for secondary pupils who did not achieve level 4 at age 11;
- Age 13: "world class" tests in maths and problem-solving for "top" 10 per cent;
- Age 14: Key Stage 3 externally marked tests;
- Age 16: GCSEs;
- Age 17: GCSE re-takes and AS exams. The government expects pupils to take five AS subjects before proceeding to take three forward to A-level;
- Age 18: A-levels. Post 2002 Advanced Extension Awards are to be introduced for the "brightest" students.

An estimated 90 per cent of young people now take Optional Tests at ages 8, 9 and 10. Of course these aren't optional for the pupils. The numbers doing so proliferated when performance-related pay was imposed (Woodward, 2000). This time the tests are taken for teachers' financial benefit, but before judging staff too harshly it should be noted that in almost every instance tests are employed for others' benefit, never the students. The so-called "world class tests" are to enable planners and politicians to produce international comparisons; Baseline tests were manufactured to measure value-added performance and prevent schools in low-income areas crying foul when the league tables invariably place them at or near the bottom. Key Stage 2 tests were required to produce the league tables needed for a free market system between schools to operate. Given that the results arrive too late to be used for selection purposes "popular" secondary schools frequently employ their own "diagnostic" tests. Finally GCSEs, A-levels and Advanced Extension Awards are necessary for secondary league tables and to enable employers and universities to select and filter. Rarely do tests tell teachers anything new about pupil progress or learning.

Where is this obsession leading? Some consequences are evident. First it creates a great deal of stress and anxiety. The evidence is not conclusive but it is probably contributing to the sharp increase in diagnosed mental illness amongst young people (see chapter 7). Already we have calls for stress management to be added to the curriculum to help students cope with the tests and some primary schools are introducing it to improve their test scores (Burke, 2000: Luxmoore, 2000). Second, ever more time is stolen from young people to achieve imposed outcomes. Compulsory homework is augmented by weekend, evening and holiday cramming; Taylor Road Primary (Leicester), for example, had pupils in school the Sunday prior to Stage 2 tests and during mornings in the Easter holidays (Woodward, 2000). Third, it fosters a climate that sponsors cheating. Results are so crucial for teachers, schools, LEAs and communities (National Strategy for Neighbourhood Renewal funding, to "help" our poorest 88 communities, is dependent on achievement of "outcomes" including designated test scores) that predictably widespread (perhaps wholesale) cheating occurs since nobody benefits from exposure, including the senior officials and politicians policing the system who profit from the "improved results" cheating delivers (Davies, 2000). Finally it discourages dialogue within schools, thereby de-humanising the educational experience. Abundant evidence exists that teachers now spend more time cramming and "telling pupils facts and ideas or giving directions" (Galton *et al.*, 1999: 67). Treating them as receptacles, not learners, objects to be fed a script and denied the voice dialogue offers (Mroz *et al.*, 2000: Duffield *et al.*, 2000). Activities that should be endowed with value are cheapened, becoming chores designed to meet targets. As an HMI recently told the author: "this week I sat in on six Literacy Hours. I saw the teachers hear dozens of children read, but not once did they discuss what was being read to them. Not once did they make sure the child under-stood what they had read".

Young people have a right to education but we deceive them and delude ourselves if we pretend what is currently on offer is worthwhile or life enhancing. Being forced to sit in classrooms and trained like circus animals to perform on command is not an education. Elements of it may possess intrinsic worth and many students endure school because their certificates have negotiable labour market value. Students also enjoy meeting friends and often like their teachers. So schools survive the regime of tests and assess-ment. But getting by is not good enough. Davies and Kirkpatrick's (2000) comparative survey of British, Danish, Dutch and German schools highlights how Britain has lagged behind in giving young people a creative role to play in their education and this gap is probably growing. Meaningful engagement must extend beyond the play therapy of school councils and consultative groups discussing the design of school uniforms, menus and choosing prefects into opportunities to shape the content and delivery of the learning experi-ence. We need to create Fisher's (1998) "communities of enquiry" wherein students can engage as partners in a dialogue about their own and others' education. Places where this happens exist and the evidence confirms they are "academically" and "socially" successful (Harber, 1996: Apple and Beane, 1999). However such institutions are incompatible with a highly centralised system and compulsion. They require teachers to be free to enter into dialogue with their students about the fundamentals that count – what should we study? How should we study it? Centralised control of the curriculum and compulsory attendance make that impossible. Therefore whilst these features remain the administrative cornerstones of our educational system progress regarding children's rights in schools will remain minimal.

Opting out

During the last decade, notably post-Bulger, truancy has attracted heightened attention. There are no authoritative data available to establish whether truancy has risen, or not, in recent years. Unfortunately, according to Davies (2000), fiddling of the figures to achieve arbitrary targets is now so prevalent contemporary data is probably worthless. Those setting the policy agenda clearly believe it is increasing. The consistent message is that truants are a threat to themselves and others, as one minister, explained: "at risk of becoming one of the malingering employees of tomorrow, or worse still of drifting into a life of crime. Show me a persistent young truant, and there is a potential young criminal" (Patten, 1993). Fighting truancy is equated with fighting crime, even though research fails to provide substantive evidence to support this assumed relationship (O'Keefe, 1993). Nevertheless it is Section 16 of the 1988 Crime and Disorder Act, that came into effect in February 2000, which is at the heart of the anti-truancy strategy. This allows police to remove young people from the streets if they have "reasonable cause" to suspect they are absent without good reason. Truancy patrols comprising police, educational welfare officers and youth workers "stop young people" and either deliver them to school or the police station if they cannot prove they are old enough to be at large. Other initiatives linked to the £500 million programme to reduce truancy by a third before 2003 include: raising maximum fines for parents to £5,000; awarding the 50 schools achieving the highest reductions in truancy a £10,000 bounty; funding to build fencing and install CCTV cameras on perimeters, at exits and in corridors to prevent escape attempts and the skipping of lessons; and the introduction of Connexions "smart cards". The latter serve a number of functions. Schools with the technology in place use them to "swipe" young people into every lesson, allowing pupil movement to be continuously monitored and to exclude students from parts of a campus; they also serve as identity cards for truancy patrols, and verifiers of age for publicans, bus companies and shopkeepers; and finally as a sop they entitle holders to discounts in certain fast-food outlets and similar ventures anxious to relieve young people of their cash. Some schools have introduced their own incentives. One gives classes with ten weeks' full attendance a trip to Alton Towers, others offer free burgers for each full week (White, 2000). It says much about a school's self-image and lack of faith in the intrinsic value of the educational experience it offers when it resorts to bribing children to attend.

One of the most heartening developments for those concerned with children's rights is the phenomenal growth of home-schooling and autonomous learning networks. In Britain around 150,000 children with the active collaboration of their parents have chosen to opt out. Significantly over half the parents choosing this route are teachers (Webb, 1999). In the USA proportionately more young people are home educated, over 10 per cent in some states. The reasons for doing so are varied. For some it is the result of unhappy school experiences, for most though it appears to be a positive choice. According to one study it usually emanates from a desire to secure a more enriching education founded upon "an understanding of the interests, drives and aptitudes" of the young person (Fortune-Wood, 2000: 22). One follow-up study of home-educated adults found they led normal social lives, possessed exceptional social skills, matured earlier, were more likely to be involved in community and voluntary work and post-school learning (Webb, 1999). Perhaps the most articulate advocacy for this model comes from a participant:

> Children have no choice over their education, you tell us, but for as many as 150,000 home-educated children this isn't true. These children don't want any kind of school. School is a training ground for bullies and victims. School is a place where you learn what someone else has decided for you. School is a place where parents can leave their children for free, without taking responsibility for their education. Having a say in the type of building or the uniform or even some small say in what is taught or how teaching is done won't make much difference. The choice that children need is whether to be there or not. If more parents realised it or allowed it, children already have this choice.
>
> I like to choose what and how to learn. I don't want to be in a place where my property can be confiscated. For me learning is about living. I learn from everything I do and I make choices all the time. Choices are what growing up is all about and the choices have to be real, not just a bit of consultation to make you feel better. Home education doesn't give you the school you want, it gives you the education and life you want.
>
> (Tamsyn Fortune-Wood, aged 12 –
> letter to the *Guardian*, 23 January 2001)

Conclusion

Discontent with our authoritarian, repressive and standardised school system is growing. With good reason young people are getting more and more difficult to control within it. Slater (2001) reports that 66 per cent of teachers believe school discipline has deteriorated in the last five years, and it is difficult to contradict their judgement when scrutinising the ways schools have cut lunch-hours, break-times (in some cases eliminated them) and installed technology to enhance pupil supervision (Scott, 2000). Increasingly students are treated as actual or potential criminals requiring constant surveillance as schools acquire the appearance of a Northern Ireland police station. Rarely today are they places in which civilised or cultured persons of any age would elect to linger. We can only expect greater not less repression, according to Adcock, as ever more control of movement, learning and behaviour will be required for these creaking Victorian institutions to survive in a changing world. Home schooling and autonomous learning may be one answer (Dowty, 2000); small democratic schools another (Harber, 1996; Toogood, 1991), or possibly Adcock's preferred option of a "school-free system in which parents are encouraged to work with professional tutors in the provision of a personalised education for each child" (2000: 27). Perhaps if we seriously changed the way our schools operate to match the requirement of a Danish Education Act that "the teaching of the school and its daily life must [therefore] build on intellectual freedom, equality and democracy" (quoted Davies and Kirkpatrick, 2000: 22) we might avoid the dramatic upheavals Adcock views as inevitable. But that would require a complete overhaul of the current orientation of education policies, and the bulk of recent legislation.

Whatever solution is espoused the question of children's rights in relation to schooling and education will remain stalled until the thorny issue of compulsion is addressed. Compulsion ensures young people are axiomatically second-class members of the school community; they must "put up and shut up". Compulsion demands schools find ways of keeping some, perhaps many, young people in the building against their will. It corrupts the education process, as Godwin predicted, making teaching a role "not fit for a freeman" (quoted McCallister, 1931: 267–268) and forcing teachers to behave in ways that contradict their prime role as educators and mocks all discussion of the rights, freedoms and dignity of their students. It brings schools, and by association education and teaching, into disrepute. All in order to achieve the dubious end of incarcerating within the system some young people who actively wish to be somewhere else and many more, who, like working adults, want to miss the odd session when they have something better to do.

Compulsion also allows parents to abuse the education system, to use schools as warehouses where they can deposit their children, to gain the freedom to work or play whilst deluding themselves it is for the child's benefit. Young people are being sent to school earlier, for no good educational reason, but to get single mothers off welfare and allow employers to impose flexible working. For some the length of the school day is now intolerable. Only 19 per cent of young people attending breakfast and after-school clubs, which keep some incarcerated for 10 hours a day, would do so if given the choice (Smith, 2000). Some parents like such provision and schools find them profitable, but little evidence exists to show that these increased hours on school premises have any educational value whatsoever. Using schools as warehouses infringes the rights of young people and again devalues the standing of teachers. However it is not a new role merely the extension of a traditional one – the keeping of children off the streets and away from adults.

Perhaps the future of schools as institutions depends on a willingness to reject compulsion and the need to make allies of their students, on their readiness to accept young people as free and autonomous partners, to embrace children's rights not as an optional extra but as their very raison d'être? If not then John Gatto may be correct in predicting

> the defiant personal decisions of simple people, like the quiet revolution of the homeschoolers taking place under our noses right now which may be the most exciting social movement since the pioneers, not least because it is leaderless; a revolution in which our type of factory schooling has been treated as irrelevant, which it most certainly is.
>
> (quoted Fortune-Wood, 2000: 12)

The prospects for reforms concerning the rights of young people in the school setting are not good for those who advocate that students must be given opportunities to make collective and individual decisions relating to the content and structuring of their educational experiences. This however should not deter those committed to children's rights from trying. No institution impinges upon the daily lives of the overwhelming majority of children more than the school and none is so contemptuous of their opinions or the concept of democracy. That state of affairs must be constantly challenged and if we cannot create schools that respect the rights of children and actively foster democracy then we must not flinch from actively supporting alternatives that do.

References

Adcock, J. (2000) *Teaching Tomorrow: Personal tuition as an alternative to school* Nottingham: Education Now Books

Apple, M. and Beane, J. (1999) *Democratic Schools: Lessons from the chalk face* Buckingham: Open University Press

Birmingham Post (2000) "Purists win the day on English spelling" *Birmingham Post* 25 November

Burke, J. (2000) "Children suffer stress over their 'love lives'" *Observer* 29 October

Davies, L. and Kirkpatrick, G. (2000) *The EURIDEM Project: A review of pupil democracy in Europe* London: Children's Rights Alliance

Davies, N. (1931) *Education For Life: A Danish Pioneer* London: Williams and Norgate

—— (2000) *The School Report: Why Britain's schools are failing* London: Vintage

De la Cour, P. (1988) "Diversity in one country: the Danish example" *Education Now News and Review* May/June

DfEE (1997) *Excellence for All Children: Meeting Special Educational Needs* London: DfEE

Dowty, T. (2000) *Free Range Education: how home education works* London: Hawthorn Press

Duffield, J., Allen, J., Turner, F. and Morris, B. (2000) "Pupils' Voices on Achievement: an alternative to the standards agenda" *Cambridge Journal of Education* 30(2) pp. 263–289

Fisher, R. (1998) *Teaching Thinking: Philosophical enquiry in the classroom* London: Cassell

Flekkøy, M.G. (1991) *A Voice for Children: Speaking out as their Ombudsman* London: Jessica Kingsley Publishers

Fortune-Wood, J. (2000) *Doing it Their Way: home-based education and autonomous learning* Nottingham: Educational Heretics Press

Galton, M., Hargreaves, L., Comber, C., Wall, P. and Pell, A. (1999) *Inside the Primary Classroom: 20 years on* London: Routledge

Gledhill, K. (2001) "The Year of the Child?" *Community Care* 4 January

Godwin, W. (1797) *The Enquirer, Reflections on Education, Manners and Literature* (second edition 1823) London: G.G. and J. Robinson

—— (1976) *An Enquiry Concerning Political Justice, and its Influence on General Virtue and Happiness* Harmondsworth: Penguin

Griffith, R. (2000) *National Curriculum: National Disaster? Education and Citizenship* London: Routledge Falmer

Hackett, G. (2001) "MPs rekindle childminder row" *Times Educational Supplement* 5 January

Harber, C. (1996) *Small Schools and Democratic Practice* Nottingham: Educational Heretics Press

Henry, J. (2000) "New threat to slap-case head" *Times Educational Supplement* 15 December

—— (2001) "Dressing down for expensive uniform rules" *Times Educational Supplement* 12 January

Home Office (2000) *Study Guide to the Human Rights Act 1998* London: Home Office Communication Directorate

Jeffs, T. (1986) "Children's rights at school" in B. Franklin (ed.) *The Rights of Children* Oxford: Blackwell

—— (1995) "Children's educational rights in a new era" in B. Franklin (ed.) *Children's Rights: Comparative Policy and Practice* London: Routledge

—— (1999) *Henry Morris: Village colleges, community education and the ideal order* Nottingham: Education Now

Koch, H. (1952) *Grundtvig* (trans. Llewellyn Jones) Yellow Springs Ohio: Antioch Press

Lovett, W. and Collins, J. (1840) *Chartism: A new organization of the people,* (reprinted 1969) Leicester: Leicester University Press

Luxmoore, N. (2000) *Listening to Young People in School, Youth Work and Counselling* London: Jessica Kingsley Publishers

McCallister, W.J. (1931) *The Growth of Freedom in Education* London: Constable

Mroz, M., Smith, F. and Hardman, F. (2000) "The Discourse of the Literacy Hour" *Cambridge Journal of Education* 30(3) pp. 378–390

Newell, P. (2000) *Taking Children Seriously: Proposals for a Children's Rights Commissioner* London: Calouste Gulbenkian Foundation

O'Keefe, D. (1993) *Truancy in English Secondary Schools* London: Truancy Research Project, University of North London

Patten, J. (1993) "Truancy – Time for the Responsible Citizen to Strike Back" *DFE Press Release* 26 November

Ross, A., Hutchings, M. and Menter, I. (2001) "Heads will roll" *Guardian Education* 23 January pp. 8–9

Scott, C.A. (2000) " 'Going Home with the Chaps': Concerning the degradation of young urbanites and their social space and time" *Youth and Policy* (69) pp. 17–41

Slater, J. (2001) "Unhappy? No we still enjoy the job" *Times Educational Supplement* 12 January

Smith, F. (2000) *Child-Centred After School and Holiday Childcare* London: ESRC Research Briefing

Smithers, A. and Robinson, P. (2000) *Attracting Teachers* Liverpool: Centre for Employment Research, University of Liverpool

Smithers, R. (2000) "Blunkett to have last word on new literacy test" *Guardian* 30 August

Toogood, P. (1991) *Small Schools* Nottingham: Education Now Books

Wainwright, M. (2000) "Football chief to run school body" *Guardian* 3 October

Walker, J. (2000) "Schools reject problem pupils" *The Birmingham Post* 25 November

Ward, C. (1991) *Influences* Bideford: Green Books

Webb, J. (1999) *Those Unschooled Minds: Home educated children grow up* Nottingham: Educational Heretics Press

Wheen, F. (2000) "Wallop? It's more like codswallop" *Guardian* 13 December

White, P. (2000) "Teaching the truants a lesson" *The Journal* 20 October

Willow, C. (2001) "The Year of the Child?" *Community Care* 4 January

Woodward, W. (2000) "Testing ... testing ... testing" *Guardian* 20 May

—— (2001) "Pretty vacant" *Guardian* 18 January

3 The Children Act 1989 and children's rights

A critical reassessment

Jeremy Roche

In this chapter I consider the background to the Children Act 1989 and outline those provisions of the legislation which can be seen as promoting the welfare and liberty rights of children. I then examine some of the case law on the Children Act and, using recent research findings, attempt a critical reassessment of the legislation. I argue that what the promotion of children's rights requires is not so much amendments to the Children Act, though some useful amendments could be made, but a shift in adult thinking and practice concerning children. The demand for children's rights is a social and political project and while the Children Act 1989 can be seen as providing a framework for significant change it cannot bring this about by itself.

The demand for reform

The origins of the Children Act 1989 are complex. On one level the legislation was informed by a series of official reports including the Department of Health and Social Security review of childcare law (DHSS, 1985) and the Law Commission report on guardianship and custody (Law Commission, 1988) The message of these reviews was that the current law was unclear, unnecessarily complicated and characterised by procedural and substantive injustice. The government White Paper described its purpose in bringing forward proposals for change in the law relating to childcare and family services as the achievement of "greater clarity and consistency" to help "parents and children who may be affected by the law and those who work professionally within it" (DHSS/Home Office, 1987: para. 4).

Running alongside these institutional reviews of the legal framework were the child abuse scandals of the 1980s which centred on local authority social services practice (See generally Reder *et al.* 1993). The inquiry into the death of Jasmine Beckford found, amongst other things, that the social workers involved treated the parents as the client rather than the child: "Jasmine's fate illustrates all too clearly the disastrous consequences of the misguided attitude of the social workers having treated Morris Beckford and Beverley

Lorrington as the clients first and foremost" (London Borough of Brent, 1985: 294).

Further the social workers were found to have "had no idea what the legal implications of a care order were" (p. 207); failings of professional practice were a major cause of the "inevitable disaster" of Jasmine Beckford's death. The media response to this event was one of condemnation of the social workers involved for their failure to take timely action to protect the child.

In contrast the Butler Sloss report into the Cleveland case criticised those involved (paediatricians, police and social workers) for their over-zealous approach to protecting the children believed to be at risk of sexual abuse. However here the "villains" were the consultant paediatricians not the social workers. In the words of the Report:

> By reaching a firm conclusion on the basis of physical signs and acting as they would for non-accidental injury or physical abuse; by separating children from their parents and by admitting most of the children to hospital [Dr Higgs and Dr Wyatt] compromised the work of the social workers and the police.
>
> (Butler-Sloss, 1988: 243)

None the less Cleveland was seen as an instance of the local authority over-reaching itself even though it took the actions it did on the basis of the diagnoses of the two doctors. Earlier the report had noted that for some children the child protection process itself was experienced as abusive – as Butler-Sloss observed "the voices of the children were not heard".

Also in the mid 1980s the House of Lords gave their famous decision in the Gillick case. This case was concerned with whether the DHSS could lawfully issue a notice to the effect that while it was desirable to consult the parents of a person under 16 years of age who sought contraceptive advice and treatment, in some circumstances the doctor, exercising his or her clinical judgement, retained the right to provide such advice and treatment without informing the parents. Mrs Gillick sought a declaration from the High Court that this notice was unlawful. The case reached the House of Lords and in his oft-quoted judgement Lord Scarman held that: "The underlying principle of the law ... is that parental right yields to the child's right to make his own decision when he reaches a sufficient understanding and intelligence to be capable of making his own mind up on the matter in question" (*Gillick* v *West Norfolk and Wisbech AHA* [1985] 3 WLR 830 at 855)[1]

So, prior to the Children Act 1989 the law was seen as ineffective in promoting appropriate child protection practice and preventive work with families and as failing to involve parents and children sufficiently in decision-making. It was also seen as being too complex and as failing to strike the right balance between family privacy and the power of the state to intervene to protect children.

The Children Act 1989

In the words of the Lord Chancellor the legislation was the "most far reaching reform of childcare law ... in living memory".[2] Section 1 of the Act laid down three key decision-making principles. Under the Children Act the welfare of the child was the paramount consideration,[3] unnecessary delay was seen as prejudicial to the child's welfare and to be avoided, and the so-called no order principle required the court not to make an order unless it considered that "doing so would be better for the child than making no order at all". In addition the Act provided a "welfare checklist", i.e. a list of factors the court was required to take into account when hearing any contested application for a section 8 order and applications for orders under part IV of the Act.[4] With two exceptions the checklist was derived from existing case law. First, under section 1(3)(a) the court had to have regard to the "ascertainable wishes and feelings of the child concerned (considered in the light of his age and understanding)". Whilst this was within the spirit of the Gillick decision it was both less and more than that decision.[5] It was less in the sense that on one reading of Lord Scarman's judgement the common law was recognising the decision-making autonomy of children – under the Act the court merely has to take the child's wishes and feelings into account. The court's view of the child's welfare will prevail. It is more in that the court has to consider the child's wishes and feelings as a matter of routine. Second, under section 1(3)(g) the court was required to have regard to the range of powers available to it in the proceedings in question. This provision allowed the court to make an order different from the order applied for and thus underlined the courts' new decision-making flexibility.[6]

The Act introduced the concept of parental responsibility. This concept can be seen as promoting a new model of parenthood – once a parent always a parent.[7] For example, in the field of private law under the Act, parental responsibility for the child survived the making of an order for divorce. In the area of public law, even when a child was being "looked after" by the local authority under a care order the child's parents "shared" parental responsibility with the local authority. This was of symbolic and practical importance. Symbolically it served to reinforce the idea that you were always a parent – you still had the responsibility, even though in certain circumstances it could be circumscribed. Practically the concept was important because it linked either with other provisions in the Act or developments outside of the legislation.[8] The intended net effect of the concept was to reduce the likelihood of matrimonial disputes over children and to promote partnership between the local authority and the parents of children in need and "looked after" children.

Children and parents acquired new procedural and substantive rights under the Act. Parents whose children had been taken from the home under an emergency protection order could challenge the order after 72 hours. There was a presumption of contact between children and their parents both when the child was the subject of an emergency protection order (EPO) and when in care; children and parents had the right to take disputes about contact to court. Local authorities could not acquire compulsory powers over a child without the approval of the court.[9]

The Act also envisaged a different kind of relationship between local authorities and families experiencing difficulties in bringing up their children.[10] Under section 17 of the Children Act the local authority was under a general duty to "safeguard and promote the welfare of children within their area who are in need" and "so far as is consistent with that duty to promote the upbringing of such children by their families, by providing a range of services appropriate to those children's needs". Under Part III of the Act the local authority was thus under a duty to provide support to families with children in need thereby safeguarding and promoting their welfare and avoiding the need for more coercive forms of intervention later. Such support was to be arranged on the basis of partnership between the local authority and the family (Thoburn, 1995). When children did end up in care parents still had a right to be involved, section 22 imposing a duty on the local authority to consult with the child and the child's parents before making any decision in respect of the child.

Furthermore section 22(5) of the Act imposed a duty on the local authority to give due consideration to "the child's religious persuasion, racial origin and cultural and linguistic background" in making any decision about a child they were looking after. There were other provisions in the Act aimed at fostering respect for such identity rights of the child.[11]

Finally the Act repositioned the court, in some instances making it the key decision-making forum,[12] in others withdrawing judicial scrutiny.[13] In the public law field the role and powers of the guardian ad litem (GAL) were redrawn in order to secure for the court the availability of a report from an independent welfare professional which was thorough and based on access to all the relevant information.[14]

Children's rights

So in what ways can the Children Act 1989 be said to have advanced children's rights. The Act can be said to have advanced the "welfare rights"[15] of children through its endorsement of the paramountcy principle,[16] the provision of the "welfare checklist" and the no order principle. The threshold criteria[17] can be seen as an attempt to limit state intervention into family life by requiring a minimum threshold of harm to be established before any compulsory powers over a family can be acquired by the local authority. Lord Mackay argued:

> It is not proper to intervene on any level of harm. The fundamental point is that State intervention in families in the shape of the local authority should not be justified unless there is some level – "significant"

is a good word for it – at which significant harm is suffered or is likely to be suffered.

(cited in Allen, 1992: 125)

Such a "threshold" could be argued to promote the welfare rights of children by limiting the discretion of the local authority to intervene in the name of the welfare of the child – a concept that has been used and can be used to legitimate a very wide range of actions. Many of these, with the benefit of hindsight and from a more critical vantage point, appear to have undermined the welfare of the children involved (Robertson and Robertson, 1989). Even when a child did end up being "looked after" by a local authority under a care order this did not severe the parent–child link. The local authority acquires "parental responsibility" under the provisions of the Act but not such as to extinguish the parental responsibility of the parents in its entirety. The Act, also through its emphasis on the local authority providing supportive services to families with children "in need", promoted children's welfare rights. Children are best looked after in their own families and the role of the local authority should be to support families in bringing up their children. Children are thus spared the trauma of having to leave their home with all the resultant damaging consequences for their education, self-esteem and identity. However, "welfare rights" while important are not the only concern of the modern children's rights movement – such rights do not in any way challenge "adultist"[18] assumptions about what children are like.[19] The liberty rights of children[20] raise very different issues.

There are four aspects of the legislation that can be seen as supportive of children's liberty rights. First, the Act allowed for the possibility that children themselves may want to make applications for one of the new section 8 orders.[21] Section 10 specifically provided for the eventuality in which a child applied to the court for permission to make an application for a section 8 order. The court can only grant the child leave to apply if "it is satisfied that he has sufficient understanding to make the proposed application". None the less the Act in its contemplation of the possibility of the child becoming a litigant could be seen as advancing and extending the child's autonomy.

Second, and linked to the above, is the departure from the settled rule that a child could not bring or defend an action except via a guardian ad litem or "next friend", i.e. via an adult intermediary. Rule 9.2A of the Family Proceedings Rules 1991[22] provided that a child could prosecute or defend proceedings without a "next friend" in two situations: where the proceedings are not "specified proceedings" and the child has the leave of the court and where a solicitor has accepted instructions from the child having considered in the light of the child's understanding that the child is able to give instructions.[23] These two provisions opened up the possibility for the first time of the child having unmediated access to legal services and the courts.

Third, a number of provisions of the Act gave the child, if he or she was of sufficient understanding to make an informed decision, the right to refuse to submit to a medical or psychiatric examination or assessment.[24] Thus section 44(7) provides that even where a court has directed that the child undergo a medical or psychiatric examination or other assessment the "child may, if he is of sufficient understanding to make an informed decision, refuse to submit to the examination or other assessment".[25]

Finally, under section 26 of the Act the child was given the right to complain about the local authority's discharge of their functions under part III of the Act. This applied to children in need as well as children who were being "looked after". Prior to the Act there had been no legal requirement on local authorities to set up complaints procedures. Local authorities were now required to set up such procedures and they had to have an independent element.[26]

So while the Act can be said to have been concerned with the welfare of children, with much of the change focused on altering the power relations between local authority and parents and recasting the responsibilities of courts and local authorities, it also moved towards a recognition of the child as a legal subject. How does this assessment measure up in the light of subsequent events.

Ten years on – a critical assessment

Since 14 October 1991 when the Act was brought fully into force there have been a number of developments. Research has shown that some of the positive hopes for the Act have failed to materialise. Later I will consider whether this is due to shortcomings in the Act's framework or whether the roots of the "failure" lie in the practices and attitudes of adults and professionals. But first I want to provide a brief summary of some of the research findings on the operation of the Act as a whole before exploring some of the case law and the research which examines how children fare when engaged with the law and legal processes.

Under section 17 of the Act families with children in need should have had access to support services from the local authority; the provision of such services was seen as key to the safeguarding and promotion of children's "welfare rights". However support on the basis of partnership for families with children in need as envisaged by section 17 has been undermined by wide variations among local authorities in their interpretation of children in need. Instead local authority practice concentrated on children "at risk" – a resource hungry strategy which was singularly unsuccessful as a preventative strategy.[27] Aldgate and Statham in their review of the research observe: "Several of the studies on family support services show clearly that in some cases that had been 'closed' by social services the children could be identified as 'in need' within the Children Act definition" (2001: 22).

The Framework for Assessment provides an estimate of the numbers of children in need. It estimates that there are over four million children "living in families with less than half the average household income" (Department of Health, 2000: para. 1.1). Of these four million "vulnerable children" there are between 300,000–400,000 children in need (para. #1.6). The research by Thoburn *et al.* (2000) into family support revealed that 98 per cent of families whose children were at risk of suffering emotional maltreatment and neglect were characterised by the "extreme poverty of their material environment". None the less according to Brandon *et al.* (1999) it is child protection concerns which constitute the gateway to support services. This is despite the wording of the guidance to the Act, which stated that the definition of children in need was deliberately wide to emphasise "preventive support and services to families".[28] Clearly, in a context of substantial child poverty, the variations in the definition of children in need and the failure on the part of local authorities to comply with their statutory duties under section 17 has resulted in a lottery as far as support services for children in need are concerned.[29]

In relation to the liberty rights of children there are three issues which capture the direction of the judicial wind in the interpretation of the Act; these are child litigants, children in court and the child's right to refuse medical treatment.

Early on there was anxiety about the so-called "children divorce their parents" scenario. The social unease over the child litigant is neatly captured in an *Observer* article in 1993 by Polly Ghazi:

> Parents who turn up their noses when their children bury themselves in Viz, Smash Hits or Just 17 may be making a big mistake. The magazines may soon contain advertisements for a booklet entitled Your Say in Court, which could have a significant effect on family relationships. Aimed at 10-to-16 year-olds it provides a step-by-step guide on how to "divorce" parents.
>
> (*Observer*, 25 July 1993)

There was also judicial unease about such child litigants. As a result in 1993 the High Court issued a practice direction in which it states that all applications for leave to apply for a section 8 order should be heard by the High Court (Practice Direction [1993] 1 FLR 668). The High Court has also decided that in considering such applications the court will have regard to three issues; what is in the child's best interests, if leave is granted is the child's application for a section 8 order likely to be successful, and the jurisdiction to allow child applications should be cautiously applied and only exercised when matters of importance are raised. In *Re S* [1993] 2 FLR 437 Sir Thomas Bingham MR, referring to the Act requiring a balance to be struck between two principles, observed:

> First is the principle to be honoured and respected, that children are human beings in their own right. ... A child's wishes are not to be

discounted or dismissed simply because he is a child. He should be free to express them and decision-makers should listen. Second is the fact that a child is, after all, a child. The reason why the law is particularly solicitous in protecting the interests of children is because they are liable to be vulnerable and impressionable.

So the judiciary have imported further requirements which had to be satisfied before the High Court would give leave to a child to apply for a section 8 order; they did so on the basis of the child's vulnerability. This high threshold seems to conflict with the spirit and the letter of the Gillick decision.

Linked with this anxiety about the child as a legal subject is a concern with the child who is a party to proceedings being visible, being in court. Section 95(1) of the Act provides that when hearing any proceedings under parts IV and V of the Act the court has the discretion to decide whether or not the child should attend the hearing or a specified part of the hearing. The Rule 16(2) of the Family Proceedings Courts (Children Act 1989) Rules 1991 provides that the proceedings can take place in the absence of a child who is a party if the court "considers it in the interest of the child, having regard to the matters to be discussed or the evidence likely to be given" and the child is represented by a GAL or solicitor. Rule 11(4) states that the GAL must advise the court on a number of matters including the child's wishes regarding attendance at court. In *Re C* [1993] the GAL supported the 13-year-old girl's wish to attend the care proceedings; she was present throughout the proceedings before the family proceedings court. When this case went to the High Court on appeal, even though no party objected to the presence of the child, Waite J ruled that "young children should be discouraged from attending High Court appeals from the justices in family proceedings". He urged GALs to give very careful thought beforehand to whether children should be present and that they should be prepared to explain their reasons to the judge. The more recent case of *Re H (Residence Order: Child's Application for Leave)* [2000] 1 FLR 780 reinforces this image of the absent/silent child object. In this case a 12-year-old boy wanted to intervene in his parents' divorce proceedings in order to ensure that he ended up living with his father. The High Court refused his application for leave to apply for a residence order on the ground that as father and son were of one mind on this matter there was no argument that might be put to the court on behalf of S which would not be advanced on behalf of the father. In the course of his judgement Johnson J. stated (p. 783):

I would wish to assure S that the judge ultimately deciding where he shall live will take full and, indeed, generous account of his wishes, but I see no advantage to the court in making that difficult decision or advantage to S himself in his being legally represented. Whether or not he would be allowed to be in court is a matter that would be decided by the judge hearing the final issue, although, speaking for myself, I would doubt that the judge would allow S to be in court.[30]

The paradoxical message is clear; the child who is the very reason for the court sitting need not necessarily be heard or seen directly. The advice given to GALs and the extra barriers put in the way of children applying for leave to apply for a section 8 order testify to the judicial disquiet with the idea of the visible participating child. In their own interests children should not be witness to the resolution of the conflict in which they are central.

The case law on the seemingly clear-cut right given to children by the Children Act to refuse to submit to a medical examination or assessment provides further proof of the difficulty judges experience when faced with the imagery of the autonomous child. As noted above, under the Act children were given the right to refuse to submit to a medical or psychiatric examination and assessment, and in so doing the Act was merely putting on a statutory footing the House of Lords decision in Gillick.[31] However in *South Glamorgan County Council* v *W and B* [1993] 1 FLR 574 the High Court gave leave to the local authority under section 100(3) of the Act to bring proceedings to invoke the High Court's inherent jurisdiction in the event of the 15-year-old girl's refusal to submit to the psychiatric assessment ordered under an interim care order (see s.38(6) of the Act). She did not consent and High Court exercised its inherent jurisdiction to order that the assessment proceed and therefore by-passed the "right" given to mature minors under the Act. Brown J. stated: "In my judgement, the court can, in an appropriate case … when other remedies within the Children Act have been used and found not to bring the desired result, can resort to other remedies." So the "mature minor" enjoys the right under the Children Act to refuse to submit to a court-ordered assessment but this right can be "trumped" in "appropriate cases" by the High Court's exercise of its inherent jurisdiction.[32]

Perhaps we are asking too much of the judiciary. Required as they are to give paramount consideration to the welfare of the child it is perhaps not surprising that they err on the side of caution.[33] In addition to the judicial caution evidenced by such cases the research into the operation of the Act paints a picture in which it is not just courts but professionals who are uneasy and struggle with notions of children's rights once they extend beyond the right to welfare.

The Act gave to children the contingent right to instruct a solicitor. Research has revealed how fragile this right is. Sawyer (1995) in her research into the way solicitors assess the competence of children to participate in family proceedings found that they varied in their approach. The process of assessing competence was seen as neither simple nor clear-cut, for instance age was one factor but not the only one. Sawyer found that lawyers went beyond what was demanded of them in their legal role when it came to assessing the competence of the child with welfare considerations regularly intruding, especially in private law cases (1995: 95–96).[34] In considering the question of the separate representation of children in family proceedings she notes that two concerns are raised. First "there is the question of whether having a right to state 'wrong' opinion is so good in itself that it necessarily outweighs the risks inherent in the advocation of a view of the child's welfare which may be incorrect" (1995: 168) In the public law context this concern is resolved by the involvement of the guardian ad litem – who can put a "better view". There is also the issue "whether having the right to speak out and be heard ... gives rise to any risks in the child's position outside the proceedings, including his or her own individual family relationships" (1995: 168). In the private law context this is the familiar "children should not have the burden/responsibility put on them" argument.[35] According to Sawyer the idea of Gillick competence "cut little ice" with the practitioners in the context of private family proceedings (Sawyer, 1997: 20). Sawyer observed (1995: 169)

> Few believed that even a competent child's view should always be followed; even the interviewees committed in principle to "children's rights" appeared to proceed with considerable paternalist – or parentalist – assumptions in practice, albeit they used different formulations to justify the exercise of the function.[36]

In Sawyer's more recent research (1999) into the role and work of the court welfare officer (CWO) in the context of private law disputes she confirms earlier work which depicts their role as one of promoting parental agreement wherever possible in order to avoid a formal trial of matters relating to the children (see also Piper, 1993). Only where this is not possible will they report to the court on the child's welfare. While they saw contact as the "child's right" and believed in principle in seeing the child, very few actually did so. Further, "Some CWOs would only see children if effectively forced to do so in the final stages of preparing a welfare report for a contested hearing; this was then done in order to avoid criticism or re-referral by the court" (Sawyer, 1999: 262). Sawyer also writes that (1999: 261):

> The idea of involving the children as an active participant in the process was not on the everyday agenda at all. Even when an older child was seen and listened to this was often unwillingly and for the practical reason that some older children are capable of disrupting arrangements parents have been helped by CWOs to make.

Lyon *et al.* (1999) explored the support needs of children when their parents break up. In their examination of the way in which the present system supported children they found a number of serious shortcomings. Children were given little information about the process or their rights. Some of the young people involved in the research were angry "that they were being denied access to a crucial service of information concerning the issue of parental relationship break down and the potential impact of divorce proceedings on children and young people" (para. 2.06).[37] There was no information available informing young people of their rights in relation to divorce and its aftermath, in particular their right to make an application to vary the post-relationship breakdown arrangements which did not meet their self-defined needs. One respondent said:

> Looking back, I think that we should have been given much more infor-
> mation. We didn't have a clue as to what was going on and the whole
> thing was just a muddle in my head. I think that I should have had
> someone to talk to, and maybe have some influence on the custody
> arrangements.

Children might want to be included in some way and to have access to proper information about the divorce or separation process, to know where they stand in relation to this and what their rights are in such situations. On occasion they might want separate representation and the services of a lawyer – though as Sawyer concludes much will depend on the lawyer they approach (Sawyer, 1997: 21). However perhaps a key stumbling block to seeing children as legitimate legal actors lies in the idea of family privacy. Feminists have already radically altered our understanding of the idea of family privacy, asking amongst other things "whose privacy?" Okin argues (1989: 184):

> the family in which each of us grows up has a deeply formative influence
> on us. … This is one of the reasons why one cannot reasonably leave the
> family out of the "basic structure of society," to which the principles of
> justice are to apply.

She goes on to observe that if we properly address the question of justice within the family it will be a "better place for children to develop a sense of justice". However while Okin is concerned first and foremost with gender, considerations of children rights should prompt a rethink on two issues. First, that it should no longer be assumed that women's interests are always coincident with those of children. Second, children may have their own view on a host of issues associated with family life and their life within the family. Beck alerts us to the democratisation of family life and argues that "equality of rights for the child certainly collides with the protection of the family and requires or allows the deprivatisation of privacy to a certain extent" (1997: 162).

In the public law context, Masson and Winn Oakley in their research into the representation of children in care proceedings found that "neither children's interests nor their wishes are strenuously advocated by their representatives" in every case (1999: 136). They found that despite having

party status in care proceedings children were not on "an equal footing" with the other parties (1999: 144). They write:

> Representation of children and young people in these proceedings is largely based on shielding them from the process rather than assisting them to participate ... their party status does not help to make the proceedings real for them.[38]

The unsatisfactory aspect of this situation in both the private and public law fields is expressed by Sawyer in her rehearsal of the arguments in favour of children having access to legal services. She writes:

> The essential advantage of involving the legal process, from the partici- pants' point of view, may be seen as ensuring that people have a chance to speak on matters which concern them so that everyone may be satis- fied that justice is done.

(1995: 163)

Perhaps what is at stake here is the idea of actually listening to children and treating them with the same equality of concern and respect you would adults. The practical and symbolic issues raised by this are particularly awkward and controversial when it is the child who wants to make a public issue out of a private trouble.[39]

These findings should not surprise us. In the widespread distrust of welfare professionals so fashionable since the 1980s perhaps we have lost sight of the sociology and socio-legal literature of the 1960s and 1970s which explored the myriad ways in which clients were routinely vulnerable to profes- sionals working to their own agendas. In the midst of the concern about the abuse of power by welfare professionals, lawyers and courts were elevated to the only guarantors of procedural and substantive justice. No longer was law a "con game" (Blumberg, 1969), it was the only process whereby the decisions of welfare professionals could be held accountable. If adults are vulnerable to the imposition of agendas by professionals how much more so are children. What the above discussion of professional practice on the part of some lawyers and court welfare officers reveals is a paternalistic disregard. Too often children do not count – and certainly not enough to displace the systemic inducements to do other than fully advocate for one's client.

Smart and Neale in their research into children's perspectives on post- divorce parenting (2000) refer to a "newer debate" as to whether professionals working in the family justice system are adequately "ascer- taining the wishes and feelings of the child". They observe in the context of recent research and policy debates that the

> shift away from seeing the child as an inevitable victim whose welfare must be safeguarded, towards a framework within which the child is

seen as a potentially active participant in his or her own family's progress is probably only slight, yet it is potentially important.

Smart and Neale found that children wanted to share in a certain amount of information, but they did not necessarily want to carry the burden of adult responsibilities. "They wanted to be respected as children and young people, not as if they were adults" (2000: 165). Later they observed that the children in their research distinguished between participation and choice though where "children were frightened of, or disliked a particular parent, they were often much more forceful in insisting that a child should decide on his own who he should live with". They conclude that the invitation to participate (not as yet extended to children) might "oblige us to start to approach the whole issue of ascertaining the wishes and feelings of the child in a different way".

Conclusion

What underpins much "law talk" about children is a concern to protect them (from others, themselves and their own choices) and an anxiety about them. Children are idealised and demonised (Griffin, 1993), there is little space in between for a more honest conversation about children, family life and social justice. The suspicion which surrounds children is undermining of the UNCRC but is also being resisted and challenged. The demand for inclusion, for the right to participate, is central and integral to the project of imagining different kinds of adult–child relations – though the form such conversations might take is uncertain, especially in professional settings. Children's rights are about rethinking and redefining adult–child relations and are a means "with which to articulate challenge and hold to account relationships of power". As Federle argues (1994: 355–356):

> rights claims challenge existing hierarchies by making the community hear different voices. Community and claiming are part of a slow historical process that will invigorate the debate about children's rights and will, someday, lead to a better life for children through the articulation of ideal relationships between children and adults in the larger community.

There is debate as to whether the Children Act 1989 still provides an acceptable framework for children's rights.[40] Some changes have been argued for and legislation introduced. For example the Care Leavers Act 2000 seeks to improve on the Children Act by imposing more carefully defined duties towards care leavers on local authorities. There have been calls for the role of GALs to be extended to private as well as public law matters.[41] This looks as if it has been superseded by the plans to establish the Children and Family Court Advisory and Support Service.[42] The

"Children are unbeatable" campaign has argued for the end of the parental right to chastise their children. Given that the UN Committee on the Rights of the Child recommended in its response to the UK government's first Report to the Committee that the UK tackle the question of the parental right to chastise it is perhaps time that a provision was enacted bringing this right to an end.[43] However the direction of change seems to be quite different. Two recent consultation papers reveal the government's concern to emphasise notions of parental right rather than children's rights. First, in *Protecting Children, Supporting Parents* (DoH, 2000) the government in response to the decision of the European Court of Human Rights in *A* v *UK* ([1999]) 27 EHRR 611 asks where the line should be drawn in law as to the acceptable physical punishment of children. The consultation paper ruled out outright abolition of this parental right on the grounds that public opinion[44] was against such a ban, it would be contrary to "common sense', it would bring the law into disrepute and fails to see that smacking has an educative role.[45] As if this was not bad enough the government more recently has issued a consultation pack on National Standards for the Regulation and Inspection of Day Care and Childminding. In this it is suggested that childminders subject to parental agreement should be able to smack a child in their care and smoke. Both proposals have been condemned (Haynes, 2000) and taken together can be seen as reinforcing notions of children as the property of their parents. How else is one to understand the proposal about smoking which contradicts the governments own campaigning on the subject.

I am left with two observations: the way in which we think about children and children's rights has to shift and in that process adult practices including professional practice centring on children will shift. Continued reliance on the language of children's rights is part of this shifting process but one that does not necessarily lead to direct change in the law. The rhetoric of rights is as much about shifting our imagination as it is about specific demands for legal change. We might all benefit from taking children and their rights more seriously. Masson and Winn Oakley suggest (1999: 144) that "greater opportunities to participate, where they wished to do so, might encourage some children to engage with the proceedings". This would necessitate "changes in court practice, such as clearer use of language, shorter hearings and more attention to the needs of ordinary people" – this would also benefit parents, relatives and carers. Perhaps the law reduces "us" all to children. We also need to follow through the implications of Smart and Neale's observation that "the subtleties of family relationships may not be captured by such a brief and alien intervention in which children may apparently be quizzed on their views for the first and only time in their childhood" (2000: 168).[46]

Finally, these shifts in thinking about children will be uneven, contested and championed in different ways, in different places and in this sense the "politics of childhood" (and "children's rights") will intensify. Increasingly children themselves are challenging and resisting adult constructions of incompetence (see Anderson, 2000). If we do not grapple with the negative ideas associated with children, and their imprisonment between innocence and threat, to socially include children in public and private spaces they will remain distrustful of irregular and sporadic adult invitations to participate, on adult terms, for adult purposes and within adult agendas. The children's rights project involves both the law and agitation around the law and legal processes. Some of the disappointing jurisprudential and policy developments since the Children Act 1989 came into force testify to the fragility of the children's rights project.[47] They serve to underscore the idea that it is also a cultural project which necessarily straddles the public and private sphere and requires adults to rethink their attitudes towards children and childhood.

Notes

1 One concrete consequence of the House of Lords judgment was that those who worked in family planning settings were now reassured that they would not be acting unlawfully in providing such advice and treatment – this was of practical significance for many young women – see "Victory for Mrs Gillick is a tragedy for thousands of young people" *Guardian* 30 January 1985.

2 It has also influenced childcare legislation in a number of jurisdictions, e.g. Malta, Ghana.

3 Under the previous legislative framework the welfare of the child had been the "first and paramount" consideration.

4 These were applications for care and supervision orders and education supervision orders.

5 Lord Mackay said in Committee: "This Bill does nothing to change the underlying Gillick principle, which has to be taken into account by all who exercise parental responsibility over a child mature and intelligent enough to take decisions for himself" (*Hansard*, House of Lords, Vol. 502, Col. 1,351).

6 The Act also blurred the boundary between public and private law in part through the ability of the court to make any order, not just the order applied for, in family proceedings.

7 I am indebted to Katherine Gieve for using this phrase in an interview with me on the Children Act conducted in 1990.

8 For instance, changes to divorce procedure whereby there is less judicial scrutiny of post divorce arrangements relating to the children and the development of mediation services both link with the concept; as the Booth Committee commented on conciliation: "It is of the essence of conciliation that responsibility remains at all times with the parties themselves" (1985, para. 3.10).

9 The local authority is still the gatekeeper to the system. In *Nottinghamshire County Council* v *P* [1993] 3 All ER 815 the Court of Appeal stated that the court cannot force a local authority to apply for a care order even though, as in this case, the local authority had applied for a prohibited steps order.

10 The White Paper referred to the provision of services by a local authority as a "positive response" and not as a mark of failure either on the part of the family or the professional involved. "An essential characteristic of this service should be its voluntary character, that is it should be based clearly on continuing parental agreement and operate as far as possible on a basis of partnership and co-operation" (White Paper, para. 21).

11 For example, section 74(6) provides that in considering the needs of any child for the purposes of deciding whether the care provided by a child minder is "seriously inadequate" the local authority must have regard "to the child's religious persuasion, racial origin and cultural and linguistic background".

12 With the ability to control its own proceedings.

13 For example, the retreat from divorce. See Bainham, 1990 and Roche, 1991.

14 Under section 42 the GAL was given extensive rights of access to records held by the local authority and the NSPCC.

15 By welfare rights I am referring to the child's right to basic provisions such as shelter, food and clothing as well as the care and protection of children.

16 Though the welfare principle has been subject to substantial criticism – see for example Reece, 1996.

17 Section 31(2) of the Act provides that a court may only make a care or supervision order if "it is satisfied – (a) that the child concerned is suffering, or likely to suffer, significant harm; and (b) that the harm, or likelihood of harm, is attributable to – (i) the care given to the child, or likely to be given to him if the order were not made, not being what it would be reasonable to expect a parent to give to him; or (ii) the child's being beyond parental control".

18 See Dalrymple and Burke, 1995.

19 See, for example, Kohm and Lawrence, 1997–98, who see Articles 12 and 14 of the UNCRC as blurring the line between adulthood and childhood (at p. 369).

20 By liberty rights I am referring to those rights associated with the child's autonomy interest, e.g. the right to make their own decisions on matters that concern them.

21 These are contact orders, prohibited steps orders, residence orders and specific issue orders. These orders are very flexible and the court can make a section 8 order on its own motion as well as on application.

22 This came about as a result of amendments to the Family Proceedings Rules in April 1992. At the time the change was not seen as particularly important (see Thorpe, 1994).

23 The solicitor is under a duty to take instructions directly from the child where the child is in conflict with the GAL. In *Re H (A Minor)(Care Proceedings: Child's Wishes)* [1993] 1 FLR 440 the court referred to the solicitor's failure to take instructions exclusively from the child when there was clearly a conflict between the child and the GAL as constituting "a fundamental forfeiture of the child's right".

24 For example, under an interim care or supervision order – section 38(6).

25 This is again consistent with the Gillick decision.

26 The Representations Procedure (Children) Regulations 1991 laid down minimum standards with which local authorities had to comply.

27 Another consequence of such an approach was the failure to invest in innovative preventive support work with families.

28 The Guidance continued (Department of Health, 1990: vol. 2 para. 2.4): "It would not be acceptable for an authority to exclude any of [the three categories of children in need] – for example, by confining services to children at risk of significant harm which attracts the duty to investigate under section 47."

29 Other aspects of the legislation's emphasis on partnership have also failed to materialise. The Act required the local authority to have regard to the racial, cultural, religious and linguistic background of any child they are looking after. However social work as a profession is not immune from the institutional racism which pervades many social institutions. Dutt (2000) and Dutt and Phillips (2000) analyse the problem of racism within social work practice. See also Barn *et al.* (1997).

30 The court had accepted that he had sufficient understanding to make the application for leave. Later Johnson J. refers to the "spectre" of the "mother being faced across a courtroom by solicitor or counsel acting on behalf of the child she bore". Clearly such an image is more compelling than that of a child rendered silent and invisible by judicial practice – of course justified on the basis of the child's welfare – though this is far from self-evident.

31 The courts had started the retreat from Gillick before the Children Act 1989 came into force – see *Re R* [1991] 3 WLR 592 (see generally Roche, 1996). More recent cases on medical treatment and the rights of the mature minor include *Re L* (*Medical Treatment: Gillick Competence*) [1998] 2 FLR 810 and *Re M* (*Medical Treatment: Consent*) [1999] 2 FLR 1097.

32 In contrast the Children (Scotland) Act 1995 inserted into the Age of Legal Capacity (Scotland) Act 1991 the following provision:

> A person under the age of sixteen years shall have legal capacity to consent on his own behalf to any surgical, medical or dental procedure or treatment where, in the opinion of a qualified medical practitioner attending him, he is capable of understanding the nature and possible consequences of the procedure or treatment.
>
> (see section 2(4) of the Age of Legal Capacity (Scotland) Act)

33 O'Donovan (1993) reminds us of the ways in which the law denies children's subjectivity. It does so by seeing only those aged 18 years and over as full legal subjects, by seeing children as lacking those attributes which are the prerequisite of legal subjectivity, e.g. capacity, and by dealing with children via a paternalistic discourse. O'Donovan also comments on the double-edged quality of the welfare principle, noting that welfare itself is often a good reason for ignoring what the child says (p. 95).

34 Again the Scottish legislation provides a nice contrast. The Age of Legal Capacity (Scotland) Act 1991 as amended by the Children (Scotland) Act 1995 provides (s.2(4A), that "a person under the age of sixteen shall have legal capacity to instruct a solicitor, in connection with any civil matter, where that person has a general understanding of what it means to do so". Later it states the presumption that children aged 12 years or over have such understanding.

35 However children might not welcome "enforced intimacy" in whatever professional/formal setting it takes place. The meaning and feel of professional intervention may be very different for child and professional. For many children having some control over both agendas and outcomes is what matters – hence the appeal of Childline, whose success is based upon offering a confidential service. Research carried out by Childline confirms that it is this confidentiality that is so important to children who phone about all kinds of issues including relationship breakdown. It is of note that children who make use of their service often just want a totally safe place to talk about a matter that concerns them and often children are able after such a confidential conversation to decide for themselves what they will do.

36 See also Diduck (2000) who writes of lawyers' support for limiting children's involvement in divorce disputes.

37 This echoes Lyon and Parton's (1995) question "how do children find out about their rights to use Section 8 orders?"

38 Piper (1999) argues that the "good" family lawyer sees him- or herself as amongst other things being involved in "client-handling". See also Smart and Neale, 1999, chapters 8 and 9, for an analysis of changing role of family lawyers.

39 Where the family is together and it is the child who is seeking to bring an issue before the courts the anxiety raised is understandable – but I would argue this is not a good enough reason for denying children a right of access to legal advice and representation (Roche, 1999 and Lim and Roche, 2000). Where the parents are separating this privacy argument gives way to a paternalistic concern to protect the child from full knowledge of all that is involved in the period of transition and redefinition.

40 For example the Mostyn Report (1996) argued that change to the law was needed in order to make a more positive contribution to the prevention of child abuse. It also recommended that legislation based on the UNCRC should be introduced in order to secure the rights and needs of children.

41 In *Guarding Children's Interests* (The Children's Society, 2000) the children interviewed in the research made it clear that they valued the role of the GAL and saw the ideal GAL as someone who listened to them and explained the legal process. However some children did have a negative experience – e.g. one child thought that confidentiality had been breached.

42 At this early stage it is hard to state whether this move will be of any benefit to children. There is a suspicion that the changes are driven by cost-cutting considerations rather than the desire to refine the mechanisms whereby the child's voice can be heard in the legal process.

43 This would both signal and be a sign that there had been a shift in the way children are viewed though the "success" of such a move would be dependent on other initiatives centring on children. See for example Durrant and Olsen's (1997) interesting analysis of the Swedish experience.

44 They did not include children in this.

45 For useful review and summary see Roberts, 2000.

46 This links with ongoing debates about what is happening to the family. See Beck, 1997 and Roche, 1999. Note also the different direction taken in Scotland. The Children (Scotland) Act 1995 departed radically from the legislation in England and Wales and was influenced by the provisions of the UNCRC. Section 6 of the Act imposes a duty on parents to consult with their child on any major decision. The Scottish Law Commission had consulted on this matter. It stated (1992: paras 2.62–64):

> The question as we saw it was whether a parent or other person exercising parental rights should be under a similar obligation to ascertain and have regard to the child's wishes and feelings as a local authority was in relation to a child in its care. ... There are great attractions in such an approach. It emphasises that the child is a person in his or her own right and that his or her views are entitled to respect and consideration. ... On consultation there was majority support for a provision requiring parents in reaching any major decision relating to a child, to ascertain the child's wishes and feelings so far as practicable and give due consideration to them having regard to their age and understanding. ... Many respondents clearly regarded such a provision as an important declaration of principle.

The Act also provides that children aged 12 or over are presumed to be capable of forming a view.

47 But not all; the current war on child poverty is a good example of a positive development which might provide space for other children's rights initiatives, e.g. enhanced participation in their local communities.

References

Alanen, L. (1994) "Gender and Generation: Feminism and the 'Child Question'" in Qvortrup, J., Bardy, M., Sgritta, G. and Wintersberger, H. (eds) *Childhood Matters Social Theory, Practice and Politics* Aldershot, Avebury

Aldgate, J. and Statham, D. (2001) *The Children Act Now Messages from Research* London, The Stationery Office

Allen, N. (1992) *Making Sense of the Children Act* (Second edition) London, Longman

Anderson, J. (2000) "Stop Smacking Us!" *childRight* no. 168 p. 15

Bainham, A. (1990) "The Privatisation of the Public Interest in Children" *Modern Law Review* 53 (2) p. 206

Barn, R., Sinclair, R. and Ferdinand, D. (1997) *Acting on Principle: An Examination of Race and Ethnicity in Social Services Provision for Children and Families* London, BAAF/CRE

Beck, U. (1997) "Democratisation of the Family" *Childhood* vol. 4 (2) pp.151–168

Blumberg, A. (1969) "The Practice of Law as a Confidence Game" in Aubert, V. (ed.) (1971) *The Sociology of Law* Harmondsworth, Penguin

Booth Report (1985) *Report of the Matrimonial Causes Procedure Committee* London, HMSO

Brandon, M., Thoburn, J., Lewis, A. and Way, A. (1999) *Safeguarding Children with the Children Act 1989* London, Stationery Office

Butler-Sloss (1988) *Report of the Enquiry into Child Abuse in Cleveland* Cm. 412 London, HMSO

Children's Society (2000) *Guarding Children's Interests* London, The Children's Society

Dalrymple, J. and Burke, B. (1995) *Anti-Oppressive Practice Social Care and the Law* Buckingham, Open University Press

Department of Health (1990) *The Children Act 1989. Guidance and Regulations, Volume 2. Family Support, Day Care and Educational Provision for Young Children* London, HMSO

—— (2000) *Protecting Children, Supporting Parents* London, Department of Health

Department of Health, DfEE and the Home Office (2000) *Framework for the Assessment of Children in Need and their Families* London, Stationery Office

DHSS (1985) *Review of Child Care Law: Report to Ministers of an Interdepartmental Working Group* London: HMSO

DHSS/Home Office (1987) *The Law on Child Care and Family Services* London, HMSO

Diduck, A. (2000) "Solicitors and Legal Subjects" in Bridgeman, J. and Monk, D. (eds) *Feminist Perspectives on Child Law* London, Cavendish

Durrant, J. and Olsen, G. (1997) "Parenting and Public Policy; contextualising the Swedish corporal punishment ban" *Journal of Social Welfare and Family Law* 19 (4) pp. 443–461

Dutt, R. (2000) "Racism and Social Work Practice" in Cull, L. and Roche, J. (eds) *The Law and Social Work Contemporary Issues for Practice* Basingstoke, Palgrave

Dutt, R. and Phillips, M. (2000) "Assessing Black Children in Need and Their Families" in Department of Health *Assessing Children in Need and their Families* (Practice Guidance) London, Stationery Office

Federle, K. (1994) "Rights Flow Downhill" *International Journal of Children's Rights* 2 p. 343

Griffin, C. (1993) *Representations of Youth: The Study of Youth and Adolescence in Britain and America* Cambridge, Polity Press

Haynes, G. (2000) "New National Standards on Registered Childminding *childRight* no.170 p. 21

Kohm, L. and Lawrence, M. (1997–98) "Sex at Six: The Victimisation of Innocence and Other Concerns over Children's Rights" *Journal of Family Law* 36 pp. 361–406

Law Commission (1988) *Family Review of Child Care Law: Guardianship and Custody* Report No. 172 London, HMSO

Lim, H. and Roche, J. (2000) "Feminism and Children's Rights" in Bridgeman, J. and Monk, D. (eds) *Feminist Perspectives on Child Law* London, Cavendish

Lyon, C. and Parton, N. (1995) "Children's Rights and the Children Act 1989" in Franklin, B. (ed.) *The Handbook of Children's Rights Comparative Policy and Practice* London, Routledge

Lyon, C., Surrey, E. and Timms, J. (1999) *Effective Support Services for Children and Young People When Parental Relationships Break Down* Liverpool, Calouste Gulbenkian Foundation, NYAS, Liverpool University

London Borough of Brent (1985) *A Child in Trust. The report of the panel of enquiry into the circumstances surrounding the death of Jasmine Beckford*, Wembley, London Borough of Brent

Masson, J. and Winn Oakley, M. (1999) *Out of Hearing* Chichester, John Wiley

O'Donovan, K. (1993) *Family Law Matters* London, Pluto Press

Okin, S. Moller (1989) *Justice, Gender and the Family* New York, Basic Books

Piper, C. (1993) *The Responsible Parent: A Study in Divorce Mediation* Hemel Hempstead, Harvester Wheatsheaf

—— (1999) "How do you define a family lawyer?" *Legal Studies* 19 (1) pp. 93–111

Reder, P., Duncan, S. and Gray, M. (eds) (1993) *Beyond Blame. Child Abuse Tragedies Revisited* London, Routledge

Reece, H. (1996) "The Paramountcy Principle Consensus or Construct?" *Current Legal Problems* 49 pp. 267–304

Roberts, M. (2000) "Protecting Children, Supporting Parents: government consultation on physical punishment" *childRight* no. 163 pp. 3–5

Robertson, J. and Robertson, J. (1989) *Separation and the Very Young* London, Free Association Books

Roche, J. (1991) "The Children Act 1989: Once a Parent Always a Parent" *Journal of Social Welfare and Family Law* 5 pp. 345–361

—— (1996) "Children's Rights: A Lawyer's View" in John, M. (ed.) *Children in Our Charge The Child's Right to Resources* London, Jessica Kingsley

—— (1999) "Children: Rights, Participation and Citizenship" *Childhood* 6 p. 475

Sawyer, C. (1995) *The Rise and Fall of the Third Party Solicitors assessments of the competence of children to participate in family proceedings* Oxford, Gulbenkian Foundation

—— (1997) "The Mature Child – How Solicitors Decide" *Family Law* January, pp. 19–21

—— (1999) *Rules, Roles and Relationships. The structure and function of child representation and welfare within family proceedings* vols 1 and 2, Oxford, Centre for Socio-Legal Studies

Smart, C. and Neale, N. (1999) *Family Fragments?* Cambridge, Polity

—— (2000) "It's My Life Too" – children's perspectives on post-divorce parenting" *Family Law* March, pp. 163–169

Thoburn, J. (1995) "The Children Act 1989 and Children 'In Need' " in Bainham, A., Pearl, D. and Pickford, R. (eds) *Frontiers of Family Law* Chichester, John Wiley, pp. 219–227

Thoburn, J., Wilding, J. and Watson, J. (2000) *Family Support in Cases of Emotional Maltreatment and Neglect*, London, The Stationery Office

Thorpe, J. (1994) "Independent Representation for Minors" *Family Law* 20

4 Children's rights and youth justice

John Muncie

Introduction

Ever since the early nineteenth century, when the troubled and troublesome young were first thought to deserve a different formal response to that afforded adults, it has become commonplace to describe youth justice as riddled with complexity, confusion, ambiguity and unintended consequences. The aims of acting in a child's "best interests", ensuring offenders get their "just deserts" and protecting children's rights have always sat uneasily together. This chapter examines the extent to which children's rights are present in systems of youth justice which are based on welfare principles (as in Scotland) or those based on the principle of "just deserts" (as in England and Wales). By exploring recent legislative reform, particularly in England and Wales, it questions how far the "new youth justice" is any better equipped to prioritise and uphold more than a rhetorical commitment to children's rights.

Welfare and rights: the infantilisation of youth justice?

Much of the welfare principle in youth justice derives from the reforming zeal of philanthropists and "child-savers" in the 1850s. Then, young people were believed to be in need of treatment within moral re-education programmes designed to both deter *and* prevent offending. "Justice" was delivered through confinement in reformatories and legitimised in the language of care. As a result, such intervention was directed not only toward the offender, but also toward those thought likely to offend – the orphan, the vagrant, the runaway, the independent and those with a "deviant" street lifestyle. The prevailing argument that age and the neglect and vice of parents should be taken into account when adjudicating on juveniles opened the way for a plethora of welfare-inspired legislation in the twentieth century. The 1908 Children Act created a separate and distinct system of justice based on the juvenile court; the 1933 Children and Young Persons Act formally required the court to place welfare considerations paramount; and the 1969 Children and Young Persons Act advocated the phasing out of criminal, in favour of civil, proceedings. By the 1960s custodial institutions were also being criticised as stigmatising, dehumanising, expensive, brutalising, and as criminogenic rather than rehabilitative agencies. "Justice" for juveniles was considered best delivered through the abolition of custody and the establishment of a range of treatment units located in the community. The care and control of young offenders was to be handed over from judicial agencies to social service professionals. Again intervention was couched in the language of welfare and rehabilitation rather than correction.

As a result the principle that the rights of young people in trouble were best served by removing them from their home and placing them in care "for their own good" occupied a central place in youth justice policy throughout much of the twentieth century. Welfarism though has never been universally accepted as the most suitable way of dealing with young offenders. A strong law-and-order lobby ensured that a range of punitive custodial options – borstals, detention centres, youth custody centres – remained firmly in place. Consequently, in practice, traditional principles of punitive justice were never seriously undermined by the 1969 Act. Welfarist principles were simply added to the range of interventions and disposals available to the court. Welfarism was generally employed with a younger age group of, for example, low school-achievers, "wayward girls" and truants from "problem" families designated as "pre-delinquent" – the social workers' domain – whilst the courts continued their old policy of punishing offenders – the magistrates' domain. The two systems became vertically integrated. Moreover the concept of welfare in law was, and remains, characteristically narrow and circumscribed. At best it may allow for an acknowledgement of the reduced culpability of children, but this in turn has been used to justify early intervention against those considered to be "at risk". Rarely, if ever, has it meant that they are dealt with more leniently (King and Piper, 1995).

Indeed in England and Wales a legal discourse of guilt, responsibility and punishment has remained dominant in the definition and adjudication of young offending. However there is no intrinsic reason why youth justice should mimic such adult procedures. In Scotland, for example, a different outcome was reached from the welfare/punishment debates of the 1960s. The 1968 Social Work (Scotland) Act established new social work departments, gave local authorities a general duty to promote social welfare for children in need and established the children's hearing system (which came into operation in 1971). Children's hearings are not a criminal court but a welfare tribunal serviced by lay people from the local community. They deal with criminal cases but in recent years have become increasingly focused on child neglect, abuse and protection. Cases are initially referred to a reporter from a range of bodies which may include education authorities and social work departments, but is usually the police. The role of the reporter is to sift referrals and decide on a future course of action. There are wide-ranging grounds governing referral to a hearing. They include not only committing an offence but also:

- being beyond the control of parents;
- falling into bad associations and being exposed to moral danger;
- lack of parental care causing suffering or ill health;
- having been the victim of a sex or cruelty offence;
- living in a household where there is, or is likely to be, the perpetrator of such an offence;
- having failed to attend school regularly.

When a case reaches a hearing it is deliberated upon by three lay members of a panel, the parents or guardians of the child, social work representatives and also the child. Legal representation is not encouraged but "safe-guarders" such as teachers and solicitors may be present. Paid legal representation is not allowed. The hearing cannot proceed unless all parties understand *and* accept the grounds for referral. The hearing does not deter-mine guilt or innocence (it can only proceed if guilt is admitted, except in child protection cases where grounds must be shown) and is solely concerned with deciding on future courses of action. Before reaching any decision, reports on the child from the social work department are heard thus granting the social worker a more pivotal role than in the English youth courts.

Following a hearing one of three decisions is made: to discharge the referral, to make a supervision order or to make a residential supervision order. The most frequent (and increasing) disposal is a social work supervi-sion requirement. About 15 per cent of disposals result in residential supervision. The latter usually involves committal to a list D school (the equivalent of an English Community Home with Education). However for a significant minority whose offences are considered "serious" the hearing system is bypassed and referred directly to the adult Sheriff and High Court system (Norrie, 1997). In this respect Scottish welfarism is reserved only for less serious offences and some routes into adult justice have remained unchallenged. Moreover the hearings system only deals with those up to the age of 16. Whilst in Scotland there are almost no penal options for those under the age of 16, there remains a continuing presence of custodial insti-tutions for those over the age of 16 whose regimes are far removed from the promotion of welfarism. As in England some of Scotland's most punitive systems still appear to be reserved for its young. And welfarism always remains prey to shifts in the broader political climate. McGhee *et al.* (1996: 68–69) have, for example, argued that by the 1990s: "Increased public pres-sure to make children accountable for wrong doing, plus a growing concentration on the needs of victims, have contributed to the public focus shifting from the welfare of the child to offending behaviour and its conse-quences."

Nevertheless McAra and Young (1997) maintain that the Scottish hearing system continues to stand, in contrast to justice-based systems such as in England and Wales, as "an object lesson" in prioritising welfare and individualised attention and without increasing crime rates. However, the merging of criminal and care cases, the treatment of 17-year-olds as adults and the lack of automatic legal representation do place the Scottish system at odds with various articles of the UN and European Conventions on the Rights of the Child.

Justice and rights: the adulteration of youth justice?

In the rest of the UK, liberal lawyers, civil libertarians and radical social workers were by the 1980s becoming increasingly critical of "welfare-based" procedures and sentencing. They argued that "meeting needs" acted as a spurious justification for placing excessive restrictions on individual liberty, particularly for young women, which were out of proportion either to the seriousness of the offence or to the realities of being in "need of care and protection". Indeterminate sentencing schemes, in general, mean that length of sentence rests on discretionary psychological assessments of how far an offender has "improved" rather than with reference to the actual crime committed. As a result minor offenders can serve longer sentences than those convicted of more serious offences, particularly if they decline the "offer" of treatment. It has also been argued that the investigation of social background is an imposition: that social work involvement not only preserves explanations of individual pathology, but also undermines the young person's right to natural justice. Young people are placed in double jeopardy – sentenced for their background as well as for their offence – and as a result their movement up the sentencing tariff tends to be accelerated (Morris *et al.*, 1980)

In the wake of these criticisms a new justice-based model of corrections emerged. Its leading proponent, Von Hirsch (1976), proposed that the following principles be reinstated at the centre of youth and criminal justice practice:

- proportionality of punishment to crime, or the offender is handed a sentence that is in accordance with what the act deserves;
- determinacy of sentencing and an end to indeterminate, treatment-oriented sentences;
- an end to judicial, professional and administrative discretion;
- an end to disparities in sentencing;
- equity and protection of rights through due process.

The idea of punishing the crime, not the person, had clear attractions for those seeking an end to the abuses of discretional power and initially this approach did appear to have some successes. From the mid 1980s, the numbers sent to custody in England and Wales were dramatically reduced, whilst informal cautioning and the use of intensive supervision burgeoned. Notions of "just deserts" and proportionate sentencing were formalised by the 1991 Criminal Justice Act. A focus on "deeds" rather than "needs" formally expunged many of the last vestiges of welfarism from the system.

However the liberal critique of welfare also coalesced with the concerns of traditional retributivists that rehabilitation was a "soft option". For them tougher sentencing would also enable criminals to get their "just deserts". Within the political climate of the 1980s notions of "just deserts" and "anti-welfarism" were indeed politically mobilised by the right. The language of "justice and rights" was appropriated as one of "individual responsibility and obligation". Accordingly Hudson (1987) has argued that the "just deserts" or "back to justice" movements that emerged in many Western jurisdictions in the 1980s was evidence of a "modern retributivism" rather than necessarily heralding the emergence of new liberal regimes and a positive rights agenda. The 1991 Criminal Justice Act may have helped to expand non-custodial measures, but their retributive edge was considerably sharpened. The favoured rhetoric and practice became that of delivering *punishment in the community*. Moreover, renewed fears of persistent young offenders, and in particular the political fallout from the murder of James Bulger by two 10-year-olds in 1993, enabled the youth justice system to take a decisively retributive turn. Custody was once more promoted through the slogan "prison works". The dominant strategy became that of punishing all young offenders, whatever their age and whether their punishment was to be delivered in community or custodial settings (Muncie, 1999b).

Since the early nineteenth century, most young offender legislation has been promoted and instituted on the basis that children and young people should be protected from the full weight of the criminal law. It remains widely assumed that under a certain age young people are *doli incapax* (incapable of evil) and should not be held fully responsible for their actions. But the age of criminal responsibility differs markedly. Across Europe, for example, in Scotland the age of criminal responsibility is 8, in England and Wales 10, in France 13, in Germany 14, in Spain 16 and in Belgium 18. How certain age groups – child, juvenile, young person, young adult, youth, young defendant, young offender – are perceived and constituted in law is neither universally agreed upon nor easily and consistently defined. In England and Wales, whilst the under 10s cannot be found guilty of a criminal offence, the law up to 1998 presumed that those under 14 were also incapable of criminal intent. To prosecute this age group the prosecution had to show that offenders were aware that their actions were "seriously wrong" and not merely mischievous. During the mid 1990s, however, the principle of *doli incapax*, which had been enshrined in law since the fourteenth century, came under attack from both the left and right. The doctrine was placed under review by the Conservative government following a High Court ruling in 1994 that it was "unreal, contrary to common sense and a serious disservice to the law". Three years later, the Labour Home Secretary announced that "children aged between 10 and 13 were plainly capable of differentiating between right and wrong". This was in direct contradiction to a United Nations recommendation that the UK give serious consideration to *raising* the age of criminal responsibility and thus bring the UK countries in line with much of Europe. However the Home Secretary's view held sway. In 1998 the Crime and Disorder Act abolished the *doli incapax* presumption, thus removing an important principle which, in theory at least, had acted to protect children from the full rigour of the criminal law (Bandalli, 2000). In other respects too the distinction between adult and youth justice has been eroded in the past decade. Fionda (1998) cites a series of legislative changes and reformulations of policy that have "an almost stubborn blindness" to welfare principles and the mitigating circumstances of age. The "adulter-ation" of youth justice is most marked for 10–13-year-olds who now face almost the same sentencing powers as were previously restricted to those aged 14 or over (see below). As a result by the end of the 1990s the youth justice system was offering neither welfare nor progressive justice to those who came before it (Goldson, 1999).

Legislative powers of the new youth justice

In the late 1990s New Labour's reformulation of youth justice rested on the principal aim to *prevent* offending by children and young people. It claimed to be "drawing a line under the past". This section outlines the powers of the new youth justice in England and Wales (Goldson, 2000) that were made available to the police and the youth court following implementation of the 1998 Crime and Disorder Act, the 1999 Youth Justice and Criminal Evidence Act, the 2000 Criminal Justice and Court Services Act and the 2001 Criminal Justice and Police Act. These pieces of legislation have, in the main, augmented, rather than overturned existing legislation. Nevertheless they have been heralded as marking the most radical "shake-up" of the youth justice system in a century.

Cautioning, reprimands and final warnings

Following arrest, and before taking any formal action, the police must inter-view the young person. A parent or an "appropriate adult" (usually a social worker) must be present. The 1998 Crime and Disorder Act replaced the previous practice of police cautioning with a system of reprimands and a final warning. A first offence can be met with a reprimand, a final warning or criminal charges depending on the seriousness of the offence. In 1994 guide-lines had already been issued to discourage the use of second cautions even though they had been successful in diverting many young people out of the system altogether. Now, on a second offence, a final warning (akin to caution plus schemes that had previously operated in some parts of the country) will usually involve some community-based intervention whereby the offender is referred to a youth offending team for assessment and allocation to a programme designed to address the causes of offending, even though no formal prosecution has taken place. Non-compliance with a programme may be announced in court on the committal of future offences. The danger, as frequently voiced, lies in young people being consistently "set up to fail".

Discharge

If the young person faces a criminal charge and is prosecuted in the youth court an extensive range of sentencing options are available. An absolute discharge is given when the court decides to take no action usually because the offence is "technical" or extremely "trivial". As in an adult court a conditional discharge can be imposed for up to three years on the understanding that the offender does not commit another offence in that time. If another offence is committed then the defendant may face sentencing for both the old and the new offence. Young offenders cannot receive a conditional discharge, unless there are exceptional circumstances, if they have had a formal police warning in the previous two years.

Fines, compensation and reparation

The court can impose a fine on offenders or their parents. For a 10–13-year-old child the maximum is £250. For a 14–17-year-old young person the maximum is £1,000. For a person under the age of 16 the order is usually made against a parent or guardian. Compensation orders may relate to injury, loss or damage and are designed to provide recompense to victims, rather than to punish the offender. The maximum is £5,000. In addition the 1998 Crime and Disorder Act introduced the reparation order which requires the young offender to make reparation to a victim or to the wider community by, for example, apologising personally, writing a letter of apology, cleaning graffiti or repairing damage. The reparation may not exceed 24 hours and must be completed within 3 months of the order being made. Breach may result in a £1,000 fine or the court can re-sentence for the original offence.

Referral orders

Introduced by the 1999 Youth Justice and Criminal Evidence Act, referral orders are intended to be the *mandatory*, standard sentence imposed on all offenders, no matter how relatively minor the offence, who are under 18 years old, have no previous convictions, and who plead guilty. It has the clear potential to make all conditional discharges redundant. Offenders will be referred to a youth offender panel, established by a local youth offending team, to agree a programme of behaviour to address their offending. There is no provision for legal representation. It is not a formal community sentence but does require a contract to be agreed to last from a minimum of 3 months to a maximum of 12. The programme may include victim reparation, victim mediation, curfew, school attendance, staying away from specified places and persons, participation in specified activities, as well as a general compliance with the terms of the contract for supervision and monitoring purposes. Failure to agree a contract or breach of conditions results in the case being referred back to court to sentence the young offender afresh.

Parenting orders and parental bind over

Since the 1991 Criminal Justice Act parents and guardians can be ordered to exercise proper care and control over young offenders in their charge. To ensure that the requirements of a community sentence are met parents can be required to forfeit up to £1,000 if the young person reoffends. In addition the 1998 Crime and Disorder Act introduced new powers to require a parent or guardian of a convicted young person to attend counselling or guidance sessions and to comply with certain specified requirements (such as ensuring the child goes to school each day and is indoors by a certain hour in the evening). The stated aim is to encourage parents to address a child's anti-social and offending behaviour. A social worker, probation officer or a member of a youth offending team supervises the order. Breach is a criminal offence with a liability of up to a £1,000 fine.

Community sentences

Following the 1998 Crime and Disorder Act and the 2000 Criminal Justice and Court Services Act there are 9 different types of community orders:

- *Attendance centres* available for 10–20-year-olds, offenders are required to report to a centre on a weekly basis for a range of activities including military drill, gym, social skills training and discipline training. Usually run by the police, offenders must attend for two hours, twice a month, with a sentence usually lasting between 12 and 36 hours.
- *Action plan orders* established by the 1998 Crime and Disorder Act, these have been described as a short intensive programme combining punishment, rehabilitation and reparation to change offending behaviour and prevent further crime. The court specifies the particular "tailor-made" requirements and may include specified activities, attendance centre, schooling attendance and reparation. Each order is prescribed for a fixed term of 3 months.
- *Curfew orders* powers to impose a curfew on offenders aged 16 and above were introduced in the 1991 Criminal Justice Act but are only available in those areas where monitoring arrangements, for example through electronic tagg-ing, have been established. A curfew of different places or different periods can be made for a maximum of 6 months and between 2 and 12 hours a day.

- *Exclusion orders* introduced by the Criminal Justice and Court Services Act 2000, these prohibit the subject from entering specified places for a period of 3 months if under 16 and for 2 years if over 16. Compliance can be monitored electronically.
- *Drug treatment and testing orders* established by the 1998 Crime and Disorder Act, these may be imposed on offenders aged 16 and over where the court decides that the offender is dependent on, or has a propensity to misuse, drugs, that such misuse is related to the offence and that the offender is susceptible to treatment. The order can only be made with the offender's consent to undergo treatment (as an outpatient or resident in a hospital or clinic) and to submit to further testing of drug usage during the course of the order. Such an order can last between 6 months and 3 years.
- *Supervision orders* these can be imposed on 10–17-year-olds. Offenders have to report to a social worker or probation officer and engage in certain activities such as intermediate treatment, involving up to 90 days instruction in social, community, domestic and creative skills. Other possible requirements include living in a particular place, refraining from taking part in certain activities and providing reparation to individual victims or the community at large.
- *Probation orders* available for those aged 16 or over, offenders are placed under the supervision of a probation officer for a period of between 6 months and 3 years. During that time the offender must comply with any specified conditions which may include residence requirements, attending a probation centre or participation in cognitive behavioural programmes such as an anger management group, an alcohol offender group or a sex offender group. Breach may result in fine, additional community sentences or a re-sentencing for the original offence. Renamed as community rehabilitation orders in 2001.
- *Community service orders* available for those aged 16 and above, their main purpose is to punish and reintegrate the offender into the community through demanding unpaid work and keeping to a strict disciplined timetable. They last for between 40 and 240 hours and must be completed in 12 months. Once envisaged as an "alternative to custody" they are now sentences in their own right. Renamed as community punishment orders in 2001.
- *Combination orders* these combine elements of a probation order with those of a community service order. Renamed as community punishment and rehabilitation orders in 2001.

Custodial sentences

For many years the standard custodial provision available to the youth court for those aged 15 to 17 was detention in a young offender institution, Following the 1994 Criminal Justice and Public Order Act the maximum sentence was increased from 12 to 24 months. The same Act also introduced secure training orders for 12–14-year-olds who had been convicted of three or more offences which would be imprisonable in the case of an adult. The minimum sentence length in a secure training centre was for 6 months with a maximum of 2 years. By 2000 only three such centres were available. However the 1998 Crime and Disorder Act abolished the sentences of secure training and detention in a young offender institution and replaced them with a generic sentence of a detention and training order (DTO). This came into force in April 2000 and, significantly, extends the custodial option to 10-year-olds. A DTO can be given to 15–17-year-olds for any offence considered serious enough to warrant a custodial sentence; to 12–14-year-olds who are considered to be "persistent offenders"; and to 10-year-olds and 11-year-olds at the discretion of the Home Secretary. The orders are for between 4 and 24 months. Half of the order is served in the community under the supervision of a social worker, a probation officer or a member of a youth offending team. These age reductions in the detention of young people coupled with increases in maximum sentence appear directly at odds with the UN Convention on the Rights of the Child. This states at Article 37 that imprisonment of a child "shall be used only as a measure of last resort and for the shortest appropriate period of time". Moreover as there are no separate young offender institutions for girls, they are held in adult prisons often sharing the same facilities as adults. The DTO raises the possibility that 12–14-year-old girls could now also find themselves in adult jails. Again this is in contravention of the UN Convention that states that "every child deprived of liberty shall be separated from adults unless it is considered in the child's best interests not to do so" (Howard League, 1999).

A custodial sentence of detention (without the training component) is now restricted to those aged 18, 19 and 20. However in cases of homicide, causing death by dangerous driving and "grave" crimes, the youth court can pass its jurisdiction to the Crown Court. Under the powers of Section 53 of the Children and Young Persons Act a 10–17-year-old can be detained for a longer period than the normal maximum of 2 years, at the discretion of the Home Secretary, either in a local authority secure unit or a prison service establishment. This practice is also under review. Following a decision in 1999 of the European Court of Human Rights in the case of *T and V* v *United Kingdom*, a practice direction was issued to ensure that young defendants (in this case the murderers of James Bulger who were aged 11 at the time of the trial) are not subjected to adult style court proceedings. The two defendants – Venables and Thompson – had been sentenced to be detained for a minimum of eight years. This was raised to ten years by the Lord Chief Justice and to 15 years by the Home Secretary (a decision subsequently declared to be illegal in July 1996). As a result the European court also stipulated that decisions over length of sentence in such cases should be decided by the judiciary and not politicians.

Preventive measures

One of the most radical initiatives of the 1998 Crime and Disorder Act is the availability of new orders and powers that can be made other than as a sentence following conviction. Child safety orders, local child curfews, anti-social behaviour orders and sex offender orders do not necessarily require either the prosecution or indeed the commission of a criminal offence.

Child safety orders can be made by a family proceedings court on a child below the age of criminal responsibility if that child is considered "at risk". Justified as a "protective" measure it places the child under the supervision of a social worker or a member of a youth offending team for a period of up to 12 months. The court can specify certain requirements such as attending specified programmes or avoiding particular places and people. Breach may result in the substitution of a care order under the powers of the 1989 Children Act. In addition local authorities can, after consultation with the police and local community, introduce a local child curfew to apply to *all* children under the age of 10 in a specific area. This places a ban on unsupervised children being in a specified area between 9 p.m. and 6 a.m. In these ways children can be targeted as "offenders" before they are old enough to be criminally responsible. Child curfews were extended to 15-year-olds in 2001. Similarly an anti-social behaviour order is a civil order which can be made by the police/local authority on anyone over the age of 10 whose behaviour is thought likely to cause alarm, distress or harassment. The order lasts a minimum of 2 years and breach is punishable by up to 5 years' imprisonment. Though justified as a means to control "nuisance neighbours" there is increasing evidence that they are primarily targeted at youthful "rowdy and unruly" behaviour. Sex offender orders may be less applicable to young people but can be imposed on anyone over the age of 10. Again it is a community-based order, applied for by the police, against any sex offender whose present behaviour is considered to be a cause of serious harm. It lasts for a minimum of 5 years and breach is punishable by imprisonment.

Restorative or punitive justice?

The new youth justice (as outlined above) has been described as a "melting pot of principles and ideologies" (Fionda, 1999), as "institutionalised intolerance" (Muncie, 1999a) and as a "misconceived and misguided" over-reaction (Gelsthorpe and Morris, 1999). It is clear that any number of inclusionary and exclusionary practices can be legitimated within the general rubric of crime prevention. But, throughout, the goal of securing welfare, justice or rights for young people has become increasingly obscured. Moreover the new youth justice that is being offered to young people is marked not only by the "new" but by a series of reinventions of some familiar themes of the past:

- *Just deserts* – the erosion of age considerations by focusing on the gravity of the offence and formulating a proportionate response.

- *Risk assessment* – acting on the possibility of future crime and on the non-criminal as well as the criminal, thus drawing younger populations into formal systems of control.
- *Managerialism* – the rewriting of the purpose of youth justice to achieve measurable and cost-effective outcomes that are amenable to audited accounting.
- *Community responsibilisation* – maintaining that certain families and communities are implicated in criminality and that they have a responsibility to put their own houses in order. If they "fail" then stringent and intrusive community penalties are warranted.
- *Authoritarian populism* – the resort to overtly punitive measures to respond to and channel perceptions of public punitiveness for the purposes of short-term political expediency and electoral gain.
- *Restorative justice* – the attempt to increase offender awareness and ensure they make amends to victims and communities.

(Gelsthorpe and Morris, 1999; Newburn, 1998;
Muncie, 1999a; Bottoms, 1995; Garland, 1996)

Yet New Labour is well aware that the key formal principle underlying all work with young offenders remains that of ensuring their general welfare. The Children and Young Persons Act 1933 established that all courts should have primary regard to the "welfare of the child" and this has since been bolstered by the 1989 Children Act's stipulation that a child's welfare shall be paramount. Similarly the UN Convention on the Rights of the Child requires that in all legal actions concerning those under the age of 18, the "best interests" of the child shall prevail. However the 1998 Act gives no direction to the courts or youth offending teams that child welfare should be of primary consideration. Instead New Labour's reform programme, often involving early intervention and action against non-criminal behaviour, is couched in the language of crime prevention and child protection. Erosion of civil liberty is presented as an enabling, new opportunity and, even more paradoxically, as an "entitlement" (Scraton, 1999). In the 1997 White Paper, *No More Excuses*, and in response to the UN Committee on the Rights of the Child in 1999, Labour has claimed that:

> Children need protection as appropriate from the full rigour of the criminal law. The United Kingdom is committed to protecting the welfare of children and young people who come into contact with the criminal justice process. The government does not accept that there is any conflict between protecting the welfare of the young offender and preventing that individual from offending again. Preventing offending promotes the welfare of the individual young offender and protects the public.
>
> (Home Office, 1997, para. 2.2)

if a child has begun to offend they are *entitled* to the earliest possible intervention to address that offending behaviour and eliminate its causes. The changes will also have the result of putting all juveniles on the same footing as far as the courts are concerned, and will contribute to the *right* of children appearing there to develop responsibility for themselves.

(UK government, 1999, para. 10.30.2, italics added)

It is hoped that this representation of criminalising measures, that penetrate deep into the everyday lives of young people and their families, will be enough to ward off criticism and potential contradiction with the 1998 Human Rights Act implemented in 2000. This Act incorporates the European Convention on Human Rights into British law. Article 6 provides for the right to a fair trial with legal representation and a right to appeal. Youth offender panels deliberating on referral orders would appear to be in denial of such rights. Article 8 confers the right to respect for private and family life and protects families from arbitrary interference. Parenting orders, child curfews and anti-social behaviour orders, in particular, would again appear to be in contempt (Dinham, 1999). Moreover, many of the principles of restorative justice, in particular the powers of the Youth Justice and Criminal Evidence Act, only confer rights on the victim or the community to receive reparation, but "does not confer, nor does it appear to even recognise, that children have rights and that these are protected in law. [It] establishes only that children have responsibilities" (Haines, 2000: 64). The contractual language of referral orders masks their fundamentally coercive, compulsory and potentially authoritarian nature (Wonnacott, 1999; Ball, 2000).

Much has been made of the principles of restorative justice – responsibility, restoration, reintegration – that ostensibly underpin some of the new legislative initiatives. For some, such principles hold a potential to transform a system that in other major respects is governed by punitive values (Dignan, 1999). Restorative principles are typically cited as being present in referral, reparation and action plan orders. The often quoted reference point is the experience of Family Group Conferences (FGCs) pioneered in New Zealand in 1989 and based on traditional systems of conflict resolution within Maori culture. FGCs involve a professional co-ordinator, dealing with both civil and criminal matters, who calls the young person, their family and victims together to decide whether the young person is "in need of care and protection" and if so what should be provided. The outcome is usually some form of apology or community work. The key element of progressive restorative practice is that the offender is not marginalised but accepted as a key contributor to decision-making. Moreover in New Zealand FGCs are not simply involved in trivial cases but also serious offences involving burglary, arson, rape and so on. In contrast, as Morris and Gelsthorpe (2000) point out, the restorative elements of the new youth justice in England and Wales appear partial and peripheral.

They are additions to, rather than core defining components of, a system that is also intent on punishment and retribution.

There are other grounds for considering that the rights of children and parents are being bypassed by the new legislation. Whilst it is acknowledged that crime prevention and reduction are best achieved through community-based interventions, any communitarian rationale is made to work with and through a series of authoritarian measures. The legislation claims to be supportive of parents and protective of children but its preventive rhetoric is driven by coercive powers. Civil orders are backed up by stringent criminal sanctions. Similarly, by equating "disorder" with crime it significantly broadens the reach of criminal justice to take in those below the age of criminal responsibility and the non-criminal as well as the known offender. Above all the numbers of young offenders incarcerated have continued to grow since 1993 and there is evidence to suggest that detention and training orders are accelerating, rather than reversing, this trend (Nathan, 2000). Growing penal populations inevitably undermine any commitment to promoting rehabilitation and preventing reoffending. By implementing the Conservatives' plans for a network of secure training centres for 12–15-year-olds, and by drawing 10-year-olds into the subsequent detention and training order, the extension of custody to young children is confirmed. Indeed in the three years following the passing of the 1998 Act, New Labour moved further to substantiate its authoritarian credentials by advocating the withdrawal of benefit for those who fail to comply with community sentences; extending electronic monitoring to 10-year-olds; implementing the "three strikes and you're out" rule for burglars; introducing mandatory drug testing of all those arrested; extending child curfews to 15-year-olds; urging greater use of anti-social behaviour orders; advocating on-the-spot fines for drunken, noisy, loutish and anti-social behaviour; imposing "lifestyle" sentences, such as driving licence confiscation, for public order offences; and sentencing on the basis of past crimes.

All of this seems far removed from the principles of either restorative justice or just deserts. It is more a reflection of how youth justice policy is driven by short-term political expediency and ever-desperate measures to placate tabloid and mid-market newspaper law-and-order campaigns. As a result, whilst there have been important shifts in discourse and practices, the dominant terms of the political debate over crime and punishment have not been disputed. New Labour's "modernisation" of youth justice holds authoritarian and remoralisation discourses firmly in place. Pragmatism, efficiency and the continual requirement to "get results" by any means necessary continues to take precedence over any commitment to due process, justice and democratic accountability. It is not simply that children's rights are being ignored in this new reforming zeal; in numerous key respects they are being explicitly undermined.

References

Ashworth, A., Gardner, J., Morgan, R., Smith, A., Von Hirsch, A. and Wasik, M. (1998) "Neighbouring on the oppressive: the government's anti-social behaviour order proposals", *Criminal Justice*, vol. 16, no. 1, pp. 7–14

Ball, C. (2000) "The youth justice and Criminal Evidence Act 1999: a significant move towards restorative justice or a recipe for unintended consequences?", *Criminal Law Review*, April, pp. 211–222

Bandalli, S. (2000) "Children, responsibility and the new youth justice" in Goldson, B. (ed.) *The New Youth Justice*, Lyme Regis, Russell House

Bottoms, A. (1995) "The philosophy and politics of punishment and sentencing" in Clarkson, C. and Morgan, R. (eds) *The Politics of Sentencing Reform*, Oxford, Clarendon

Dignan, J. (1999) "The Crime and Disorder Act and the prospects for restorative justice" *Criminal Law Review*, January, pp. 48–60

Dinham, P. (1999) "A conflict in the law?", *Youth Justice Matters*, December, pp. 12–14

Fionda, J. (1998) "The age of innocence? – the concept of childhood in the punishment of young offenders" *Child and Family Law Quarterly*, vol. 10, no. 1, pp. 77–87

—— (1999) "New Labour, old hat: youth justice and the Crime and Disorder Act 1998" *Criminal Law Review*, January, pp. 36–47

Garland, D. (1996) "The limits of the sovereign state: strategies of crime control in contemporary society", *British Journal of Criminology*, vol. 36, no. 4, pp. 445–471

Gelsthorpe, L. and Morris, A. (1999) "Much ado about nothing – a critical comment on key provisions relating to children in the Crime and Disorder Act 1998", *Child and Family Law Quarterly*, vol. 11, no. 3, pp. 209–221

Goldson, B. (1999) "Youth (in)justice: contemporary developments in policy and practice" in Goldson, B. (ed.) *Youth Justice: Contemporary Policy and Practice*, Aldershot, Ashgate

—— (ed.) (2000) *The New Youth Justice*, Lyme Regis, Russell House

Haines, K. (2000) "Referral orders and youth offender panels" in Goldson, B. (ed.) *The New Youth Justice*, Lyme Regis, Russell House

Home Office (1997) *No More Excuses: A New Approach to Tackling Youth Crime in England and Wales*, Cm 3809, London, HMSO

Howard League (1999) *Protecting the Rights of Children*, London, The Howard League for Penal Reform

Hudson, B. (1987) *Justice through Punishment*, London, Macmillan

King, M. and Piper, C. (1995) *How the Law Thinks About Children*, Aldershot, Ashgate

McAra, L. and Young, P. (1997) "Juvenile justice in Scotland", *Criminal Justice*, vol. 15, no. 3, pp. 8–10

McGhee, J., Waterhouse, L. and Whyte, B. (1996) "Children's hearings and children in trouble" in Asquith, S. (ed.) *Children and Young People in Conflict with the Law*, London, Jessica Langley

Morris, A. and Gelsthorpe, L. (2000) "Something old, something borrowed, something blue, but something new? A comment on the prospects for restorative justice under the Crime and Disorder Act 1998", *Criminal Law Review*, January, pp. 18–30

Morris, A., Giller, H., Geach, H. and Szwed, E. (1980) *Justice for Children*, London, Macmillan

Muncie, J. (1999a) "Institutionalized intolerance: youth justice and the 1998 Crime and Disorder Act", *Critical Social Policy*, vol. 19, no. 2, pp. 147–175

—— (1999b) *Youth and Crime: A Critical Introduction*, London, Sage

Nathan, S. (2000) "Detention and training orders: further experimentation in juvenile incarceration", *Youth Justice Matters*, June, pp. 3–11

Newburn, T. (1998) "Tackling youth crime and reforming youth justice: the origins and nature of 'new labour' policy" *Policy Studies*, vol. 19, nos 3/4, pp. 199–211

Norrie, K. (1997) *Children's Hearings in Scotland*, Edinburgh, Green/Sweet and Maxwell

Scraton, P. (ed.) (1997) *"Childhood" in "Crisis"?*, London, UCL Press

—— (1999) "Threatening children: politics of hate and policies of denial in contemporary Britain", paper presented to the Organisation for the Protection of Children's Rights, Quebec, October

UK Government (1999) *Convention on the Rights of the Child: Second Report to the UN Committee on the Rights of the Child by the United Kingdom*, London, HMSO

Von Hirsch, A. (1976) *Doing Justice: The Choice of Punishments*, New York, Hill and Wang

Wonnacott, C. (1999) "The counterfeit contract – reform, pretence and muddled principles in the new referral order", *Child and Family Law Quarterly*, vol. 11, no. 3, pp. 271–287

5 Children's rights ten years after ratification

Michael Freeman

Childhood in England has a negative image. It tends to be associated with boarding schools, nannies, "six of the best" and expressions like "children should be seen and not heard" (Voice for the Child in Care, 1998). When Lloyd de Mause referred to childhood as a "nightmare" (1976: 1) he wrote in general terms, but many would confirm that childhood as experienced by English children comes close to this description. Of course, things have changed since the graphic portrayals in *Jane Eyre*, *The Water Babies*, *David Copperfield* or *The Way of All Flesh*, but these changes in childrearing and in attitudes have been recent – school-beatings were the norm a generation ago – and, perhaps, not all that profound.

This must be borne in mind by anyone approaching the question of children's rights in England. True, there are references to the importance of children's rights in English case law and increasingly so. And it is ten years since the United Kingdom ratified the UN Convention (see Walsh, 1991). But its support for this was half-hearted, a number of reservations were entered[1] and no legislative or other changes were introduced to promote compliance. An aura of complacency greeted its ratification – the government minister in charge, Virginia Bottomley, said publicly on any number of occasions that "of course" English law went further than the Convention. She was referring principally to the Children Act of 1989 (on which see Freeman, 1992), hailed, as each Children Act has been, as a "children's charter".[2] As we shall see, there are features of the Act which highlight a child's autonomy, but other values dominate the Act and, it may be thought, trump children's rights (see Fox Harding, 1991). The judiciary, as it has since the early 1970s, has continued to assert, as one of its number Dame Elizabeth Butler-Sloss did in the *Cleveland* report (HMSO, 1988), that children are persons and not objects of concern (see for example *Re B* [1992]). But such a principle has not been upheld consistently, even by judges, like Butler-Sloss, who proclaim it most vociferously (cf. *Re T* [1997] and *Re C* (*HIV test*) [1999]). Smug self-satisfaction still oozes from the government: a reading of the Second Report to the UN Committee would give the impression that a child's England is more like Nirvana (United Kingdom, 1999).

This chapter looks at some of the key provisions in the Convention and measures English law against them. In doing this it is not intended to endorse the Convention as the final word on children's rights. Indeed, there are many provisions in it, often reflections of international compromise (see Johnson, 1992), which could be redrafted to show distinct improvements (see Freeman, 2000a). But that is not the goal of this chapter. This is rather to show ways in which English law can be improved in the light of, what is supposedly, world consensus on the status of children. The chapter does not purport to be exhaustive of the issues raised. Each Article of the Convention could occupy a paper itself. All that can be done here is to highlight, to point to shortcomings and to suggest improvements and modifications in English law and practice.

The best interests of the child

Article 3 of the Convention is, together with Article 12, arguably the most important provision in the Convention. It provides in sub-paragraph 1:

> In all actions concerning children, whether undertaken by public or private social welfare institutions, courts of law, administrative authorities or legislative bodies, the best interests of the child shall be a primary consideration.

It will be observed that the Convention says that the children's best interests are "a primary consideration", not *the* primary consideration or *the paramount* consideration. It is regrettable that the Convention does not set a *standard* as high as that found in English law (see the Children Act 1989, Section 1(1)). Where the child's interests are paramount, they "determine" the course to be followed (*J* v *C* [1970] *per* Lord MacDermott). But, on the other hand, the *scope* of the provision far exceeds the range of decisions within the remit of English law (see the Children Act 1989, Section 1). English law applies the paramountcy principle only to courts and not even to all court decisions. In adoption the child's welfare is only the "first consideration" (Adoption Act 1976, Section 6, and this is in line with the UN standard). In divorce, the child's welfare is not as yet considered at all,[3] though it is the "first consideration" (again congruent with the UN standard) when matters of money and property are considered (Matrimonial Causes Act 1973, Section 25(1)) – at least that is the theory, for the Child Support Acts of 1991 and 1995 have clearly prioritised the rights of taxpayers over the interests of children.[4] In situations where one parent is trying to oust the other from the family home, because of violence or other molestation, the child's welfare is merely one consideration (Family Law Act 1996, Section 33(6) and (7): see also Freeman, 1996). The Court of Appeal was quick to point out that the Children Act had not changed the law on this (*Gibson* v *Austin* [1992]). In immigration matters the child's welfare is certainly not paramount (*R* v *Secretary of State ex parte T* [1995]). Nor is it where a decision is being taken to place a child in secure accommodation (*Re M* [1995] and see Bates, 1995 and Smith and Gardner, 1996). Even in wardship (see *Re D* [1977]), where the "golden thread" is that the child's welfare comes "first, last and all the time", the courts have found questions relating to children which are not governed by the paramountcy rule.

Outside "courts of law", as narrowly construed, there are a vast range of tribunals dealing with matters affecting children which in no way are bound by the "best interests" principle. The Thompson and Venables case (on which see Sereny, 1995: 273) reminded us that criminal courts are not so constrained: in what sense can the trial processes and, indeed, the sentence in that case be said to be impressed by the best interests of the two boys involved? It tends to be forgotten that in most European countries Thompson and Venables could not have stood trial: indeed, even in England had they had the foresight to commit their frightful murder six months earlier they would have been presumed conclusively to lack the capacity for criminal activity.

As far as tribunals are concerned, the list is endless, and only a few will be picked out for comment. Tribunals hearing nationality and immigration appeals are not bound by any best interests principle. Tribunals in the education system, hearing appeals on such matters as school choice, school exclusions and special educational needs are not so bound. Nor are social security tribunals, though these may hear appeals from young people of 16 and 17 denied benefits.

Outside the courts, the absence of the "best interests" principle in any number of areas demands critical examination. Perhaps most glaring of all is the way successive Education Acts have shamefacedly refused to acknowledge children's rights in the area of education. The principle in Article 12 (see below) is virtually ignored in the education system (Alderson, 1999; Roche, 1999). The message conveyed by recent education legislation is very clear: the consumers of education are the parents, not the children. There is not even a legal requirement to hold school councils (and see Alderson, 2000). Similarly, housing legislation contains no "best interests" principle: the placement of a child in "bed and breakfast" accommodation can thus not be challenged by reference to any principle such as that in the Children Act (or UN Convention). This leaves unanswered the question as to whether a judicial review examining such a decision would be governed by the paramountcy principle, but, though an interesting argument, it is difficult to see it succeeding.

Even social services departments' obligations do not necessarily extend to giving first consideration to children's interests. Section 17 of the Children Act 1989 requires them to "safeguard and promote the welfare of children within their area who are in need". But "in need" can be, and in practice is, interpreted restrictively (Barber, 1990; Clements, 1994). There is a thin line between setting priorities and reinterpreting the legislation. The latter is unlawful, but a successful challenge to it would be difficult to mount.

The Children Act has gone a long way towards ensuring that institutions dealing with children act in the best interests of such children. There are duties on community homes, voluntary homes, private children's homes, independent boarding schools (see Sections 61, 64, 67, 86, 87), though the duties as regards these have already been diluted. But these duties – to safeguard and promote the child's welfare – do not apply to maintained schools or to non-maintained special schools.

There is no best interests principle in the health service or in the penal system or in the system dealing with the absorption of refugees. And, since the United Kingdom has ratified the Hague Convention on the Abduction of Children, it can operate somewhat perversely when a child is improperly removed from his or her habitual residence to the United Kingdom (Freeman, 2000c).

The child's rights of participation

Article 12 of the Convention requires States Parties to:

> assure to the child who is capable of forming his or her own views the right to express those views freely in all matters affecting the child, the views of the child being given due weight in accordance with the age and maturity of the child.

For this purpose, the child is to be given the "opportunity to be heard in any judicial and administrative proceedings affecting the child".

In formulating this right the Convention goes well beyond earlier international documents. It is the first explicitly to state that children have a right to have a say in processes affecting their lives. Marta Santos Pais has argued that this converts the child into a "principal" in the Convention, an act of enormous symbolic importance (Pais, 1992, at 76). Article 12 can be seen as a development from the child liberation philosophy of the 1970s (see Farson, 1978; Holt, 1975), and is in line with the *Gillick* decision of the House of Lords in 1985 [1986]. In Lord Scarman's words in that case "parental right yields to the child's right to make his own decisions when he reaches a sufficient understanding and intelligence to be capable of making up his own mind on the matter requiring decision" ([1986] at 189).

The initial impression is thus that English law complies with Article 12. There is a lot in the Children Act to reinforce this impression. Thus, for example, courts making decisions about a child's upbringing, albeit in a limited range of circumstances, are required to have regard to the "ascertainable wishes and feelings of the child concerned" in the light of that child's age and understanding (Section 1(3)(a)). As a second example, local authorities, before making any decision as regards a child whom they are looking after or are proposing to look after, are to ascertain the wishes and feelings of the child, so far as this is reasonably practicable (Section 22(4)). A third positive example is the range of provisions in the Children Act allowing a child of sufficient understanding to make an informed decision, the right to refuse to submit to a medical or psychiatric examination or other assessment in the context of a child assessment order, emergency protection or other similar protective measure (Sections 38(6), 43(8), 44(7), Schedule 3, para. 4).

And yet as soon as this third example is given, and it is itself a logical progression from the *Gillick* ruling, we come up against a sustained interpretational backlash, as represented by a series of decisions which began with *Re R* [1992] and *Re W* [1993]. As a result of these decisions, it would seem that the *Gillick* principle does not confer upon a competent child a power of veto over treatment, but merely allows him (or her) to give valid consent to such treatment. A girl of 14, if *Gillick*-competent, can thus consent to an abortion, but should she refuse to consent her pregnancy can nevertheless be terminated. That in practice this is unlikely to happen is because of the ethical standards of the medical profession, not English law. The *consent* of a *Gillick*-competent child cannot be overridden by those with parental responsibility, except the court, but *refusal* to accept treatment by such a child can be overridden by someone who has parental responsibility. The Master of the Rolls, Lord Donaldson, did, however, concede that "such a refusal is a very important consideration in making clinical judgements and for the parents and the court in deciding whether themselves to give consent" [1992 at 27]. Lowe and Juss have said that "in this way ... the court fuses the principle of child autonomy with the practice of intervention" [1993]. Perhaps so. But what is left to child autonomy? It is hardly surprising that in *South Glamorgan C.C.* v *W and B* [1993] a first instance judge should hold that despite the statutory right of veto in Section 38(6) of the Children Act (and, presumably, also that conferred by Sections 43(8), 44(7) and Schedule 3, para. 4), the court could exercise its inherent jurisdiction to override the child's refusal. These cases show a judiciary unable to grasp the implications of the Children Act – and, it should be added, the UN Convention (and see Thomas and O'Kane, 1998; Yamamoto *et al.*, 1987).

The Children Act is quite positive on Article 12, but not consistently so. It offers considerable scope for the representation of a child's wishes and feelings in the public welfare area (see Section 41). The emphasis on the guardian ad litem in public law is, however, quietly overlooked in private law disputes (Roche, 1991). It seems to be forgotten that the child may need independent representation as much when his or her parents are at war as when there is some conflict between them and the local authority, for example when abuse or neglect is alleged. There is, as yet, the implementation of Part II of the Family Law Act 1996 now having been shelved, no voice for the child in divorce (Douglas, Murch and Perry, 1996; Trinder, 1997). In relation to divorce, the Children Act is parent-centred, not child-centred, legislation. The Family Law Act 1996 effects a considerable improvement but this has not been implemented and may never be implemented. It would direct decisions about arrangements relating to children to be governed by the paramountcy principle (see Section 11(3)). Whether this would encourage courts to become more interventionist where children are affected by divorce is in the realm of speculation and is likely to remain so.

But then it might be asked why children should be able to express their views at the point of a divorce when the law provides no mechanism for them to have a say at home. In English law, as in virtually every other legal system, parents do not have to ascertain or have regard to their children's wishes before making decisions, even major ones, which affect the child. I remember as a 10-year-old being moved from one school to another and not even being told that this was going to happen until a new uniform was put out the evening before! My parents thought I'd be happier at the new school or so at least they rationalised. It does not have to be this way. In Finland the Child Custody and Right of Access Act of 1983 states that before a parent who has custody

> makes a decision on a matter relating to the person of the child, he or she shall, where possible, discuss the matter with the child taking into account the child's age and maturity and the nature of the matter. In making the decision the custodian shall give due consideration to the child's feelings, opinions and wishes.

This model has now been embraced in Scotland (Children (Scotland) Act 1995). The Scottish Law Commission thought there might be value in such a provision "even if it was vague and unenforceable" for it could have an influence upon behaviour. There is considerable force in this argument. If parents were expected to take their children's opinions and wishes seriously, it is likely that they would demand similar attention to the rights of children to participate by public authorities. And this, despite the Children Act, certainly does not happen at present.

A clear example of this failing is the field of education. There is a certain irony in this, since one of the aims of education is to enhance the capacity for decision-making. In crucial areas participation in major decisions is removed from those most affected by those decisions. Article 12(2) provides that children should be given an opportunity to be heard in judicial and administrative proceedings affecting them, but such provision is egregiously absent from school exclusion procedures, in the procedures for choosing a school and in school choice appeals and in all the discussion over such matters as the school curriculum. There are rarely any clearly defined complaints procedures, so that children who suffer bullying, abuse, discrimination or other forms of injustice lack a forum at which these issues can be aimed and the problem investigated. English education law bears little resemblance to the participatory model spelled out in Article 12.

Abuse and neglect

Article 19 of the UN Convention requires States Parties to:

take all appropriate legislative, administrative, social and educational measures to protect the child from all forms of physical or mental violence, injury or abuse, neglect or negligent treatment, maltreatment or exploitation including sexual abuse.

English law clearly targets abuse and neglect (Lyon, 2000a). Parents who abuse or neglect children may be prosecuted and protective measures using emergency protection (Children Act 1989, Section 44) and care and supervision orders are available (Sections 33 and 35). The linchpin of the protective system is "significant harm" (see Freeman, 1990). A care order (or a supervision order) may be made if a child is suffering significant harm or is likely to suffer significant harm if no order is made, and this is attributable to the quality of parental care not being what a reasonable parent could give. The Children Act extended the ambit of care to include suspicion that a child is at risk. Other statutory changes recently have made it easier for children's accounts of sexual abuse in particular to be brought before a criminal court. American research findings indicate that the introduction of these innovatory techniques to assist the abused child to give evidence are not working successfully – prosecutors for example being reluctant to use them for fear that juries will believe they have a weak case. There is no replicating evidence in England, but there is a suspicion that similar patterns of under-use would be found here too. The lesson is clear: changing laws (in this case procedures) changes nothing unless you also convert those who are able to operate the new laws or administer the processes as to their value.

And questions must be asked as to whether English law takes child abuse seriously. Legislation does not spell out parental responsibilities: it clearly could give greater guidance on good parenting practices. The reluctance to intervene in families may also be questioned. We should not be deceived by the increase in care orders: too many children are still left in abusive homes. Care orders need to become easier to obtain, and they have become more difficult since *Re H* [1996] which rejected a simple balance of probabilities test. In practice it now means that "the worse the danger the child is in, the less likely the courts are to remove her from it" (Spencer, 1994; see also Hayes, 1997). If this is to be the standard, then the threshold test for intervention may need to be lower. As things stand, efforts to protect children are being obstructed and often the inevitable is being delayed. There is at least a suspicion that children are being sacrificed to an ideology which ring-fences the family.

But laws also achieve little without the injection of resources. And one of the lessons of the English struggle to conquer child abuse is of the failure to address the resources question. Social services departments still commonly report that they have children on child protection registers with no social worker allocated to them. Reports of inquiries into child deaths have constantly reiterated the need for greater resources to target families at risk.

Article 19, though, goes beyond abuse in its narrow and accepted sense. It pledges states to protect children from "all forms of physical ... violence" (Freeman, 1999a; Lyon, 2000b). English law, however, permits parents to use "reasonable chastisement" (*R* v *Hopley* [1860]). The provision in the Children and Young Persons Act 1933 which makes cruelty an offence (Children and Young Persons Act 1933, Section 1) specifically excludes physical punishment (Section 1(7)). Studies point to prevalence of physical punishment in England, and to the fact that the use of an implement or its threat is by no means uncommon. Eight European countries and Cyprus have prohibited all physical punishment of children (Sweden in 1979 followed by: Finland, Denmark, Norway, Austria, Cyprus, Latvia, Croatia and Germany). A recommendation of the Council of Europe Committee of Ministers in 1985 urged Member States (the United Kingdom is one) to "review their legislation on the power to punish children in order to limit or indeed prohibit corporal punishment, even if violation of such a prohibition does not entail a criminal penalty".

The Children Act, while it continued the progress to outlaw corporal punishment outside the home, did not take up the issue of physical chastisement by parents. And yet nothing is a clearer statement of the position that children occupy in society, a clearer badge of childhood, than the fact that children alone of all people in society can be hit with impunity. There is probably no more significant step that could be taken to advance both the status and protection of children than to outlaw the practice of physical punishment. Much child abuse is, we know, punishment which has gone awfully wrong. Sweden goes even further: their Parenthood and Guardianship Code outlaws "other humiliating treatment" as well. Is it too much to hope that England will follow the lead of Sweden and the other European countries that have declared the hitting of children to be unacceptable? For how much longer will this rite against children be allowed to continue?

Certainly there is no prospect of this change in the immediate future. The government has ruled out the Swedish model as "quite unacceptable" (Department of Health, 2000: cf. Children Are Unbeatable! Alliance, 2000). Acceptable physical chastisement will be redefined in the light of *A* v *United Kingdom* [1998] which ruled that English law insufficiently protects children, but parents will retain the right to hit their children (see also Newell, chapter 23).

Article 19 needs also to be read in conjunction with Article 34, under which States Parties are to protect the child from "sexual exploitation and sexual abuse". Awareness of, and sensitivity to, these phenomena have increased enormously in the years since the Convention, and the English legal system has responded to a variety of the forms of sexual exploitation that exist. But gaps remain.

Legislation (the Street Offences Act 1959) does not distinguish child from adult prostitutes. However, guidelines were published at the end of 1998 recommending that child prostitutes should be treated as victims of crimes rather than as offenders. Some believe this does not go far enough and would like child prostitution to be totally decriminalised (Ayre and Barrett, 2000).

It took the world a long time to wake up to the evil of sex tourism. After the World Congress in Stockholm in 1996, the UK passed the Sexual Offences (Conspiracy and Incitement) Act 1996 and this gave the UK courts jurisdiction to deal with those who conspire or incite others in the UK to commit sexual acts against children abroad. A year later the Sexual Offences Act 1997 made it possible to prosecute UK citizens for sexual offences against children committed outside the UK. These are important measures but they have not eradicated the problem. Very few prosecutions have been mounted and very little done to tackle the problem at source. Nor has much been done to target the importation of sex slaves (from Eastern Europe and the Far East in particular) into the UK.

Some measures have also been taken to target paedophiles and other sex offenders. The Criminal Justice Act 1991 extended supervision of sex offenders with their release from prison, but this remains weak and ineffective. The Sex Offenders Act 1997 created a register of sex offenders. Critics complain that this is not widely enough available, and there have been calls for a new law to be modelled on the US's "Megan's law" so that a community can be alerted to the presence of known paedophiles. There were major protests in Portsmouth in particular in 2000. The Crime and Disorder Act 1998 introduced sex offender orders to help the police manage sex offenders in the community. Whether any of the measures or the three collectively are sufficient may be doubted but it is sufficient to see what else can be done consistently with the principles of a liberal society. But the reality remains that few children suffer at the hands of stranger perverts and many are abused within their own homes and within community homes (Waterhouse, 2000; Myers, O'Neill and Jones, 1999) and by teachers, priests and others whom society has not hitherto demonised. The establishment of a central register of those unsuitable to work with children, if adequately policed, may do something to stem this problem. But the state can only do so much. More requires public vigilance and responsiveness to the cries of children, which for long have gone unheard.

Freedom of expression

The UN Convention provides that the child is to have the right to "freedom of expression" (Article 13). This right is to include

> freedom to seek, receive and impart information and ideas of all kinds … either orally, in writing or in print, in the form of art, or through any other media of the child's choice.

The only restrictions (Article 13(2)) are to protect the rights and reputations of others (the law of defamation, for example) and to protect national security and public order, as well as public health and morals. The Convention states that the child's right to freedom of expression *includes* the forms of expression listed, and it is therefore not exhaustive of them. The "freedom to hold opinions" in the European Convention on Human Rights (now embodied in English law by the Human Rights Act 1998) is thus arguably also embraced within Article 13.

There are a number of ways in which English law fails to sustain this freedom. Governmental intrusions on school curricula, limiting teaching about homosexuality (the notorious Local Government Act 1986, Section 28 remains on the statute book, despite efforts to remove it). Forbidding "the pursuit of partisan political activities by pupils" and the "promotion of partisan political views in the teaching of any subject in the school" (how one conjectures is modern history to be taught?), restricting sex education (Monk, 1998), are all breaches of Article 13.

The insistence by schools on the wearing of school uniforms is a further potential breach of Article 13. English courts have upheld head teachers' insistence on the wearing of uniforms, in one case agreeing with a head who sent home a girl who wore trousers (she had had rheumatic fever, but no doctor's letter was offered in support of her mother's decision to send her to school so dressed) (*Spiers* v *Warrington Corporation* [1954]). The European Commission in the *Stevens* case in 1986 rejected a mother's application alleging that the rules on school uniform breached her and her son's rights under the European Convention. But it admitted that "the right to freedom of expression may include the right of a person to express his ideas through the way he dresses". The Commission did not think it had been established on the facts that the child had been prevented from expressing a particular "opinion or idea by means of ... clothing". The American Supreme Court upheld school students' rights to wear black arm bands to protest against the Vietnam war. "It can hardly be argued", it pronounced, "that either students or teachers lose their constitutional rights to freedom of speech or expression at the schoolhouse gate" (*Tinker* v *Des Moines Community School District* [1969]). English schools regularly breach both the letter and spirit of this and hitherto have got away with it. But there is a strong arguable case that judged against the Convention many of their practices would be found unacceptable. It is difficult to see how they could be defended in terms of Article 13(2).

Freedom of thought, conscience and religion

The UN Convention Article 14 requires States Parties to respect the right of the child to freedom of thought, conscience and religion. Freedom to manifest religion may be subjected only to such limitations "necessary to protect public safety, order, health or morals or the protection of the rights and freedoms of others". The European Convention on Human Rights lays down a similar right, though it does so in stronger terms, emphasising the right to change religion and to "manifest" religion in worship, teaching, practice and observance.

The European Convention is now, of course, part of English law. There thus is statutory confirmation of the rights set out in the UN Convention. Schools which deny Muslim children the opportunity to pray on Fridays or insist upon Jewish children attending schools on Saturday clearly breach both the UN Convention and the Human Rights Act. English education law which gives parents a right to withdraw their children from religious worship and instruction in schools and even allows them to request special lessons in a particular religion also breaches the UN Convention because it does not give children similar rights. The continuing reluctance of British governments to approve funding for voluntary-aided Muslim schools – while allowing this for Church of England, Catholic and Jewish schools – is a breach of both the "religion" Article and of Article 2 of the UN Convention. Arguments by some (Miller, 1990; Newell, 1993), allegedly in the cause of children's rights, to ban circumcision of male babies clearly also fly in the face of the freedom of religion Article (and see also Freeman, 1999b). The British government has resisted the weak arguments proffered to outlaw the practice – as indeed has every other government today save Sweden. The Nazis banned it of course: need one say more?

Children in care may not be brought up "in any religious persuasion other than that in which [they] would have been brought up if the order had not been made" (Children Act 1989, Section 33(5)(a)). On one level this is right, but what of the child who does not wish to be brought up in care in the religion of his (or her) family, perhaps associating it with the abuse to which s/he has been subjected? Or the child who does not wish to be brought up in any religion? In theory, the *Gillick* case should cater for such children, provided, of course, they are deemed to have sufficient understanding of the issues and sufficient maturity and intelligence to have thought rationally about them. And, certainly, regulations under the Children Act (Children's Homes Regulations, 1991) should satisfy this requirement (see para. 11), but in practice the Christian ethos of many childcare organisations may not make this particularly easy.

It may be noted also that wards of the court are, at least in theory, also denied freedom of religion, since the court may direct this. In practice, it is doubtful whether the problem exists. Nevertheless, it ought to be made clear by statute that the powers of the wardship court, in effect the inherent jurisdiction of the High Court, cannot be used in derogation from the principle set out in the UN Convention on the Rights of the Child.

Freedom of association

Article 15 of the UN Convention recognises the right of the child to freedom of association and to freedom of peaceful assembly, subject only to restrictions necessary in a democratic society in the interests of national security or public safety, public order, the protection of public health or morals or the protection of the rights and freedoms of others.

The refusal of schools to allow union activity or, for example, CND meetings or anti-apartheid meetings or meetings to celebrate a particular national day of an ethnic group within a school breaches this Article. We have had an Education Act almost annually in recent years. Is it too much to hope that the next one will encode some basic rights for school children? Similar problems arise in the context of local authority care: it is known that the National Association of Young People In Care (NAYPIC) has had difficulty organising in some areas. Again, it has to be stressed that local authorities which obstruct such activity are in breach of the UN Convention.

It is doubtful whether British Public Order Legislation, in particular the restrictive Public Order Act of 1986, satisfies the Convention. The new offence of "disorderly conduct" is wider than the exceptions allowed in this Article. Certainly, the police could interpret it, and have done, to restrict gatherings by young people.

These policies have continued – and intensified. The Crime and Disorder Act 1998 introduces powers for local authorities to impose curfews for children under the age of 10 (Walsh, 1999). The imposing of a curfew denies a child the right to be out even though he has committed no offence (in law, of course, he cannot do so anyway) and even though he has not been identified as someone at risk of so doing. Curfews are blanket bans on a child's freedom. They are incompatible both with Article 15 and also Article 16. There is no evidence that curfews will either cut down on potential criminal activity or in any way protect these children. But it could lead to more children being abused, as well as criminalising children under 10 and reinforcing the image that the public space is off bounds for children. "Seen but not heard" could swiftly become "Neither seen nor heard".[5]

The protection of privacy

Article 16 of the UN Convention states:

No child shall be subjected to arbitrary or unlawful interference with his or her privacy, family, home or correspondence, nor to unlawful attacks on his or her honour and reputation.

To a large extent a child's privacy is controlled by parents or other caretakers, and to a large extent also the privacy that parents can offer is related to their income and other resources. The poor have never had much privacy: their lives have always been more public than that of more affluent people. The privacy provision cannot, therefore, be entirely disentangled from another Article in the Convention which proclaims the right of every child to an adequate standard of living (Article 27). Children condemned to live in bed and breakfast accommodation have neither an adequate standard of living, nor any degree of privacy. It may be added that they are hardly likely to have the opportunities for play and recreational activities set out in the Convention (Article 31) or, indeed, to find the right to education, guaranteed by the Convention (in Articles 28 and 29) of much import.

A child's privacy is interfered with in a number of ways. Within the home this may be difficult to provide for, but in institutions, where there is widespread abuse of privacy, English law has done far too little to protect the freedom guaranteed by Article 16. Even where attempts have been made, for example, by Regulation under the Children Act, there is growing evidence that these attempts are frustrated in practice. The right to private correspondence is not protected in all institutions which house children and young persons. In some residential institutions children cannot even use toilets in complete privacy. There may be communal bathing facilities only. There are institutions in which the periods of young women are monitored by staff. In some children's homes, notably but not exclusively secure accommodation, closed circuit video cameras and two-way mirrors are used to observe children. This may be done without their knowledge, let alone their consent.

There are many other ways in which a child's privacy is invaded and to which all too little attention has been given. For example, the growing practice of advertising children for adoption with exposure of biographical details and the use of a photograph is a clear breach of this Article of the Convention. Whether it should be stopped is another matter. If adoption or another form of permanent placement is in the best interests of the child concerned, it may be thought unduly legalistic to insist upon this "lesser" right and therefore sacrifice a "greater" one. The Convention does after all, in Article 21, mandate those countries which permit adoption to "ensure that the best interests of the child shall be the paramount consideration" (a provision with which, as we shall see, English law does not currently comply). At the very least I would hope that the current "advertising" practice would be subjected to sustained scrutiny and reasoned debate.

Adoption

As already indicated, English law falls short of its Convention obligations in relation to Article 21, the adoption Article.

First, the "best interests" of the child are only the "first consideration" in adoption proceedings in England (Adoption Act 1976, Section 6). The Convention requires them to be the "paramount" consideration. "First" suggests, as is indeed the case, that there are other considerations, such as the rights of biological parents: "paramount" suggests, by contrast, that the best interests of the child should be determinative. If the report of the Departmental Review on Adoption is implemented, English law will be brought into line with the Convention, but there are no immediate plans to do so.

Second, the Convention requires that the "persons concerned [should] have given their informed consent to the adoption on the basis of such counselling as may be necessary" (Article 21(a)). In England, counselling is not always available and, where given, often is offered after the adoption has taken place. Furthermore, English law (unlike that in Scotland) has never required the consent of the person most concerned, namely the child. Again, the Adoption Review will, if and when implemented, remedy, at least to some extent, this defect. But it proposes the age of 12 as the appropriate one. This is unduly cautious: a child can clearly express a desire for or against a particular adoption at a much earlier age than this. I would advocate fixing the age no higher than 7. A transplant to a new family is too important a step to contemplate against the wishes of a child able to express wishes and feelings about its desirability.

Third, there is the issue of inter-country adoption. This was one of the more controversial areas covered by the Convention, with some countries notably Venezuela being understandably unhappy with the whole concept. It needs to be said that if other provisions in the Convention were universally fulfilled (adequate standard of living (Article 27), adequate health care for mothers and children (Articles 24(2)) being the most obvious examples), there would be little need for inter-country adoption. But in the foreseeable future and particularly in the light of the collapse of infrastructures in many parts of the world, there will be a felt necessity to rescue children from orphanages and bring them to more prosperous and stable countries like the United Kingdom. In the light of this it may be said that English law is insufficiently geared to assist the process of inter-country adoption. The *Luff* decision ([1992]), in particular, showed an insensitivity to the needs of Romanian orphans. But where inter-country adoption is allowed, it is clear that English law, and practice, falls short of the Convention obligation to ensure that the safeguards and standards are "equivalent" to those existing in the case of national adoption. With the implementation of the Hague Convention on inter-country adoption this should change. But we must wait and see.

Health and health services

Article 24(1) of the Convention states that:

> States Parties recognize the right of the child to the enjoyment of the highest attainable standard of health and to facilities for the treatment of illness and rehabilitation of health.

States are to "strive to ensure that no child is deprived of his or her right of access to such health care services". The United Kingdom sets no standards as such for children's health services. There is no sense that the allocation of resources within the National Health Service reflects the needs of children. There are known to be wide regional variations in provision too. Further, poverty is strongly associated with increased risk to child health, so that full implementation of this Article requires sustained measures to eradicate child poverty. But this increased steeply during the eighteen years of Tory misrule, and, although there is a commitment by the Labour administration to end child poverty by 2019, it has continued to increase in its first three years (by 100,000).

Part of the problem is that the health of children, indeed, the population generally, is the responsibility of unelected health authorities.

In particular Article 24 requires a number of measures. It requires measures to be taken to diminish infant and child mortality. This has declined, but the decline has slowed, is slower than many comparable countries and is high in comparison with, for example, France, Italy and Sweden. The UK has the highest post-neonatal mortality rate of seven European countries as reported in a 1990 study. It also requires an emphasis on primary health care. There is concern that recent changes in the delivery of health services may work to the detriment of this, particularly as regards children.

The Article further requires measures to tackle the "dangers and risks of environmental pollution" (Article 24(3)). There is evidence of an association between respiratory illnesses in children and the amounts of pollution in the areas where they live. Much more could be done to tackle smoking now that the evidence of the effects of passive smoking is incontestable. Smoking could be banned in public places. Cigarette advertising could be stopped, including sponsorship of sporting and other events. On this the current government has hesitated. Taxation on tobacco products could be vastly increased. More could be done to discourage smoking by children. The right to a smoke-free environment must "trump" the so-called freedom of smokers to destroy themselves and others. Questions must also be raised about nuclear installations in the growing light of clear association between them and childhood leukaemia. More also could be done to cut air pollution: again the association between the prevalence of respiratory illnesses in children and the amount of pollution in the areas they live is clear. An EEC Directive of 1980 was supposed to be implemented by 1982: Britain was not fully in compliance with this in the early 1990s – there were promises of full compliance by 1993 – but it is doubtful whether in the north of England in particular the air is yet satisfactory.

The Article also requires appropriate pre- and post-natal health care of mothers. There are regional variations here as well as class differences and little doubt that more could be done. Health education is also inadequate. It is not, however, in the National Curriculum.

Article 24 also contains one of the most controversial provisions in the Convention. In paragraph 3, States Parties are required to take "all effective and appropriate measures with a view to abolishing traditional practices prejudicial to the health of children". There is legislation prohibiting female genital mutilation (Prohibition of Female Circumcision Act 1985): this was the main target of the provision. It cannot, however, be said that the legislation is working very effectively. As many as 3,000 young girls in Britain may be genitally mutilated each year, the number increasing as asylum applications from Somalia escalate (*Observer*, 24 September 2000). France takes a more heavy-handed approach to the problem and parents and others have been imprisoned. Education may be thought to be a better approach, but there is little evidence of any such campaign among the communities concerned in England. There is no evidence that male circumcision, properly carried out, is prejudicial to the health of male babies. To associate this with female genital mutilation is crass, though a number of children's rights advocates continue to do so (Miller, 1990) (its lawfulness has been upheld in *Re J* [1999]). Other traditional practices have been targeted at various times: for example, the Yoruba practice of making excisions in the faces of male children was the subject of a well-publicised prosecution in 1974 (*R v Adesanya* [1974]), though there can be little doubt that the practice continues. Ear and nose piercing arguably also falls within the purview of this Article but, in a world where children are victimised in so many more harmful ways, it hardly warrants attention.

Education

References have already been made to failures within the education system to address children's rights issues. It took until 1999 for corporal punishment finally to be abolished in schools (School Standards and Framework Act 1998, Section 131).

The UN Convention (in Article 28) recognises the right of the child to education and emphasises "equal opportunity". States Parties have a number of obligations, which include to "take measures to encourage regular attendance at schools and the reduction of drop-out rates" (Article 28(1)(e)). Truanting is a major and increasing problem. So are temporary exclusions (which now exceed 100,000 a year) and permanent exclusions (which increased five-fold in the 1990s). Afro-Caribbean boys, children in public care and children with special educational needs make up the highest proportion of pupils excluded. There is no simple cause (perceived irrelevance of the curriculum, poor relationships with teachers, dim employment prospects, racism, bullying (Smith and Shu, 2000) may be contributory factors). Another factor – indirectly government-induced – is the introduction of performance league tables for schools which naturally encourage schools to exclude under-achievers. There is now a Social Exclusion Unit but this will tackle the problem only at the level of pupil disaffection. If more thought was given to the implications of Article 12, it might be recognised both that more input by children into school structures might cut truanting and the need for exclusions and that measures to tackle exclusions need to focus on schools as well as pupils (Wyness, 1999).

Juvenile justice

The English approach to children who do wrong falls far short of Convention expectations. The UN Convention (see Article 40(3)(a)) does not set a minimum age of criminal responsibility, but England in setting this at 10 imposes criminal liability at a much younger age than most other European countries (though it is, of course, 8 in Scotland, though this does have a system of children's hearings (but see Murray and Hallett, 2000). This was to some extent mitigated by the presumption of *doli incapax* – when a crime was committed by a child between the age of 10 and 14 the prosecution had to prove that he understood that what he had done was seriously wrong as opposed to just naughty – but this presumption was abolished by the Crime and Disorder Act 1998. Children as young as 10 can thus be held fully accountable for their actions just as adults. Three years earlier the UN Committee on the Rights of the Child had asked the UK Government to give serious consideration to raising the age of criminal responsibility – this was some riposte.

The UN Convention also provides (Article 37(b)) that where a child is detained or imprisoned it should be "only as a measure of last resort and for the shortest appropriate period of time". But in England now (see Criminal Justice and Public Order Act 1994, Section 17) 15–17-year-olds can spend 24 months in custody (it was previously 12 months). The 1994 Act also gave courts powers to convict a child aged 10 to 14 of a "grave offence". Before this legislation the only grave offence of which those under 14 could be convicted was homicide. The result is that younger children can be convicted of a wider range of offences and in this way be given longer sentences.

The 1994 Act also introduces the "secure training order" (see Section 1) and the secure training centre. These are in effect prisons for 12–14-year-olds. There are now five secure training centres. The UN Committee on the Rights of the Child (in 1995 – three years before the first centre opened) questioned whether they would comply with the UN Convention. Early experience has borne out the Committee's fears. There has been evidence of inappropriate control and restraint techniques, poor education provision, bullying and attempted suicides. Not only do the centres fail to comply with Article 37(b); they also show scant consideration for the basic principle enunciated in Article 3.

Article 37(c) requires States Parties to ensure that

> every child deprived of his or her liberty shall be treated with humanity and respect for the inherent dignity of the human person, and in a manner which takes into account the needs of persons of his or her age...

It may not be clear to the government that young offenders' institutions are in flagrant breach of this Article, but Her Majesty's Chief Inspector of Prisons is no doubt. He has been consistently scathing. In his indictment of

Feltham Young Offenders Institution, he describes the conditions he found as "unacceptable in a civilised country". His concerns included inmates being locked up for 22 hours a day in cold, dilapidated cells, with a lack of opportunity for exercise, unwashed linen and pitifully inadequate provision of personal clothing. He could have added the number of suicides (and see Rayner, 2000). One who could testify to the gross undermining of humanity and dignity to be found in Feltham – or who could have had he lived to tell his story – was Zahid Mubarek who was an Asian of 19 from East London in Feltham for stealing £6 worth of razor blades. The authorities put him in a cell with a violent racist who beat him to death with a wooden table leg (*Guardian*, 2 November 2000: 1–2).

The latest legislation (Youth Justice and Criminal Evidence Act 1999) may conform to the UN Convention but it too raises serious concerns. It introduces the referral order. This is intended to become the standard sentence for children convicted of an offence for the first time. Children will be referred to a Youth Offender Panel (YOP). Although judicial proceedings are not avoided (cf Article 40(3)(b) of the UN Convention), the practice should be more child-centred, and more expeditious (in line with Article 40(2)(b)(iii) of the Convention and Rule 20.1 of the Beijing Rules). In theory the best interests of the child should be a "primary consideration", thus complying with Article 3 of the UN Convention. And, if YOPs are able to facilitate the active participation of children, Article 12 too may be observed. Concerns however remain. Children (as young as 10) will be required to sign contracts agreeing a "programme of behaviour". This child cannot be legally represented: this, we are told (Home Office, 1997, para. 9.37) "would put an obstacle in the way of the panel dealing directly with the defendant". An "appropriate person" (normally a parent) should be present (but see Williams, 2000), and the child may choose an adult to be present as well (the Panel must approve and agree this). Neither is a satisfactory substitute for a legal representative (and see Wonnacott, 1999).

A concluding comment

This survey has shown that complacency about children's rights in England is totally misplaced. It has directed attention to some of the areas where legislative change is required, where practice needs to be better monitored, where greater thought has to be given to protecting the interests and furthering the rights of children. Progress towards these ends needs a structure. The development of this is beyond the scope of this chapter, but the following tentative suggestions will be made.

First, the UN Convention should be incorporated into English law: breach of a provision of the Convention should be an infringement of English law with all the implications that this would have. Second, the concept of a child impact statement should be introduced (Freeman, 1997; Newell, 2000). All legislation, including subsidiary and local, should be accompanied by an assessment of its effect on children. This should apply also to health plans, education innovations (the National Curriculum for example) and other policy changes. Third, we should follow the example of Norway (see Flekkøy, 1991) and the other countries which have introduced the concept of an *ombudsman* for children. The details of this are again beyond the scope of this article, but essentially the office would, I believe, be information-gathering, complaint-receiving and litigation-initiating. The structure sketched here would give some teeth to the Convention in England. The Convention has to be seen as a beginning but the lives of children will not change for the better until the obligations it lays down are taken seriously by legislatures, governments and all others concerned with the daily lives of children.

Notes

1 Notably on immigration and citizenship.
2 This was particularly the case with the Children Act 1975.
3 If the Family Law Act 1996 s.11 is ever implemented, the child's welfare will take a much more prominent position.
4 Though the legislation was based on a report called *Children Come First* (HMSO, 1990).
5 The Government now accepts that imposing curfews on children under 10 was a bad policy and understands why local authorities have not invoked the powers given to them to do this (see *The Independent*, 11 December 2000). Nevertheless, it plans legislation in 2001 to introduce curfews for 10–16-year-olds.

Cases cited

A v *United Kingdom* [1998] 2 FLR 959
Gibson v *Austin* [1992] 2 FLR 349
Gillick v *West Norfolk and Wisbech Health Authority* [1986] AC 112
J v *C* [1970] AC 668
M v *M* [1973] 2 All ER 81
R v *Adesanya* [1974] *The Times* 16, 17 July
R v *Hopley* [1860]
Re B [1992] 2 FLR 1
Re C (HIV Test) [1999] 2 FLR 1004
Re D [1977] Fam. 158
Re H [1996]
Re J [1999] 2 FLR 678
Re M [1995] 1 FLR 418
Re R [1992] Fam. 11
Re T [1997] 1 FLR 501
Re W [1993] Fam. 64
R v *Secretary of State ex parte T* [1995] 1 FLR 293
R v *Secretary of State for Health ex parte Luff* [1992] 1 FLR 59
South Glamorgan County Council v *W and B* [1993] 1 FLR 574

Spiers v *Warrington Corporation* [1954] 1 QB 61
Tinker v *Des Moines Community School District* [1969] 503 U.S.

References

Alderson, P. (1999) "Human Rights and Democracy in Schools – Do They Mean More Than 'Picking Up Litter and Not Killing Whales?' ", *International Journal of Children's Rights* 7: 185
—— (2000) "School Students' Views on School Councils and Daily Life at School", *Children and Society* 14: 121
Ayre, P. and Barrett, D. (2000) "Young People and Prostitution: an End to the Beginning?", *Children and Society* 14: 48
Barber, S. (1990) "Heading Off Trouble", *Community Care* 840: 23
Bates, P. (1995) "Secure Accommodation Orders – In Whose Interests?", *Child and Family Law Quarterly* 7: 70
Cameron, C. and Moss, P. (1995) "The Children Act 1989 and Early Childhood Services", *Journal of Social Welfare and Family Law* 17: 417
Children Are Unbeatable! Alliance (2000) *Moving On From Smacking: Children Are Unbeatable*, Children Are Unbeatable! Alliance: London
Clements, L. (1994) "House Hunting", *Community Care* 28 July–3 August: 20
Department of Health (1991) *Children Act Guidance and Regulations Residential Care*, Vol. 4, Part I, HMSO: London
—— (1992) *Review of Adoption Law: Report to Ministers of Interdepartmental Working Group*: para. 7(1)
—— (2000) *Protecting Children, Supporting Parents*, Department of Health: London
de Mause, L. (1976) *The History of Childhood*, Souvenir Press: London
Douglas, G., Murch, M. and Perry, A. (1996) "Supporting Children When Families Separate – A Neglected Family Justice or Mental Health Issue", *Child and Family Law Quarterly* 8: 121
Farson, R. (1978) *Birthrights*, Penguin: Harmondsworth
Flekkøy, M. (1991) *A Voice for Children*, Jessica Kingsley: London
Fox Harding, L. (1991) "The Children Act 1989 in Context: Four Perspectives on Child Care Law and Policy", *Journal of Social Welfare and Family Law* 179, 285
Freeman, M. (1990) "Care After 1991" in D. Freestone (ed.) *Children and the Law*, Hull University Press, Hull
—— (1992) *Children, Their Families and the Law*, Macmillan: Basingstoke
—— (1996) *The Family Law Act 1996*, Sweet and Maxwell: London
—— (1997) *The Moral Status of Children*, Kluwer: The Hague
—— (1999a) "Children are Unbeatable", *Children and Society* 13: 130
—— (1999b) "A Child's Right To Circumcision", *British Journal of Urology* 83 (Supplement 1): 74
—— (2000a) "The Future of Children's Rights", *Children and Society* 14: 277
—— (2000b) "The End of the Century of the Child?", *Current Legal Problems* 53: 505
—— (2000c) "Images of Child Welfare in Child Abduction Appeals" in J. Murphy (ed.) *Ethnic Minorities, Their Families and The Law*, Hart: Oxford
Hayes, M. (1997) "Reconciling Protection for Children with Justice for Parents", *Legal Studies* 17: 1
Holt, J. (1975) *Escape from Childhood*, Penguin: Harmondsworth

HMSO (1988) *Report of Inquiry into Child Abuse in Cleveland* (Cm. 412), HMSO: London

—— (1990) *Children Come First* (Cm. 1264), HMSO: London

—— (1991) *Children's Homes Regulations*, S.I. No. 1506, HMSO: London

Home Office (1997) *No More Excuses – A New Approach to Tackling Youth Crime in England and Wales*, Stationery Office: London

Johnson, D. (1992) "Cultural and Regional Pluralism in the Drafting of the UN Convention on the Rights of the Child" in M. Freeman and P. Veerman (eds) *The Ideologies of Children's Rights*, Martinus Nijhoff: Dordrecht

Kelly, L. and Mullender, A. (2000) "Complexities and Contradictions: Living With Domestic Violence and the UN Convention on Children's Rights", *International Journal of Children's Rights* 8

Lowe, N. and Juss, S. (1993) "Medical Treatment – Pragmatism and the Search for Principle", *Modern Law Review* 56: 865, 870

Lyon, C. (2000a) "The Definition of, and Legal and Management Responses To, the Problem of Child Abuse in England and Wales" in M. Freeman (ed.) *Overcoming Child Abuse: A Window On A World Problem*, Ashgate: Aldershot

—— (2000b) *Loving Smack or Lawful Assault? A Contradiction In Human Rights and Law*, Institute of Public Policy Research: London

Miller, A. (1990) *Banished Knowledge*, Virago: London

Monk, D. (1998) "Sex Education and HIV/AIDS: Political Conflict and Legal Resolution", *Children and Society* 12: 295

Morrow, V. (1999) " 'We Are People Too': Children's and Young People's Perspectives on Children's Rights and Decision-Making in England", *International Journal of Children's Rights* 7: 149

Murray, C. and Hallett, C. (2000) "Young People's Participation in Decisions Affecting Their Welfare", *Childhood* 7: 11

Myers, J., O'Neill, T., Jones, J., (1999) "Preventing Institutional Abuse: An Exploration of Children's Rights, Needs and Participation in Residential Care" in Violence Against Children Study Group, *Children, Child Abuse and Child Protection*, Wiley: Chichester

Newell, P (1993) *The UN Convention and Children's Rights in the UK*, National Children's Bureau: London

—— (1994) "Beyond Child Abuse: A Child's Right to Physical Integrity" in A. Levy (ed.) *Refocus on Child Abuse*, Hawksmere: London

—— (2000) *Taking Children Seriously*, Calouste Gulbenkian Foundation: London

Pais, M. (1992) "The United Nations Convention on The Rights of the Child", *Bulletin on Human Rights* 91/2: 75

Rayner, J. (2000) "Killing Time In Britain's Jails", *The Observer* 24 September 2000

Roche, J. (1991) "The Children Act 1989: Once a Parent Always a Parent?, *The Journal of Social Welfare and Family Law* 345

—— (1999) "Children: Rights, Participation and Citizenship", *Childhood* 6: 475

Savolainen, M. (1986) "More Rights for Children", *Journal of Family Law* 25: 113, 117

Sawyer, C. (1999) "Conflicting Rights for Children: Implementing Welfare, Autonomy and Justice in Family Proceedings", *Journal of Social Welfare and Family Law* 21: 99

Sereny, G. (1995) *The Case of Mary Bell*, Pimlico: London

Smith, C. and Gardner, P. (1996) "Secure Accommodation under the Children Act 1989", *Journal of Social Welfare and Family Law* 18: 173

Smith, P. K. and Shu, S. (2000) "What Good Schools Can Do About Bullying", *Childhood* 7: 193

Speight, N. and Wynne, J. (2000) "Is The Children Act Failing Severely Abused and Neglected Children?" *Archives of Disease in Childhood* 82: 192

Spencer, J. (1994) "Evidence In Child Abuse Cases – Too High A Price For Too High A Standard", *Journal of Child Law* 6: 160

Thomas, N. and O'Kane, C. (1998) "When Children's Wishes and Feelings Clash With Their 'Best Interests' ", *International Journal of Children's Rights* 6: 137

Trinder, L. (1997) "Competing Constructions of Childhood: Children's Rights and Children's Wishes In Divorce", *Journal of Social Welfare and Family Law* 19: 291

United Kingdom (1999) *Second Report to the UN Committee on the Rights of the Child*, The Stationery Office: London

Voice for the Child in Care (1998) *Shout To Be Heard*, VCC: London

Walsh, B. (1991) "The United Nations Convention on the Rights of the Child: A British View", *International Journal of Law and the Family* 5: 170

Walsh, C. (1999) "Imposing Order: Child Safety Orders and Local Child Curfew Schemes", *Journal of Social Welfare and Family Law* 21: 135

Waterhouse (2000) *Report of Inquiry into Child Abuse in North Wales*, Stationery Office: London

Williams, J. (2000) "The Inappropriate Adult", *Journal of Social Welfare and Family Law* 22: 43

Wonnacott, C. (1999) "New Legislation: the Counterfeit Contract – Reform, Pretence and Muddled Principles in the New Referral Order", *Child and Family Law Quarterly* 11: 271

Woodroffe, C. and Glickman, M. (1993) "Trends in Child Health", *Children and Society* 7: 49

World Health Organisation (1992) *Health for All Indicators*, Eurostat/PC: Copenhagen

Wyness, M. G. (1999) "Childhood, Agency and Education Reform", *Childhood* 6: 353

Yamamoto, K., Soliman, A., Parsons, J. and Davis, O. (1987) "Voices in Unison – Stressful Events In Lives of Children In Six Countries", *Journal of Child Psychology and Psychiatry* 28: 855

6   The Human Rights Act 1998

Human rights for children too

Jane Fortin

The Human Rights Act and the European Convention on Human Rights

The Human Rights Act 1998, which became fully operational on 2 October 2000, incorporated the European Convention on Human Rights into our domestic law. Many lawyers considered the 1998 Act to be one of the most significant events in the history of English law. Others doubted this, claiming that it would be a damp squib. After all, they said, we are already familiar with the provisions of the Convention; indeed the United Kingdom ratified it many years ago in 1951. But, as this chapter will endeavour to demonstrate, the doubters will assuredly be proved wrong – the Human Rights Act will have a dramatic and far reaching effect on all existing and future law.

Even incorporating the European Convention into English law marked a radical change of approach to protecting the rights and freedoms of all British residents. In the past, it had been argued that because the United Kingdom was 'a free country', peoples' innate freedoms were best protected by a democratically elected Parliament, rather than by being embodied in a written constitution, as in the USA and France. Now that argument is in the past and everyone, regardless of age, is entitled to all the rights listed by the European Convention.

The European Convention on Human Rights must be placed in its own historical context; its provisions then become more easily comprehensible. It was drafted in the aftermath of World War II and the rights it contains reflect the determination of those living in post-war Europe to prevent a recurrence of the type of atrocities and persecution experienced by so many. Its provisions protect an individual's private life and secure his freedom from undue state interference. It guarantees the basic liberties deemed essential to a free and civilised society, including freedom from imprisonment without a fair trial, freedom of expression and religion and the right to peaceful assembly. The United Kingdom signalled complete commitment to its ideals by being the first European country to ratify the Convention in March 1951

(Home Office, 1997: 1.2). But the rights it contained were not then made part of our internal law – nearly fifty years later, in 2000, the Human Rights Act 1998 took this final step.

Although not made part of English law back in the early 1950s, the European Convention has undoubtedly had an important influence on the development of our laws. This is because, through the act of ratification, the government signalled an international intention to observe its objectives. So when faced with any domestic legislation with an uncertain meaning, our courts were entitled to assume that all legislative provisions should be interpreted in a way which was consistent with the Convention's terms. Of far greater significance however, was the existence of a powerful mechanism for its enforcement. Other international conventions like the United Nations Convention on the Rights of the Child provide no form of redress for those whose rights are infringed by their governments. The European Convention was, however, always different. Individuals unable to get a remedy in their own countries for infringements of their rights under the Convention, could, as a last resort, petition the European Court of Human Rights in Strasbourg. A finding in their favour forced the governments involved to amend their domestic laws to avoid further breaches of a similar kind (*W* v *UK* and *A* v *UK*, both discussed below).[1]

Until relatively recently the Strasbourg decision-making process was a complicated one. Petitions were investigated first by the European Commission of Human Rights and in the event of its being satisfied that the petitioner had exhausted all domestic remedies and that the petition had some merit, it would then refer the case to the European Court of Human Rights to obtain a legal ruling. The system was later simplified and in November 1998 the part-time Commission and Court were replaced by a single full-time Court which decides both on the admissibility and merits of each case.

Children are people too

In the past, the United Kingdom has often been required to respond to claims taken by its residents to the European Court of Human Rights arguing that the government has infringed their rights protected by the Convention. The government has been obliged to amend English law when the Court found in favour of such petitioners. But getting a case to Strasbourg has not been a simple task; unless the procedure was specially expedited, it took an average of five years and cost at least £30,000. Now that the Human Rights Act has been implemented, matters are very different. British residents can have Convention claims considered by their own courts. In purely practical terms, this saves considerable time and expense. Put so mundanely, the change does not appear particularly dramatic. Nevertheless, by making it unlawful for any "public authority" to act in a way which is incompatible with any Convention right (HRA 1998: s6), the Human Rights Act forces all branches of government to consider how their day-to-day operations affect individuals' human rights. Failure to do so may be challenged by anyone in the British courts.

Summarised briefly, the new system enables people of any age, including children, to apply to the domestic courts, arguing that their rights under the Convention have been infringed by the government or other public agency. If the court agrees with such a claim, it may grant whatever remedy within its powers it considers appropriate. In some cases the infringement may stem from a piece of legislation, past or present, which the court considers takes no account of the Convention rights claimed. It is then for the government to put matters right through a "fast-track" Parliamentary procedure to amend the legislation as swiftly as possible, to bring it into conformity with the Convention (HRA 1998: s4(2), 10, Sch. 2).

In many cases, however, litigants may claim that it is the existing principles of the common law itself which infringe their Convention rights. A mentally handicapped patient might, for example, object to the principles of case law built up by the courts over the centuries which govern a patient's consent to treatment. The patient might claim that they do not adequately protect his or her right to freedom from inhuman or degrading treatment, as protected by Article 3, or to physical integrity, as protected by Article 8. If the domestic court finds in the litigant's favour, it, as a "public authority" (HRA 1998: s6), must not act in a manner incompatible with the Convention. It must therefore produce a legal judgment amending the principles of common law in a way that ensures compatibility with the Convention. The court may feel obliged to override case law dating back hundreds of years, irrespective of the level of court from which it emanated. From then on, consent to medical procedures will be governed by the principles and terminology of human rights law, rather than those attaching to the law of assault and battery which presently govern this area of medical practice. It is this feature of the Human Rights Act which will, in time, have a truly seismic effect on all legal principles established by judges down the ages. The implications of such a change are enormous since it will, of course, gradually oblige the courts to recast many aspects of our law in a human rights mould.

The European Convention and children's claims

Incorporation of the European Convention into domestic law has already made people think far more about their entitlement to the rights it protects. Without doubt, children can benefit from this heightened rights consciousness. To date, the notion that children have rights and that these must be fully acknowledged and promoted has been regarded with some suspicion in the United Kingdom. Even the government's ratification (in 1991) of the

UN Convention on the Rights of the Child failed to ensure that legislators took full account of the rights of this minority group. This was noted by the Committee on the Rights of the Child, who in 1995 responded in critical terms to the United Kingdom's initial report on implementation of the UN Convention. It drew detailed attention to the widespread improvements in British law and policy still required to accomplish the aims of the UN Convention in this country.[2]

The Human Rights Act demands a more sympathetic government response to calls to fulfil children's rights. The terms of old legislation, declared by the courts to be incompatible with children's rights under the European Convention, require swift amendment, thereby promoting much needed reform of many of the legislative principles already in existence. The Human Rights Act also forces government departments to review carefully any new draft legislation which directly or indirectly affects children in every context, to ensure its compatibility with their rights, as secured by the European Convention. Any government Minister introducing draft legislation into either House of Parliament must now annex a written statement confirming that it is in his view compatible with the terms of the European Convention (HRA 1998: s19). More dramatically, as explained above, the Act enables the domestic courts to achieve at least some improvements in the law without waiting for Parliament to introduce amending legislation. They may adjust the principles of common law themselves, in order to accord with the demands of the Convention.

Above all, when considering children's claims, the courts must adopt a far more rights-oriented approach. Indeed, all those involved in children's proceedings, practitioners and the judiciary alike, are rapidly becoming expert on the large body of very technical case law produced by the European Commission and Court in Strasbourg, when called on to interpret the scope of the Convention's "Articles". This is due to the Human Rights Act directing the domestic courts, when considering any alleged infringement of Convention rights, to be guided by the way in which the Articles of the Convention have been interpreted in the past by the Strasbourg institutions (HRA 1998: s2).

Practitioners keen to familiarise themselves with Convention concepts must also acquaint themselves with two important principles which are crucial to its interpretation. The first is the "margin of appreciation" which enables the Strasbourg institutions to allow a degree of flexibility over the manner in which the rights protected under the Convention are fulfilled. When considering complaints the European Commission and Court have recognised that governments cannot be expected to interpret all their obligations under the Convention in a precisely identical fashion. States are therefore entitled to a measure of latitude or "margin of appreciation" when ensuring that Convention rights are duly observed, in the light of local conditions and requirements. The second is the principle of "proportionality". This acknowledges that in relation to provisions like Article 8, which are not absolute but can be infringed in certain clearly defined circumstances, a fair balance must be established between the demands of the general interests of the community and the need to fulfil the individual's rights under the Convention. In other words, a restriction on the right itself may at times be justified, as acknowledged by the qualifying words of the Article itself, but only as long as the restriction (or infringement) is *proportionate* to the legitimate aim pursued by the government imposing the restriction.

Despite its importance, the domestic courts are not obliged to follow the Strasbourg case law slavishly, if they can be persuaded that it is anachronistic. As the European Court has itself stressed, the Convention is a "living instrument" and its interpretation must keep abreast with changes in societies' needs. Even so, the existing body of case law is obviously extremely influential and children's lawyers, in particular, must use it carefully. A brief examination shows that, until recently, the Commission and Court have often adopted a very cautious approach to the notion of children having rights of their own, independent of those of their parents.

Can the European Convention rights help children?

As explained above, to use the rights listed in the European Convention to best effect, children's legal advisers must assess the way its Articles have been interpreted, on behalf of children in the past, by the European Commission and Court of Human Rights. They are hampered by the dearth of case law focusing on children's rights. This is not surprising, given the Convention's history and objectives. It never obviously catered for activities which concern children. Indeed, there are three aspects of the European Convention which undermine its ability to promote children's rights very effectively. The first is its narrow scope. Because it is concerned with civil and political rights, its interpretation has principally revolved around the basic freedoms deemed essential to individual autonomy and privacy from state interference, such as freedom from torture and the right to a fair trial. Since children are brought up in the protected environment of the home, these kind of rights are usually far less important to them than to adults, and in many respects, less important than their social and economic rights. By contrast, the UN Convention on the Rights of the Child makes detailed provision for both sets of rights. It not only provides children with the right to basic freedoms but also aims to secure their rights, for example, to a reasonable standard of living, to a good health service and to free education.

A further restriction of the European Convention's ability to promote children's rights is that although its provisions apply to all individuals, whatever their age, it was self-evidently never designed to provide specifically for children as a group. Whilst at least some of its articles can be utilised on their behalf, applications concerning children have to be fitted into provisions that could have been far better worded had the Convention been designed with them specifically in mind. For example, how many step-fathers think in terms of employing "torture or inhuman or degrading treatment", if and when they beat their charges with a stick? (*A* v *UK*, discussed below).[3]

Finally, even applications which focus on children's rights will inevitably be brought on their behalf by adults, quite simply because children are too young to cope with the procedural complications of making claims themselves. The adults acting for children are often their parents, and the adult perspective of the Articles of the Convention may, at times, be exploited by parents to promote their own rights, at the expense of those of their children. In particular, there are concerns that the wording of Article 8, which promotes the value of family privacy, will often be utilised by parents to oppose court orders keeping them away from their children, despite the express intention of these orders being to promote their children's best interests.

Despite these limitations, the Human Rights Act 1998 can deliver a great deal for children. Children, just like adults, can now complain to the domestic courts if any right listed in the European Convention on Human Rights is infringed by any public authority, such as a hospital trust, a local education authority, or a department of social services. Similarly they can complain if the state, through its laws, has failed to protect them adequately from the behaviour of some private individual – even a parent. Nor do they have to wait until they are well into adulthood before receiving a decision from Strasbourg.

Although many of the Articles in the Convention have a particularly adult perspective, this does not mean that they cannot protect children. The Articles that children's lawyers are most likely to consider employing are briefly discussed below. Longer works provide more detailed discussions of the European Convention case law applying to children's claims (e.g. Fortin, 1999a and 1999b and Kilkelly, 1999).

Article 2: the right to life

Article 2 was obviously intended to protect people from being killed unlawfully. For example, the European Court of Human Rights famously declared that the United Kingdom had infringed Article 2 when three members of the IRA were killed by a British undercover team in Gibraltar (*McCann* v *UK*).[4] It is unlikely that many children would make claims of this kind. Nevertheless, Article 2 may support applications like that brought by Jaimee Bowen against the Cambridge District Health Authority in 1995. She was suffering from terminal leukaemia and tried to force the health authority to fund experimental treatment which might give her a chance of life. She could only get her claim looked at by the courts by using judicial review law, a particularly technical branch of administrative law (*R* v *Cambridge Health Authority ex parte B*).[5] Ultimately, her application failed because the Court of Appeal did not think the health authority's decision was "unreasonable" in the circumstances. Now that the Human Rights Act has been implemented, a patient like Jaimee might claim that a health authority is obliged to take positive steps to promote her right to life under Article 2. On balance, it seems unlikely that such an argument could succeed, since health authorities would be forced to prioritise their spending using chances of survival as an overriding criterion. The courts may consider that such an approach would not necessarily promote the well-being of patients of any age.

Article 3: freedom from torture or inhuman or degrading treatment or punishment

Like Article 2, Article 3 seems to have a particularly adult orientation. As its phraseology makes clear, only very serious types of treatment will fall within its scope. It can, for example, protect criminal suspects from being subjected to inhuman treatment whilst under interrogation. But although its wording suggests that it is not particularly relevant to children, applicants claiming its protection have had dramatic success in combating corporal punishment in British schools (Fortin, 1998: 235–238). The British government finally responded to this pressure in 1998, by introducing legislation prohibiting the use of corporal punishment in all schools, state funded and private alike (Education Act 1996: ss548–549, as amended by School Standards and Framework Act 1998: s131).

More dramatically, in autumn 1998, the European Court of Human Rights reached a decision against the United Kingdom which showed that the Articles of the Convention can protect children even in the privacy of their own homes. It agreed with a 9-year-old boy that the English law was deficient and needed changing. Although the boy had been beaten by his step-father at intervals over a week with a garden cane, in a way prohibited by Article 3, a jury had acquitted the step-father of criminal assault (*A* v *UK* (*Human Rights: Punishment of Child*)).[6] The European Court considered that by allowing parents to use "moderate and reasonable" corporal punishment on their children, English law fails to protect children adequately from Article 3 infringements. The European Court's decision meant that the government was obliged to find a way of prohibiting parents from punishing their children in an "inhuman or degrading" way. The Department of Health responded by producing a consultation document seeking views on how to reform the law (Department of Health, 2000). Many consider that this consultation process was marred by the government's firm view that the reformed law must retain for parents the right to use physical punishment as a form of discipline (Department of Health, 2000: 2.14). In any case, can a legislative formula really be devised which will provide parents with comprehensible guidance on what physical punishment falls into the "torture or inhuman or degrading treatment" category and what does not? If legislation simply prohibited all forms of corporal punishment there would be no room for argument.

Article 3 can also provide children with protection from child abuse. This was made clear by the European Court of Human Rights when it considered the applications brought by the Official Solicitor on behalf of some of the children involved in the *"Beds Cases"*.[7] There a social services department, although fully aware of the situation, had failed to intervene to protect five children suffering from very severe parental abuse and neglect. The European Court stressed that the local authority should have complied with its positive duty under Article 3 to protect the children from ill-treatment which it knew or ought to have known about (*Z and others* v *UK*).[8] It is arguable that section 47 of the Children Act 1989 should now be amended to impose more rigorous duties on local authorities to intervene to protect children in obviously abusive situations.

Article 5: the right to liberty and security of person

Article 5 was principally intended to protect citizens from being deprived of their liberty unlawfully, particularly when accused of a crime. It certainly was not designed to deal with private disputes within the home during which, for example, parents restrict a child's liberty in an unacceptable manner. The Convention was, after all, drafted in post-war Europe at a time when family privacy from state interference was particularly prized and, as discussed below, this is particularly emphasised by the terms of Article 8. But there are risks attached to family privacy. Children will not thrive if they are brought up in an atmosphere of adult bullying, criticism and petty restrictions. Nevertheless, neither the wording of Article 5, nor of the other Articles, make it easy for them to complain about the behaviour of over-authoritarian parents.

Take the issue of children being hospitalised on a "voluntary" basis for psychiatric treatment. The principles of domestic law currently applying to their situation are confusing and unsatisfactory (Fortin, 1998: 116–130). The law implicitly recognises that forcible detention of a child, particularly if he or she is well into adolescence, is a Draconian measure. So a child should not be locked up for more than 72 hours, even for the purpose of ensuring that he or she receives essential treatment, without a secure accommodation order being obtained first (Children Act 1989: s25) or the mental health legislation being used. But the secure accommodation regulations can be side-stepped if a young patient requiring treatment is admitted on a voluntary basis, to a ward which does not adopt very formal methods for preventing him or her leaving. Once in residence, a regime of tranquillising medication may result in the patient, though being on an "open ward", feeling unable to leave.

Less subtle methods have been used to ensure that adolescents needing assessment remain where adults put them. By the time a 12-year-old girl absconded from a psychiatric hospital, she had been there over two weeks, during which time she had been kept on an adult ward, in a hospital nightdress, with her daytime clothes locked in a locker (*R* v *Kirklees Metropolitan Borough Council ex parte C*).[9] She failed both in her claim for judicial review of the local authority's decision to place her in the hospital and in her claim for damages for false imprisonment. According to the Court of Appeal, there is no principle of common law which prevents the admission of a voluntary patient to hospital for assessment, as long as the admission has the patient's consent. Ironically her "consent" in this case had been supplied by the local authority, on her behalf, she having been the subject of a care order. It is obviously important that psychiatrists can discover what is underlying adolescents' disturbed behaviour. But there are many critics of the present law, in so far as it apparently allows them to be "volunteered" for admission to hospital by their parents or others, without any additional check, such as an automatic review by a mental health tribunal (see *inter alia* Kennedy, 1994: 365; Hoggett, 1996: 9, 65).

Could a child use Article 5 of the European Convention to complain about this type of treatment? The European Court was not particularly sympathetic with such a claim in the late 1980s. A 12-year-old boy complained that his rights under Article 5 had been breached by his placement in a psychiatric ward for 5½ months on his mother's request. In their view, although he was not mentally ill, he was still at an age where it was normal for decisions to be made by a parent even against his wishes (*Nielsen* v *Denmark*).[10] The Court implied that it might have reached a different conclusion had the boy been older. Even so, it seems strange that the Court was sanguine about a parent arranging for her son's liberty to be restricted against his will for so long. A domestic court faced with a similar claim may be encouraged to interpret the provisions of Article 5 more liberally; after all views about the decision-making abilities of adolescents have changed considerably since the late 1980s.

Article 6: the right to a fair trial

The main focus of Article 6 is on ensuring that those accused of crimes are given a fair trial. For example, the two killers of James Bulger successfully argued before the European Commission and Court that the form of their trial was unfair under Article 6 (*T* v *UK* and *V* v *UK*),[11] thereby forcing the government to adjust the procedures used for trying very young children accused of serious crimes.[12] But Article 6 can deliver far more than this and may provide the means for challenging the law relating to children and their families in a variety of contexts outside the criminal. It guarantees the right of access to any court or tribunal, and once there, the right to a fair hearing. Many of its constituent parts have been interpreted broadly. For example, the European Court has ruled that the right of access to any court or tribunal must be an effective right in practice. Consequently, Article 6 may, depending on the circumstances, be infringed when withholding legal aid undermines the litigant's ability to participate effectively in the litigation (*Airey* v *Ireland*).[13]

The right to a fair hearing encompasses a variety of rights. When considering parents' complaints about the procedures adopted by the Scottish children's hearing system, the European Court made it clear that despite the special nature of hearings involving children's issues, there are certain procedural requirements, such as full disclosure of documents filed with the court, fundamental to the concept of a fair trial. These must be complied with to enable all parties to participate properly in the proceedings (*McMichael* v *UK*).[14] A litigant also has a right to a hearing within a reasonable time, without procedural delay resulting in a de facto determination of the issue before the court (*H* v *UK*).[15] Delay, of course, has a particular relevance to cases involving very young children.

The Strasbourg case law surrounding the interpretation of Article 6 may well suggest that the part that children themselves are allowed to play in litigation which involves them should be reconsidered. It certainly raises doubts about whether the judiciary should maintain their current reluctance to allow children to attend court when the court hears an application for a care order (*Re C (a minor) (care: child's wishes)*)[16] or a secure accommodation order (*Re W (secure accommodation order: attendance at court)*).[17] It is further questionable whether the existing system denying legal representation to mature children in private disputes over their upbringing can continue without challenge. Doubtless these issues will be addressed by the Children and Family Court Advisory and Support Service (CAFCASS) once it becomes operational.

In other respects, the usefulness of Article 6 is undermined by the extremely technical nature of the Strasbourg jurisprudence interpreting its scope. In particular, the Article only guarantees procedural fairness in the determination of a person's "civil rights and obligations". Early Convention case law interpreted this phrase to mean only those rights attaching to "private" rather than "public" activities and disputes. At first sight, this restricted interpretation of the Article's scope does not cause problems for any disputes relating to children. This is because all rights protected by Article 8, the right to respect for family life, are "civil rights" and so all formal decision-making processes interfering with those rights are safe-guarded by Article 6 (*McMichael* v *UK*).[18] In practice, most disputes over the extent to which an adult member of a family can enjoy his or her children's company, such as contact and residence disputes, and child protection litigation could trigger Article 8 claims. Therefore the litigation must automatically comply with the due process requirements of Article 6. Consistent with this approach, British parents successfully challenged the procedures used by local authorities to restrict their rights to visit their children whilst in care, these rights being considered important "civil rights" (e.g. *W* v *UK*).[19]

Unfortunately, not all disputes focusing on children are so easily defined as being within the protection of Article 6. For example, Strasbourg case law suggests that the right to remain in a country rather than face deportation is not a "civil right" and is not therefore within the scope of Article 6. Consequently, unless linked with Article 8 claims, in the way discussed below, some of the more unsatisfactory aspects of the immigration law's treatment of children cannot be addressed by challenges claiming incompatibility with the aims of Article 6. Strasbourg case law also suggests that any educational rights connected with state education are not of a civil nature, since they fall within the domain of public law. On this interpretation, Article 6 cannot cure the procedural unfairness of the system established by the education legislation which excludes children under 18 from being parties to appeals heard by education tribunals (School Standards and Framework Act 1998: s65(5), Sch. 18, para. 17). By giving parents and not their children the right of appeal, the current legislation withholds an important right of appeal from the child whose parents are, for example, incapable of presenting his or her case satisfactorily or are too uninterested to do so. Children's legal advisers might, in future, attempt to persuade the domestic courts that the scope of Article 6 should be broadened to produce an interpretation more in tune with children's real needs.

A further limitation is that Article 6 can only guarantee procedural safeguards in cases involving a formal dispute over civil rights and obligations, leading to a "determination" of those rights. Consequently, although most independent tribunals would be governed by its requirements, child protection conferences would not be; unless it could be argued, perhaps rather tenuously, that the conference decision to register the child was an integral part of later child protection proceedings. Nevertheless, as discussed below, child protection conferences may be bound by the obligations of procedural fairness imposed by Article 8.

Article 8: the right to respect for a person's private and family life, his home and his correspondence

Article 8 is the one most likely to provide children and their families with the greatest protection from state interference. An important aspect of the concept of freedom is that states must respect an individual's right to individual privacy and family life. An Article 8 claim can be strengthened if combined with a claim under Article 14 that the applicant is being badly treated because he or she is a member of a minority group (under Article 14, all Convention rights must be secured "without discrimination on any ground such as sex, race, colour, language, religion").

The state can at times justify infringing rights to family life by arguing under Article 8 (2) that its action "is in accordance with the law and is necessary in a democratic society in the interests of national security ... for the protection of health or morals, or for the protection of the rights and freedoms of others". As the scope of Article 8 is far broader than its wording might infer, its constituent elements are briefly discussed below.

Private life

Family lawyers are familiar with the notion that the law should promote children's psychological need to know about their biological origins. The *Gaskin* decision indicates that children's claims to be given whatever information is available about their family background can be supported by Article 8. The European Court agreed with Gaskin that his rights under Article 8 had been infringed by Liverpool City Council when it refused him access to the full file of documents relating to his childhood in local authority care (*Gaskin* v *UK*).[20] Legislation has gradually been introduced enabling individuals to gain access to personal information held by public bodies, such as social service departments and health authorities. This is particularly important to children who have spent many years of their childhood cared for by local authorities.

An important aspect of private life is the ability to form sexual relationships without unjustifiable state interference. The European Commission has acknowledged that sexual privacy is as important to adolescents as it is to adults. It concluded that English law violates the rights of homosexual males between the ages of 16 and 18 under Articles 8 and 14 of the Convention (*Sutherland* v *UK*).[21] It criminalised their sexual activities, whilst respecting the privacy of 16-year-old heterosexual males and females and lesbians. Despite the House of Lords' reluctance to reform this aspect of the law, new legislation was eventually introduced, reducing the age of consent for homosexual males from 18 to 16 (The Sexual Offences (Amendment) Act 2000).

Family life – implications for immigration practice

Article 8 can sometimes be used to protect families facing being split up by deportation orders. A parent's opposition to deportation may be strengthened by the child arguing that losing a parent in this way will infringe his or her own right to family life and that the child should not be expected to accompany the parent abroad. Claims can be further strengthened by a child arguing that if the whole family returns to their country of origin they will live in conditions so severe as to be "inhuman and degrading", thereby infringing the child's own rights under Article 3.

Although arguments like these may certainly assist some families facing deportation, Article 8 has clear limitations. In particular, Article 8 (2) allows family rights to be balanced against the government's right to maintain a firm system of immigration control. Nevertheless, incorporation of the European Convention may encourage the adoption of a policy consistently taking greater account of children's own rights in immigration cases.

Family life – parent v the state v the abused child

Balancing parents' rights against children's rights is particularly difficult for the courts who hear local authority applications for care orders intended to protect children against parental abuse. Under domestic law, the court considers whether the care order can be justified under sections 1 and 31 of the Children Act 1989. The Human Rights Act now allows parent to reinforce their opposition to a care order by arguing that it will infringe their rights to family privacy under Article 8 (1) of the European Convention. Their lawyers will point to the European case law stressing that such interference with parents' rights to family life can only be justified if it is "necessary" to make an order of this kind, to protect the child's health and morals and the child's own rights. In other words, the domestic courts can now only make a care order if, in addition to the requirements of the Children Act 1989, the provisions of Article 8 (2) of the Convention can also be satisfied.

Hopefully, this change will not provoke a swing towards strengthening parents' rights at the cost of protecting children. When considering cases of this kind, the European Court has itself shown a growing appreciation of the dangers of allowing the scales to be weighted in favour of parents' claims, weakening those of their children (*Johansen* v *UK* and *Scott* v *UK*).[22] It has accepted that an interference with parents' rights may be necessary, as long as it is not too heavy handed and is *proportionate* to the degree of likely harm to the child if not removed from home. It has even begun to refer to the UN Convention on the Rights of the Child to justify its increasing concern with the child's own rights in such disputes. This trend should enable the domestic courts to feel justified in weighing up the competing interests of family members, but ultimately favouring the children's best interests. Conceivably, the process of satisfying the requirements of the Children Act 1989 and Article 8 (2) of the Convention will become inextricably bound up with each other, with the domestic courts normally maintaining that any order deemed to be in the child's best interests can be justified because it will also protect his or her health or morals.

Procedural fairness

As noted above, the requirements of procedural fairness imposed by Article 6 are broadly confined to formal litigation processes. So the sort of decisions reached by practitioners outside a litigation context, for example those reached at child protection conferences, are probably outside its scope. Nevertheless, departments of social services and other agencies, such as adoption panels, should bear in mind that Article 8 imposes procedural obligations of its own. The European Court has emphasised that all decision-making processes leading to interference by the state with family life and privacy must ensure a proper respect for the interests of family members – and these procedural requirements cover administrative as well as judicial procedures (*W* v *UK* and *McMichael* v *UK*).[23]

Articles 9, 10 and 11

To date there is little Strasbourg case law which indicates that children or their advisers have often thought in terms of their being able to claim any of the rights protected by Article 9 (freedom of thought, conscience and religion), Article 10 (freedom of expression) or Article 11 (freedom of assembly) on their own behalf. Applications have been brought by parents, ostensibly on behalf of children. Many have really involved complaints about parents' own religious or philosophical convictions being infringed, for example by their children being forced to undergo religious or other forms of instruction in schools (e.g. *Angelini* v *Sweden*).[24] It will be interesting to see whether children begin to complain about their parents' behaviour, for example, parents enrolling children at denominational schools, using Convention rights to support their arguments.

Article 2 of the First Protocol: educational rights

One of the few parts of the Convention to secure a right of specific importance to children, as opposed to adults, is Article 2 of Protocol One which proclaims that:

> No person shall be denied the right to education. In the exercise of any functions which it assumes in relation to education and to teaching, the State shall respect the right of parents to ensure such education and teaching in conformity with their own religious and philosophical convictions.

As the wording of this provision makes clear, an important objective was to protect parents from religious and racial persecution by the state attempting to indoctrinate their children through their schooling. Consequently, its terms may provide little obvious scope for challenging the principles of domestic education law which currently give educational choices to parents rather than to children. Indeed, in many ways, Article 2 of Protocol One seems to reinforce this approach by directing states to 'respect the right of *parents* to ensure such education and teaching in conformity with their own religious and philosophical convictions".[25] Domestic law currently supports parents who wish to dictate to their children their views on religion and sex education in that it protects their right to withdraw their children from the religious instruction and collective school worship (Education Act 1996: s389) and from the sex education classes provided in maintained schools (Education Act 1996: s405). It is now conceivable for adolescents to challenge these provisions claiming that whilst these statutory exemptions comply with their parents' rights under Article 2 of Protocol One of the Convention, their own rights to freedom of expression, of religion and to receive and impart information are all being infringed. Fortin provides a more detailed assessment of the impact of the HRA on education law elsewhere (1999a: 364–366).

Conclusion

The Human Rights Act provides an exciting challenge for all those who work closely with children. Used skilfully, at least some of the provisions of the European Convention can be utilised very effectively to promote children's rights. Undoubtedly some adults, particularly parents, will attempt to argue that its Articles reinforce the common view that the value of family life lies in its privacy from state interference, even that family privacy involves parental autonomy. Article 8 of the Convention carries this message most clearly, but the wording of the other Articles provide little obvious encouragement to view children as independent individuals, separate from their parents and other family members. Nevertheless, a growing familiarity with the precise terms of the Convention and the jurisprudence surrounding it should enable those working with children, particularly children's legal advisers, to support such a view. Above all, parents and other adults must not be allowed to exploit the terms of the Human Rights Act to promote their own rights at their children's expense. The real difficulty will be to make children and their advisers aware of what the new legislation offers and what they can achieve through its imaginative use.

Acknowledgement

This chapter draws upon materials from an earlier paper by Fortin published in *Seen and Heard* (2000) Vol. 10, No. 3, pp. 13–31.

Notes

1 For example, *W v United Kingdom* [1987] 10 EHRR 29 and *A v United Kingdom* (*Human Rights: Punishment of Child*) [1998] 2 FLR 959.
2 See *Concluding Observations of the Committee on the Rights of the Child: United Kingdom of Great Britain and Northern Ireland*, CRC/C/15/Add 34 Centre for Human Rights, Geneva, 1995.
3 *A v United Kingdom* (*Human Rights: Punishment of Child*) [1998] 2 FLR 959.
4 *McCann v United Kingdom* [1995] 21 EHRR 97.
5 *R v Cambridge Health Authority ex parte B* [1995] 1 FLR 1055.
6 *A v United Kingdom* (*Human Rights: Punishment of Child*) [1998] 2 FLR 959.
7 Full title – *X and others (minors) v Bedfordshire County Council, M (a minor) and another v Newham Borough Council and others, E (a minor) v Dorset County Council and other appeals* [1995] 3 All ER 353.
8 *Z and others v United Kingdom* [2001] ZFCR 246.
9 *R v Kirklees Metropolitan Borough Council ex parte C* [1993] 2 FLR 187.
10 *Nielsen v Denmark* [1988] 11 EHRR 175.
11 *T v United Kingdom* [1999] Application no 24724/94 and *V v United Kingdom* [1999] Application no 24888/94.
12 See *Practice Direction – Trial of Children and Young Persons in the Crown Court*, issued 16 February 2000 by the Lord Chief Justice.
13 *Airey v Ireland* [1979] 2 EHRR 305.
14 *McMichael v United Kingdom* [1995] 20 EHRR 205.
15 *H v United Kingdom* [1987] 10 EHRR 95.
16 *Re C (a minor) (care: child's wishes)* [1993] 1 FLR 832.
17 *Re W (secure accommodation order: attendance at court)* [1994] 2 FLR 1092.
18 *McMichael v United Kingdom* [1995] 20 EHRR 205, at para. 87.
19 *W v United Kingdom* [1987] 10 EHRR 29.
20 *Gaskin v United Kingdom* [1989] 12 EHRR 36.
21 *Sutherland v United Kingdom* [1997] 24 EHRR CD 22.
22 For example, *Johansen v Norway* [1996] 23 EHRR 33 and *Scott v United Kingdom* [2000] 1 FLR 958.
23 *W v United Kingdom* [1987] 10 EHRR 29 and *McMichael v United Kingdom* [1995] 20 EHRR 205.
24 *Angelini v Sweden* [1988] 10 EHRR 123.
25 Emphasis supplied.

References

Department of Health (2000) *Protecting Children, Supporting Parents – A consultation document on the physical punishment of children*, The Stationery Office, London

Fortin, J. (1998) *Children's Rights and the Developing Law*, Butterworths, London

—— (1999a), "Rights Brought Home for Children", *Modern Law Review* Vol. 62, pp. 350–370

—— (1999b), "The HRA's Impact on Litigation Involving Children and Their Families", *Child and Family Law Quarterly* Vol. 11, pp. 235–253

Hoggett, B. (1996) *Mental Health Law*, Sweet and Maxwell, London

Home Office (1997) *Rights Brought Home: The Human Rights Bill*, Cm 3782, HMSO, London

Kennedy, I. (1994) "Informal Admissions to Psychiatric Hospital: Child", *Medical Law Review* 365

Kilkelly, U. (1999) *The Child and the European Convention on Human Rights*, Ashgate, Dartmouth

Swindells, H., Neaves, A., Kushner, M. and Skilbeck R. (1999) *Family Law and the Human Rights Act 1998*, Family Law, Bristol

Part III

Children's rights

Cases for action

7 Medicalising children's behaviour

Vicki Coppock

Introduction

On 10 April 2000 viewers of the BBC TV current affairs programme *Panorama* were informed of an alarming increase in the numbers of children and young people in Britain being diagnosed with Attention Deficit (Hyperactivity) Disorder (ADHD) and prescribed stimulant medication such as methylphenidate (Ritalin) to treat it. UK statistics from the Department of Health (2000) show a staggering increase in the prescription rates for Ritalin during the 1990s. From just 2,000 prescriptions in 1991, the figure had risen to 14,700 by 1995; by 1996 it rose to 47,900 and by 1999 it had reached a remarkable 158,000. These figures do not include prescriptions from private practice, nor do they take account of prescriptions for other psychoactive medications used in the treatment of ADHD such as Dexadrine and Clonadine. Overall it is estimated that some 190,000 children in the UK are being given psychiatric drugs to control their behaviour (*Observer*, 9 April 2000). Clearly such a dramatic statistical trend warrants closer examination and an understanding of the context of change.

This chapter will focus on the power of adults, as parents and professionals, to describe and define the oppositional behaviour of children and young people as "illness" or "disorder". It will be centrally concerned with theoretical knowledge and professional discourses emanating from psychology and psychiatry since these professions perform an authoritative function as arbiters of what is constitutive of "normal" and "abnormal" human behaviour. Professional discourses contain both written and unwritten assumptions about the nature of "childhood" and "adolescence" which inform judgments concerning what is deemed "acceptable" and/or "appropriate" behaviour for children and young people. These judgments, and the various interventions that flow from them, can have profound consequences for the lives of children and young people. In many circumstances they may actually undermine or overtly breach the core principles of those initiatives intended to secure the rights of children and young people in law and through convention.

The chapter begins with an historical and theoretical discussion of constructions of the mental health of children and young people. The problems associated with the process of defining mental "health" and "illness" in children and young people are explored, and its consequences in the form of inconsistent institutional responses. From here the chapter moves on to examine critically the increasing tendency to medicalise the oppositional behaviour of children and young people through the application of diagnoses such as ADHD. The implications of such diagnoses, and use of psychiatric drugs in their treatment, are discussed in the context of the child's or young person's right to be involved in decisions about their health, and bodily integrity. The chapter concludes with a consideration of the need for fundamental changes in the power relationships between adults and children as a basis for securing the positive mental health of children and young people.

Historical and theoretical contexts

The behaviour of children and young people has been the focus of enduring adult scrutiny and debate. While the character and form of adult concern changes over time, reflecting prevailing constructions of childhood, the assumed and legitimated power and authority of adults to define what is appropriate and acceptable behaviour for children and young people remains constant. Originally this power and authority was derived from the church, underpinned by religious discourse and ideology. However, since the late nineteenth century the behaviour of children and young people has been constructed, interpreted and responded to primarily within the hegemony of scientific discourse and professional practice.

Constructions of normality and abnormality have been institutionalised in the state's response to children and young people and operationalised through professional practice. A mushrooming network of institutions and academic/professional disciplines has emerged to give legitimacy to the social regulation of children and young people. As Goldson (1997: 16) argues:

> The professionalisation of childhood and the emergence and development of discrete specialisms – each with its own corpus of knowledge and power – demands, maintains and reproduces a process whereby "technicians" (doctors, psychiatrists, psychologists, teachers, social workers) have been able to penetrate and regulate the social world of the child.

Each of these technicians operates within the traditions of their own distinctive professional and institutional frameworks. However, their practices converge at the site of discourse and knowledge derived from within "the psychology complex" (Rose, 1985) – that is a professional hegemony can be identified within which the lives of all children and young people are constructed through the dominant discourses of development and socialisation. A range of theoretical models of human behaviour has developed within and between the various academic and professional disciplines, usually polarising around the nature v. nurture debate. Nevertheless, professional practice has evolved within and has been shaped by the overarching application of the medical or disease model.

The evolution of the medical model facilitated a shift in explanations of human behaviour from an essentially moral framework of meaning to an illness framework. Foucault (1977) suggested that this reflected the imperialist project of the medical profession insofar as it extended its authority from the physical body to the psychological mind. Thus the state was increasingly able to maintain order through the surveillance and monitoring of the population under the ostensibly benevolent gaze of health and welfare professionals. In this sense the therapeutic discourse of the medical model is able to disguise its potency as a means of social control. It deflects attention away from the operation of social and political processes in the conceptualisation of normality and abnormality and obscures the way in which values and customs enter into the definition of "disorder". In particular the power of the medical model lies in its potential to divest a person's behaviour of any political significance, rendering their actions meaningless "symptoms".

For children and young people the significance of this is amplified since the maintenance of order is woven into the fabric of daily interactions between adults and children (Grimshaw and Berridge, 1994). Children and young people are rarely considered to be independent actors within their environments. Indeed, such independence is often considered potentially dangerous: "Children are not naturally good. They need firm tactful discipline from parents and teachers with clear standards. Too much freedom for children breeds selfishness, vandalism and personal unhappiness" (Cox and Boyson, 1975: 1).

Resistance to adult control is not considered a legitimate option for children and young people and can invariably lead to their behaviour being pathologised, medicalised or criminalised, depending upon the arena in which it occurs and the professional discourse within which it is constructed. This is not to suggest that the challenging behaviour of children and young people is unproblematic or that parents and professionals are engaged in a conspiracy of ill-will towards them. Rather it is argued that the medical model is not always a reliable indicator of, nor an appropriate response to, the distressed behaviour of children and young people (see also Coppock, 1997).

Deconstructing the defining process

To the lay person the processes involved in defining, identifying, explaining and responding to "problem" behaviour in children and young people are governed by the objective, rational application of academic and professional knowledge. This can be a misleading assumption. Children are routinely diagnosed with a whole array of behavioural disorders on the basis of personal, subjective impressions of parents and other professionals. As Schrag and Divoky (1981: 36) note:

> Most simply reflect behaviour that some adult doesn't like, but they are nonetheless discussed and attributed to individual children as if they were medically demonstrable organic ailments. As a consequence, millions of children are no longer regarded as part of the ordinary spectrum ... but as people who are *qualitatively* different from the "normal" population.

The diagnostic process is underpinned by the utilisation of a range of professional tools for assessing "problem" behaviour. For example, psychiatric classifications systems (such as the *Diagnostic and Statistical Manual of Mental Disorders* (DSM IV) of the American Psychiatric Association (1994) and the World Health Organisation's (1992) *ICD 10 Classification of Mental and Behavioural Disorders*) are intended to be objective mechanisms which guide the diagnostic process. Yet these systems, and the categories of disorder therein, are replete with adult assumptions of what is acceptable, appropriate and normal behaviour for children and young people. Although they are modelled on the scientific paradigm, the clinical judgments that follow are not valid objective observations, but inferences influenced by attitudes and beliefs. Subjective factors are not eliminated since the process relies on the interpretation of human emotions and behaviour, reflecting a whole range of social, political and cultural biases (see Fernando, 1988; Loring and Powell, 1988). Therefore it comes as no surprise that research has demonstrated a wide discrepancy between criteria used for the identification of problem behaviour, confirming "fundamental disagreements between the professions over issues as basic as the definition of a disorder or the concept of treatment" (Hersov in Kurtz, Thornes and Wolkind, 1994: 3).

Professional intervention in the lives of children and young people operates in four main institutional settings – education, health, social services and criminal justice. Significantly, research has indicated that each of these systems deals with broadly the *same* types of presenting behavioural difficulties. For example, research undertaken by Steinberg (1981) and Jaffa and Deszery (1989) examined the reasons for adolescent admissions to institutional psychiatric care. In some cases the reasons for admission appeared appropriate – albeit not unproblematic. These included cases of deliberate self-harm and severe psychosis. However in a substantial number of other cases the reasons for admission were identified as truancy, disobedience, staying out late, lying, running away and verbal abuse, implying that the oppositional behaviour of these young people had been medicalised and presented as a psychiatric disorder. Grimshaw and Berridge (1994) identified very similar behavioural characteristics in their research sample of children and young people referred to educational psychology services for assessment. Presenting "problem" behaviours included control difficulties at home and disruption, physical aggression, verbal abuse, temper tantrums and attention seeking at school. In these cases, however, the behaviours were constructed within the professional discourse of special educational needs and so attracted a diagnosis of "emotional and behavioural difficulty".

Not only does such research demonstrate the power of adults to define the non-conforming behaviour of children and young people as problematic in the first instance but also the power of the medical model to translate non-conformity into "disorder". It also points to the significance of the referral process in constructing the problem behaviour as distinctively psychiatric or educational. Malek (1991) has demonstrated the arbitrariness of the processes surrounding the definition of problem behaviour in children and young people by parents and professionals. She reveals how the diagnostic label and its application is invariably contingent upon the first point of contact, identification and referral. Furthermore, within each institutional setting and at each stage of the defining process, assessments of behaviour operate within the determining contexts of class, gender, race and ethnicity, producing fundamentally different patterns and outcomes for children and young people.

The fact that the oppositional behaviour of children and young people is subject to inconsistent institutional responses also brings into question the legitimacy of the "treatments" that are contingent upon them. Interventions in the lives of children and young people because of their "problem" behaviour can vary widely, depending on which institutional setting is dealing with it. This may have profound consequences for their lives and opportunities.

The disturbing case of ADHD

Attention Deficit (Hyperactivity) Disorder is a diagnostic category of the *Diagnostic and Statistical Manual of Mental Disorders* (DSM IV) of the American Psychiatric Association (1994). As such it is conceptualised as a "mental illness" and the professions of psychiatry, behavioural psychology and education dominate its assessment and treatment. Children and young people are diagnosed with ADHD if they demonstrate particular behavioural characteristics (notably inattention, impulsivity and hyperactivity) to such a degree and so persistently as to indicate the presence of a "disorder". The educational context is frequently the focus of multi-disciplinary professional concern and activity since ADHD behaviours are identified as contributing to academic failure in otherwise "able" pupils. However, as with other behavioural disorders of childhood, ADHD is beset with many definitional and diagnostic problems following from the historical vagaries of differential professional discourses and systems as identified above.

Since the indicators for ADHD cover behaviours that are ostensibly quite innocuous (such as fidgeting, being easily distracted, disliking schoolwork, talking excessively and interrupting), concerns have been expressed that the diagnostic criteria read more like a crime sheet of child and adolescent behaviours objected to by adults than any genuine disorder. None of the behaviours listed in the DSM IV criteria for ADHD is intrinsically abnormal. What behaviour constitutes a "fidget"? How much talking is "excessive"? Diagnosticians differ considerably in their interpretations of these behaviours:

> Through these criteria, describing common, everyday behaviours of children, the rhetoric of science transforms them into what are purported to be objective symptoms of mental disorder. On closer inspection, however, there is little that is objective about the diagnostic criteria.
>
> (Kirk and Kutchins, 1992: 221)

There is a strong suggestion that boys and children and young people from ethnic minorities may be over-represented in diagnoses of ADHD, reflecting the institutionalisation of differential gendered and cultural expectations of behaviour. In this sense it has been argued that ADHD is a culturally created diagnosis, "a pathology only in the interaction between a culture's values, demands and expectations for individual demeanour or performance" (Ideus, 1994: 188).

Ideus (1994: 180) uses Wren's notion of "cultural encapsulation" to describe the process whereby professionals promote a particular ideological interpretation of a "problem" or "disorder" without demonstrating any awareness of the significance and influence of cultural values, assumptions and biases in professional practice. For example, there are significant differences in the rates of diagnosis cross-culturally. Countries such as Norway and Sweden rarely diagnose ADHD and rarely administer psychiatric drugs to children (Breggin and Breggin, 1995). Traditionally ADHD has been more frequently diagnosed in the USA than in Britain and Europe (Rutter, 1983). However, the statistical evidence cited at the beginning of this chapter suggests that this trend is rapidly changing (Department of Health, 2000).

Notwithstanding the fact that its very existence has been heavily contested within and outside of the professional sphere since the 1960s, there has been continual disagreement amongst clinicians themselves about what to call "it" and indeed what its core features are. Rather than investigate the reasons for such disagreements, the various professionals involved "have coalesced around the agenda of legitimizing and codifying the disorder" (Ideus, 1994: 173). Thus the terminology adopted has frequently changed (Brain-Injured Child Syndrome, Minimal Brain Damage, Minimal Brain Dysfunction, Hyperactive Child Syndrome, Hyperkinetic Reaction of Childhood, Attention Deficit Disorder, Attention Deficit (Hyperactivity)

Disorder, Hyperkinetic Disorder) depending on which classification system is being used and the current fashionable trend in professional discourse.

The similarities between the diagnostic criteria for ADHD and related and overlapping diagnoses such as "conduct disorder", "disruptive behaviour disorder", "emotional and behavioural difficulty" and "oppositional defiant disorder" cast doubt over the validity of differentially diagnosing ADHD at all. For example, Kewley (1994) cites a study by Prendergast *et al.* who found that clinicians in the UK tend towards a diagnosis of conduct disorder in the same child who in the USA would have been diagnosed with ADHD. Other practitioners have expressed worries about misdiagnosis in that the so-called symptoms of ADHD are identical to those exhibited by children who have experienced or are experiencing emotional trauma (Howes, 1999). Such research clearly casts doubt over the fervent assertions of doctors and psychiatrists that their professional judgments are grounded in objective, medical science. Indeed, it is precisely the illusion of scientific objectivity that diverts attention away from the ethical implications of drugging children.

Just fixing the broken brain?

Although the dominant discourse within psychiatry is that ADHD is a genetic brain disorder, no direct evidence of neurological damage has been demonstrated in the children and young people who are supposedly suffering from it:

> There is no *physical* test that can detect the supposed existence of ADHD. There are no specific *physical* symptoms associated with it. The ADHD diagnosis is made by comparing the child's *behaviours* with a description of the disorder as defined and accepted by experts and practitioners in the field.
>
> (Breggin, 1998: 121)

Current thinking centres on the notion of chemical imbalance affecting the functioning of the frontal lobe of the brain. Medication is thought to act as a chemical facilitator, regulating the imbalance and "normalising" the individual's emotional and behavioural responses. Indeed some clinicians use the analogy of prescribing spectacles to correct short-sightedness or insulin for diabetes. But is it this straightforward? Although clinicians often give reassurances to the contrary, the way stimulant medication affects the brain is complex and not fully understood. There is sufficient cause for concern that research pointing to the potentially negative effects and/or limited usefulness of stimulant medication has been played down in the mainstream academic and professional literature.

Of particular concern is what is referred to as the "zombie" effect. Stimulant medication can suppress the child's or young person's mental activity in such a way as to produce a "zombie-like" appearance and robotic behaviour. This inhibition of feeling and spontaneity also facilitates obedience and conformity and for this reason has raised ethical concerns about the use of a "chemical cosh" to control non-compliant children and young people. Reports of other adverse effects include: palpitations, abnormally increased heart rate, increased blood pressure, excessive central nervous system stimulation, toxic psychosis, depression or sadness, dizziness, headache, insomnia, nervousness, irritability, attacks of Tourette's or other tic syndromes, anorexia, nausea, vomiting, stomach pain, dry mouth, weight loss, growth suppression, blurred vision, low white blood cell count, hypersensitivity reaction and anaemia (Drug Enforcement Administration, 1995).

In 1978 the World Health Organisation declared Ritalin a Schedule II drug – the most addictive in medical usage. Indeed, in 1996 the International Narcotics Control Board (an agency of the United Nations) stated:

> Methylphenidate's (Ritalin) pharmacological effects are essentially the same as those of amphetamine and metamphetamine. The abuse of methylphenidate (Ritalin) can lead to tolerance and severe psychological dependence. Psychotic episodes (and) violent and bizarre behaviour have been reported.
>
> (cited in Breggin, 1998: 11)

As is the case with many psychoactive medications, Ritalin and other stimulants have been found to have an iatrogenic effect – that is they can exaggerate the very symptoms they are supposed to be treating – hyperactivity, impulsivity and inattention. The following quotes from parents highlight this problem:

> In a sense it was a miracle drug because I could do things around the house for the first time. But he deteriorated. When the medication wore off he'd be really hyper.
>
> (cited in 'Mag', *The Mirror*, 16 May 2000)

> He was like something out of *The Exorcist*, or Damien in *The Omen*. He stabbed his brother in the foot with scissors. I was frightened to go to sleep sometimes. He used to demand the pills and was definitely addicted. I find it incredible they're giving a class A drug to a five-year-old.
>
> (cited in 'Focus', *Observer*, 9 April 2000)

Rather than recognising these behaviours as a warning sign of the drug's negative effects, the deterioration is all too often simply taken as confirmation of the presence of disorder (and thereby the legitimation of the clinician's diagnostic prowess). It can also lead to an increase in dosage of medication, or indeed the introduction of a further drug, propelling the child or young person into a potentially dangerous cycle of multiple drugging. Indeed concerns from the USA have suggested a possible connection between the use of Ritalin and other psychiatric medications and recent high profile cases of child/teen suicide and extreme acts of violence (Breggin, 2000).

The prescribing practices of physicians have also been called into question. British children as young as 4 have been prescribed Ritalin even though the drug is contraindicated below the age of 6 years by its manufacturer, Novartis. There is very little research evidence on the effects of such powerful drugs on young children, but that which does exist indicates severe negative emotional reactions. There have been studies on animals showing that manipulating the chemical messengers in the developing brain (as occurs with the administration of stimulant medication) may permanently alter normal brain development (Breggin, 1998). Concerns worldwide have prompted the United Nations to call on governments to seek out over-diagnosis of ADHD and over-prescription of medication. In the UK the Department of Health has instructed the National Institute for Clinical Excellence (NICE) to establish "best practice" and issue definitive guidelines on the prescribing of Ritalin (*Young Minds Magazine*, Sept./Oct. 2000: 11).

Notwithstanding these potentially harmful effects, when the research literature is scrutinised more closely, it appears that there is little evidence of the *long-term* effectiveness of psychostimulant medication in the treatment of behavioural disorders in children and young people:

> Thirty years of scientific literature generated by ADHD/Ritalin advocates affirms that Ritalin and other stimulants have, at best, a very short-lived "positive" effect on children. The effect lasts no more than four to eighteen weeks. During that brief time, stimulants control or subdue the child's behaviour without improving learning or academic performance.
>
> (Breggin, 1998: 115)

Thus, on the basis of the research findings, the medical profession's claims for Ritalin cannot as yet be substantiated. This lends support to the argument that the use of medication is unnecessary and unjustified. Nevertheless, so strong is the professional belief that a response (even if negative) to medication in and of itself indicates the presence of biochemical abnormality, such objections are invariably nullified.

The child's right to Ritalin?

Those who are pro-ADHD/Ritalin would argue that the negative effects have been exaggerated and that scaremongering is undermining the efforts of clinicians. Moreover, through the powerful benevolent discourse of medicine, those who oppose the diagnosis of ADHD and use of medication are accused of denying the child or young person their *right* to be treated. In a societal culture where the demand for compliance and formal educational achievement is high, there is an assumption that the child or young person has the right to benefit from anything that would enable him or her to "adjust" and overcome any "deficits" that might impede the ability to compete for "success". The alternative scenario is presented as potentially catastrophic, with the child or young person destined to a future of educational and social failure. It is essentially a middle class world-view that only measures "success" in narrowly defined terms and naively assumes a meritocratic society offering equal opportunities for all. In this context, however, it is easy to see the positive appeal of such a discourse to parents. What genuinely caring parent would not want their child to "fit in" and reap society's rewards? Additionally the medicalisation of problem behaviour can appear attractive insofar as it ostensibly removes the stigma of "blame" either from the individual child or young person or their parents.

This is not to suggest that parents should be "blamed". Rather it reflects the considerable pressure on parents in our society to "get it right". Parents have rights, duties and responsibilities in relation to their children which means that they are usually held responsible when things go wrong, as in the case of the child's "inappropriate", "abnormal" or "illegal" behaviour. Therefore it is understandable, given the authoritative status of the medical profession in Western societies, that many parents acquiesce to medical authority, even in the face of evidence suggesting that their child is reacting negatively to medication: "When he first took Ritalin I didn't question it. He just sat there all day, not joining in, but I thought the doctor knew best" (parent, cited in 'Mag', *The Mirror*, 16 May 2000: 9).

On the other hand, where parents do vehemently oppose the medicating of their children, they may stand accused of neglecting or obstructing their child's health needs and can be threatened with legal proceedings (Breggin, 1998; 'Mag', *The Mirror*, 16 May 2000).

Parents have become more aware of ADHD through the media and from the networking activities of parent support groups such as The Hyperactive Children's Support Group (HACSG) and The National Learning and Attention Deficit Disorders Association (LADDER). These groups represent an extremely powerful parental lobby in favour of ADHD diagnosis and they have become instrumental in articulating demands for clinical and educational services for their children. Indeed, one of the most important motivations for getting an ADHD diagnosis is the fact that the medicalising process entitles the individual to services that without the designation would not be forthcoming. Children and young people can receive extra educational help of various kinds and in some cases financial support is available to parents through the payment of attendance allowance (Tracy, 1999). With the promise of such potential benefits parents have been known to "physician shop" until an ADHD diagnosis is made (Reid, Maag and Vasa, 1993).

A flourishing trade in private practice has emerged both in the USA and Britain to fulfil the growing consumer demand led by energetic pressure groups of parents. As Ideus and Cooper (1995: 52) state:

> It is clear that consumers of medical services have the choice as to whether they follow the professional's prescription or reject it. The client's right to choose is vitally important, and essential to the effective running of helping and caring services.

However, this obscures the important question of who is being identified as the "consumer" here – the parent(s) or the child or young person? All too often it is assumed that the interests of both parties are mutual, when in reality they may be in conflict. In the majority of circumstances it is the wishes of parents that are acceded to and children and young people are left powerless in the decision-making process.

Defending the right to bodily integrity

Some commentators and practitioners have expressed concern that the rapidly expanding diagnosis and pharmacological treatment of ADHD is a worrying indication of the increasing social control of children and young people through medication, amounting to a breach of their human rights. While disorders such as ADHD are constructed humanistically through the benevolent discourse of medicine, the means by which children and young people are "normalised" and "treated" remain deeply controversial. From the point of view of children and young people themselves, it is not difficult to perceive the use of medication and/or behaviour "therapies" as tools of adult social control, or even violence. As Fennell (1992: 312) reminds us:

> Pindown provides a salutary example of the dressing up of oppressive control in the rhetorical garb of therapy, and of the capacity of that rhetoric to convince those running the regime that what they where doing was in the best interests of children.

The majority of children and young people undergoing such "treatment" do so not having given their informed consent. It is their parents or other adults acting *on their behalf* who give permission for them to be treated. Such practices are rooted in the dominantly paternalistic framework governing child health and welfare interventions – the belief that adults invariably know better than children and young people what is "in their best interests". It is an adult-led process to which the child or young person is expected to submit and conform. Failure to do so is invariably understood as confirmation of the presence of "disorder", giving further justification for the enforcement of "treatment".

The Family Law Reform Act 1969, the Age of Majority Act (Northern

Ireland) 1969 and the Age of Legal Capacity (Scotland) Act 1991 give young people aged 16 and over the right to consent to surgical or medical treatment. Additionally, since the landmark ruling in *Gillick* v *West Norfolk and Wisbech Area Health Authority* [(1986) AC 112], those under 16 also have an independent legal right to consent to surgical or medical treatment (without parental knowledge or consent) provided they have "sufficient understanding and intelligence". This ruling was thought to have marked a new era in relation to children and young people's rights as it dismissed the idea that parents have absolute authority over their children until they reach 18. The principle that parental rights must be exercised in line with the evolving capacities of the child was consolidated in the 1989 Children Act and the 1989 UN Convention on the Rights of the Child.

It had been assumed that a "*Gillick* competent" child is able to give and to refuse consent to treatment. However, the Court of Appeal decided that any person with parental responsibility, or the High Court with its inherent jurisdiction, in certain situations, is able to override a child's or young person's right to refuse treatment. The cases of *Re R*, *Re W* and *Re H* (see Bates, 1994) each involved consideration of the compulsory treatment of "disturbed" children and young people. In each case the right to refuse medical treatment was overridden. Moreover, their refusal to consent to treatment was taken as indicative of their "*Gillick* incompetence". Fennell suggests that this is problematic:

> What is not acceptable is the automatic assumption that refusal is irrational and can be overridden whether or not the patient is competent. This is the very assumption which underlies Lord Donaldson's guidance – that children under 16 are never competent, even if they are *Gillick* competent, to refuse treatment as long as someone else with a concurrent power of consent agrees to it.
>
> (1992: 327–328)

Adults are presumed to be competent unless there is evidence to the contrary. Children and young people are afforded no such privilege. Indeed it is the severity of the test for "*Gillick* competence" that "provides the basis for decisions in individual cases which ignore the child's wishes" (Masson, 1991: 529). Masson deduces that is virtually impossible to envisage a situation where a child or young person with a mental health diagnosis could ever refuse treatment.

In matters to do with the fundamental right to bodily integrity the adult patient's autonomy is considered more or less inviolable. By contrast, children and young people have little option but to submit to medical treatment considered "in their best interests", and as such they have no veto over what happens to their bodies. As Roberts (1999: 15) states: "meaningful consent implies the possibility of saying 'no' and having this refusal respected". Both the Children Act 1989 and the UN Convention clearly place a duty on health professionals to seek the views of children and young people "in accordance with their age and maturity". This means that they should be consulted over all forms of treatment, including any potentially negative effects, or possible alternatives. There is no valid excuse for a child or young person to be excluded from actively participating in this decision-making process. To ensure that a child or young person has sufficient understanding and intelligence to make an informed decision about their treatment requires that adults allow them the information and opportunities for discussion they require (British Association for Community Child Health, 1995).

Breggin's (1998: 82) critique of the uses and abuses of the drug Ritalin reveals that children's and young people's views are rarely sought:

> The feelings and attitudes of the children themselves have been system-
> atically excluded from nearly all studies ... with a few exceptions, the
> literature doesn't even comment on what the children themselves feel
> about any aspect of being diagnosed and drugged.

For Breggin (1998: 117) the drugging of children to control their behaviour amounts to "technological child abuse" and "should raise profound spiritual, philosophical and ethical questions about ourselves as adults and about how we view the children in our care".

Conclusion

> We claim to be a child-centred society, but in reality there is little evidence
> that we are. In many ways we are a ruthlessly adult-centred society where
> children are defined almost exclusively in terms of their impact on adult
> lives. Our adult-centred society has tried to contain and limit the impact of
> children on adult life by either excluding them from much of it (or) blaming
> them for disturbing it.
>
> (Mental Health Foundation, 1998: 4/5)

As adults increasingly dictate how children and young people should behave in specific contexts, the spaces and opportunities for them to freely dispel their natural energy diminish. As long ago as 1970 the child liberationist John Holt questioned the pathologising of a child or young person's energy level as a "disease": "The energy of children is 'bad' because it is a nuisance to the exhausted and overburdened adults who do not want to, or know how to, and are not able to, keep up with it" (cited in Breggin, 1998: 181).

This chapter has demonstrated the problems inherent in the conceptualisa-tion of the oppositional behaviour of children and young people as "illness" or "disorder". It has challenged the validity of medicalising discourses which render children and young people powerless and enforce their dependency on adults to act "in their best interests". Specifically it has raised objections to the rapidly escalating practice of medicating children and young people who present with behavioural problems designated ADHD. It has been argued that the use of medication is potentially harmful and is an inappropriate response to the distressed behaviour of children and young people.

Contemporary evidence indicates that adults are prepared to tolerate an increasingly narrow band of behaviour from children and young people. Year on year more children and young people are excluded from our schools and at younger and younger ages. Indeed, it is suggested that children in Britain are expected to start formal education much too early, before they are emotionally and developmentally ready to benefit from it (Wolff, 1999). Nevertheless they are still expected to be "on task" for lengthy periods and when, unsurprisingly, they demonstrate frustration and restlessness, *they* are identified as having a behaviour problem. The demands of the National Curriculum and the obsession with management systems, performance indicators and league tables are preventing schools from attending to the *emotional* literacy of children and young people (Orbach, 1998, 1999).

A bitter contempt for "childhood" and "youth" as a whole has emerged and an unprecedented attack has been launched on those children and young people who are deemed to have stepped outside of the bounds of adult definitions of "acceptable" and "appropriate" behaviour (Scraton, 1997). Instead of finding better ways of meeting the needs of all children, those who most openly express their distress are labelled and in too many cases drugged. As Breggin (2000) argues, by the time children and young people begin to demonstrate distress they are often already alienated from the adults in their lives.

Successive UK governments have failed to adequately invest in the holistic well-being of *all* children and young people. In a context where child poverty is endemic (Joseph Rowntree Foundation, 2000) the challenging behaviour of children and young people should perhaps come as no surprise. The emotional distress of children and young people must be located in the structural reality of their experiences of exclusion and marginality.

The components of positive mental health – "the ability to develop psychologically, emotionally, intellectually and spiritually; the ability to become aware of others and how to empathise with them; the ability to use psychological distress as a developmental process" (NHS Health Advisory Service, 1995: 15) – will only be realised in a context where all children and young people are valued and respected, both individually and collectively. It is incumbent on adults to build stronger, child and young person-centred, nurturing relationships – in the home, at school and within the community. As Professor Steve Baldwin, clinical psychologist (cited in *Panorama*, BBC TV, 10 April 2000) states:

> What children need is our understanding. Occasionally they need psychotherapy, they need counselling, they need us to provide them with our best services and our best efforts to meet their needs, their health

needs, their social needs, their educational needs, and their interpersonal needs. What they don't need is to be drugged.

References

American Psychiatric Association (1994) *Diagnostic and Statistical Manual of Mental Disorders*, fourth edition (DSM IV), Washington DC: American Psychiatric Association

Bates, P. (1994) "Children in secure psychiatric units: Re K, W and H – 'out of sight, out of mind'?", *Journal of Child Law*, 6, 3: 131–137

Breggin, P. (1998) *Talking Back to Ritalin: What Doctors Aren't Telling You About Stimulants for Children*, Monroe: Common Courage Press

—— (2000) *Reclaiming Our Children: A Healing Plan for a Nation in Crisis*, Cambridge, MA: Perseus Books

Breggin, P. and Breggin, G.R. (1995) "The hazards of treating 'Attention Deficit/Hyperactivity Disorder' with methylphenidate (Ritalin)", *Journal of College Student Psychotherapy*, 10, 2: 55–72

British Association for Community Child Health (1995) *Child Health Matters: Implementing the UN Convention on the Rights of the Child within the National Health Service. A Practitioners' Guide*, London: BACCH

Coppock, V. (1997) "Mad, Bad or Misunderstood?", in P. Scraton (ed.) *"Childhood" in "Crisis"?*, London: UCL Press

Cox, C.B. and Boyson, R. (eds) (1975) *Black Paper 1975: The Fight for Education*, London: JM Dent

Department of Health (2000) *Prescription Cost Analysis Data*, London: The Stationery Office

Drug Enforcement Administration (1995) *Methylphenidate (A Background Paper)*, Washington DC: US Department of Justice

Fennell, P. (1992) "Informal compulsion: the psychiatric treatment of juveniles under common law", *Journal of Social Welfare and Family Law*, 4: 311–313

Fernando, S. (1988) *Race and Culture in Psychiatry*, London: Croom Helm

Foucault, M. (1977) *Discipline and Punish: The Birth of the Prison*, London: Allen and Unwin

Goldson, B. (1997) "'Childhood': an introduction to historical and theoretical analysis", in P. Scraton (ed.) *"Childhood" in "Crisis"?*, London: UCL Press

Grimshaw, R. and Berridge, D. (1994) *Educating Disruptive Children: Placement and Progress in Residential Special Schools for Pupils with Emotional and Behavioural Difficulties*, London: National Children's Bureau

Howes, N. (1999) "Hyperactivity can indicate trauma", *Young Minds Magazine*, 42: 15

Ideus, K. (1994) "Cultural foundations of ADHD: a sociological analysis", *Therapeutic Care and Education*, 3, 2: 173–192

Ideus, K. and Cooper, P. (1995) "Chemical cosh or therapeutic tool? Towards a balanced view of the use of stimulant medication with children diagnosed with attention deficit/hyperactivity disorder", *Therapeutic Care and Education*, 4, 3: 52–63

Jaffa, T. and Deszery, A.M. (1989) "Reasons for admission to an adolescent unit", *Journal of Adolescence*, 12: 187–195

Joseph Rowntree Foundation (2000) *Poverty and Social Exclusion in Britain*, York: Joseph Rowntree Foundation

Kewley, G. (1994) "Medical aspects of assessment and treatment of children with attention deficit disorder", *Therapeutic Care and Education*, 3, 3: 284–293

Kirk, S. and Kutchins, H. (1992) *The Selling of DSM: The Rhetoric of Science in Psychiatry*, New York: Aldine De Gruyter

Kurtz, Z., Thornes, R. and Wolkind, S. (1994) *Services for the Mental Health of Children and Young People in England: A National Review*, London: Maudsley Hospital and South Thames (West) Regional Health Authority

Loring, M. and Powell, B. (1988) "Gender and DSM III: a study of the objectivity of psychiatric diagnostic behaviour", *Journal of Health and Social Behaviour*, 29: 1–22

Malek, M. (1991) *Psychiatric Admissions: A Report on Young People Entering Residential Psychiatric Care*, London: The Children's Society

Masson, J. (1991) "Adolescent crisis and parental power", *Family Law*, December, 528–531

Mental Health Foundation (1998) *The Big Picture: Promoting Children and Young People's Mental Health*, London: Mental Health Foundation

NHS Health Advisory Service (1995) *Together We Stand: The Commissioning, Role and Management of Child and Adolescent Mental Health Services*, London: HMSO

Orbach, S. (1998) "Emotional Literacy", *Young Minds Magazine*, 33: 12–13

—— (1999) *Towards Emotional Literacy*, London: Virago

Reid, R., Maag, J.W. and Vasa, S.F. (1993) "Attention Deficit Hyperactivity Disorder as a disability category: a critique", *Exceptional Children*, 60, 3: 198–214

Roberts, M. (1999) "R v M: Refusal of medical treatment", *childRight*, 159: 14–15

Rose, N. (1985) *The Psychological Complex: Psychology, Politics and Society in England 1869–1939*, London: Routledge and Kegan Paul

Rutter, M. (1983) "Behavioural studies: questions of findings on the concept of a distinctive syndrome", in M. Rutter (ed.) *Developmental Neuropsychology*, New York: Guilford Press

Schrag, P. and Divoky, D. (1981) *The Myth of the Hyperactive Child: and other means of child control*, Harmondsworth: Penguin

Scraton, P. (ed.) (1997) *"Childhood" in "Crisis"?*, London: UCL Press

Steinberg, D. (1981) "Two years referrals to a regional adolescent unit: some implications for psychiatric services", *Social Science and Medicine*, 15

Tracy, E. (1999) "Wonder drug or playground curse?", *Guardian*, 12 October, 2–3

Wolff, S. (1999) "Starting school: do our children start too young?", *Young Minds Magazine*, 42: 10–11

World Health Organisation (1992) *The ICD 10 Classification of Mental and Behavioural Disorders*, Geneva: WHO

8 Young children's health care rights and consent

Priscilla Alderson

The main concern of this chapter is to examine how children's rights to health care, and their rights within health services and everyday health care, illuminate other important rights. Especially relevant here is Article 12 of the UN Convention on the Rights of the Child (1989): children's rights to express their views freely in all matters affecting them. Article 24 on health rights is one of the most detailed articles in the Convention. This, and other related articles, will be reviewed briefly.

A central question to address is at what age children can begin to form and express views which have due weight in health matters that affect them, and when they are able to give legally valid consent. Health carers often lead the way in respect for younger children's rights, far more so than teachers or social workers tend to do. This may be because children are treated singly by doctors rather than in class groups. Doctors can respond to individual children, whereas teachers worry about the effects on the larger group if they grant certain pupils extra freedoms, or even when they spend time listening to a child. Unlike school pupils, child patients share a status with adult patients, whose views and consent are increasingly respected. Child patients also tend to be treated in their own right, whereas young social work clients are seen much more in the context of the whole family and of child protection. Doctors have greater authority and legal protections than any other profession when they respect the views and informed consent or refusal of their young patients if, in the treating doctor's clinical judgement, the child is competent (Age of Legal Capacity (Scotland) Act 1991, s.2(4)). For all these reasons, the experiences of children who have complex, dangerous conditions and health treatments can vividly illustrate the extent of their provision rights to health care and their participation rights to information and shared decision-making. Examples will be discussed to illustrate when children begin to be involved actively in their health care and when their rights become relevant.

Modern concepts of rights are only 300–400 years old. Authors of rights treaties spoke of the "inalienable rights of man" (Paine, 1790, 1792) within notions of rational autonomous manhood which denied rights to women and children (Mendus, 1987). Women who asserted their own rights could do so either by claiming to be as rational as men or else by expanding the meaning of rights and of the kind of human beings who could be rights-holders. This chapter takes concepts of rights and humanity further by considering how human rights are inalienable and integral to all human beings, including babies.

Article 24 and related rights

Article 24 of the UN Convention is unusual in being ten sections long, and in giving specific details, such as the child's right to "adequate nutritious foods and clean drinking water". The Article states the importance of "access to education and ... support in the use of basic knowledge of child health and nutrition, the advantages of breast feeding, hygiene and environmental sanitation and the prevention of accidents". The Article illustrates crucial strengths in the Convention. It deals with necessities and not with luxuries. It delicately skirts round the minefields of maternal versus babies' rights over breast feeding by emphasising women's rights to knowledge about the advantages of breast feeding. The Article balances global with local perspectives by poignantly acknowledging how aspirational some children's rights are. Section 1 enshrines "the right of the child to the enjoyment of the highest attainable standard of health and to facilities for the treatment of illness". Children do not have the (unrealistic and often unattainable) right to be healthy. Neither do they have the right to every type of health care, but to what is available, and Article 24 concludes by exhorting international cooperation in "achieving progressively the full realisation" of children's health rights, which depend on redistributing resources from wealthy to poor countries. Article 24 also illustrates the Convention's themes that rights need not be expressions of selfish individualism, or of competition for power and resources when one person's gain is another person's loss. Instead, the vision of rights is of win-win, of each person's equal entitlement to respect and to resources such as clean water when the group benefits and not simply the individual. This moves towards realising the Convention's vision of rights as collective respect for everyone's equal claim, dignity and worth, promoting "social progress and better standards of life in larger freedom and in the spirit of peace, dignity, tolerance, freedom, equality and solidarity", conditions in which physical and mental health flourish.

The Convention is so coherent that most articles reinforce and expand one another and can be related, for example, to health. There is the preamble and also the articles on quality of life and relationships, non-discrimination, best interests, survival and development, identity, family life, respect for every child, protection from neglect, abuse or discrimination, and inclusion of disabled children. All these and other articles link to each child's physical and mental integrity and well-being. This chapter concentrates on showing how Article 12 is especially relevant to children's health.

The first and basic rights involve respect for each person's mental and bodily integrity, and freedom from violation. Modern societies were especially reminded of this principle by the Nuremberg Code written by lawyers following the Nuremberg trials. The Nuremberg Code (1947) opens: "The voluntary consent of the human subject [to medical research] is absolutely essential". This means "free power of choice, without the intervention of force, fraud, deceit, duress, overreaching, or other ulterior form of constraint or coercion". Ordinary people are assumed to be able to have "sufficient knowledge and comprehension of the elements of the subject matter involved as to enable [them] to make an understanding and enlightened decision".

Children were assumed not to have the independence or comprehension to be able to make free, informed decisions. The English Family Law Reform Act of 1969 stated that minors over 16 years could give legally valid consent to medical treatment, but said nothing of children under 16. Some case law in England, Scotland and many Commonwealth countries respected younger teenagers' views and, in an attempt to ensure that minors under 16 could only access health care with their parents' consent, Mrs Gillick took her health authority to court. However, the eventual ruling in the Gillick case (1985: 423) was that the parental right to decide for a child "terminates if and when the child achieves sufficient understanding and intelligence to understand fully what is proposed" and "sufficient discretion to enable him or her to make a wise choice in his or her own interests". Unlike adults, children must take account of their own best interests. The ruling did not specify an age when children begin to have these two vital capacities: understanding and discretion or wisdom.

The UN Convention states (Article 41) that any standards in a nation's law which are higher than the Convention's standards shall apply. The Gillick ruling which influences many Commonwealth countries goes beyond the Convention. (It seems that Scandinavian and most European countries do not use Anglo-American hospital consent forms. Children and adults are not routinely asked formally to make and signify a decision about their treatment. They seem to tend to assume that they should take their doctors' advice, so that Article 12 is less overtly relevant to their medical care.) Article 12 is the nearest article to the key right for adults, autonomy. But Article 12 is partial; children's participation rights are about taking part, not taking charge. Four levels are involved in decision-making, and the Convention covers the first three (Alderson and Montgomery, 1996). The child has the right (1) to be informed, and (2) to express views freely in matters which affect the child (there is no age limit). (3) Adults give "due weight" to the child's views, "in accordance with the age and maturity of the child", and give the child "the opportunity to be heard in any judicial or administrative proceedings affecting the child", such as decisions about major health treatment. The "Gillick" level, which is missing from the Convention, is (4) the competent child has the right to be the main decider, such as about proposed surgery. Like the Convention, English law does not specify a lower age limit.

Bodies, minds and rights

Philosophers have traditionally identified humanity with the aspects in which human beings appear to differ from animals, especially their intellect (Kant, 1796). This approach strongly influences medicine and psychology, which tend to assume that children slowly emerge from an animal state into a rational consciousness that qualifies them to become adult rights-holders (Morss, 1990). Respect for children's Article 12 rights depends on accepting that all human beings are bodies as well as minds, and they learn everything through their senses, feelings and physical experiences (as many philosophers accepted). Acknowledging this is the basis for appreciating in young children and babies, as well as adults, two abilities necessary for forming and expressing valid views – understanding and wisdom.

Babies express realistic views such as happiness or anxiety very strongly, and surely no one has the right to deny them this freedom. Giving due weight to babies' views is essential for sensitive and efficient baby care. For example, when Amy aged 18 days was hungry, she sucked her hand and looked hard into her mother's eyes. Usually placid, she protested if held by someone other than her mother at these times. When she was held against her mother, she moved around until she found the breast. In breast or bottle feeding, the baby is the active partner, the adult simply sits and waits. Babies are expert not only in sucking, but in regulating the milk supply. Amy fed often on some days, and seldom on others and her mother trusted her to "be in charge". If these skills are dismissed as "instincts" then instincts have to be redefined with far more profound and subtle meanings (Midgely, 1994). Similarly, when given opportunities, young children soon learn to feed, wash and dress themselves, and to choose appropriately warm or cool clothing. During their first five years they learn the basic knowledge they will rely on for a life time (Gardner, 1993) usually without professional supervision. They are active learners and self-health carers from the start, with wisdom through being in tune with their body.

Young children's capacity to understand distressing and complex knowledge is shown especially when they have serious illness or disability. Children as young as two years can name their cancer drugs, and have the moral and intellectual understanding to co-operate with harrowing treatment (Kendrick *et al.*, 1986). Children with conditions such as thalassaemia or cystic fibrosis have to endure painful treatment everyday and, unless they are informed, they may well assume that the treatment is worse than the disease, and seems like torture deliberately inflicted by their parents. It is vital that the children understand the nature and purpose of the treatment as soon as possible, to avoid misunderstandings which could induce grief and terror. It is not a question as to whether 2-year-olds can understand, because they are interpreting and making sense of their experiences all the time. The question is how skilled and respectful are the adults in listening to the child and ensuring that clear relevant information is exchanged with them. Gaining children's informed co-operation reduces the child's initial resistance and fear as well as the daily stress on families. This is especially critical when children hold their health and life in their hands in co-operating with daily medication or physiotherapy.

Active co-operation

Children's co-operation may go well beyond rather passively "complying" with prescribed treatment, towards actively managing daily life. For example, Susan developed diabetes when she was 4 years old. She knew how ill she felt when her blood sugar levels were too low or too high, and she learned to do frequent blood tests. She knew that her twice daily insulin injections were "the key to change sugar into energy" and she was expert in filling the syringe and injecting herself. Yet it was more complicated for her to manage her high carbohydrate and low fat and sugar diet, in the timing and type of every meal and snack, to refuse sweets while watching other children enjoying them, to strive to be as like other people as she could, and to cope with being different. She gracefully achieved all these everyday challenges, which are very hard at any age. Her friends helped her by instructing their mothers in the kinds of food to serve when Susan visited them.

Undue concentration on personal decisions when discussing Article 12 can inadvertently suggest that it is a self-centred right which feeds children's supposed egoism (Piaget, 1932). However, children may at least inadvertently influence policies. The intense distress of babies and children in hospital decades ago who were separated from their parents was gradually heard by health staff. Parents began to be encouraged to stay with children in the wards, and later be with them in intensive care units, in treatment rooms and anaesthetic rooms. The policies were guided by children's voices (Robertson and Robertson, 1989).

Article 12 is about "all matters affecting the child" not simply decisions, and it potentially extends to the broadest political and economic issues which children may deliberately influence. So, for example, young children have been involved in replanning housing estates and the wider environment, and in tackling poverty, racism and injustice which affect the health of all their community. Three-year-olds can plan, budget for, buy and cook the midday meal at playgroup (for a review see Alderson, 2000). The logical and effective way to raise standards of physical and mental well-being in schools, such as by improving behaviour and reducing vandalism and violence or by making the inclusion of disabled and refugee children really work, is to involve every child in the school as a responsible member, as schools demonstrate (Highfield School, 1997; Cleves School, 1999). Reports from Africa, Asia, and South America of children who competently run households or market stalls, who work in the home, on farms or in factories, also challenge the minority wealthy world notions of very limited children's capacities.

Altruism and reciprocal concern

Young children, moreover, often express views which show clear concern for other people's well-being. Babies are troubled when their mother looks sad or distracted, and soon begin to try to offer solace or comfort. At 6 months, Susan passed round her soggy biscuit wanting everyone to have a taste. By 2 years of age, children argue about who should have the largest piece of apple and about "being fair" and about distributive justice. After a day spent reading about young children's supposed inability to appreciate another person's point of view, on a dark winter evening outside a shop I saw a baby sitting in a pram crying while a toddler reached up with a look of deep concern gently wiping away the tears. Possibly the youngest example of comforting another person, intentionally or not, is of premature twins when the sister who was strong enough to go home came back to visit her brother in hospital every day. When they lay in the same cot he curled his fingers round hers and the watching adults felt that she was giving him strength and hope (anon., 1999: 11).

Such examples raise questions about the respect, nurturing and trust which underlie children's rights and whether these can ever be one-way or are always partly reciprocal. A doctor who cared for children with leukaemia once described emotions as contagious; he caught the anger or distress of the parent he spoke with and carried the emotions through the day. If this notion has some reality, it may explain how there is perhaps always some return, some mutual reward, in the care and respect expressed between adults and children. Human autonomy is not realised solely in lonely isolation, but also through reciprocal interdependent relationships. Children's health care decisions may be complicated by their altruism, their wish to please and not to worry their parents, by concealing their own knowledge and anxieties (Bluebond-Langner, 1978). The next sections give further examples of young children's understanding, wisdom, and ways of exercising their health care rights. The intention is to try to see civil liberties through children's eyes and to listen to their voices, especially those who are disadvantaged and excluded.

Examples of young children's serious decisions: understanding and deciding

During research about children's consent to surgery (Alderson, 1993), 120 young patients were interviewed. They were 8 to 16 years old, and they, their parents, and the health practitioners caring for them gave some examples of experiences of children younger than 8, which will be recounted here. Brenda aged 9 years was waiting for her third hip operation when the anaesthetist arrived. Before he spoke, remembering an occasion when she might have been thought to be barely aware, and when she was 6 years old, Brenda said, "Please can I have gas? I don't like the injection and please can I have I have the mint flavoured gas like I had last time?" Brenda shows how adults and children often have strong views on wanting to influence "minor" aspects of their treatment.

Adults were asked, during the consent to surgery research, at what age they thought children could begin to understand the relevant information to a level when it was important to explain the condition and treatment to them. Psychologists and play workers gave young ages. One psychologist thought that explanations with a doll helped a 3-year-old to prepare for her leg amputation. Another psychologist recalled a 3-year-old who understood that his liver biopsy was for investigation not for treatment. He knew they would take "a little piece so it would not matter. And it would be looked at under a glass (he didn't seem to know the word for microscope) to see if it was good or not". When told of this example, a 4-year-old quickly said "You mean a microscope".

A third psychologist remembered "an exceptionally brilliant 3 year old with haemophilia. He explained the nature of his illness and how he could do his injections himself, and what they meant and why he was doing it. ... I asked him questions to check that [he really understood]".

A doctor described the interest of 3-year-olds and 4-year-olds "in parts of their body, how the parts relate to each other, about their muscles and bones, and about things breaking and needing repairing. When my son was 7 he had reimplantation of the ureters" and he understood the drawings and explanations. Children's imaginative sense-making is illustrated by a 6-year-old who worried that "taking blood" meant taking all the blood. The play specialist who gave this example added, "We looked at a body book and he could see that it wouldn't be dangerous." The play specialist continued to describe children's awareness, and how respecting children by sharing information with them can help them to overcome fear.

> I like them to be familiar with what will happen. This morning I had gone through things like EMLA cream [a pain reliever which numbs the skin before injections]. When we'd gone down to theatre, the anaesthetist was wiping the cream off and, in so many words, the child said, "Oh, we'll wipe that away, this is numb, I won't feel anything now."

On a more abstract level, surgeons described how they explained risk.

> You can give children down to 5 or 6 years old having spinal surgery some ideas of what spinal cord injury means. Even though the risks of paralysis are so small, if it happens it totally destroys a child's life. And I explain, "Well, you can't cross the road without some risk," and I say, "It's rare," or "very very rare". ... If we don't inform children, and they

then have to face something they weren't expecting, that's something they carry with them for the rest of their lives. They're resentful and rightly so. I'd never operate on a child whose parents says, "Don't tell my child about spinal cord injury."

Children are believed to be limited in their ability to reason responsibly because they think in the short term, whereas adults think in the long term (although many adults give up unhealthy habits only when they begin to feel the unhealthy effects and not well in advance as long-term prevention). However, several interviewees aged about 8 or 9 years spoke of accepting painful treatments: "So that I'll look normal when I'm 18", or "So I won't have to be in a wheelchair when I'm 20". Surgeons described now they explained preventative treatment in terms of "putting money in the bank" to enjoy in the future and they felt that young children understood.

Beyond understanding information is the more complex and active process in consent of forming and expressing a decision. The following examples give extreme instances of adults' respect for children's consent or refusal. When Niki was 11 years old, in describing her past battles with schools and her younger sister's views, she showed the strong views which disabled children and their families acquire early on. She was very thin because of her anterior horn cell damage condition. Leaning on her crutches she said earnestly during her interview before surgery (Alderson, 1993) "It's so important to be normal". Niki and her mother fought for access to the local school. "It's stupid to go to a handicapped school, because I'm normal and that's that. One day I'm going to have to go out into that big wide world and do what normal people do, but in a handicapped school you don't get that." Niki said she wanted to have the two operations to straighten her spine and her mother respected her view, "It's her body, her life. ... I reckon kids understand what you tell them from whenever, there isn't an age."

NIKI: I don't want to look horrible. I've got a hump as well. And if your spine's twisted and your ribs go in, it would squash my lungs and all my inside, and then kill me after a while. I'll be going like that. [She bent over further, then looked at the tape recorder and added] You won't be able to tape that. My sister, she's 8 years old, she says that the hospital is practically saving my life. I said to Mum, "You'll be okay Mum."
INTERVIEWER: Was your Mum worried?
NIKI: Yes. That's why I said that to her.
INTERVIEWER: Did that cheer her up?
NIKI: Yes, she started laughing.

Niki illustrated children's awareness of balancing their own interests with other people's, such as their parents. During a research interview about children's consent (Alderson, 1993) a family liaison sister in a heart–lung transplant unit described some the concern for their parents among some children with cystic fibrosis.

> One mother said to her son after his brother had died, "We owe it to your brother for you to have a transplant." He was very distressed. I said to him, "If you didn't want that operation would you tell us?" He said, "No, because my mother would be so sad if I said that."

Some children retain control. The sister described how:

> We believe the child always has to be involved. We know that they literally have their life in their hands afterwards. If they stop taking their medications, for example, they will die. One, previously active little 7 year old girl with cystic fibrosis became desperately ill .... She cried desperately when she was told she needed a transplant. She died two weeks later. She had developed an infection, but medically there was no reason for her to deteriorate quite so dramatically. I think that if children don't want something, then they give up.
>
> (Alderson, 1993)

The sister considered that these children's long experience of severe illness gave them an exceptional understanding of the value of life, that at 4 or 5 years they understood their illness and treatments, as long as these had been explained to them. They understood the lung transplant procedure, and that death meant "total separation" from their parents and that they would "never come back". "Their understanding is greater than mine", said the sister, because of their bodily experiences and knowledge.

Another reason for dismissing children's decision-making abilities is the belief that they can only hold one or two ideas in their mind at a time (Buchanan and Brock, 1989: 220) and therefore they cannot weigh up a list of pros and cons and make a rational cost–benefit calculation. Observations during the research about children's consent to surgery rapidly dispelled this belief, because the children would not take part in interviews when soap operas were being shown on television. Obviously, they clearly understood and distinguished the many complicated characters, plots and relationships in each soap, or they would merely have been confused and bored by the dramas. The children narrated the nature and purpose of their planned surgery and the effects they hoped to benefit from. The transplant unit sister gave a detailed list, from a 7-year-old, who considered having a heart–lung transplant. The girl listed the risks that the transplant might not work well, it would be very unpleasant, and she might die while on the waiting list or during the operation, but she concluded,

> There's a chance that I could feel really good and I could come first in a race on my pony. ... All those other things [being ill and possibly dying]

are going to happen to me anyway, so please ask them to give me some new lungs.

(Alderson, 1993)

The mention of the pony might be seen as a child's limited superficial thinking. And yet adults often give simple examples for wanting to undergo risky treatment, such as "I want to see my grandchildren". Such examples symbolise that person's sense of identity, the meaning and value in their life which makes risking painful mutilating treatment seem to be worthwhile.

Working with and learning from these children had transformed the sister's views, and those of other nurses. "Working with these children is a real eye opener." The nurses cited younger ages, than the ages they said they would have given a few years previously, for when they thought that children could understand and when they could be come involved in making the most serious decisions. These examples have been given because they illuminate how healthy "normal" children might also be involved far more in decisions which affect them, and at earlier ages, if the adults and children could consider this to be possible and worthwhile.

Occasionally children's wish to reject treatment is respected. Samantha aged 6 years wanted to have a recommended liver transplant, so that she could be pink instead of yellow, have a new body shape so that she could wear nice clothes, and be able to run. She explained the surgery to her class at school. After the first transplant failed she willingly accepted a second transplant. This transplant was also rejected and Samantha became very frightened, unhappy and resisting. She stopped eating. With great reluctance her parents gradually decided to respect Samantha's obvious wish. They refused the offer of a third operation with such a slight chance of success, and took her home. Her mother wrote: "Samantha died three days later. They were the most stressful days of my life, but I do not regret the decision. They were very important days to us. … We must learn to listen to our children in whatever way they are capable of telling us their views" (Irwin, 1996). Samantha probably knew from years of experience of illness what her decision entailed.

Research and policy: cases for action on children's health rights

Research about children's capacities and consent has tended to underestimate them, for several reasons. Traditionally, psychologists have worked with children in laboratories and used standardised tests, instead of seeing children in the familiar context of their own lives where they are more confident and knowledgeable about their own experiences. Researchers have administered questionnaires to large groups of "representative" mainly healthy children, who may know very little about illness and complex treatments. From finding that these children are ignorant, adults often then mistakenly conclude that children do not know, cannot know, and should not have to know about distressing complex matters. Researchers have linked higher intelligence and success at school with the greater possibility of maturity to make complicated decisions. Yet fortunately for them, healthy successful children have often been sheltered from the painful experiences through which some children gain the essential wisdom and courage for making hard choices. The disadvantaged children often miss school through being ill or excluded and do poorly in tests.

Researchers also question parents and teachers for their views about children's understanding and behaviour, and take little account of how adults might be repeating stereotypical views of children as ignorant, instead of describing a child's known or potential abilities. Many questionnaires emphasise negative failings, and leave little space for reporting children's strengths and their immensely varied interests and abilities. Understandably, researchers also concentrate on the observable and measurable. So research about consent tends to concentrate on the medical information which patients recall and recount. Yet the central features of consent are how people inwardly digest information, weigh it in the light of personal values, waver between opposite options, and gradually gain the resolve to make and stand by a risky decision. These invisible thoughts and feelings are hard to research, except through in-depth interviews with relatively small samples. People then query how worthwhile or generalisable such small-scale research can be. Generalisations cannot be drawn from a few examples, but generalisations can be challenged by only two or three instances. A few 3-year-olds and 4-year-olds who show a mature grasp of their complex condition and treatment refute beliefs that children cannot have such understanding until they are 7 or 12 years old.

To discover how children exercise their agency, it is necessary to look in close detail at their everyday life. Yet as well as the routine and mundane, we have to look at how children respond to exceptional circumstances such as serious illness. They are not exceptional children, but extraordinary events and their unusual knowledge and experience may reveal capacities in them which remain latent and undetected in most children. Another unusual aspect of consent to surgery is when children are exposed to distressing, complex and dangerous decision-making (because of medico-legal traditions) in contrast to the heavy protection that shields most children, and the way adults often decide for children in many other areas of life. Through moving outside the boundaries of normal childhood, young patients challenge how normal and realistic these boundaries are. If the physically weakest children, including ones with learning difficulties, are able to make complex decisions, why are their seemingly more highly achieving peers denied their Article 12 rights to express views and influence decisions in matter affecting them?

Examples set by some young children who make decisions about high risk treatment urgently call for revisions to health care policies and the training of health professionals in how to inform and involve all children who wish to be involved. New guidance from the British Medical Association (BMA, 2000) fully supports listening to and involving children. This is not to say that children must be involved. Like adults, a few children do not want to take any part, most want to share in decision-making to a greater or lesser extent, and a few children want to be "the main decider" about proposed treatment. Health practitioners are responsible for ascertaining with each child the appropriate degree of involvement. English law assumes an all-or-nothing approach. People are either competent to consent or, if judged to be incompetent, left without agreed standards concerning how they should be informed and partly involved. The BMA now offers guidance on respecting the rights of all children, at whatever level they are able and willing to be involved.

New policies which respect children's health rights work when common underlying assumptions are revised. These involve encouraging greater respect for babies and young children's knowledge about their bodily needs, and on learning from children's feelings, such as of trust or anxiety, so that adults can share in planning appropriate care with children. This is illustrated by Samantha's parents' respect for her as a full human person with unique and essential knowledge about her best interests. "Rights" is shorthand for huge assumptions about everyone's moral status and the appropriate relationships that underlie all behaviour. Although rights are social constructs, and were initially men's and later adults' prerogative, through the UN Convention's broader interpretations human rights may be seen as inalienable and integral to all human life from birth. Babies' rights to freedom of expression are inevitably either honoured or disrespected by other people, and they cannot be treated as if they do not exist. Rather than trivialising rights, questions of babies' health care rights can illuminate what it means to be a human being and why rights matter so much.

References

Alderson, P. (1993) *Children's Consent to Surgery*, Open University Press: Buckingham

—— (2000) *Young Children's Rights*, Jessica Kingsley: London

Alderson, P. and Montgomery, J. (1996) *Health Care Choices: Making Decisions with Children*, Institute for Public Policy Research: London

Anon. (1999) "Some sisterly love gives baby Daniel strength to get better", *London Metro Newspaper*, 8 August 1999

Bluebond-Langer, M. (1978) *The Private World of Dying Children*, Princeton University Press: Princeton, NJ

British Medical Association (2000) *Health Care for Children and Young People: Consent, Rights and Choices*, BMA: London

Buchanan, A. and Brock, D. (1989) *Deciding for Others*, Cambridge University Press: New York

Cleves School (1999) *Learning and Inclusion: The Cleves School Experience*, David Fulton Books: London

Gardner, H. (1993) *The Unschooled Mind: How Children Think and How Schools Should Teach*, Fontana: London

Gillick v *Wisbech and W Norfolk AHA* [1985] 3 All ER

Highfield School (1997) *Changing Our School: Promoting Positive Behaviour*, Highfield School: Plymouth

Irwin, C. (1996) "Samantha's wish", *Nursing Times*, 4: 92 (36): 30–1

James, A. (1993) *Childhood Identities*, Edinburgh University Press: Edinburgh

Kant, I. (1796/1972) "Groundwork of the metaphysic of morals", in H. Paton (ed.) *The Moral Law*, Hutchinson: London

Kendrick, C. *et al.* (1986) "Children's understanding of their illness and treatment within a paediatric oncology unit", *ACP Newsletter*, 8 (2): 16–20

Mendus, S. (1987) "Kant: an honest but narrow-minded bourgeois?", in E. Kennedy, and S. Mendus (eds) *Women in Western Political Philosophy*, Wheatsheaf: Brighton: 21–43

Midgley, M. (1994) *The Ethical Primate: Humans, Freedom and Morality*, Routledge: London

Morss, J. (1990) *The Biologising of Childhood: Developmental Psychology and the Darwinian Myth*, Lawrence Erlbaum Associates: Hove

Paine, T. (1790, 1792/1945) "The Rights of Man", in P. Foner (ed.) *Complete Writings of Thomas Paine*, New York

Piaget, J. (1932) *The Moral Judgement of the Child*, Routledge: London

Robertson, J. and Robertson, J. (1989) *Separation and the Very Young*, Free Association Books: London

9 Children's rights to public space

Environment and curfews

Virginia Morrow

The French sociologist Jacques Donzelot argued that Western childhood was transformed by the state during the nineteenth century into a kind of "supervised freedom", initially of bourgeois children, but later extended to working-class children. The problem of working-class childhood was excessive freedom – "being left to the street" – and this had to be limited and controlled, "by shepherding the child back to spheres where he [*sic*] could be more closely watched: the school and the family" (Donzelot, 1979: 47). The object of the plethora of parliamentary measures during the nineteenth century that attempted to enforce standards for protecting children, including child labour laws and the introduction of compulsory education, was both "hygienic and political in nature, the two ... being indissociable" (Donzelot, 1979: 78). Thus childhood in developed countries has become a "quarantine period" (Aries, 1960); a preparation for adulthood that has led to a marginalisation of children in time and space (see Ennew, 1994).

During the last half of the twentieth century these metaphors have become literal, as children have been increasingly expected to spend their time in their homes and their schools and their rights to, and consequent experiences of, public space, have become problematic. This needs to be seen in the context of increasingly punitive attitudes towards children "out on the streets", both in reality and in rhetoric – in policy statements on a range of issues, but encapsulated by periodic rants about "child curfews" – for example, the Home Secretary "is poised to introduce a 9pm to 6am curfew for teenagers in troubled areas" (*Guardian*, 11 October 2000). This rhetoric is accompanied by a general demonisation of youth in the media (Holland, 1992), and a policy commitment to reinforcing and restating the responsibility of parents to "control" their young. But what do these tendencies mean to children themselves?

This chapter explores the exclusion of children from the public sphere from children's perspectives. In aggregate, the issues they describe serve to exclude them from the public sphere not in the strict sense of citizenship, but the literal sense of exclusion from public spaces. It looks at their accounts of practical problems they encounter, such as increased traffic; the increasing lack of appropriate places for them to go, especially as they become older;

planners' neglect of play space provision; their views about "child curfews", and their views about parents' responsibilities.

Background

The chapter draws on data collected in a research project conducted for the Health Education Authority.[1] This project was exploring the relevance of (Putnam's) concept of "social capital" in relation to children and young people: "Social capital" consists of the following features: social and community networks; civic engagement or participation; community identity and sense of belonging; and norms of co-operation, reciprocity and trust of others within the community (Putnam, 1993). The premise is that levels of "social capital" in a community have an important effect on people's well-being. The research explored 12–15-year-olds' subjective experiences of their neighbourhoods, their quality of life, the nature of their social networks, and their participation in their communities (see Morrow, 1999, 2000, 2001a). Research was conducted in two schools in relatively deprived wards in a town in South East England. One ward consisted of "suburban sprawl" on the outskirts of the town, with post-war housing and factories; the second consisted of a mixture of industrial development, and Victorian, inter-war and post-war housing developments. The sample comprised 101 boys and girls in two age bands: 12–13-year-olds and 14–15-year-olds, with a significant proportion from minority ethnic groups.

The research used a variety of qualitative methods: (a) written accounts of out-of-school activities, who is important, definitions of "friend", future aspirations and social networks; descriptions of where they "feel they belong"; (b) visual methods including map drawing and photography by the participants of "places that are important" (this generated 17 maps/drawings and 100 photos); and (c) group discussions exploring use of and perceptions of neighbourhoods, how they would improve their neighbourhoods, and their community and institutional participation. As a "prompt" in group discussions, children were shown two newspaper cuttings: one depicting their town in negative terms, and one on "child curfews" (see Morrow, 2001b).

Drawing on findings from this research, this chapter explores children's perspectives on their use of public space. Firstly, it highlights the problematic nature of their experiences of communal areas; secondly, it explores their views of child curfews; and thirdly, it explores their lack of participation in their communities. The research reflects children's perspectives on the concerns found by Hillman (1991) in his study of children's declining independent mobility in the UK. As many writers have pointed out, children need opportunities to do things on their own, and the lack of these opportunities is likely to have adverse effects upon their social and emotional development as well as their quality-of-life in the here and now.

Perceptions of public space

Many children perceived their neighbourhood environments as unsatisfactory. They described a strong sense of exclusion on a number of levels, because of a lack of appropriate places to go; cost barriers; and practical problems caused by traffic and other forms of fear.

Firstly, all children described not having enough to do in terms of appropriate facilities. Very few described involvement in organised voluntary activities (6 boys mentioned being members of a formal sports team; 10 children mentioned using the local youth clubs). Most children, especially boys, described playing out with friends in local parks. However, these parks were often not pleasant places to go for a number of reasons. Harry, age 13, described how:

> there's a park where we live, we call it "Motorway Field" because its right by the motorway, and its just covered in dogs' muck, you just don't like to go there, people let their dogs go anywhere, so we like to play football there, but cos you don't know where the dogs muck is, you don't play because you don't want to get covered in it.

Dog mess was nearly always mentioned as a problem in the context of playing in local parks. Wasef described how: "The parks are dirty ... cos people's dogs go in there and everything, and people don't stop 'em". Rock, 15, photographed a primary school playing field near where he lived, and described how he plays football there: "It's good, because there are no dogs, and no adults screaming at you to stop".

Several younger children described a lack of wild places to "make dens". One girl mentioned "we used to have a den, in the woods there, and me and my friend found loads of like drugs and stuff, packets and things, so we took them to the police". One 12-year-old boy mentioned that he didn't like his area:

> cos its so built up, there's not much to do, and like, where my sister lives, she lives in [another town], and just across the road there's a big forest, and my brother likes to go over there with their dog, and they'd be out for hours and hours, and that's what I like when I go there.

Local youth clubs were seen by older children as unsuitable for younger children, though a few of the younger children did use them and liked them. Youth clubs were not particularly popular with girls, and some felt there was not enough for girls to do at the respective youth clubs: "all they do is play football and basketball", or "there's nothing for girls". Cameron explained:

> There's two up Hill Ward ... all the little kids hang about, and all the smokers, and the people who think they're it, hanging about, and there's one down Hill Ward, they had it all built, and I used to take my cousin.

And then they split it from 12 year olds to 16 year olds and they split my cousin, she was only 8, I couldn't go in with her, and she wouldn't go in on her own. She didn't like it.

Casey added: "There's two round my area, that's no good. ... Darren used to hang about there, he thought he was IT, and his gang, and they were like ... all tall, and no-one would go in there, and then there's one down the road ... and that's just boring. That's just completely boring." On the other hand some of the boys in the same year group did use the youth club: Fred: "its open three times a week, I go there most times, sports, play games, listen to music". A lack of things to do and places to go was a general explanation by participants for "anti-social" behaviour: "we're only getting into trouble because we're hanging around on the street because there's nothing for us to do".

Many children mentioned an explicit exclusion they felt that was encapsulated by "No Ball Games" signs. These prevented them from playing football near their homes on patches of communal grass. These signs were photographed, depicted on maps and discussed in groups: Isabelle, age 15, explained of her photograph: "this is a sign that is on a piece of greenery on my road. It stops children from playing typical games, but little children need somewhere to play ... they may not be allowed to go to the park". In discussion she said "They've got 'No ball games' signs all over our streets, and there are loads of little pieces of grass where kids could just play, and be fairly happy and fairly safe, but they put up 'No ball games' signs and then they can't play there, and its like stopping them from ... enjoying themselves." Another girl, Katie, age 13, included the sign on her map, and wrote underneath "not fair".

Exclusion by cost

In both schools, the cost of activities was frequently mentioned as a barrier to participating fully in community life. A Year 8 group had the following discussion:

CAMERON: If there was a swimming pool, or a cheaper cinema, we'd be there ...

DION: If they made more ... like adventure centres, ... and things like that, then we'll be down there nearly every weekend, and things like that, but since they don't have anything like that we wander about the streets and get in trouble for it.

SHANNON: The most fun thing we can do, without our parents having to pay for it, is just go and walk round the shops in town.

DION: Exactly.

ANGELINA: And we can't afford it, cos we can't get jobs at the moment.

CASEY: It's hard, cos me mum don't get paid that much.

In both schools the town centre was an attraction. Older children described how "I like town better, there's much more action" but were very preoccupied with the issue of the bus fare that rises to an adult fare when they are 13 or 14, but they don't necessarily have much money; the only entertainment is in town, and it is expensive. One girl said: "the thing that annoys me is that the police always moan that we're on the streets, so they build places like the new clubs and stuff, but we have to pay to get into that". Further, when they did go into the town centre, they felt they were regarded with suspicion by security guards and shop keepers who gave them "dirty looks" because they thought they would be shoplifting (Morrow, 2000). Valentine suggests that children and teenagers are "among those undesirable 'others' being driven out of space by private security forces" (1997: 65).

Practical exclusion and the problem of road traffic

Traffic was a major preoccupation for younger children. Often it was difficult for them to cross the road:

KELLIE: Nothing to do much, we live on a main road, its quite busy, its hard to cross the road ...
REBECCA: I don't like the person across the road, because we have to make sure when we cross the road, there's this man, that lives across the road, and he zooms round and he nearly hit my brother ...

Others complained about motorbikes joyriding or riding on pavements:

KERRY: We have motor bikes that come straight onto the mud track of the field, they go straight past the houses and down and you have little kids walking sort of like on the path and that, and they have motorbikes that go down there ...

In both schools, the issue of traffic led to long discussions and graphic descriptions of accidents and near-accidents:

CAMERON: My brother got run over a couple of weeks ago, by a bus driver, and the bus driver just opened the window and swore at him, but ... [my brother] was on his bike, and he gave way, because they come so fast round the corner, he hit him, and just started shouting at him, through the thing, and left him in the road ...
DION: It's getting worse, like now, cos like when it was in my mum's, and your time, it would have been safer, out on the streets, now its even worse ...
CASEY: I babysit two twins and a little boy, and I can't take'em anywhere, because [the little boy] runs around the streets, and one time he was

crossing the road ... he was about that much away from getting knocked over ...

GIRL: Round our area, the roads aren't safe either, cos everyone like speeds, yeah, they should put humps to make it slower.

And a group of 12–13-year-olds described how:

SONIA: Miss, there's traffic lights, you know down town there's that road, there was a car going by, there was a lot of traffic, the light was red, it just went past.

CHARLES: I was nearly run over outside school walking across the zebra crossing! A car speeded up and just missed me ...

IFTIKHAR: When they're turning they should use the little yellow light [i.e. indicator] because they don't use it.

Traffic and busy roads can constitute practical constraints on children's environments and may impinge on their social interactions. The responsibility of adults to drive safely, use their indicators, and keep to speed limits is rarely given much attention, yet individualised health promotion messages emphasise the responsibility of children to learn to cross the road safely. Hillman's (1991) study showed how increased traffic was used by parents as a reason not to allow their children out on the streets on their own.

Exclusion by fear

The fear of crime from drunks, gangs on the street, and racist neighbours also made children people feel unsafe in their neighbourhoods. Children mentioned not feeling safe in local parks and on the streets:

AMY: Like someone was assaulted down [in the local park], I mean, that makes you scared to go down there, and that was in broad daylight, so God knows what its gonna be like at 10 o'clock at night. ... I live in like a secluded road, hardly anyone comes down my road, but there's nothing there, there's like a little park down the road, but someone was assaulted there, you're scared to go there. So if I was, like, 20, and I had two little kids, I'd have nowhere to take them in [this area], that was safe.

This kind of account was mostly from girls, but some boys also described feeling unsafe in the parks:

GIZMO: Me and Tom are like hard, man, you live in [Estate], don't yer, Tom?

TOM: Yeah.

GIZMO: Like you've got the shops, and they're right next to the park, and there's all trouble over at the shops, and then they bring it on to the park, so you ain't really got that much places to go, I mean there's two parks, and both of the parks int so ... cos you've got all the gangsters walking through there ...

Gangs hanging around the shops at night were also a preoccupation. Drunk people on the streets, and gangs on the streets ("gangsters") near where they live bothered all age groups.

KELLIE: I think my area's unattractive because there's a pub just up the road, and whenever you go out you just see all these drunk people walking down the road, all the time.

And in another group:

AMY: We have one youth club, and that's here. I mean walking round West Ward shops at night, you get a lot of like gangs hanging round there, and you don't fancy walking to like the youth club up here.
GIZMO: Same at [Estate], same at [other part of town], any big [inaudible ?shops] you're gonna have gangs hanging round.
DAVE: My best place is my house, man ...
AMY: It's hard to explain, but its dangerous like walking round the shops and stuff, like I don't like walking past there at night, all the shops are shut but there are still loads of people hanging around ... even if you're walking in a gang, its like, even if you've got 20 people, you're still scared.

Older children expressed a strong sense that if they were on their own territory, they were OK:

ISABELLE: It depends what part of Springtown you go to, some parts, if you like don't live there, you don't feel safe.
JOSEPH: You don't know the territory.
MARIA: People who live in [Hill Ward], they're not going to be scared in [Hill Ward], but then other people who ... don't, might be.

In another group the boys seemed to feel safe in their area, but the girls less so. One girl said "Sometimes, there's trouble round our area". Another girl said: "Its alright when you know everybody, if we don't know them and one of our friends knows them, so then they get to know us." Others said:

TAMISHA: If anybody gets into trouble and stuff, we just like go round the corner.
GEMMA: We've got ... alcoholics who like sit in the park, all the little kids playing there and stuff, and its during the day, as well ... they come up to you and like, they follow you around the park.

Several children described racial harassment in their neighbourhoods. One girl, whose family was originally from Pakistan, described how her house had been vandalised before they moved in:

GIRL In West Ward area, I don't think its safe ... because before we moved in we were living with my mum's brother, because I don't have a dad, he died, yeah, so because we didn't have a house, my mum wanted to look for a house, so she got it in the Ward area, so its near all of our family, and before we moved in, somebody, it was snowing then, and somebody chucked loads and loads of snowballs at our window, and it smashed. So we couldn't move in there, and then because all the people in our road are quite racist.

RESEARCHER: Was that what the snowballs were about?

GIRL It was just our house, cos our house was a mess as well, smashed glass and everything, everything was alright before we moved, but as soon as we were getting in, then the glass was all smashed. I don't think it was right.

Another boy (family originally from Bangladesh) described how he did not play outside his flats: "if I've got nothing to do I play inside with my own computer, [not] outside [because] usually people are quite racist to me, because that's why I don't like my area that much".

In one group discussion, four southern Asian girls described attacks on their homes, often from neighbours, and how they were taunted with the words "Paki", "go back to your own country". This made them feel angry, they said, and added "But this is where we were born". In a different group, Jamel described how:

Next door ... there's a father, and a mother, well, the mother passed away, and they're grown ups, 20, or 30, there's three brothers living there. One of them, he's fine with us, he doesn't swear, he's very kind to us, but the others, they like argue with him, like "why do you talk to these people"? ... The older brother, he was racist to us, and one time he got some dogs come round our house, but the police came and they took 'em away ... our window was broken quite a lot of times, when we first moved in, but now, its safer, no-one really swears at us or nothing.

The word children used to describe how racist attacks made them feel was "angry". However, fear of racial harassment must have implications for their overall psychological and emotional well-being. These processes must impact on children's use of public spaces, effectively keeping them in their homes.

Exclusion from participation

Participation in community decision-making for children was virtually non-existent. Only one boy in the study felt he could go to his local residents association and make suggestions about his local area (when he said this in the group discussion, someone whispered that "ah, but that's a posh area"). If the council did come and ask about local facilities, they felt that their parents were consulted, not them. Amy said: "they send questionnaires to our parents but its not our parents who want to go to the Youth Club, its us. So they should ask us". One girl said "I don't think people are really bothered about kids"; in another group a boy said "They just do things like little tiny parks for little kids ... we don't want little parks". This had led to some direct action in the past:

MIKE: 'Cos I remember, I was living in my old house, and it was like the woods, in Riverside, there was the woods like over to the side, and they knocked it down to build more houses, and we didn't [want that] we used to play there and have our like tree houses, dens and things, but they didn't ask us. We tried slashing their tyres and things like that, nicking keys, and stuff but it didn't work. We was young then, so ... [laughter].

There was virtually no sense of community participation, and one girl commented that she felt they should have a say in the community, "because what happens does affect us as well as the adults and they don't seem to think about that when they're making decisions". The town council has recently started a "Youth Forum", but children in the study were not aware of it:

GEMMA: No-one knows about it, if there is one.
TAMISHA: I think there should be one, but ...
MIRANDA: ... but they'd chose the people who do all the best in school, and everything, and they're not average people, are they?

The children who participated in the study were resourceful and reflective commentators on their environments, and they put forward many reasonable suggestions for improving their areas. One of the problems facing this age group is that they have no formal channels through which to communicate their views, or to convert their energy into a positive resource for their neighbourhoods. Youth forums are the most common way of facilitating children's views, but they don't necessarily work effectively (see Fitzpatrick *et al.*, 1998). Matthews *et al.* (1998: 29) have suggested that they have often failed "because of a lack of clarity of purpose and tokenism".

Child curfews: "It makes us feel like babies!"

How did children perceive proposed curfews? The news cutting used as a prompt had the headline: "Youth crime crackdown targets parents": and described a policy to make parents "impose a 'curfew' on their children, keeping them off the street after 9pm". This provoked a good deal of discussion within the groups; the majority were initially offended and thus were highly negative towards the idea. Some saw curfews as a threat to individual liberty and freedom: Amy said "They're not letting people have their own choice"; Gavin said "the police can't really stop us from going out, because we've got rights as well, just cos we're not adults, it doesn't mean we haven't got rights". Others pointed out that night time is the time they can hang around together; and parents won't let their children out on their own. Mike, age 14, said he thought they were "a cheek, because its *our* childhood, night time is when all of us really hang around together".

SIMON: We should be going out, like clubs.
MIKE: We're young adults.
SONIA: It's the only time we can be ourselves outside of school ...
MIKE: When there's no older people around, you can like sit in the park and play, not play [correcting himself].
SIMON: Socialise.
MIKE: Without people watching ...

Some described a strong sense of distrust from adults around them, and this was reinforced by media imagery of their age group: "insulting" ... "cos people expect you to be no good" ... "they don't give you the benefit of the doubt, they just write you off before they've even met you". Some children felt it was up to parents to decide what time they had to be in, and indeed this is what already happens for most of them: "it's up to the parents. I'm allowed out, if I'm with loads of friends, then I'm allowed out till later, but if I'm walking home on my own, then [my mum]'ll say an earlier time, because in broad daylight my brother got jumped, in an alleyway, near where we live, so, in some ways I feel that my mum is doing the right thing".

Others could see a good side to curfews. Carlos said "maybe on school nights, but not on Saturdays, on school nights I have to be in at 9, but on other nights I just go in at half 11, 12". Amy suggested that "I say that I don't think it's right, but it's good, cos it can also like help people with their schoolwork, cos if they're not allowed out, they've got nothing else to do but do their homework". Some children suggested that curfews could be appropriate in certain cases, as Amy (age 15) put it: "If it's individual people that have constantly done things wrong, then I think it's ok, but if they done it for all 15 year olds, I don't think it's really fair, cos not all 15 year olds go round trashing cars and that." Similarly Charles, 13, said: "I can understand that for some, like young offenders who do like vandalism, or something, then I can understand that, but other than that, what's the point?" Sabrina, on the other hand, in the same group as Charles, was cynical and said: "But, Miss, they've been planning it for ages, it's not even gonna take place, they're just making it all up so that parents think the government's really good, and that this government's much better than the other one." Research conducted in Cardiff suggests that such legislation is likely to be highly problematic in practice (Drakeford and Butler, 1998).

As noted, most children could see the problem from the parents' perspectives, and argued that it was up to parents to decide what time they should be in.

PETER: My mum thinks the curfew's a good idea, because when I used to hang around with my friends a lot, but now I've changed, cos I got caught by the police like about three times, I have, honestly.

GIRLS: Yeeeah [sarcastically].

PETER: I've run from 'em once and got caught, the other two times I just stood there cos I knew I was gonna get caught anyway, my mum found out, but my dad still doesn't know, … my dad would go mad, but my mum said they'd better put a curfew in or else all the kids and that will always be up, always have the police knocking on the door …

JOHN: In a way, I think it's a good idea …

GAVIN: I understand why the parents want it, because they're always worried about their kids being out late at night, and that's when like all the gangsters come out.

In another group, in response to the suggestion that "its up to your parents" what time you come home, one boy suggested "yeah, but some parents don't even care". Mike said: "cos the source of the problem is the parents, if the parents can't handle the children, there's no point in bringing them in early, cos they can still do the crime before 9 o'clock". Parents clearly set boundaries and provided a source of stability and moral guidance to children (or not) as the case may be. A recurring view expressed particularly by girls, was that of concern for younger children, and how parental duties should be fulfilled. Kerry commented "I'm not saying that people in Moss Hills are careless, but some mothers in Moss Hills just let their little kids go everywhere" (see also Valentine, 1997).

Children as stakeholders?

In summary, children in the study appeared to have limited self-efficacy and participation in their communities/neighbourhoods. They did not seem to feel they shared in community life; there were physical, social and economic barriers to their full participation. In terms of civic participation, this is not really surprising given that they are positioned outside of democratic structures by their very nature as children, in that they do not attain the right to full adult citizenship, at least in terms of voting rights, until the age of 18. But surely they have "spatial rights" to the use of public space? Further, their experiences of lack of civic participation may have implications for their perceptions of democratic institutions and structures later on when they do leave school, and this begs the question of whether or not a "healthy scepticism" is learnt early on in life.

This chapter has highlighted how a range of practical, environmental and economic constraints were felt by children in this small-scale study, for example, not having safe spaces to play, not being able to cross the road because of the traffic, having no place to go except the shopping centre, but being regarded with suspicion because of lack of money. While caution needs to be exercised about generalising, it is likely that children in many other urban and suburban settings face similar constraints (see e.g. O'Brien, 2000; Percy-Smith, 1999, Matthews and Limb, 2000). Issues such as the physical geography of the built environment, community safety, fear of crime and traffic, as well as access to financial resources have implications for children's general well-being that are rarely addressed in public policy discourses (see also Davis and Jones, 1996, 1997).

In conclusion, social policies that are aimed at improving children's well-being need to pay attention to children's quality of life, in the broadest sense, in the present, rather than be driven by a perspective which prioritises children as future citizens, in terms of human capital. In other words, we need to consider the processes by which spatial exclusion takes place, rather than just pronouncing about the outcomes (anti-social behaviour, juvenile crime rates etc.). A focus on the "here-and-now" of children's lives shows how they are excluded from the social life of the community by virtue of their age. The needs of 12-year-olds (for example, for places to make dens) are likely to differ from the needs of 15-year-olds (for example, for places to socialise away from the sometimes hostile gaze of adults), let alone the needs of older people.

Most of English social policy relating to children is about seeing them as successful or unsuccessful outcomes, rather than as "stakeholders", whether in their communities or wider society. Local government policies in some parts of the country do attempt to incorporate children and young people, and these policies may aim to contribute to greater social inclusion (whether or not they succeed is another matter, see McNeish 1999; Fitzpatrick, Hastings and Kintrea, 1998; Matthews *et al.*, 1998; Matthews and Limb, 2000) but this is not matched by an equivalent shift at national level. Implicit in many national social policy discourses is the idea that children should conduct their lives in home and school under the watchful gaze of parents or teachers – clearly this is problematic from the points of view of children themselves; parents' and teachers' views have not been sought.

A framework for action already exists in the form of the UN Convention on the Rights of the Child. In particular, Articles 12.1; 13; 24(1); 24(2)(c); 27(1); 31(1) are relevant to the issues raised in this chapter. Children themselves seem to be well aware that they are effectively denied a range of participatory rights that adults take for granted. This awareness becomes more problematic as they get older; and is likely to limit their sense of self-efficacy. They are not as rebellious and disaffected as dominant imagery depicts them to be. They have a strong sense that they need their educational qualifications, and that school is important, and at the same time, they would like to have access to safe local streets and neighbourhood spaces, but they are well aware that their needs and rights are neglected. Many of their experiences seem likely to have an impact on their well-being. Yet "currently, the UK does not monitor the well-being of its children adequately" (Bradshaw, 2000: 1). If social justice for children and young people is about equalities and opportunities, with the aim that unjust inequalities should be reduced and where possible eliminated, then implementation of the UN Convention constitutes a clear way forward.

Notes

1   This was then the health promotion arm of the England and Wales Department of Health; now the Health Development Agency.

References

Aries, P. (1960) *Centuries of Childhood*. Harmondsworth: Penguin

Bradshaw, J. (2000) "Poverty: the outcomes for children". *ESRC Children 5–16 Research Briefing. July 2000, No. 18*. Swindon: ESRC.

Davis, A. and Jones, L. (1996) "Children in the urban environment. An issue for the new public health agenda". *Health and Place*, 2: 107–113

—— (1997) "Whose neighbourhood? Whose quality of life? Developing a new agenda for children's health in urban settings". *Health Education Journal*, 56: 350–363

Donzelot, J. (1979) *The Policing of Families. Welfare versus the State*. London: Hutchinson

Drakeford, M. and Butler, I. (1998) "Curfews for children: testing a policy proposal in practice". *Youth and Policy*, 62: 1–15

Ennew, J. (1994) "Time for children and time for adults". In J. Qvortrup, M. Bardy, G. Sgritta, and H. Wintersberger (eds) *Childhood Matters. Social theory, practice and politics*. Aldershot: Avebury

Fitzpatrick, S., Hastings, A. and Kintrea, K. (1998) *Including Young People in Urban Regeneration. A lot to learn?* Bristol: The Policy Press

Hillman, M. (1991) *One False Move. A study of children's independent mobility*. London: Policy Studies Institute

Holland, P. (1992) *What is a Child? Popular images of childhood*. London: Virago

Matthews, H. and Limb, M. (2000) "Exploring the 'Fourth environment': young people's use of place and views on their environment". *ESRC Children 5–16 Research Briefing No. 9*. Swindon: ESRC

Matthews, H., Limb, M., Harrison, L., and Taylor, M. (1998) "Local places and the political engagement of young people: youth councils as participatory structures". *Youth and Policy*, 62: 16–31

McNeish, D. (1999) *From Rhetoric to Reality. Participatory approaches to health promotion with young people*. London: Health Education Authority

Morrow, V. (1999) "Conceptualising social capital in relation to the well-being of children and young people: a critical review". *The Sociological Review* 47, 4: 744–765

—— (2000) " 'Dirty looks' and 'trampy places' in young people's accounts of community and neighbourhood: implications for health inequalities". *Critical Public Health* 10, 2: 141–152

—— (2001a) "Networks and neighbourhoods: children's and young people's perspectives". *Social Capital for Health Series*. HDA: London

—— (2001b) "Using qualitative methods to elicit young people's perspectives on their environments: implications for community health promotion initiatives". *Health Education Research: Theory and Practice* 16, 3: 255–268

O'Brien, M. (2000) "Childhood, urban space and citizenship: child-sensitive urban regeneration". *ESRC Children 5–16 Research Briefing No. 16*. Swindon: ESRC

Percy-Smith, B. (1999) "Multiple childhood geographies: giving voice to young people's experience of place". Unpublished doctoral thesis, University College Northampton

Putnam, R. D. (1993) *Making Democracy Work. Civic traditions in modern Italy*. Princeton NJ: Princeton University Press

Valentine, G. (1997) " 'Oh yes I can'. 'Oh no you can't': children and parents' understandings of kids' competence to negotiate public space safely". *Antipode* 29, 1: 65–89

Ward, C. (1978) *The Child in the City*. London, Architectural Press

10 Children's rights to sex and sexuality education

Deena Haydon

Introduction

Moral panics concerning "childhood innocence", "family breakdown", loss of "traditional values" and the costs of "promiscuity" (Corteen and Scraton, 1997) are consistently promoted by politicians and media commentators. Reactionary headlines fuel public outrage, demanding political responses to untypical but highly publicised and emotive accounts of young people's active sexuality. These include pre-teen and teenage pregnancies, access to contraception and "irresponsible" young fathers. Simultaneously, popular discourses emphasise children's vulnerability, and the need to protect their assumed innocence, via highly charged campaigns targeting suspected sex offenders. It is in this context that sex education policy has developed.

As "operational statements of value" (Ball, 1990), legislation and guidance identify requirements and recommendations validated by governments. This chapter outlines official policy from the late 1980s to the early 2000s; illustrating how successive governments have accepted and reinforced dominant ideologies about children, sex and sexuality. Recurring themes are identifiable in statutory and non-statutory policy, including: responsibility for and content of sex education, moral values, "controversial issues" such as homosexuality, HIV/AIDS and advice to under 16s. Shifts in emphasis are also evident, reflecting political agendas and contradictory philosophies underpinning education and health policies. While the "Thatcher era" reaffirmed "Victorian values" (marriage, family, parenthood), conflict between education and health policies led to confused and confusing messages. Since 1997, New Labour initiatives have attempted to resolve these contradictions while failing to address the implementation of children's rights. In conclusion the chapter proposes adoption of a rights-based agenda for sex education policy and practice, using implementation of the UN Convention on the Rights of the Child as a starting point.

The New Right Agenda: a return to Victorian values

Until 1986, sex education in English schools was ad hoc. Responsibility for provision was placed in the hands of governing bodies of county, controlled and maintained special schools by the 1986 Education (No. 2) Act. Having considered whether sex education should form part of the secular curriculum, the governing body was required to write and maintain a policy statement. If provided, the statement required an outline of the content and organisation of the sex education curriculum. If not, the statement was expected to confirm this decision. The Act made no separate provision for sex education in voluntary aided or special agreement schools. It was anticipated, however, that head teachers and governing bodies would consider non-statutory Circular 11/87 (DES, 1987) in discharging their responsibilities. This guidance expected governing bodies to be "strongly influenced" by the "widely accepted view" that schools had a responsibility to offer pupils some education about sexual matters; ensuring that education about health was not impaired. It specified that pupils should understand the relationship between certain forms of sexual behaviour and AIDS.

Parents were defined as key figures "in helping their children to cope with the physical and emotional aspects of growing up and in preparing them for the challenges and responsibilities which sexual maturity brings". While it was acknowledged that some parents may feel inhibited about discussing sexual matters with their children, teaching offered in schools was expected to complement and support the role of parents. Under the 1986 Act, however, governing bodies were given discretion to accept or reject parent's requests for their children to be withdrawn from sex education.

Outlining content for primary children, the guidance suggested that sex education should help them to cope with growing up and to gain an elementary understanding of human reproduction. Emphasis was placed on matching provision to maturity, not necessarily indicated by age, and answering children's questions sensitively. At secondary school, physical aspects of sexual behaviour were encompassed within biology while sex education was subsumed in personal and social education (PSE) or health education. Special schools were perceived as having a "particularly sensitive role", given assumed parental difficulty in understanding the experiences of "the disabled" or in accepting that disabled children could be sexually active. The guidelines stated that "children with learning difficulties" may require additional help to cope with the emotional and physical aspects of growing up, learning about "acceptable" behaviours and being warned about unacceptable behaviour by adults.

Affirming the Thatcher agenda, the 1986 Act specified that school sex education should encourage pupils "to have due regard to moral considerations and the value of family life". Circular 11/87 defined a moral framework for sex education. "Facts" were expected to be presented objectively, enabling pupils to understand different sexual attitudes and behaviours; know what was legal; consider their own attitudes; make informed, responsible decisions about personal attitudes at school and in adulthood. These objectives prioritised the values of self-restraint, dignity, respect for themselves and other people. Promoting a specific version of sexuality, the guidance suggested that pupils should be helped to recognise the physical, moral and emotional risks of casual and promiscuous sexual behaviour, and to appreciate the benefits of stable married family life and the responsibilities of parenthood.

The guidance noted that schools could not avoid tackling "controversial issues", such as abortion and contraception, but should offer balanced, factual information while acknowledging ethical issues. Yet its recognition that religion-based schools might present such subjects differently undermined commitment to provision of a "balanced" curriculum. Religion was also used to substantiate negative advice concerning homosexuality: "for many people, including members of various religious faiths, homosexual practice is not morally acceptable". The Circular stated: "deep offence may be caused to them" should the issue be handled insensitively by teachers.

Reflecting reactionary arguments presented during political and media debates about homosexuality and the age of consent, the guidance reinforced popular assumptions that open discussion about homosexuality constituted its promotion as a sexual orientation, enabling predatory gay men to exploit impressionable young men. An explicitly prohibitive sentence stated: "There is no place in any school in any circumstances for teaching which advocates homosexual behaviour, which presents it as the 'norm', or which encourages homosexual experimentation by pupils." Further undermining teachers' professionalism was the inflammatory comment: "encouraging or procuring homosexual acts by pupils who are under the age of consent is a criminal offence". No similar statement concerning heterosexual acts was deemed necessary.

The 1988 Education Act specified the contemporary purposes of education – a broad, balanced curriculum promoting the spiritual, moral, cultural, mental and physical development of pupils and preparing them for the opportunities, responsibilities and experiences of adult life. There was a contradiction between these general purposes and statutory curriculum content relating to sex education. The science orders for the National Curriculum introduced by the Act covered knowledge about human reproduction at Key Stages 1 (5–7 years) and 2 (7–11 years), and education about HIV, AIDS and other sexually transmitted diseases at Key Stage 3 (11–14 years). Consequently, the formal curriculum focused on biological "facts" and a scientific approach to the body as a system rather than personal and social development.

During the early 1990s, education legislation and guidance continued to prioritise parental responsibility for sex education, the delivery of biological facts and moral values in school-based provision. The 1993 Education Act established the right of parents to withdraw their children from sex education other than instruction within the National Curriculum. Replacing previous guidance, Circular 5/94 (DFE, 1994) confirmed parents as the arbiters of their children's sex education. Schools were expected to "ensure that parents understand the right of withdrawal and how to use it". Parents were not required to account for their decision, nor specify alternative arrangements.

The purpose of sex education was confirmed as providing knowledge about loving relationships, the "nature" of sexuality, and the processes of human reproduction. Loyalty and fidelity were added to the list of important values, and Circular 5/94 stressed that sex education "must not be value free". A patronising statement suggested that teachers needed to acknowledge that many children come from backgrounds which do not reflect such values or experiences. While avoiding offence, teachers should help pupils "whatever their circumstances, to raise their sights".

Under the 1993 Act, primary school governing bodies retained responsibility for deciding whether or not to provide sex education. Circular 5/94 confirmed primary sex education as preparation for the challenges of growing up and understanding human reproduction. Provision was expected to take into account children's capacity to absorb sensitive information and the extent to which it was essential for them to have such information at that point in their development. The Circular stated: "provision should be geared to the needs of the class or group as a whole ... not ... determined by the pace of the most precocious pupils". Prioritising parental wishes, Circular 5/94 suggested that a teacher asked an explicit question should normally discuss the child's concerns first with the child's parents, to see how they would like the matter to be handled. The teacher could then respond to the child outside the classroom situation if agreed by the parents. Speaking to the child before consulting her/his parents was considered appropriate only in exceptional circumstances (where the teacher believed the child may be distressed or in danger).

The 1993 Act made sex education in secondary schools mandatory. Education about HIV/AIDS and STDs was removed from the science curriculum at Key Stage 3 and placed within sex education. It was affirmed by Circular 5/94 that secondary sex education should encompass the broader emotional and ethical dimensions of sexual attitudes plus facts about human reproductive processes and behaviour, with balanced information about "sensitive" matters. Although making no direct reference to homosexuality, Circular 5/94 included a paragraph about Section 28 of the 1988 Local Government Act. This stated that Section 28 "prohibits local authorities from intentionally promoting homosexuality or publishing material with that intention, and from promoting the teaching in any maintained school of the acceptability of homosexuality as a pretended family relationship". Despite acknowledging that this prohibition applied to the activities of local authorities, as distinct from governing bodies and staff of schools on their own behalf, inclusion of a reference to Section 28 within the Circular reinforced teacher and governor concerns about discussion of homosexuality.

Education and health: a clash of ideologies

Throughout successive Conservative administrations, objectives promoted by educational and health policies were contradictory. Circular 11/87 confirmed the role of schools in limiting the spread of AIDS via enhanced public awareness. In fact, schools had "a clear responsibility" to warn pupils about the health risks of casual, promiscuous sexual behaviour – whether heterosexual or homosexual – and the dangers of drug abuse. Whatever its policy on sex education, each school was expected to draw attention to forms of behaviour carrying a risk of HIV/AIDS infection and risk reduction strategies. In contrast, guidance about provision of advice to under 16s noted that, while "good teachers" were expected to take a pastoral interest in the welfare and well-being of pupils, this "should never trespass on the proper exercise of parental rights and responsibilities".

The controversial "Gillick" case exemplified tensions between parental and professional responsibilities, illustrating how the concept of "protection" can undermine a child's access to information and their ability to make decisions for themselves. In 1981 Victoria Gillick, a committed Catholic and mother, demanded guarantees from her local authority that girls under 16 would be refused contraception or abortion without parental knowledge or consent. The local authority rejected her demands and she mounted a legal campaign, claiming that prescription of contraceptives by a doctor increased the likelihood of under-age sex. She argued that this promoted, encouraged and facilitated unlawful sexual intercourse. A 1986 House of Lords judgement rejected this argument, suggesting that a doctor's intention would be to protect the young woman from pregnancy rather than to promote or encourage sexual intercourse. The subsequent "Gillick ruling" stated that, while it would be unusual for a doctor to prescribe contraceptives to a girl under 16 without parental knowledge or consent, a doctor would be justified provided that: it was in the girl's best interests; she understood the advice; she could not be persuaded to tell her parents; without advice or treatment her health would suffer; she would begin or continue sexual activity.

Although a health professional was responsible for deciding whether a young woman understood advice in these circumstances, the ruling prioritised her needs regardless of parental consent. However, the ruling was interpreted negatively in educational policy; polarising the roles of education and health professionals. Circular 11/87 stated that the medical context had "no parallel in school education". Provision of advice on sexual matters without parental knowledge or consent was defined "an inappropriate exercise of a teacher's professional responsibilities", which "could ... amount to a criminal offence". The Circular suggested that a teacher approached by a pupil for advice about aspects of sexual behaviour should redirect the pupil to their parents. If the teacher believed the pupil had embarked on or was contemplating conduct likely to lead to physical or moral danger, or breach of the law, the teacher had a general duty to warn the pupil of the risks involved. Whether the teacher should inform the head teacher, and whether the head teacher should consider involving the pupil's parents, specialist support services, or the local education authority, was discretionary – determined by the circumstances and the professional judgment of staff.

Conflicting ideologies were also evident within education policy. In contrast to the emphasis on knowledge about biological "facts" within the National Curriculum science orders, guidance about the non-statutory cross-curricular theme "health education" (incorporating sex education) prioritised personal development, skills and attitudes. Key objectives included: promoting quality of life; the physical, social and mental well-being of the individual; provision of information about what was good/harmful; and the development of skills to help individuals use knowledge effectively, resist social pressures and respect the needs of others (National Curriculum Council, 1990). This guidance recognised that provision of suitable information and activities designed to develop skills for maintaining personal safety, managing relationships and making positive choices, required matching the curriculum to a learner's age, developmental stage and background as well as the social pressures they were likely to encounter, their interests and needs.

The Conservative government's "Health of the Nation" strategy (Department of Health, 1992) identified HIV/AIDS and sexual health as one of five key areas. Major objectives included reducing the incidence of HIV infection and other sexually transmitted diseases (STDs), decreasing the numbers of "unwanted" pregnancies and conceptions amongst under-16s, and ensuring the availability of effective family planning services. *The Key Area Handbook* (Department of Health, 1995), outlining strategies for education and prevention at local levels, emphasised Sex Education Forum (1992) recommendations that sex education should: be integral to the learning process; begin in childhood and continue into adult life; provided for all children, young people and adults. It was acknowledged that biological information alone "is not adequate in enabling people to act responsibly if they decide to become sexually active". Also necessary were development of interpersonal and negotiating skills, and a sense of self-worth.

The significant contribution that sex education could make to realising Health of the Nation targets was noted in Circular 5/94. Legislative changes to provision, however, undermined these objectives. Although sex education at secondary school (including education about HIV/AIDS and STDs) was made mandatory by the 1993 Act, the parental right of withdrawal meant that a young person could leave school at 16 having received no formal sex education. Further, previous guidance about provision of contraceptive advice to under-16s was confirmed in Circular 5/94, which warned that the legal position of a teacher giving advice had never been tested in the courts. The professional judgment of teachers and autonomy of the child were significantly undermined by this guidance since a teacher who believed that a pupil had engaged in, or was thinking about, risky or illegal behaviour was expected to inform the head teacher. If the pupil was under age, the guidance suggested that the parents be made aware, preferably by the pupil, and that the head teacher should check this had been done. In 1997, the British Medical Association (BMA, 1997: 2) adopted the resolution that DFE guidelines on sex education in school contravened Health of the Nation objectives and would not promote children's health. The BMA argued that education guidelines showed "scant respect for young peoples' rights and confidentiality", and that resource allocations for sexual health were inadequate.

The social democratic agenda: resolving the contradictions?

Since its election in 1997, the Labour government has refocused attention on sex education and appears to have aligned education and health policies. Although criticised for not making it statutory, the government has developed a framework for PSHE which incorporates sex education (QCA, 1999). This emphases the development of personal confidence and responsibility, a healthy lifestyle, good relationships and respect for others. The "Saving Lives: Our Healthier Nation" strategy (Department of Health, 1999) recognises schools as key settings for the promotion of better health and well-being; to be achieved through local programmes based on education and health partnerships providing accessible, relevant information and equipping children with the skills to make informed decisions. A specific theme within the "Healthy Schools" programme, jointly led by the DfEE and Department of Health, is sex and relationships education (SRE).

Non-statutory SRE Guidance has replaced Circular 5/94 (DfEE, 2000), defining SRE as lifelong learning about physical, moral, emotional development; understanding the importance of marriage for family life, stable and loving relationships, respect, love and care; and the teaching of sex, sexuality and sexual health. SRE "is not about the promotion of sexual orientation or sexual activity – this would be inappropriate teaching". Challenging suggestions that sex education provision promotes sexual activity, the guidance states: "Effective SRE does not encourage early sexual experimentation." It should teach young people to understand sexuality; enabling them to build confidence, self-esteem, knowledge and skills to cope with conflicting pressures. Partnership with parents is still considered essential, including their involvement in policy development and in the planning and delivery of sex education programmes, thus reassuring them about content and the context in which it will be presented. Schools are expected to support parents in developing appropriate vocabulary, talking with their children about feelings and relationships, and answering their children's questions.

The role of pupils in implementation of effective policy and practice has also been recognised in recent policy documents. For example, the criteria for assessing a school's achievements in SRE (DfEE, 1999) include: a policy owned and implemented by all members of the school, including pupils, and a planned SRE programme which identifies learning outcomes appropriate to pupils' age, ability, gender, level of maturity and is based on pupils' needs assessment. The guidance states that a school's SRE policy should reflect the views of pupils; acknowledging that listening and responding to their opinions will strengthen their confidence and self-esteem. It is anticipated that the new school inspection framework will reinforce evaluation and reporting about pupils' personal, spiritual, moral, social and cultural development and the effectiveness of support and advice offered by a school to all its pupils.

Outlining content for different phases, the SRE guidance recommends that early years education about relationships should focus on friendship, bullying and the building of self-esteem. In the transition year, preceding the move to secondary school, primary schools should have clear parameters concerning what will be taught. Content should focus on changes in the body relating to puberty; what issues may cause young people anxiety and how they can deal with these; how a baby is conceived and born. Guidance emphasises that teaching methods should take account of developmental differences between children. Schools should establish what is appropriate in whole class, small group or one-to-one discussion. It is suggested that teachers may require support or training in handling sensitive questions.

Addressing previous criticism of school sex education, the guidance notes that SRE programmes should focus on boys as much as girls at both primary and secondary levels. Since SRE policies should be "culturally appropriate and inclusive of all children", consultation with pupils and parents is required to establish what is appropriate and acceptable for them in terms of content and delivery. The specific needs of children with special educational needs and learning difficulties are highlighted, and schools are reminded of their duty to ensure that *all* pupils are included in SRE. Secondary school sex education should be within the context of self-esteem and responsibility for actions, particularly regarding sexual activity and parenthood. Young people should understand arguments for delaying sexual activity, and the guidance proposes that SRE should be connected to issues of peer pressure and other risk-taking behaviour.

Schools are advised to prescribe their intentions concerning "sensitive issues", outlining the agreed values framework within which those contributing to SRE are expected to work. The guidance links specific issues to government strategies aimed at reducing teenage pregnancies and the incidence of HIV/AIDS and sexually transmitted infections (STIs). It proposes that trained staff in secondary schools should provide information about different types of contraception (including emergency contraception), and their effectiveness, plus information about where confidential advice, counselling and treatment can be obtained. Teaching about safer sex is a priority, including knowledge about HIV, AIDS and STIs – what constitutes risky behaviour; how to prevent infection; diagnosis and treatment. Assertiveness skills are prioritised, to enable pupils to negotiate relationships, avoid being pressured into unwanted or unprotected sex, and become effective users of services which help prevent or treat HIV and STIs. While acknowledging that the religious convictions of pupils and parents should be respected, the guidance emphasises that the purpose of SRE is preparation for the responsibilities and challenges of adult life. Using abortion as an example, it is argued that provision of information, opportunities to explore dilemmas, and development of communication skills should be given precedence.

The SRE guidance does not define a moral framework. Acknowledging research findings, it notes that young people often complain about the focus on reproduction and neglect of meaningful discussion about feelings, relationships and values in school sex education. It is argued that rooting SRE within the PSHE framework will address this balance. The 1986 requirement that sex education provision should encourage moral considerations and the value of family life remains statutory. However, the SRE guidance states: "The government recognises ... that there are strong and mutually supportive relationships outside marriage. Therefore pupils should learn the significance of marriage and stable relationships as key building blocks of community and society. Care needs to be taken to ensure that there is no stigmatisation of children based on their home circumstances."

While the Labour government promotes the nebulous concept of "social inclusion", there has been fierce opposition to its proposed repeal of Section 28 leading to a compromise within the SRE guidance. Section 28 is not mentioned and the guidance states that young people, whatever their developing sexuality, need to feel that SRE is relevant and sensitive to their needs. Specifically, schools "need to be able to deal with homophobic bullying". However, having stated that teachers should be able to deal honestly and sensitively with sexual orientation, answering questions and offering support, the guidance continues: "there should be no direct promotion of sexual orientation". This implies that "sexual orientation" is confined to homosexuality.

Recommendations concerning confidentiality are considerably less prohibitive and emphasise meeting the needs of the pupil. The guidance notes that effective SRE helps pupils identify and understand what constitutes acceptable behaviour. This may lead to disclosure of child protection issues. Consequently, teachers need to be familiar with procedures for reporting concerns and the school's child protection policy. However, the guidance states that teachers are not legally bound to inform parents or the head teacher of disclosure, unless specifically requested by the head teacher. Pupils should know that teachers cannot guarantee unconditional confidentiality, and be encouraged to talk to their parents. But they should be reassured that their best interests will be maintained. If confidentiality has to be broken, pupils should be informed first and then supported as appropriate. Pupils should also be informed about sources of confidential help. Although health professionals working in schools have to abide by school policies, the guidance confirms that they are bound by their professional codes of conduct to maintain confidentiality and can give advice or information to a pupil about health-related matters (including contraception) outside the classroom context.

Implementing children's rights: future directions

It is difficult to assess the achievement of specific objectives unless they have been agreed and a commitment to their implementation has been demonstrated. The UN Convention on the Rights of the Child establishes the civil, political, social and economic rights of children. Ratification by the UK government in 1991 represented an obligation to review national legislation to ensure compliance with its articles. However, national policies and practices have consistently breached a number of articles. For example, neither Conservative nor Labour administrations established mechanisms to ensure promotion and implementation of the Convention (Article 4), or made the principles and provisions of the Convention widely known to adults and children (Article 42). Despite obvious disapproval by the UN Committee (1995), the Labour government has retained the right of parents to withdraw their children from sex education. This contravenes the right of children to express their views in all matters affecting them and to have their views taken seriously (Article 12).

But implementation of the Convention is not just about ensuring that legislation explicitly incorporates its Articles. As evidenced by the 1975 Sex Discrimination Act and 1976 Race Relations Act, the existence of laws does not guarantee enforcement. Implementation of all rights to all children, without discrimination of any kind (Article 2), remains an ideal. Children's personal experiences and access to opportunities are affected by their gender, age, sexuality, class, culture, religion, abilities, and geographical location. Individual and institutional stereotyping and discrimination reinforce, and are reinforced by, legislation and guidance which reproduce specific socio-cultural "norms" and values. As far as sex education is concerned, children's rights will continue to be denied unless contemporary constructions of childhood, sex and sexuality are contested. This means changing attitudes towards, and expectations of, children and young people and a cultural shift in popular assumptions about the role of adults in children's lives. It also means challenging the dominant ideologies of childhood, sex and sexuality, and their institutionalisation (in schools, religions, health and welfare services, the criminal justice system).

The UN Convention establishes the right of children to seek, receive and impart information and ideas (Article 13), and affirms the right to the highest attainable standard of health (Article 24). Implementation requires a commitment to sex education provision which addresses the needs and interests of children and young people on *their* terms. This includes discussion about feelings and emotions, the pleasures of sexual intimacy, the skills of negotiation, positive self-esteem, and respect for, as well as sensitivity towards, others. Health educators recognise that young people, like adults, engage in risky behaviour. They need to understand the potential consequences of their actions in non-judgmental environments. They require information about relevant preventive health care, family planning education and services.

Although the latest SRE guidance recommends the participation of children in policy and practice development, as discussed above, parental wishes and involvement have been prioritised, and parents still determine access to sex education. Article 12 establishes that children's views be given "due weight in accordance with the age and maturity of the child". In English legislation, children under the age of 16 are considered too young to be able to express themselves or make rational, informed choices (although the age of criminal responsibility is 10). Non-statutory guidance has consistently emphasised the need to match provision to the maturity of children and young people. However, judgements about "maturity" are made by adults operating within their professional frameworks. Usually, these are based on age-related stages linking sexual development to the onset of puberty and reinforcing the social construction of children as asexual innocents. Children who use explicit language, ask questions about sex, sexuality or sexual behaviour, or behave in what are considered overtly sexual ways, are defined as "deviant", "promiscuous" or "at risk" (especially if female).

Article 3 establishes the principle of the "best interests of the child" as a primary consideration in all actions concerning the child. Like many adults, children need support to develop an understanding about their rights and to receive protection from exploitation, abuse or neglect. Unlike adults, however, children are perceived as inexperienced, incompetent, egocentric and therefore incapable of recognising the complexity of situations, appreciating the implications of decisions, and making rational choices. It is assumed that adults are able to both fulfil these objectives and define a child's best interests. Consequently, policy-making excludes children and curriculum content is based on adult perceptions rather than children's knowledge and feelings. While adult personal experiences and professional frameworks inform provision, so do historical, social and cultural contexts. Current guidance, for example, assumes that it is in children's best interests to understand sexual behaviour, associated risks and how to access advice. Yet PSHE, incorporating sex education, is not a statutory requirement – state responsibility for sex education remains secondary to parental responsibility.

The relationship between sex and sexuality is highly contentious in the debate over what constitutes "best interests" sex education. Heterosexuality is positively promoted as "normal", "natural" and, in that sense "compulsory". "Appropriate" sexual activity is represented as sexual intercourse; focused on reproduction and parenthood. Diversions from these ideological constructs are condemned as "abnormal" or "unnatural". These dominant discourses about sex and sexuality determine expectations about "appropriate" knowledge, skills, behaviour, roles, responsibilities and attitudes for girls and boys of different ages. Such expectations are reinforced through curriculum content, resources, class organisation and management strategies, interactions between and among staff and pupils. Despite twenty years of debate, professional ideologies, structural procedures and personal practices continue to disadvantage, or ignore the needs of, young people who identify themselves outside the "rules" associated with gender and sexuality. In addition to personal isolation, the rejection of gender stereotypes often results in harassment and marginalisation. Provision of sexuality education, which recognises how these constructions operate and challenges stereotypes, would help young people develop their own and respect other's identities.

Official discourses, and their associated policies, promote heterosexuality to the extent of misinformation. Text book diagrams detailing the "reproductive organs" of females ignore the clitoris as it is assumed irrelevant to reproduction. Sexual activity is usually described in terms of the missionary position, with limited reference to non-penetrative sex or active participation by women. Abortion, contraception, HIV/AIDS are mentioned in guidance as "controversial" or "sensitive" issues, rather than being integral to young people's understanding about sexual relationships and ability to make informed choices. There is an implicit tension between respecting the wishes or moral, cultural and religious values of parents and provision of a balanced curriculum which might enable young people to develop personal values and effective decision-making skills.

Linked to ideological constructions of sex and sexuality is the "ideal" family promoted by the media and politicians – a heterosexual, married couple balancing work and home responsibilities while successfully parenting their biological children. This representation reinforces the assumption that the family provides a safe haven where parents care for their children; protecting them from dangerous strangers, paedophiles and harmful experiences. Social institutions are expected to support parents in their role, and state intervention in the private family domain is resisted. Recent research and campaigns reflect a very different experience, with estimates of 1 in 4 children subjected to abuse within the family or by people known to them.

The UN Convention obliges the state to take wide-ranging measures to protect children from all forms of physical or mental violence, injury or abuse, neglect or negligent treatment, maltreatment or exploitation – including sexual abuse – while in the care of parents, legal guardians, or carers (Article 19). These should include effective social programmes to support children and those who care for them; forms of prevention; and processes of identification, reporting, referral, investigation, treatment and follow up. The right to protection from sexual exploitation and sexual abuse, including coercion to engage in unlawful sexual activity and use of children in prostitution or pornography, is also established (Article 34). Fulfilment of these Articles requires an acknowledgement that children are abused and exploited by adults (parents, carers, family friends, priests, babysitters, residential care staff) who are more likely to be known to them than strangers.

Sex and sexuality education should be predicated on the principle of children's right to knowledge, information and understanding about their bodies and the processes of physical, emotional, personal and social development. Effective communication depends on shared understanding about the meanings attached to language and actions. It is therefore vital that children are actively encouraged to ask questions, and helped to develop a comprehensive vocabulary relating to sex and sexual behaviour. It is essential that they learn about the boundaries of acceptable and unacceptable behaviours; becoming familiar with definitions of abuse and exploitation. The realities of predatory relations, whether familial or external, need to be acknowledged in sex education. Otherwise the maintenance of "innocence" becomes the consolidation of "ignorance" and vulnerability.

Confidential opportunities for disclosure are also required. However hidden are the consequences, children who experience physical, emotional or sexual abuse remain traumatised. The UN Convention obliges the government to promote recovery and reintegrate neglected, maltreated or exploited children; emphasising their health, self-respect and dignity (Article 39). It is crucial to recovery that children who suffer abuse by older children or adults are identified as survivors rather than victims. Their strategies for coping with abuse, and their means of dealing with abusers, should be recognised as manifestations of strength and resistance, not ignored by an ideology of victimhood.

Development of effective sex and sexuality education is a complex issue, not resolved by moralising or reactionary responses to perceived "crises" in childhood (see Scraton, 1997). Provision of information has to be balanced with children's capacity to receive and make sense of it. Grounding sex education policy and practice in the best interests of the child, and matching provision to their maturity, necessitates using the experiences, questions, concerns and interests of children as the appropriate starting point. Within any class there will be a range of needs and interests and these should all be addressed. As in any subject, if one child raises an issue it is likely to be of interest to others in the classroom. If not, they will ignore it or seek further clarification when it becomes relevant to them.

Sex and sexuality education is premised on helping children to develop respectful and caring relationships. The emphasis, however, should be on their present needs. As well as long-term improvements in health and well-being, effective provision will enable young people to make informed decisions about parenthood. Teachers and health professionals should be entrusted with delivery of sex education based on responding directly to children and young people, using a range of strategies to enable open discussion and opportunities for development of skills and attitudes as well as acquisition of knowledge. Policy-makers at all levels should actively involve children and young people in the processes of policy development; ensuring consistency in education and health objectives, and establishing goals which are achievable. Sex education which develops self-confidence – enabling children to maintain personal safety, negotiate relationships and make informed choices while respecting individual identities and lifestyles – is the right of every child and young person.

References

Ball, S. (1990) *Politics and Policy Making in Education. Explorations in Policy Sociology*, London: Routledge

BMA (British Medical Association) (1997) *School Sex Education: good policy and practice*, London: BMA

Corteen, K. and Scraton, P. (1997) "Prolonging 'Childhood'; Manufacturing 'Innocence' and Regulating Sexuality" in Scraton, P. (ed.) *"Childhood" in "Crisis"?*, London: UCL Press

Department of Health (1992) *The Health of the Nation*, White Paper, London: Department of Health

—— (1995) *The Key Area Handbook on HIV/AIDS and Sexual Health*, London: Department of Health

—— (1999) *Saving Lives: Our Healthier Nation*, White Paper, London: Department of Health

DES (Department of Education and Science) (1987) *Circular Number 11/87. Sex Education at School* (25 September 1987), London: DES

DFE (Department for Education) (1994) *Circular Number 5/94. Education Act 1993: Sex Education in School* (6 May 1994), London: DFE

DfEE (Department for Education and Employment) (1999) *National Healthy School Standard. Guidance*, Nottingham: DfEE

—— (2000) *Sex and Relationship Education Guidance*, Nottingham: DfEE

National Curriculum Council (1990) *Curriculum Guidance 5: Health Education*, York: National Curriculum Council

QCA (Qualifications and Curriculum Authority) (1999) *The National Curriculum for England: non-statutory frameworks for personal, social and health education and citizenship at key stages 1 and 2; personal, social and health education at key stages 3 and 4*, London: QCA

Scraton, P. (ed.) (1997) *"Childhood" in "Crisis"?*, London: UCL Press

Sex Education Forum (1992) *A Framework for School Sex Education*, London: Sex Education Forum

UN Committee (1995) *Concluding Observations of the Committee on the Rights of the Child: United Kingdom of Great Britain and Northern Ireland*, CRC/C/15/Add.34 (15 February 1995), UN CRC

11 Rights and disabled children

Lesley Campbell

Introduction

As the 1990s closed there was some evidence that at the level of public policy the rights of disabled children were beginning to be acknowledged. Such an acknowledgement, however, still means that progress in realising their rights lags some ten years behind non-disabled children. Questions about the extent to which the rhetoric of public policy documents, and the fine words of inquiry reports, are translated into everyday practice, remain unanswered. There is undoubtedly a strong case to suggest that securing the rights of disabled children would bring home rights for all children.

In recent years some writers have emphasised the rights of disabled children (Cross, 1998 and Morris, 1998) but there remains a notable tendency to regard disabled children as children in need of services and protection rather than as children who have rights alongside non-disabled children.

There is, of course, a growing children's rights movement in the UK but disabled children are all too often excluded or appended as an afterthought under the banner of "all children". Within these apparently inclusive terms there is no acknowledgement of the strong pressures that militate against upholding the rights of disabled children.

The pervasive nature of the medical model within disability services serves to isolate disabled children from their peers. This isolation means that at many levels the awareness of children's rights does not penetrate the world of disabled children: they are generally unaware of their rights under the UN Convention on the Rights of the Child (UNCRC). Ruxton identifies the need to make the UNCRC more accessible to children; especially children with different impairments (Ruxton, 1998). She notes the scope for using the web as well as Braille, tape, video and sign forms of the Convention. The parents of disabled children struggle to secure (often) specialist services and the professionals in these services are themselves isolated from a rights-based perspective (Middleton, 1999).

One approach to acknowledge rights issues for disabled children has been to issue Charters of Rights that focus on disabled children. In 1997 Chailey Heritage hospital school produced a charter of children's rights as part of its child protection guidelines (Chailey Heritage, 1997). In order to mark the significance of the tenth anniversary of the UNCRC, Mencap produced its Charter of Children's Rights.

The 1989 Children Act included among its principles that disabled children should be regarded as "children first". The Guidance for disabled children is unequivocal and states that "The primary aim should be to promote access for all children to the same range of services" (Department of Health, 1989: 2). But this aspiration has not been met and the implications of this Act on the rights of disabled children are considered in the following sections.

There has been little systematic analysis of the impact of the UNCRC within the UK although the Thematic Day held by the UN Committee in 1997 began this process. There is also no research that examines the awareness of the UNCRC among disabled children. At the present time there is a degree of uncertainty about the extent to which the newly formed Disability Rights Commission will be in a position to promote and uphold the rights of disabled children. There is a similar level of uncertainty about the likely impact of the Human Rights Act on the lives of disabled children. The long-awaited extension of the Disability Discrimination Act to education holds the promise of expanded rights for children but is without the benefit of financial penalties when these rights are not upheld.

At a time of considerable change and debate about the rights of children it is useful to focus on the rights of disabled children. Rather than covering all the Articles of the UNCRC or Human Rights Act this chapter will focus on four main areas:

- right to life
- right to protection
- right to information
- right to education

This focus does not deny that all of the articles of the UNCRC or the Human Rights Act have a significance for disabled children, but it acknowledges that some rights are of particular and fundamental importance to disabled children.

Right to life

> When you are a disabled child, assumptions are made that our life is lacking in quality. These assumptions are made as soon as you are born and are used to justify discrimination.
> (Jimmy Telesford, disabled young person (Morris, 1998: 3))

Jimmy Telesford is only partially correct: assumptions are made about the value of a disabled child's life prior to birth. As more and more impairments can be detected during pregnancy and these tests come to be more widespread so terminations of affected foetuses increase. As Ward states: "prenatal testing and diagnosis raise a huge number of ethical issues" (Ward, 2001). For at least some expectant parents there is an absence of balanced information at the time of testing, little opportunity to explore the issues for their family as well as an assumption made that a "positive" result will lead to a termination (Dodds, 1997). Russell recommends that "there is a need at such times for a disability advocate – a person with full informa-tion about the lives of disabled people who can play a role in ensuring that the decisions which are made are informed decisions" (Russell, 2001).

In 1990 an amendment was made to legislation controlling human embryo research that introduced a time limit of 24 weeks for all termina-tions except when the foetus has significant impairments, when termination is legally sanctioned up to the moment of birth. In 1993 there were 457 terminations based on this amendment (Office of Population Censuses and Surveys, 1995). By 1998 this number had increased fourfold to 1,830 (Office of Population Censuses and Surveys, 1999).

As Morris points out "to give ourselves the right to judge someone else's life as not worth living is to enter the same ideological framework as the German physicians of the Third Reich" (Morris, 1991: 54).

For a disabled child the right to life assumes particular importance from the moment of birth and also throughout the childhood of some children. The value that society places on disabled children comes into sharp relief in some of the high-profile public cases and also for individual families facing difficult decisions in neonatal units up and down the country. The British Medical Association has recently issued guidance to support decision-making in this area. This guidance is based not on judgments about the quality of an individual's life but rather on the benefits of treatment in each specific case: "As with adults, the patient's best interests and an assessment of the benefits and burdens of treatment are the key factors in considering whether treatment should be provided or withdrawn" (British Medical Association, 1999: 25).

The BMA has found that with the increased prevalence of terminations on the grounds of impairment, a belief has developed among some doctors that with parental agreement secured they need not provide life-sustaining treatment for babies born with severe impairment. The Guidance empha-sises that the question is, or always should be, whether the treatment would be worthwhile and not whether the child's life is worthwhile.

The value of a disabled child's life is illustrated in some of the terms used by judges. In the case of the conjoint twins (Jodie and Mary) in 2000 the following terms were used by judges: "what is this creature in the eyes of the law"; "hideous nightmare"; "parasitic"; "so afflicted as to be intolerable" (*Re A*, 2000: 7). In this complex case, on appeal Judge Ward concluded in a more positive vein that: "each life has an inherent value in itself however grave the impairment" (*Re A*, 2000).

The Children Act 1989 charges all those with parental responsibility to act in the best interests of the child and in the main parents are the best judges of their children's interests. However in the case of Baby Alexander the court over-ruled the decision of the parents not to consent to life-saving surgery (*Re J9*, 1990). On the other side of the coin the Glass case illustrated that parents cannot necessarily enforce their preferences about the continuation of treatment where these conflict with medical evidence (*Daily Mail*, 3 August 2000).

Baby C, an 18-month-old girl is an unreported case the details of which have been given by her parents to the National Centre for Independent Living. She was diagnosed as having spinal muscular atrophy and contracted pneumonia. The hospital refused to put her on a ventilator or give her antibiotics, which would be standard treatment for non-disabled infants. The parents attempted to reverse this decision in the courts but the judge ruled that because she could not raise her head from the pillow her life was not worth living, and that in addition she would need total bodily care for the rest of her life and that this would be a burden for the state. She died in hospital of suffocation (Daw, 2000).

The Down's Syndrome Association research revealed a number of examples where children with Down's syndrome have been denied life-preserving surgery. One parent was quoted as saying: "the cardiologist said that with people with Down's syndrome they preferred not to operate, but to let nature take it's course" (Rutter and Seyman, 1999: 21).

In the case of Jo Harris, a teenager with Down's syndrome, and needing a heart and lung transplant her cardiologist was quoted as stating "there is no centre in the country that would undertake an operation on a child with Down's syndrome" (*Mirror*, 20 September 2000).

The right to life is recognised within the Human Rights Act (Article 2) as an absolute right. The HRA will give disabled children and their representatives an additional ground for challenging unlawful activity. Article 2 has a useful role for disabled children in reinforcing their rights when limited resources and technological advances might otherwise put them under threat.

Right to protection

The official acknowledgement of the particular needs of disabled children for protection is a very recent development (Department of Health, 1999). The Utting Report identified the particular vulnerabilities of disabled children living away from home (Utting, 1997).

Within the child protection field, disabled children are generally regarded as a "special group" with additional vulnerabilities rather than emphasising their right to protection. There are many reasons for their vulnerability, not least being their separation from mainstream services. Some of their specific vulnerability stems from the lack of access to "keeping safe" programmes, which tend to exclude disabled children through their messages of "run and tell". It is in the area of sex education that the rights of disabled children to information and to protection come together. Mainstream sex education programmes typically fail to address the specific needs of disabled children. Within special schools sex education has not received the attention it deserves. There are however notable exceptions, for example the whole school approach of Shepherds School in Nottingham (Shepherds School, 1998). This lack of access to appropriate sex education disempowers disabled children and increases their vulnerability.

In many parts of the country the translation of the Children Act into service development has meant the separation of disabled children teams from child protection or family support teams as if disabled children have rights to neither protection nor support. From a rights perspective this separation of both the children and the professionals attached to them means that positive developments in enhancing children's rights fail to filter through the disability barrier.

Research into child abuse indicates that care away from home is not safe for disabled children. The sheer numbers of carers involved with such children may actually increase the level of risk (Westcott and Cross, 1996 and Morris, 1996). Disabled children are estimated to be seven times more likely than non-disabled children to be living away from home. They are most likely to be living in a residential school at a considerable distance from both their parents and the placing authority. This has a significant impact on their isolation and sends a powerful message to potential abusers that here is a group of children who are not valued and can be targeted for abuse. Despite the requirement of the Children Act to provide independent visitors for all children who have lost contact with their parents only 1 per cent of eligible disabled children have allocated visitors (Knight, 1998).

Until recent years disabled children have been an invisible group within the field of child protection. Although they have now become more visible within official reports, there are serious "practice lags". There is a lack of disability awareness among investigating staff, a lack of fully accessible interviewing suites, a lack of access to the court process and a very serious shortage of specialist therapeutic skills. All of these gaps leave the rights of disabled children to protection subject to repeated violations.

The right to information

For most children, parents are the first source of information and gradually peers and other adults become increasingly important as they start school. However the vast majority of disabled children have parents who are "not like them" and who are not therefore able to share important information, for example strategies for dealing with bullying or prejudice. This has been highlighted in respect of deaf children with hearing parents but in fact applies to children with all types of impairment. This lack of access to information from parents places disabled children at a considerable disadvantage especially when considered against their lack of access to other sources of information.

Article 10 of the Human Rights Act (the right to freedom of expression) has a bearing on the disabled child's rights insofar as it prevents public authorities from restricting a person from receiving information. An example here would be the information about complaints procedures provided under the Children Act Regulations. If information about complaints procedures is not available in a fully accessible form then disabled children are disadvantaged. The Children's Society project involving young disabled researchers has highlighted the inaccessibility of local authority complaints procedures and helplines (Children's Society, 2001).

It could be argued that disabled children are excluded from information and that this would involve a denial of Article 10 in combination with Article 14 the prohibition of discrimination in the enjoyment of Convention rights.

The Children Act requires that: "young people with disabilities and their families will need clear information on the full range of services in an 'easy to read' guide in order to be able to negotiate the most effective package of care" (Department of Health, 1989: 52). Despite this requirement there are very few examples of local authorities that have gone the extra mile and made their information about services fully accessible to disabled children. A number of leaflets directed at children have been developed, some of these have been illustrated, a minority of them include symbols and even fewer are available in taped or Braille versions. Children from minority ethnic communities experience double discrimination in respect of information as they do in so many other aspects of their lives. There have been missed opportunities to involve disabled children in developing these forms of information. There is a tendency for professionals to regard all of this as "too difficult" rather than capitalise on the hunger children show for information.

The tendency to focus on different versions of information leaflets denies the significant role of play, drama, art and music in imparting information to children. A workshop for young people quoted in Russell (1998) used a range of media to inform young people about transitions. One young man who attended said: "we worked together, we used painting, video, the computer. We told each other what we wanted to do".

The limitations of parents as the providers of information was acknowledged by one of the parents: "I felt ashamed that I hadn't really talked to him about a lot of the serious things about growing up. I suppose I was afraid he would be hurt" (Russell, 1998: 20).

Many disabled children lack the opportunity to create the informal networks used by other children and so are cut off from the flow of information that relies on face-to-face contact: "The biggest barrier we face as young disabled people is isolation from other people with the same experience" (Arthritis Care, 1997: 14).

At a practical level, disabled children have useful information to share with one another. An example here would be where to find the nearest wheelchair accessible condom machine.

Consulting with children about services has become fashionable in the past decade. Before meaningful consultations can take place children need access to information. Typically, consultations are on a one-off basis about a specific service, for example targeting the children using a short-term care facility (Triangle, 1999). These consultations presuppose that the children involved already have access to information about the full range of options that might be available to them. This should include leisure services that may be more child-centred than traditionally organised short-term breaks.

Interviewing young people with physical impairments, Middleton found high levels of ignorance about even more basic issues. These young people lacked information about their own conditions and also about what this meant for their future (Middleton, 1999).

Many disabled children will have particular needs in respect of health issues. The Council for Disabled Children convened workshops for disabled young people with on-going health needs and concluded that young people need accurate information on proposed medical interventions. One young man was critical of the information provided by his GP and commented favourably on the value of information from other young people: "I mean they would really know, wouldn't they? I got to meet other young people who had the same operation. They warned me about the pills – the operation isn't always the end of things, is it?" (Russell, 1998: 58).

Children cared for by local authorities have some of the greatest needs for information. Disabled children are heavily over-represented in all forms of care away from home and yet are least likely to have information about statutory reviews or access to information held on them. Hodgson identifies the need to be provided with information before, during and after the process of being consulted about wishes and feelings (Hodgson, 1995). The consultation papers produced as part of the *Looking After Children* materials do little to include disabled children within the review process (Department of Health, 1995).

Until and unless children's rights to information is upheld, consultation exercises conducted in the spirit of Article 10 will remain at best tokenistic and in the longer term risk alienating children who will see through these adult-focused efforts. There is also a danger that consultations based on a snapshot approach fail to include children with severe and profound disabilities as these children present the greatest challenges to adult researchers. There have been some encouraging attempts to involve children as researchers and peer supporters (Children's Society, 2001). Drawing on their creativity as information-gatherers is likely to pay greater dividends for children with the most complex communication impairments (Boyden and Ennew, 1997).

Involving children in researching and developing information using all media is an obvious way of including children in shaping services (Alderson, 2000). Since personal contact is such a prevalent way of checking out services, young people could be more actively involved in information strategies, for example, developing Web sites and CD-ROMS that are accessible to disabled young people. An example here is the Mencap project, Trans-active, within which pairs of severely disabled people and students use the Internet to explore options for themselves as young adults (Mencap, forthcoming).

The focus on reasonable adjustments contained within the Disability Discrimination Act will strengthen the rights of disabled children to information in formats that are accessible to them. The right to freedom of expression will continue to have little meaning for disabled children until service providers uphold their right to information as a precursor to effective consultation.

Right to education

Education provides one of the most powerful levers in banishing stereotypes and negative attitudes towards disabled children and adults. When disabled and non-disabled children are educated together this sends strong messages to the rest of the community about the value of inclusion and diversity. It is however within the field of education that the rights of disabled children are most obviously compromised or denied. This is because of:

- the emphasis within education in the UK on parents' rights
- the investment in segregated provision
- the failure to include children in decisions about their education

All children lack information about education and disabled children are especially disadvantaged in this respect, particularly if they attend a special school. They are less likely to find out about other schools and they also lack information about after-school activities and clubs. Disabled children in both the mainstream and special school sectors are also unlikely to encounter a disabled teacher or indeed any other disabled adults. This lack of contact with the disabled world has implications for the view children have of themselves and for their preparation for transition to the adult world.

In the UK the education legislation and associated regulations and guidance have all been out of step with the UNCRC and the Children Act requirement to ascertain the wishes and feelings of children. It is especially easy to overlook the views of disabled children within the plethora of education processes and services that have been developed to meet the needs of their parents. During the assessment, statementing, appeals and exclusions processes there is currently no requirement to seek the views of the child (Children's Society, 1998).

Parent Partnership Services that provide information, advice and support to parents, by their very name exclude children. Although disabled children frequently attend some or all of the statutory annual reviews, all too often these adult-focused meetings fail to truly include children. The 2001 draft revision of the Code of Practice covering this area does indeed strengthen the rights of children within special education but has significant inconsistencies in this respect (Department for Education and Skills, 2001). An example here would be that although local authorities are expected to "be aware" of youth advocacy services there is no requirement that they make these available to young people with special educational needs. These inconsistencies demonstrate that the requirement to uphold the rights of children within education has been noted but that there is a considerable way to go before these rights are fully embedded within the culture of education.

For some disabled children the basic right to education is denied. Throughout the 1950s and 1960s parent groups like Mencap campaigned to ensure that all children had access to education. This right was finally enshrined in the 1970 Education Act. Nearly thirty years on it remains the case that some children are excluded from education on the grounds of their disability. Research highlights a number of instances where children with health needs in addition to their learning disability are denied full access to the education system (Mencap, 2001). Robinson and Jackson also found that disabled children using hospices were frequently excluded from education for significant periods of time (Robinson and Jackson, 1999).

The UNCRC states that the right to education should be recognised on the basis of equality of opportunity. An equal right to attend the school of their choice has been denied to many disabled children ever since the development of the special school sector in the UK. Despite the trend towards integration within education (placing children in the same classes or in the same sites as their peers), inclusion in terms of taking a full part in the school community is still some way off in most parts of the UK.

Following the Special Educational Needs (SEN) Programme of Action which encourages strategic planning for inclusion, many local education authorities have developed inclusion policies (Department for Education and Employment, 1998). The extent to which the fine intentions of these policy documents are matched by the experiences of disabled children has yet to be researched.

The Disability Rights Task Force Report contains the recommendation to extend the Disability Discrimination Act to education (Department for Education and Employment, 1999). In many official publications at both a national and local government level there has been a strong tendency to focus on the disabling barriers to inclusion presented by unsuitable buildings. The Task Force goes some way to redressing this balance by focusing on the content of education – the curriculum. Inclusion is not only about attendance at a mainstream school. An inclusive curriculum is also essential.

The government's response to this Task Force report has been to announce a new SEN and Disability Rights in Education Bill. This Bill promises to strengthen the rights of parents of children with statements of SEN to a mainstream school place for their child. There is however every indication that this new Bill will preserve at least one of the current caveats to inclusion contained within the 1996 Education Act. In effect, Section 316 of this Act means that disabled children can only be educated alongside their non-disabled peers as long as the latter are not disadvantaged.

The main barriers to inclusion in education are not laws or buildings or equipment but people – their attitudes and behaviour. The Disability Rights Task Force in common with other reports fails to emphasise this point. The views of teachers and parents are shaped by their experiences of disabled children and adults. We know that 61 per cent of people under 35 have no contact with disabled people (National Opinion Poll, 1999). We also know that only a tiny minority of teachers will have worked alongside a disabled colleague. In the absence of real experience, misinformation and discrimination flourish.

In the past ten years many special schools have developed links with local mainstream schools and pupils attend assemblies and selected lessons on the mainstream school site (Mencap, 1999). Despite the growth of these links at an individual pupil level, there are still limited opportunities for teachers to share knowledge and experiences across the wide special–mainstream school divide.

Children's rights within education continue to be dominated by parents' rights and the SEN and Disability Rights in Education and the Human Rights Act are no exceptions. The latter includes the "right of parents to ensure such education and teaching in conformity with their own religious and philosophical convictions". In principle this may strengthen parent's right to choose a school on the basis of their belief in the value of a mainstream education. However several European Court rulings have confirmed that the state could not be required to incur the additional cost of placement in a mainstream school. In *Simpson* v *UK* the European Commission ruled that the education authority had "a wide measure of discretion as to how to make the best possible use of resources available to them in the interests of disabled children generally" (*Simpson* v *UK*, 1989).

Conclusions

The most significant rights issue for disabled children is their invisibility and lack of contact with the mainstream world. In the foreword to Morris's work on accessing human rights for disabled children the Chief Executive of Barnados comments: "unless particular attention is paid to the inclusion of disabled children within any mainstream activity they will remain invisible and their needs and rights unmet" (Morris, 1998: 14).

No higher priority is claimed for disabled children. Upholding their rights is as simple as acknowledging these rights to be the same as for all children. The simplicity of this conclusion is however predicated on a fundamental re-evaluation of disabled children as full members of an inclusive society.

References

Alderson, P. (2000) *Young Children's Rights; Exploring Beliefs, Principles and Practice*, London: Jessica Kingsley

Arthritis Care (1997) *The Ruff Guide to Life for Young People with Arthritis*, London: Arthritis Care

Boyden, J. and Ennew, J. (1997) *Children in Focus; A Manual for Participatory Research with Children*, Stockholm: Radda Barnen

British Medical Association (1999) *Withholding and Withdrawing Life-prolonging Medical Treatment*, London: British Medical Journal Books

Chailey Heritage (1997) *Guidelines Relating to Child Protection*, Brighton: Chailey Heritage

Children's Society (1998) *No Lessons Learnt*, London: The Children's Society

—— (2001) *Ask Us: The Children's Society Multi-media Guide to Consultation for the Quality Protects Initiative*, Children's Society with Joseph Rowntree Foundation.

—— (2001) *National Multi-media Consultation with Disabled Children and Young People*, London: Children's Society

Cross, M. (1998) *Proud Child, Safer Child; A Handbook for Parents and Carers of Disabled Children*, London: The Women's Press

Daily Mail (2000) "Why Must My Son be Left to Die?" 3 August

Daw, R. (2000) *Human Rights and Disability. The Impact of the Human Rights Act on Disabled People*, London: National Disability Council and Royal National Institute of Deaf People

Department for Education and Employment (1998) *Meeting Special Educational Needs; A Programme of Action*, London: DfEE

—— (1999) *From Exclusion to Inclusion; A Report of the Disability Rights Task Force on Civil Rights for Disabled People*, London: DfEE

—— (2000) *SEN Code of Practice on the Identification and Assessment of Pupils with Special Educational Needs*, London: DfEE

Department of Health (1989) *Children Act 1989 Guidance and Regulations. Volume 6. Children with Disabilities*, London: Department of Health

—— (1995) *Looking After Children Training Resource Pack*, London: Department of Health

—— (1999) *Working Together to Safeguard Children*, London: Department of Health

Dodds, R. (1997) *The Stress of Tests in Pregnancy*, London: National Childbirth Trust

Hodgson, D. (1995) *Promoting Children's Rights in Practice*, London: National Council for Voluntary Organisations

Jones, H. (1999) *childRight*, no. 161 (Nov.). London: National Children's Bureau

Kennedy, M. (1995) In *Handbook of Children's Rights* (ed.) B. Franklin, London: Routledge

Knight, A. (1998) *Valued or Forgotten?*, London: National Children's Bureau

Mencap (1999) *On a Wing and a Prayer. Inclusion and Children with Severe Learning Difficulties*, London: Mencap

—— (2001) *Don't Count Me Out*, London: Mencap

Middleton, L. (1999) *Disabled Children; Challenging Social Exclusion*, Oxford: Blackwell Science

Mirror (2000) "To us Jo is a normal girl; she has the same right to life as anyone", 20 September

Morris, J. (1991) *Pride Against Prejudice, Transforming Attitudes to Disability*, London: The Women's Press

—— (1996) *Gone Missing? A Research and Policy Review of Children Living Away From Their families*, London: Who Cares Trust

—— (1998) *Accessing Human Rights: Disabled Children and the Children Act*, Barnados

National Opinion Poll (1999) London: Leonard Cheshire

Office of Population Censuses and Surveys (1995) *Abortion Statistics 1993* Series AB, No. 20

—— (1999) *Abortion Statistics 1998* Series AB, No. 25 1999

Re A (Children) [2000] B1 /2000/2969

Re C (Medical Treatment) [1998] 1 FLR 384

Re J 9 (A Minor) (Wardship: Medical Treatment) [1990] 3 All ER 930

Re T (A Minor) (Wardship; Medical Treatment); sub nom *Re C (A Minor) (Parents' Consent to Surgery)* [1997] 1 All ER 906

Robinson, C. and Jackson, P. (1999) *Children's Hospices: A Lifeline for Families?*, London: National Children's Bureau

Russell, O. (2001) In *Considered Choices?*, L. Ward (ed.) Wolverhampton: BILD

Russell, P. (1998). *Having a Say! Disabled Children and Effective Partnership*, London: National Children's Bureau

Rutter, S. and Seyman, S. (1999). *He'll Never Join the Army: A Report on a Down's Syndrome Association Survey into Attitudes to People with Down's Syndrome amongst Medical Professionals*, London: Down's Syndrome Association

Ruxton, S. (1998) *Implementing Children's Rights*, London: Save the Children

Shepherd's School (1998) *Feeling Grown Up*, Nottingham: Shepherd's School

Simpson v *UK* [1989] 64 DR 188 at 195

TP and KM v *The United Kingdom*, European Commission 28945/95

Triangle (1999) *Tomorrow I Go; Young People's Views about a Residential Respite Care Service*, Brighton: Triangle

Utting, W. (1997) *People Like Us; The Report of the Review of the Safeguards for Children Living Away From Home*, London: Department of Health

Ward, L. (2001) *Considered Choices?*, Wolverhampton: BILD

Westcott, H. and Cross, M. (1996) *This Far and No Further: Towards Ending the Abuse of Disabled Children*, Birmingham: Venture Press

12 Children who care

Rights and wrongs in debate and policy on young carers

Jo Aldridge and Saul Becker

Introduction

There are currently as many as 50,000 children in Britain who are providing substantial and regular care for an ill or disabled parent or other relative in the home. These children are "young carers". Research and campaign work in Britain over the past decade has identified young caring as an issue for social and political concern and has led to developments in community care policy and law. Furthermore, young carers' rights are no longer simply defined in terms of a hypothetical "wish list" as they were when young caring was first recognised in social science research, but are now firmly established in British law and social policy. This chapter examines the nature and consequences for children who are carers, and traces the social and political changes that have affected their lives and the lives of their families.

Research on young caring began in the late 1980s and identifies children in terms of the *duality* of their roles in families where parental impairment occurs. Theoretically, literature on the young carers has embraced a children's rights perspective which emerged as a consequence of a range of omissions: children were overlooked as carers in the generic carers literature and the more recent literature on the sociology of childhood. Furthermore, early evidence from small-scale studies into young caring suggested that children had been systematically overlooked as carers in both policy and practice in Britain for many years (see Becker *et al.*, 1998).

Essentially young carers are described in research and policy as children and young people who have significant or substantial care responsibilities for a sick or disabled parent, or other relative, in the home, responsibilities normally carried out by adults (see Lunn, 1990; Becker, 1995; Becker *et al.*, 1998; Becker, 2000). More than ten years of research and campaign work in Britain have contributed to this definition and to the current understanding about who young carers are, what they do, the impacts of their caring responsibilities and the numbers of children engaged in caring activities on a national scale. The growing body of qualitative and quantitative enquiry examining the lives of young carers and their families has provided us with a profile of young carers: the type of duties they undertake, the nature and extent of these and a range of consequences that can and do have far reaching effects on their lives.

Numbers and consequences

In the late 1980s two small-scale studies aimed to estimate the numbers of children who were undertaking care responsibilities in the home (O'Neill, 1988; Page, 1988). These early studies suggested that young caring was relatively uncommon. Indeed, O'Neill (1988: 2) compared the incidence of young caring at the time to that of traffic accidents: "If adult caring is on a comparable scale with unemployment, young caring is probably on a similar scale to severe road accidents."

Although empirical investigation into young caring in Britain has, on the whole, been concerned less about collating statistical evidence and more about experiential analyses,[1] estimating the *numbers* of children involved in caring has been a significant aspect of a range of research studies on young carers since the early enquiries. Through secondary analysis of 1985 General Household Survey data, Parker (1992, 1994) found that 17 per cent of carers aged 16–35 had caring responsibilities before their sixteenth birthday, and that one third of these had been assisting their parents: "This means that of the 1.2 million carers aged 35 and under in 1985, some 212,000 had been providing care since before the age of 16 and, of those, around 68,000 for a parent" (Parker, 1994: 9).

In 1995 Mahon and Higgins suggested between 15,000 and 40,000 children were caring in Britain, and the latest estimate, from the Office for National Statistics (Walker, 1996), suggests that there are between 19,000 and 51,000 young carers in the UK who are providing "substantial" or "regular" care for another family member.

As awareness of young carers' issues has grown, and support for them has increased, it has become easier to identify them in larger numbers and to conduct more detailed quantitative and qualitative studies. By contacting specialist support services it has been possible for researchers to generate statistical information about larger numbers of young carers (see Dearden and Becker, 1995, 1998), as well as to conduct in-depth interviews with young carers in different contexts (for example those caring for parents with severe mental health problems).

Thus, we know that young carers perform a range of caring and other duties, from basic domestic work to nursing tasks that include intimate caring (toileting, bathing), administering medication, lifting, as well as acting as interpreters between parents and welfare professionals (see Meredith, 1991; Bilsborrow, 1992; Aldridge and Becker, 1993; Beach, 1994, 1997; Becker, 1995; Frank, 1995; Price, 1996; Dearden and Becker, 1995, 1998, 2000a). These responsibilities may be short or long term, periodical or follow consistently routinised patterns.

The recorded impacts of caring on children are equally wide ranging. In

1992, when research into young caring in Britain was in its infancy, Meredith suggested that where children were caring, "there can be adverse effects on a child's development physically, emotionally, educationally and socially" (1992: 15). Evidence has only served to support Meredith's assertion since. We now know that when children undertake care responsibilities in the home, and where they and their families lack appropriate health and social care support and adequate income, many young carers experience a range of problems.

These problems include impaired health and psycho-social development, including physical injury (Becker *et al.*, 1998; Hill, 1999), stress-related symptoms (Aldridge and Becker, 1993; Elliott, 1992; Landells and Pritlove, 1994; Dearden and Becker, 1995, 1998, 2000b and by Imrie and Coombes, 1995), poor educational attendance, performance and attainment (Marsden, 1995; Dearden and Becker, 1998; Crabtree and Warner, 1999), restricted peer networks, friendships and opportunities (Bilsborrow, 1992; Aldridge and Becker, 1993; Dearden and Becker, 1998, 2000a) as well as difficulties in making the smooth transition from childhood to adulthood (Frank *et al.*, 1999; Dearden and Becker, 2000a). Many of these problems can also severely affect young carers in adult life. For example, many will find it difficult to enter the paid labour market if they have few, if any, educational qualifications (Dearden and Becker, 2000a).

The outcome of these research studies into the impacts of caring on children has served to raise public consciousness about young caring in the UK and alerted policy-makers and practitioners in child and family services alike to the needs of young carers and their families. In 1996 the Department of Health concluded that "helping in the care of the disabled person adversely affected [a young carer's] social life, education or restricted their freedom to take part-time jobs" (Walker, 1996: 1). Indeed, these Department of Health findings proved to be a catalyst in the ensuing policy reforms affecting young carers and their families which occurred in the late 1990s and which are discussed later in this chapter.

Young carers: a rights-based approach

One of the catalysts for the introduction of research studies into young carers in Britain was the recognition, through early small-scale and pilot surveys, that young carers had been omitted from the generic carers' literature and research, as well as from the campaign work being carried out on behalf of adult carers by the national carers' movement. What was also missing was a rights-based approach to children whose lives were affected by the particular schism presented by their caring.

Thus, early work in the UK on young carers and their families attempted to embrace a children's rights philosophy which saw young carers in need of support as children but having distinct and diverse needs as carers. However, this often proved more tractable in theory than in practice. The rights-based agenda first promoted as a result of evidence from early investigations (see Aldridge and Becker, 1993) included an inventory of children's rights[2] which recognised children's needs as children as well as their roles as carers (see Aldridge and Becker, 1995). However, at a time when young carers were still being overlooked by welfare agencies and undertaking their often significant caring duties in secrecy and isolation, the rights-based agenda proposed had all the appearance of a hypothetical wish list.

Indeed, looked at from a policy and interventionist perspective, according young carers these rights in practice seemed unworkable, not least because of the apparent difficulties involved in reconising role duality presented when children care. Such duality is echoed in a more general children's rights perspective on childhood which sees children, on the one hand, as liberated from age distinctions that serve to undermine their access to rights, and a tempered approach on the other that sees children as appropriating some degree of independence, but ultimately requiring forms of support that protect them from abuse, injury or exploitation.

In the same way, the factors that have undermined a rights-based approach to young caring have seemingly reinforced and maintained the irreconcilability of children's caring labours. Young caring transgresses the social construct of "children" as a group occupying distinctly the realm of "childhood", where they have the right to physical and emotional sustenance, protection from harm, and where they are allowed to make the gradual transition to "adulthood". Indeed, when children undertake caring at what might be deemed an inappropriate age, they occupy a distinctly "adult" realm simply on account of what they do.

Nevertheless, those working with and on behalf of young carers have continued to promote a children's rights approach to young caring. Such an approach recognises that regardless of the type and nature of children's roles when they care, they should share the same access to rights as children, as carers or as both. However, certain key factors – which are fundamentally tied up in the schism presented when children care – have challenged a fully realised rights-based approach to young caring. Essentially these challenges have come from policy and intervention strategies that have, until recently, been unsuccessful in crossing the boundaries constituted by young caring; the divisions within academic debate which have occurred as a result of challenges from disability rights authors; debates in psychiatry that define young caring in terms of "parentification"; a medical perspective that underlines the negativity of caring among children; and the promotion of the public face of young caring by the UK's national and local media.

Essentially policy responses in the UK have been caught in the duality presented by young caring, promoting neither a distinct children's rights approach nor firmly emphasising a carers' perspective. Challenges to the work on young caring in the UK (and elsewhere) in terms of academic debate have either refuted the idea of young carers as a subject for welfare classification and policy reform, or have recognised young caring as a consequence of parental impairment while emphasising the risk associations for children when they adopt caring roles. The media have promoted the view that caring by children is a brave, albeit essentially adult responsibility, worthy of public recognition by reward, but not by right. We will look at these issues in turn.

The paradox presented by young caring meant that for many years young carers were falling between the gaps in community care provision. Neither the Children Act 1989 nor the 1990 NHS and Community Care Act could accommodate the diverse yet seemingly convergent nature of their experiences and needs. Significant advances in policy for young carers first occurred when the 1995 Carers (Recognition and Services) Act was introduced. However, in 1996 the Department of Health (1996a) recognised the continuing challenges posed by the emergence of young caring on the policy agenda. The Department of Health's own research on young carers had uncovered a range of ongoing problems: families were still having to fight for recognition and services; welfare agencies were still unsure how to intervene effectively in the lives of young carers and their families because of uncertainties about legislative procedures; and resources were often hopelessly insufficient to meet the growing need:

> Most of the local authority research findings suggested that the number and needs of young carers were greater than the available resources to meet the needs ... concerns about expectations were widespread and some local research projects found local authority departments with heavy existing case loads unwilling to take on young carers as a policy issue at all.
>
> (Department of Health, 1996a: 42)

Although more recent evidence points to some small improvements in young carers' lives over the last few years in terms of what they do (see Dearden and Becker, 1998), the most significant changes have occurred in law, policy and services.

Legislative and policy developments

In the late 1980s, there was no reference to young carers in either social policy, or law. Indeed, the whole notion of a "carer" – as a concept and as a legitimate client group for state and professional intervention – was largely undeveloped and unexplored. Adult carers started to gain visibility for their contribution to family care in the research and writings of feminist and other social policy commentators from the early 1980s. This academic recognition was the catalyst which led to formal identification of (adult) carers in policy and law at the end of the 1980s, particularly with the passing of the 1990 NHS and Community Care Act. This Act, and the Griffiths report which preceded it, put carers centre-stage in the new system and structures for "care in the community" (Becker, 1997). Under the Act, in theory at least, carers were supposed to be consulted and involved in the process of needs assessment and care plan development.

The process of recognition for adult carers' needs and policy development is relatively linear: academic research exploring the experiences and needs of family carers throughout the 1980s fuelled a growing public, political and policy awareness, which was also encouraged by the development of a new but increasingly vociferous and effective carers' movement lobbying for change. These developments were largely based on an *adult* carer's rights agenda, which emphasised the rights of family carers to recognition, choice, security and support. This rights agenda was promoted by the use of a number of interrelated campaigning "cases"; the moral case – that a decent and civilised society had a moral duty to help carers; and the economic case – that if society doesn't help carers, and they "crack" under the strain, the cost to the state – to all of us – would be far greater. The political imperative to reform a community care system which was widely regarded to be insensitive to the needs of those requiring home-based care, and their carers, and which was inefficient in cost terms (promoting a series of perverse incentives), also fuelled the calls for wholesale reform (Becker, 1997).

The Griffiths report (Griffiths, 1988) and the 1990 NHS and Community Care Act are the foundations on which reform was built, but reform was specifically concerned with *adult's* needs and rights: elderly people, ill and disabled adults, and their adult carers. At this stage a *children's* rights agenda for (young) carers was virtually non-existent. Even when the NHS and Community Care Act was implemented fully, by 1993, there was still little recognition of the contribution that children made to informal care. The focus in the academic literature throughout the 1980s had been very much on adult carers; researchers continued to ignore and omit young carers from their investigations and analyses. Consequently, it is not surprising that policy developments which specifically identified and recognised young carers were some years behind parallel developments for adult carers. So, for example, the first two dedicated local young carers projects were founded in the early 1990s, whereas a network of local Crossroads schemes (providing respite care to adult carers and their families) had been in existence since the mid 1970s, with dozens of schemes operating in the 1980s and more than 200 by the 1990s. In contrast, the number of local young carers projects reached about 35 by the mid 1990s and around 120 by 1998, but even then many projects faced uncertain futures due to short-term funding arrangements (Dearden and Becker, 1998; Becker *et al.*, 1998).

While the NHS and community care reforms were essentially adult legislation, there was a clear children's rights agenda in the legislation of the 1989 Children Act. However, even here, young carers were not formally mentioned as a category of children who might be considered to be "at risk" or "in need". Indeed, as a group, they were not recognised at all. It took some years for social services departments and others to see how the

Children Act might best be used for the benefit of young carers, and in particular Section 17, which relates to "children in need" (Children's Rights Development Unit, 1994; Social Services Inspectorate, 1995).

The growth in the academic literature on young carers, from about 1992 onwards, was followed by policy developments and legislation formally establishing new rights for young, as well as adult, carers. Had the academic community recognised young carers' contributions earlier (in the 1980s) then it is conceivable that recognition in policy, but probably not in law, would have come earlier rather than later (so, for example, there would have been dedicated young carers projects in the 1980s, and more of them). The main obstacle in the timely recognition of young caring was an essentially adult perspective that constrained researchers and policy-makers from understanding that in some families care was provided not by adults but by children and young people. Hence the omission at the time of any reference to young carers in the adult legislation on community care or child welfare legislation such as the Children Act.

As we have indicated already, the early 1990s research on young carers was to have a profound impact on public and political recognition of young carers as a "new" welfare group, and subsequent policy, legislative and professional developments. But it required the efforts, campaigning work and influence of the carers' movement (in particular the Carers National Association and the Princess Royal Trust for Carers), and a number of children's charities (notably Barnardos and The Children's Society), alongside the academic evidence provided by researchers (such as the Young Carers Research Group, founded in 1993), to propel young carers firmly onto the community care and child welfare agendas. Once established, the impact of the work of these agencies and groups was relatively expeditious (in policy development terms), with young carers being formally recognised, for the first time in law, in the 1995 Carers (Recognition and Services) Act.

The Carers Act (as it is commonly referred to) confers on adult and young carers who are providing or about to provide a substantial amount of care on a regular basis the right to have their own needs assessed, and at the time when the person they are caring for is having their own formal needs assessment. The result of the carer's needs assessment must be taken into account when social services draw up a care plan of services for the care receiver. For the first time carers – and young carers – had clear rights, and it was the express intention of the Act and subsequent guidance (Department of Health, 1996b) that young carers should not be expected to sustain inappropriate levels of caring responsibilities.

Despite these rights, and the passing of time, only about one tenth of young carers in contact with dedicated projects in 1997 had ever had a formal assessment of their needs and of their ability to care (Dearden and Becker, 1998). This proportion is low considering that many of the children in Dearden and Becker's sample were involved in intimate care, had educational problems and were very young – the average age was just 12. A further weakness of the Carers Act is that it does not oblige local authorities to provide any services to carers – it is about needs' assessment, not service provision.

It required the passing of the Carers and Disabled Children Act, in 2000, to remedy this serious disjunction between assessing needs and meeting needs. Since April 2001 all carers – including young carers – have had enhanced rights to an assessment of their own needs, and local authorities have been able to provide services directly to carers, to support them in their caring role, for the first time. Moreover, some carers (including some young carers aged 16 or over) had new rights to direct payments in lieu of services.

At the same time clarification of how to recognise and assess 'children in need' was provided through a new *Framework for the Assessment of Children in Need* (Horwath, 2000). Young carers, alongside other groups of children, including children looked after by local authorities and disabled children, were to be considered as potential children in need, to be assessed as such using a new framework (Dearden and Becker, 2000b), and to be provided with access to greater family support where required.

By the turn of the millennium a children's rights agenda had fused almost seamlessly with a carer's rights agenda to establish new legal rights, and new policies and procedures, both in community care and child welfare, which recognised and benefited young carers. This fusion can be seen most clearly in the government's National Strategy for Carers (Department of Health, 1999). Here, in a series of commitments to improve the circumstances of carers – based on a carer's rights agenda – is one chapter dedicated to young carers, based on a clear children's rights agenda. The government pledges improved support for young carers, and outlines how education, social care and health authorities could do more to identify and support this group of children so they do not experience the adverse effects chronicled in the growing body of research evidence.

The National Strategy also confirms that young carers are everybody's business, not just a concern for social services and social care agencies. It took some years for this to be recognised in policy, with the first half of the 1990s being very much preoccupied with the role (and failings) of social services. However, as the educational difficulties of young carers became increasingly apparent through quantitative research (Dearden and Becker, 1998), and as the health inequalities that young carers face also became more evident, other sectors found it harder to ignore young carers in their own field of operation. So, for example, the Department for Education and Employment's Connexions strategy for 13–19-year-olds identifies young carers as a priority group for the advice and services to be provided by personal advisers, whose aim will be to enable young carers to get the most out of their education and help them access the labour market.

Challenges to children's and carers' rights

Both researchers and children's welfare campaigners have continued to promote a rights-based framework in respect of young carers, and their families. However, challenges in academic debate have emerged that have, at times, served to undermine this approach. One of the key challenges in this respect has been from a disability rights perspective, which suggests that the promotion of young carers as a "welfare category" undermines the rights of disabled parents (Keith and Morris, 1995; Morris, 1995; Olsen, 1996).

At the time, Morris argued, "it is not acceptable for children of disabled or ill parents to carry out tasks which adversely affect their emotional, social and educational development" (Morris, 1995). However, an approach based on children's rights argued for increasing focus on the distinct needs of young, as opposed to adult, carers in order to counteract any further discrimination of them by omission (in the generic academic and research work on carers) and neglect (by professionals and the welfare agencies – see Becker, *et al.*, 1998). It was further argued that a children's rights approach to young caring did not essentially negate a disability rights approach, nor undermine disabled parents and their ability to parent with efficacy (Aldridge and Becker, 1996). The summation of this debate proved effective in underlining points of convergence between the two perspectives, and in developing a model based on family rights that was congruent with a children's rights framework. In 1999, Olsen recognised that:

> The debate about appropriate responses to the issue of young carers has matured over the past few years ... The task is to identify common ground whereby the needs of children and their families are recognised and acted upon in a way which does not involve the disempowerment or silencing of either "side".
>
> (Olsen, 1999: 6)

However, an important feature of this debate between two apparently opposing camps has been that it has demonstrated a consistency among those working with and on behalf of young carers in adhering to a rights-based model. For although a more coherent *family* perspective has been incorporated into this framework over the years, work on young caring has, from the outset, emphasised the importance of an inclusive approach to parents and parenting both methodologically and analytically (see Aldridge and Becker, 1994; Becker *et al.*, 1998). A disability rights perspective on the importance of a rights-based framework for young carers remains charged with uncertainty. For example, in 1999 Olsen recognised the "different theoretical foundations" in the debate over a rights and advocacy approach to young caring and an approach which, in effect, emphasised independent living for disabled parents. He concluded: "Whilst leaning much more to the latter than the former, I have tried to articulate an approach to these issues which leaves the question of rights out of the equation altogether" (Olsen, 1999).

More recent debate in psychiatry has focused on the negative associations between childhood and caring. This debate has described young carers as "parentified" children and has underlined the risks associated with such "inappropriate" role assimilation. It is true that parent–child relationships and family hierarchy can often seem perverse when considered in the context of young caring. At its extreme young caring appears to transform relations between a child and the parent for whom that child cares. In many respects the child, as carer, becomes the nurturer, protector, domestic manager and often the nurse to the parent. Indeed, some of the research (particularly in the early 1990s) on young carers has described young caring as responsibility turned on its head, where the child becomes the parent of the parent. This aspect of young caring has resulted in further empirical investigation in psychiatry in which researchers have looked for evidence of "parentification" and considered its long-term effects (see West and Keller, 1991; Barnett and Parker, 1998; Chase, 1999). Seen essentially as an "attachment disorder", the "parentified child" is one who undertakes the physical act of caring and experiences this as role reversal. Psychiatrists have suggested that the consequences of this for children are inherently negative and damaging in the long term:

> Role-reversal is thus a specific type of parentification and, it might be argued, potentially a more pathological one, since intense or prolonged occupation of this age-inappropriate role may not only limit the individual child's development, but also adversely affect the next generation through repetition of this family pattern.
>
> (Barnett and Parker, 1998: 146)

Role reversal among children has not been a significant aspect of the effects of work on young carers, perhaps because evidence has suggested that undertaking the care management of a parent is not in and of itself indicative of role transference among children. Furthermore, defining young caring in simple "parentification" terms as children's role exchange with their parents does seem to presuppose the subjugation of parenting ability simply on the basis of the presence of impairment. As Thurman has argued, "lack of performance by an individual does not necessarily mean lack of competence on the part of that individual" (1985: 39). Although early qualitative work with young carers and their parents suggested that some *sense* of "role reversal" was often experienced by young carers as well as their ill or disabled parents (especially when support services were not forthcoming or were inadequate – see Aldridge and Becker, 1994), recognising and acknowledging these experiences was perhaps an essential prerequisite of a fully realised rights-based approach to young caring. More recently, those writing from a children's rights perspective on young carers have tried to refute the notion of role reversal or parentification. For example, Becker *et al.*, (1998) suggest that "it is important to understand young caring as one aspect of inter-generational caring, reciprocity and interdependence ... ill or disabled parents may receive care but they also provide care to their children and to others" (Becker *et al.*, 108–9).

For many years evidence-based medicine more generally has recognised young caring as one of the consequences of parental ill health or disability (see Arnaud, 1959; Anthony, 1970; O'Neill, 1985; Sturges, 1978) and has viewed this outcome, once again, as inherently negative and damaging for children's future development. Young caring was observed in general medicine as an exhibition of role transformation by children whose parents were ill in some way. It was described variously as "precocious competence" (O'Neill, 1985), "false maturity" (Arnaud, 1959), "doing defense" and as "caretaking" (Sturges, 1978).

This emphasis in general medicine, and particularly in more recent psychiatric debate, on the negative impacts of parental impairment on children as carers has served to further undermine a rights-based approach to young caring. The same could also be said of the media's representation of young carers as displaced or victimised children. As Deacon (1999: 9) has argued: "News tends to be about either elites or issues that are out of the ordinary. The young carers issue scores strongly in the latter respect, with its inversion of established and socially accepted patterns of caring."

The issue of young caring as portrayed by the media has been divided into two narratives: "the little angel" story which eulogises children as carers and "the little victim" approach – "which draws on deep rooted anxieties about the vulnerability and defencelessness of young people from adult exploitation" (Deacon, 1999: 10; see Franklin, chapter 1). A rights-based approach figures in neither narrative and would, as Deacon (1999: 11) asserts, be much more difficult to "sell" to journalists. However, despite this reluctance on the part of the media to try and "shape" public perception of young caring in terms of a more balanced and equitable narrative, and despite the emergence of other factors that have challenged the advancement of a rights-based approach to young caring, some significant progress has been made to effect change in the lives of young carers and their families over the last ten years. Nowhere is this more true than in the policy and legislative developments as outlined earlier.

Conclusion

Policy strategies in the UK have, until recently, been compromised by young carers' occupation of twin provinces – the previously assumed distinct domains of caring and childhood. Thus, policy-makers have had to reassess legislative frameworks to accommodate the ambiguity of children's roles when they provide care in order to meet their needs effectively. This reappraisal has occurred in the UK as a result of evidence from ongoing research programmes and campaign strategies by those working with and on behalf of young carers themselves, and because, as we have said, until recently the needs and rights of young carers could not be fully realised and met under British legislation or social policy. However, by the end of the twentieth century there was a convergence of interests which enabled the fusion of children's and carer's rights, for the benefit of young carers and their families.

The paradox in young caring has underpinned many of the challenges facing academics and policy-makers alike, and it is only now – after more than a decade of research and campaign effort – that the rights of young carers have finally been recognised in policy and law and in assessment procedures that offer contextualised and non-demeaning assistance to young carers, and to their families. The reasons for this delay are that a rights-based approach has been undermined by a number of key factors and for several reasons, the crux of which lies in the fundamental dichotomy presented when children care: how to reconcile and complement role duality when children undertake responsibilities that are essentially adult in nature. Despite some early problems and challenges to a rights-based approach to young caring, advances have been made over the past ten years that promote young carers' rights (and more recently, the rights of their ill and disabled parents as well). These advances have been due in part to a convergence of perspectives that were previously at odds over the issue of caring by children. There has also been a growing recognition of the continuing contribution children make to care provision as evidenced in ongoing research programmes, and in the growth of dedicated services to young carers, particularly young carers projects. More significantly recent legislative and policy reforms have had a fundamental impact on the way we view young carers and assess their needs. These have gone some way to righting the wrongs that have kept young carers hidden for so long.

Notes

1 As O'Neill argued in his early study, "One can get caught up in the numbers game. One has to look at the size of the problem in the context of the severity of impacts on individuals. It is arguably more important to identify each individual case" (O'Neill, 1988: 3).

2 Among the index of rights that were advocated at this time were the right for children to continue or stop caring and the right to a comprehensive assessment of their needs (Aldridge and Becker, 1993).

References

Aldridge, J. and Becker, S. (1993) *Children Who Care: Inside the World of Young Carers.* Young Carers Research Group, Loughborough: Loughborough University

—— (1994) *My Child My Carer: The Parents' Perspective.* Young Carers Research Group, Loughborough: Loughborough University

—— (1995) "The rights and wrongs of children who care". In *Children's Rights: A Handbook of Comparative Policy and Practice* (ed. by B. Franklin), pp. 119–30. London: Routledge

—— (1996) "Disability rights and the denial of young carers: the dangers of zero-sum arguments". *Critical Social Policy*, 16, 55–76

Anthony, E.J. (1970) "The impact of mental and physical illness on family life". *American Journal of Psychiatry*, 127, part 2, 138–146

Arnaud, S.H. (1959) "Some psychological characteristics of children of multiple sclerotics". *Psychosomatic Medicine*, 21, 1, 8–22

Baldwin, S. and Twigg, J. (1991) "Women and community care: reflections on a debate". In Maclean, I. and Groves, D. (eds) *Women's Issues in Social Policy*. London: Routledge.

Barnett, B. and Parker, G. (1998) "The parentified child: early competence or childhood deprivation?" *Child Psychology and Psychiatry Review*, 3, 4, 146–155

Beach, D.L. (1994) "Family care of Alzheimer victims: an analysis of the adolescent experience". *The American Journal of Alzheimer's Care and Related Disorders and Research*, January/February, 12–19

—— (1997) "Family caregiving: the positive impact on adolescent relationships". *The Gerontologist*, 37, 2, 233–238

Becker, S. (ed.) (1995) *Young Carers in Europe: An Exploratory Cross-National Study in Britain, France, Sweden and Germany*. Young Carers Research Group in association with the European Research Centre, Loughborough: Loughborough University

—— (1997) *Responding to Poverty: The Politics of Cash and Care*. London, Longman

Becker, S. (2000) 'Young carers'. In Davies, M (ed.) *The Blackwell Encyclopaedia of Social Work*. Oxford: Blackwell

Becker, S., Aldridge, J. and Dearden, C. (1998) *Young Carers and their Families*. Oxford: Blackwell Science

Bilsborrow, S. (1992) *"You grow up fast as well ... " Young Carers on Merseyside*. Liverpool: Carers National Association, Personal Services Society and Barnardo's

Chase, N.D. (1999) "Parentification: an overview of theory, research, and societal issues. In *Burdened Children* (ed. by N.D. Chase), pp. 3–33. California: Sage

Children's Rights Development Unit (1994) *UK Agenda for Children*. London: CRDU.

Crabtree, H. and Warner, L. (1999) *Too Much to Take On: A Report on Young Carers and Bullying*. London: The Princess Royal Trust for Carers

Deacon, D.N. (1999) "Young carers and old hacks". *The Journal of Young Carers Work*, 2, 9–11

Dearden, C. and Becker, S. (1995) *Young Carers: The Facts*. Sutton: Reed Business Publishing

—— (1998) *Young Carers in the UK: A Statistical Profile*. London: Carers National Association

—— (2000a) *Growing Up Caring: Vulnerability and Transition to Adulthood – Young Carers Experiences*. Leicester: Youth Work Press

—— (2000b) "Young carers: needs, rights and assessments". In Horwath, J. (ed.) *The Child's World: Assessing Children in Need, The Reader*. London: Department of Health, NSPCC, University of Sheffield, pp. 173–182.

Department of Health (1996a) *Young Carers: Making a Start.* London: Department of Health

—— (1996b) *Carers (Recognition and Services) Act 1995: Policy Guidance and Practice Guide.* London: Department of Health.

—— (1999) *Caring About Carers: A National Strategy for Carers.* London: Department of Health

Elliott, A. (1992) *Hidden Children: A Study of Ex-Young Carers of Parents with Mental Health Problems in Leeds.* Leeds: Leeds City Council, Mental Health Development Section

Frank, J. (1995) *Couldn't Care More: A Study of Young Carers and their Needs.* London: The Children's Society

Frank, J., Tatum, C. and Tucker, S. (1999) *On Small Shoulders: Learning from the Experiences of Former Young Carers.* London: The Children's Society

Griffiths, Sir R. (1988) *Community Care: Agenda for Action.* London: HMSO

Hill, S. (1999) "The physical effects of caring on children". *The Journal of Young Carers Work*, 3, 6–7

Horwath, J. (ed.) (2000) *The Child's World: Assessing Children in Need, The Reader.* London: Department of Health, NSPCC, University of Sheffield

Imrie, J. and Coombes, Y. (1995) *No Time to Waste: The Scale and Dimensions of the Problem of Children Affected by HIV/AIDS in the United Kingdom.* Ilford: Barnardo's.

Keith, L. and Morris, J. (1995) "Easy targets: a disability rights perspective on the 'children as carers' debate". *Critical Social Policy*, 44/45, 36–57

Landells, S. and Pritlove, J. (1994) *Young Carers of a Parent with Schizophrenia: A Leeds Survey. Leeds City Council.* Leeds: Department of Social Services

Lunn, T. (1990) "A new awareness". *Community Care* ("Inside" supplement), February 22, viii

Mahon, A. and Higgins, J. (1995) " ... *A Life of our Own" Young Carers: An Evaluation of Three RHA Funded Projects in Merseyside.* Manchester: University of Manchester, Health Services Management Unit

Marsden, R. (1995) *Young Carers and Education.* London: Borough of Enfield Education Department

Meredith, H. (1991) "Young carers: the unacceptable face of community care". *Social Work and Social Sciences Review*, Supplement to Vol. 3, 47–51

—— (1992) "Supporting the young carer". *Community Outlook*, 2, 5, 15–18

Morris, J. (1995) "Easy targets: a disability rights perspective on the 'young carers' debate". In *Young Carers: Something to Thing About. Papers presented at four SSI workshops May–July 1995*, pp. 38–62. London: Department of Health

Olsen, R. (1996) "Young carers: challenging the facts and politics of research into children and caring". *Disability and Society*, 11, 1, 41–54

—— (1999) "Young carers and the 'disability' response: identifying common ground". *The Journal of Young Carers Work*, 2, 4–7

O'Neill, A.M. (1985) "Normal and bright children of mentally retarded parents: The Huck Finn Syndrome". *Child Psychiatry and Human Development*, 15, 4, 255–268

O'Neill, A. (1988) *Young Carers: The Tameside Research.* Tameside: Tameside Metropolitan Borough Council

Page, R. (1988) *Report on the Initial Survey Investigating the Number of Young Carers in Sandwell Secondary Schools.* Sandwell: Sandwell Metropolitan Borough Council

Parker, G. (1992) "Counting care: numbers and types of informal carers". In *Carers: Research and Practice* (ed. by J. Twigg), pp. 6–29. London: HMSO

—— (1994) *Where Next for Research on Carers?* Leicester: Nuffield Community Care Studies Centre, University of Leicester

Price, K. (1996) *How do I Get them to Come? Interim Report.* Waverley, Australia: Interchange Respite Care (NSW) Incorporated

Social Services Inspectorate (1995) "Letter to all Directors of Social Services", 28 April.

Sturges, J.S. (1978) "Children's reactions to mental illness in the family". *Social Casework*, 59, 9, 530–536

Thurman, S.K. (ed.) (1985) *Children of Handicapped Parents Research and Clinical Perspectives.* Orlando: Academic Press

Walker, A (1996) *Young Carers and their Families.* London: The Stationery Office

West, M.L. and Keller, A.E.R. (1991) "Parentification of the child: a case study of Bowlby's compulsive care-giving attachment pattern". *American Journal of Psychotherapy*, 45, 3, 425–431

13 Human rights and refugee children in the UK

Mano Candappa

Refugee children are among the most disadvantaged and vulnerable in the UK. They are a very diverse group, coming from a wide range of countries and different cultural and social backgrounds, with different experiences of war, flight to safety, and attendant difficulties. They often have experienced intense disruption and upheaval in their lives. Within the UK, research suggests that they, more than any other group of children, are likely to have experienced traumatic events that may lead to a need for psychological interventions; to have parents who are unemployed, living in temporary accommodation, and thus who are economically disadvantaged; to be targeted for bullying, often of a racist nature, and to be isolated in school; and to need support in learning English (Blackledge, 1994; FEU, 1994; Melzak and Warner, 1992; Rutter, 1994). It is estimated that there are over 63,000 refugee children (including asylum-seekers and those granted exceptional leave to remain in the country (ELR) in the UK at present (Refugee Council, unpublished research)).

Refugee children and the Convention on the Rights of the Child

The United Nations Convention on the Rights of the Child entitles refugee children to the same civil, economic, social and cultural rights as other children: rights which are legally binding on governments ratifying the Convention. Of particular importance to this chapter are basic human rights, which include the right not to be discriminated against in the enjoyment of rights under the Convention (Article 2); the principle that in all actions concerning children the best interest of the child shall be a primary consideration (Article 3); the principle that signatory States shall ensure "to the maximum extent possible" the survival and development of the child (Article 6); the right to respect for private and family life (Articles 9 and 16); the right to the enjoyment of the highest attainable standard of health (Article 24); the right to freedom from torture, inhuman and degrading treatment (Articles 19 and 37(a)); the right not to be unlawfully detained (Article 37(b)); the right to a standard of living adequate for the child's development (Article 27); the right to education (Articles 28 and 29); and the right to rest and leisure (Article 31).

In addition, and specifically with respect to refugees, Article 22 of the Convention states that a child who is seeking refugee status or who is considered a refugee should receive:

> appropriate protection and humanitarian assistance in the enjoyment of applicable rights set forth in the present Convention and in other international human rights or humanitarian instruments to which the said States are Parties.
>
> (UN 1989: 22,1)

Article 22 further states that States Parties should assist the UN or other competent organisation cooperating with the UN in tracing the parents or other family members of a refugee child in order to obtain information necessary for family reunification. There are other human rights set forth in the Convention that have particular resonance for refugee and asylum-seeker children. For example, in relation to a child's right to family life, Article 10 requires States Parties to deal in a "positive, humane and expeditious manner" with applications from a child or his or her parents to enter or leave a State Party for the purpose of family reunification; Article 39 requires States Parties to take measures to "promote physical and psychological recovery and social reintegration" of a child who is a victim of, among other things, armed conflict.

The UK government's reservations

The UK government ratified the Convention in 1991, but in so doing, it entered the maximum three reservations allowed (see Franklin, 1995). Of particular relevance to this chapter is its reservation on immigration and nationality issues, where it reserved the right to apply legislation as it deemed necessary, in relation to entry into, stay in, and departure from the United Kingdom, and to the acquisition and possession of citizenship. This reservation clearly discriminates against refugee children, and is therefore contrary to Article 2 of the Convention. Additionally, and of particular concern, is its potential impact on the most vulnerable of refugee children – unaccompanied minors. For this reservation implies that they could not, as a matter of right under Articles 10 and 22 of the Convention, apply for their families to be reunited with them in the UK. Thus, potentially, the child's right to family life (Article 9) could be denied, and the best interests of the child (Article 3) are evidently not a primary consideration. Indeed, as a part of its monitoring of the Convention's implementation, the Committee on the Rights of the Child noted in its meetings on 24 and 25 January 1995, that this reservation "does not appear to be compatible with the principles and provisions of the Convention, including those of its articles 2, 3, 9 and

10" (CRC, Eighth Session). It is clear that refugee children can never be entitled to the same rights as other children in the UK until the withdrawal of the above reservation.

In this chapter I will focus mainly on the situations and experiences of refugee children in relation to other human rights in the Convention, especially Articles 19, 27, 28, 29, and 39. The discussion draws on recent research about the social lives of refugee children in the UK, which formed part of the Economic and Social Research Council's (ESRC) *Children 5–16* Programme.

The research

The research study entitled, "Extraordinary Childhoods" had two broad aims:

- to contribute to knowledge of the lives of refugee children; and
- to provide information that would be useful to policy-makers and others concerned with the welfare of refugee families.

Research questions focused in particular on refugee children's experiences in their *families*; their *friendships and social relationships*; the children's experiences of *services*, such as schools and health care; and the children's expectations of the *future*. The study began in December 1996 and covered a period of 16 months. It centred on children aged 11–14, the first years of secondary schooling and a time of significant transition in children's lives. The research proceeded through two complementary stages.

Stage 1 consisted of a series of case studies. Its main focus was a group of 35 refugee children who arrived in Britain around 1994, drawn from the main groups of asylum-seekers to arrive in the country at that time: namely, Bosnians, Somalis, Sri Lankan Tamils, and Turkish Kurds. The research issues were explored in-depth with these children, in semi-structured interviews, conducted in English. For comparative purposes, the research issues were explored at this stage with a similar number of girls and boys who were born in Britain, an ethnically mixed group, many of whom attended the same schools as the refugee children.

Stage 2 complemented the interview data, and consisted of a survey with refugee and non-refugee children, involving over 300 children, aged 12–15, from years 8, 9, and 10 in two London schools.

Children participated in the research process by assisting in the development of research instruments, and in editing their stories for inclusion in a Reader for schools on refugee issues (Rutter and Candappa, 1998). The term "refugee" was used in the study to include asylum-seekers and those granted exceptional leave to remain in the country (ELR status), as well as those granted refugee status, i.e, it was self-definition rather than a legal definition. This chapter is based on interviews with refugee children.

Children who participated in the study represent the range of experiences associated with war and political conflict, witnessing atrocities, flight to safety (often routed through three or four other countries), family separation, severe hardship, and being at the mercy of unscrupulous intermediaries. Experience of war situations meant that some children had received very little formal schooling. Some had attended school to the sound of guns and bombs. Other children came to join parents they had not seen for many years. Still others arrived in the UK as unaccompanied minors. Many children had harrowing tales to tell of escape in lorries or boats, sojourns in refugee camps, and loss of family members or friends en-route (see Rutter and Candappa, 1998).

For many refugee children, their arrival in Britain was a mixed experience: relief at being in a safe country, tempered sometimes with guilt at having fled their homes leaving friends and family behind. Many children had little knowledge of the UK when they arrived. Many experienced culture-shock and trauma on arrival. Against this background, and in the context of Article 22 of the Convention, this chapter examines whether, and to what extent, these children have been given special assistance in rehabilitation and the renewed enjoyment of their basic human rights.

Article 27: The right to an adequate standard of living

Article 27 of the Convention recognises the right of every child to a standard of living adequate for the child's physical, mental, spiritual, moral and social development. Article 27 states further that:

> States Parties ... shall take appropriate measures to assist parents and others responsible for the child to implement this right and shall in case of need provide material assistance and support programmes with regard to nutrition, clothing and housing.
>
> (Article 27, 3)

The term "adequate" may seem open to interpretation, but read along with Articles 6 and 24, a basic expected standard is clearer. Article 6.2 requires States Parties to ensure "to the maximum extent possible" the survival and development of the child; Article 24 gives the child the right to the enjoyment of "the highest attainable standard of health". The child's standard of living should, therefore, under Article 6.2 promote his/her maximum development, and under Article 24, promote the highest attainable standard of health. In addition, taken together with Article 22, Article 27 should ensure that refugee children's basic needs are well supported and provided for. This, however, does not appear to be the case. Children's accounts reveal experiences which were far from satisfactory in terms of the provision of special assistance in rehabilitation or in securing an adequate standard of living. Most children spoke of the hardships they and their families experienced in the early days in Britain, living in cramped or unhy-gienic accommodation with numerous moves before they were given permanent housing. The experiences of Fatma and Serap (two 14-year-old Kurdish girls from Turkey), and Radhika (a 14-year-old Sri Lankan Tamil girl),[1] are illustrative.

Fatma's story

> We didn't have a house for about six months or something, so we had to move on to my cousins', my uncles', my aunties'. We had one week in each house. ... I wanted to have my own house, live with my own family, be together, because you have this – have the idea that because, my auntie and uncle have a row, I always thought that it's about us, because of us, innit, they can't be happy? ... They've got three children, [and] we three children and family – it was a bit crowded, and I felt really uncomfortable. I always used to tell my mum, "Can't we have our own house?" But always we had to wait for the Council [Local Authority] to make a decision.

Serap's story

> We went to our house ... there was only one room. They [her parents] were in there and there was the TV. ... And then when we came, the man [landlord] said, ... "I don't want your children here". ... We could only stay one night ... I thought all of the house was ours, and they said "No, only this room is ours". I felt sorry then because we had to share the bathroom, kitchen.

Radhika's story

> We came to their [Grandma and uncle's] home. ... The house was all right, but it's too small. There was them two in the house, too small. And then we changed the house. We changed to another house, but it was not good. I think I changed to another house, yeah, three houses. ... I think my Mum went to Council and we talked to them that we wanted another house to live. They said, "We can't find you now." And they gave us flat ... we lived there for one week ... two weeks.

When accommodation was provided, it was often unsatisfactory, insanitary, or inadequate for the family's needs. Often accommodation was unfur-nished, and families had no means of furnishing it except by taking out a loan, which was then deducted in instalments from their benefits. This left refugee families with very little money. Some of this hardship is captured as Serap continues her story.

Serap's story

> When we came to the house, there was nothing in there. We had to buy every-
> thing. ... We stayed at my uncle's house for about two weeks, because we had
> to do everything, carpet, beds and stuff like that. ... You know we get
> Income Support? – they help us, but afterwards they cut it from the Income
> Support. ... We got carpet just for our rooms. Last year [i.e., three years
> later] ... we got carpet for the stairs and middle and corridor.
>
> It was very dirty, ... our wallpaper was ripped, some of it was coming off.
> That is why we had to clean it, it was dirty. You know, pigeon poo was
> everywhere. Bathroom was like this – all the pigeon poo. My Mum had to
> clean it all.

The children's accounts do not require additional comment; but it seems
clear that the standard of living experienced by these children was not in
keeping with their rights under the Convention.

As was noted above refugee children are very likely to have parents who
are unemployed, living in temporary accommodation, and economically
disadvantaged. The extreme poverty that many refugee children in Britain
face often contrasts with the fairly comfortable lives they led in their home
countries, since it is almost invariably wealthier people who are able to flee
to foreign countries. The situation for refugee children living in lone parent
households in the UK is particularly difficult, as Radhika explains.

Radhika's story

> I don't go to most places. My Mum don't give me money. ... Because she'd
> have to give to everyone [four siblings] if she gave it to me. ... My Mum, first
> she worked, you know, orange factory ... peeling oranges. ... She don't want
> to go there because her feet hurt there. ... She worked for us. We told her
> "Don't" because she showed her feet. ... We buy clothes after two months or
> after one year ... not really much money.

Overall, study data demonstrate that far from being given their full entitlements under Article 27 of the Convention, the standard of living of many
refugee children, especially in their early days in this country, is unacceptable.

Articles 28 and 29: the right to education

Article 28 recognises the right of the child to education, including higher
education, on the basis of equal opportunity. Article 28 is complemented by
Article 29, which states, *inter alia*, that the education of the child shall be
directed to: "The development of the child's personality, talents and mental
and physical abilities to their fullest potential."

This suggests that a child has a right to a school place, to curricular and pastoral support, and to a learning environment where the child's abilities can be nurtured and developed to their fullest potential. For refugee children, Article 22 further entitles them to protection and assistance in the enjoyment of their right to education. This right is particularly important: as Elbedour *et al.* (1993) suggest, for many children "the school serves as a second security base outside the home, or perhaps their only security base". For children who have experienced war and forced migration, the security and support the school could provide become all the more important.

Data from the study indicate that for many refugee children the school, as a universalist service, is one of the few statutory agencies from which they could derive support in settling in to their new lives. However, while there is some evidence of good practice, the level of support for refugee children varies widely and, in many areas, leaves much to be desired, from being offered a school, to the level of curricular and pastoral support given within schools. Some of these difficulties are discussed, and illustrated in the children's stories below. The first of these concerns finding a school place for a refugee child.

Waiting for a school: Humdi's story

> Humdi, a Somali boy, was 13 years old when he arrived in Britain with his mother and three younger brothers, after a harrowing flight to safety. Not long after they had settled down, his brothers were found a school, but he had to stay at home, because a school place could not be found for him. For seven months he helped his mother around the house, and sometimes went to collect his brothers from school. He wanted to go to school too, and said it felt good when he finally did get a school place.

Humdi's experience is not an isolated one. There were other children in the study who reported long waits for a school place. Recent research conducted in south London indicates that newly arrived refugee children can wait up to eight months for a school place to be found (Health Action Zone, 2000). Recent Refugee Council (unpublished) research suggests that in 1999 there were around 2,000 refugee children without a school place.

The Audit Commission report *Another Country* (Audit Commission, 2000) notes that some schools resist accepting children of asylum seekers because they can't offer the necessary support, and/or are concerned that the new arrivals might adversely affect school league tables. This, again, reveals discrimination against refugee children, which is clearly contrary to Articles 2 and 28 of the Convention. Perhaps the decision of the Department for Education and Employment (July 2000), not to include refugee children's scores in school league tables will improve this situation.

Starting school was a difficult experience for most refugee children. Many had little previous formal schooling, or their previous schooling had been interrupted and many had little knowledge of English. Most were left feeling friendless and isolated in their new schools. Some of these experiences are described by Metin, a 14-year-old Kurdish boy from Turkey.

Metin's story

> I wanted to go to school, but my first day at school, I cried and I didn't want to go to school. I didn't make any friends, nothing. I didn't understand anything and I didn't have any friends. I thought I would understand the teacher, but I didn't. The teacher was talking about all those things, but I didn't understand them. And my face was red, I think. ... After some time, about a month, because I didn't understand anything, like English, and I couldn't write anything, they took me to a special class.

Many other children in the study had similar experiences. Acquiring competence in English was seen by most children as a crucial factor in their present lives, not only for education, but also for self-confidence and social interaction. However, curricular support provided was not always adequate, or was seen as unfairly administered, as demonstrated in the stories of two Somali girls, Ihlam and Samirah, below.

Ihlam's story

> [At primary school] I found ... like it was a little bit unfair, because there's these Turkish girls, ... they find a special teacher for them, but they didn't find no teacher for me. And she [the teacher] was not even Turkish, she couldn't understand Turkish. ... I said, "At least can I join them?" but they kept saying "No". I said, "Why?" but they ... tried to find this excuse, that there's no Somalian books and stuff ... it's better if you learn with a Somalian teacher. But I don't think so, because it's better if you learn with an English teacher, [because] after you have to speak with English [people], you know.

Samirah's story

> Samirah is a 13-year-old girl, who fled Somalia with her mother, after having being displaced within the country for some time. They moved from one African country to another for over three years, before arriving in Britain. Samirah had had no formal schooling before joining primary school in Britain at Year 5. She has had inadequate support at school, and now, starting Year 9 she says, "I can't spell ... and I can't read". She has scored 3 per cent at English at her mock exams, 13 per cent at Maths, and 13 per cent at Science. Her future prospects do not look good.

Overall, the study suggests that the right to education is not fully enjoyed by many refugee children. Since, as noted above, the school is crucial to the process of rehabilitation and integration of refugee children into our society, this finding has implications for Article 39 of the Convention.

Article 39: Promotion of physical and psychological recovery and social reintegration of child victims

Article 39 of the Convention requires States Parties to take "all appropriate measures" to promote the physical and psychological recovery and social reintegration of child victims of, among other things, armed conflict. The study included some children who had been badly injured in the war situations in their countries. For example, Mohammed, a Bosnian boy, aged 9 at the time, was medically evacuated to the UK in 1993. Mohammed's story provides both a stark example of what children could experience in times of war, as well as good support for physical recovery given a child victim of war.

Mohammed's story

> Mohammed was out riding his bike in the spring of 1993, when a bomb exploded a few metres in front of him, causing severe injuries to his face and right arm. The family left Sarajevo by army plane, and when they landed in the UK, were taken straight to a hospital in London, where they stayed for one month. Mohammed had to have extensive plastic surgery to his face and arm, but, unfortunately, his left eye, which was badly damaged, could not be saved, and he now has a glass eye. A Bosnian translator supported the family in hospital, and later played an important role in helping them settle in London and in sorting out housing difficulties they experienced. Sometime later Mohammed was honoured with the award of Child of Courage. He still required more surgery at the time he was interviewed in 1997.

The strong support provided to aid Mohammed's physical recovery is certainly to be commended. However, in the great majority of cases the effects of war are not always as apparent as in Mohammed's case, and it is here that particular attention requires to be paid to the needs of refugee children. The study suggests that for a refugee child, participation in a regular school life can provide a sense of normality, which can in itself be healing for them. As shown above, this support is not always available, or not available at the required level for many children. More particularly, the pastoral support offered refugee children can be of key importance in their rehabilitation, for experiences of war and dislocation could spill over into children's present lives and manifest themselves in different ways. All too often, however, the underlying reasons for a child's behaviour are not recognised, and a child may be penalised for what is seen as malingering or "bad behaviour". This is demonstrated in the stories of Sheikh, aged 14 years, who had been severely beaten by thugs for attempting to protect his neighbours in Somalia; and Kasim, also aged 14, who arrived in Britain as an unaccompanied minor.

On living with past injuries: Sheikh's story

> [T]hey [thugs] hit me with a gun! The gun never had any bullets, they just use it to hit my legs. Now I've a problem with my legs … they start to pain. When I came to this country I had to go to hospital to get an operation. … I have to take tablets now … Sometimes … in PE when we play football, I tell teacher, "I don't like to do football today because my leg it hurts". And the teacher say to me "Do it". … Sometimes they don't believe me, they just make me do it. … When the pain's there when I play football, some people … kick your leg and you might drop down with the pain.

On coping with family separation: Kasim's story

> I come to this country in 1994. It was my birthday [and] I was a bit upset because of my Mum. I didn't see her for years, for seven years. … She didn't come, I come with my aunt [herself a minor], my Dad's sister. … She growed me up. … I got two brothers, … they're in Holland. … My big sister, she's 16 no, 17 this year, and my two little sisters, 6 and 5, three sisters – they come later. My aunt, she is looking after us, she look after my little sisters. She take them to school …
>
> Still worried about my Mum. Can't do my homework … can't do nothing because I'm worried. When I walk [down] the street, I think about my Mum. … Sometimes I cry, you know that? … Last week at school, I was thinking about my Mum and I was crying in my head. And one boy hit my head. I was so angry and I got him back. That's how I almost get expelled.

The children's accounts speak for themselves. But as these accounts demonstrate, it is where the effects of war are less obvious that refugee children are being denied the support they need, and should be able to expect as a right under the Convention. Schools, in particular, will need to reassess the support they offer refugee children in this light, and also in light of the type of environment they provide for vulnerable children, as discussed below.

Article 19: Protection of the child from all forms of physical or mental violence, injury or abuse

Article 19 of the Convention requires States Parties to take "all appropriate legislative, administrative, social and educational measures" to protect the child from all forms of physical or mental violence, injury or abuse, while in the care of any person who has care of the child. This definition includes the school as person who has care of the child, and Article 19 therefore requires schools to take appropriate measures to protect children from all forms of violence, including bullying. As noted above, however, previous research has shown refugee children to be particularly vulnerable to (often racist) bullying in schools. Indeed, many children in this study reported being bullied at school, and many perceived that their schools do not take adequate action against bullies. Below, Radhika from Sri Lanka, and Fadil (aged 13 years) from Bosnia, tell of their experiences.

Radhika's story

> That first day, they don't sit with us. They like to feel that we are separate, us two. They don't talk to us, no-one. My sister and me were just talking our language. ... There was one girl, she taking us to the coat room where we had to leave our coats. ... She said, like, "You can't talk English". ... She was like hitting us with her foot, kicking us.

Fadil's story

> There's some nasty kids to Bosnians, yeah, they just swear at us when they saw us, they bully. All big kids, ... nasty to Bosnians. ... Sometimes they hurt me ...

Here again, it seems clear that schools often fail to offer adequate protection to refugee children. This finding, taken in the light of Article 39, means that the rehabilitation of these children is often considerably impeded, rather than promoted. Overall, and generally in terms of human rights under the Convention, data presented in this chapter would suggest that these remain fully to be enjoyed by many refugee children.

Discussion and conclusions

This chapter has taken as its focus children's entitlements to basic human rights, listed in the UN Convention on the Rights of the Child, and set them against the realities of the recent experiences of young refugees in the UK. The conclusion is clear. The government's obligations to children required by the Convention are not being met in relation to refugee children. As Freeman (1995) has pointed out, the considerable disparity between the Convention and UK legislation is a major factor in allowing this to occur (see also chapter 5). For example, the best interests of the child have not been acknowledged in successive Education Acts; and housing legislation contains no "best interests" principle, so refugee children can continue to be housed in bed and breakfast accommodation. Similarly, whilst Section 17 of the 1989 Children Act requires social services departments to "safeguard and promote the welfare of children within their area who are in need", in practice interpretation of the phrase "in need" has been left to local authorities. This has led Freeman, among others, to call for the incorporation of the Convention into English law. However, under the recent Immigration and Asylum Act (1999), the Secretary of State must offer, and if the offer is accepted, must provide or arrange for the provision of "adequate accommodation" and "essential living needs" (Section 122 (3) and (4)) of children of destitute asylum-seekers. But the Refugee Council comments that the support system envisaged under this Act "will damage children's welfare and development and ... will breach both the letter and the spirit of the UN Convention on the Rights of the Child" (Refugee Council, 2000).

The recent Human Rights Act (1998) upholds rights such as freedom from torture, inhuman or degrading treatment; the right to respect for private and family life; and the right not to be discriminated in the enjoyment of these rights, discussed in this chapter in relation to the UN Convention. It remains to be seen if this Act will go further in protecting the needs and rights of refugee children. But as Drew (2000) points out, the Human Rights Act, and the European Convention on Human Rights on which it is based, were not conceived as a charter for children, so do not make reference to the best interests of the child as being a primary or paramount consideration in decisions affecting children (see chapter 6). Drew remains hopeful that since this principle appears in the UN Convention as well as the Children Act 1989, it may have some effect in issues affecting children.

The UK government's reservation on immigration and nationality issues and the effect of this on refugee children continues to be a matter of grave concern. The Refugee Council's comments on the Immigration and Asylum Act (1999) were noted above. Additionally, the Immigration and Asylum Act, in Section 122 (5), *inter alia*, restricts Section 17 of the Children Act (1989), so that local authorities may not provide asylum-seeker families with accommodation or any essential living needs while the Secretary of State is providing or arranging to provide them with such assistance. In effect, if asylum-seekers do not accept accommodation offered under the new dispersal system in the Immigration and Asylum Act, they cannot be offered other accommodation and support calling upon Section 17 of the Children Act. Anecdotal evidence suggests that many asylum-seekers are refusing to be dispersed, and are now living in destitution. This has prompted the launch of a campaign by a major children's charity for the Rights of Children Seeking Asylum, whilst commenting that immigration policy is being created at the expense of children's needs. In light of this and other evidence presented in this chapter, there is a pressing need for the government to consider the welfare of refugee children, and fulfil their human rights obligations to them, as a State Party to the UN Convention on the Rights of the Child.

Acknowledgements

I would like to thank the ESRC for funding the study (award nos L129251009 and R000222952), and very particularly the children who shared their experiences and thoughts with us. I also acknowledge the contributions of the other project team members, Itohan Egharevba, Research Officer, and Professor Peter Moss, Adviser, both from the Thomas Coram Research Unit; and Matthew Grenier, Consultant, from the Refugee Council. I am also grateful for the valued advice and support provided to the project by members of the Advisory Committee.

An article focusing on Articles 27, 28 and 29 of the UN Convention on the Rights of the Child and entitled "The Right to Education and an Adequate Standard of Living: Refugee Children in the UK" was published by the author in a special edition of *The International Journal of Children's Rights* (Vol. 8, no. 3). I would like to thank the journal's editor-in-chief for kind permission to use material from that article in this chapter. I am also grateful to voluntary sector colleagues working in the area of children's rights, in particular Kieran Breen and Anjana Bahl, for sharing their experiences in this field with me.

Notes

1   The children's accounts of their experiences have been edited, with their consent, to remove identifying features, and, where possible, children were consulted in the selection of their own pseudonyms.

References

Act of Parliament (1999) *Immigration and Asylum Act*
Act of Parliament (1998) *Human Rights Act*
Act of Parliament (1989) *The Children Act*
Audit Commission (2000) *Another Country: Implementing Dispersal under the Immigration and Asylum Act*, London: Audit Commission
Blackledge, A. (ed.) (1994) *Teaching Bilingual Children*, Stoke-on-Trent: Trentham Books
CRC (Eighth Session) Committee on the Rights of the Child, CRC/C/SR.204–206
Drew, S. (2000) *Children and the Human Rights Act*, London: Save the Children
Elbedour, S., ten Bensel, R. and Bastien, D.T. (1993) "Ecological Integrated Model of Children of War: individual and social psychology" in *Child Abuse and Neglect*, Vol. 17, pp. 805–819
Franklin, B. (1995) "The case for children's rights: a progress report" in Bob Franklin (ed.) *The Handbook of Children's Rights; Comparative Policy and Practice*, London: Routledge
Freeman, M. (1995) "Children's rights in a land of rites" in Bob Franklin (ed.) *The Handbook of Children's Rights; Comparative Policy and Practice*, London: Routledge
Further Education Unit (1994) *Refugee Education and Training*, London: FEU
Health Action Zone (2000) *The Needs of Young Refugees in Lambeth, Southwark and Lewisham*, London: Community Health South London/NHS
Melzak, S. and Warner, R. (1992) *The Integration of Refugee Children in Schools*, London: Minority Rights Group

Refugee Council (2000) "The Immigration and Asylum Act 1999", *Briefing*, London: The Refugee Council (mimeo)

Rutter, J. (1994) *Refugee Children in the Classroom*, Stoke-on-Trent: Trentham Books

Rutter, J. and Candappa, M. (1998) *"Why do they have to Fight?" Refugee Children's Stories from Bosnia, Kurdistan, Somalia and Sri Lanka*, London: The Refugee Council

UN (1989) *Convention on the Rights of the Child*, United Nations General Assembly

Part IV

Children's rights

Listening to children and
young people's voices

14 Minor rights and major concerns

The views of young people in care

Monica Barry

Introduction

Two important concepts embodied within recent Children's Acts in the UK have been informed by the UN Convention on the Rights of the Child: namely, the right to protection and the right to participation for children and young people. Protection includes safety from neglect, abuse, discrimination and exploitation, and participation includes giving children and young people a voice and the opportunity to participate in decisions which affect them.

Before introducing major legislation in 1995 which combined private and public childcare law provision in a unified Act, Scotland had enjoyed the benefit of hindsight and a lengthy period of consultation and reflection following both the Children Act 1989 in England and Wales and the ratification by the UK government in 1991 of the UN Convention on the Rights of the Child. Consequently, the Children (Scotland) Act 1995 was able to incorporate, if not extend, key principles of the UN Convention in various ways, namely, by stating in certain sections of the Act that:

- children's welfare is paramount in all decisions affecting them;
- attention must be given to children's views subject to age and maturity;
- state intervention must be limited unless in the child's best interests; and
- attention must be given to children's religion, ethnicity, culture and language.

The principles of protection and participation should have benefited, at least in theory, from this hindsight and as a result become strengthened in Scotland compared to other parts of the UK. However, in practice, research reveals that both the Children (Scotland) Act and the UN Convention are not necessarily being implemented in the interests of children and young people (Triseliotis *et al.*, 1995; Department of Health, 1999; Tisdall, 1997), and this chapter explores the contradictions between protection and participation based on the views of young people themselves.

The Scottish Act seems to contain more exceptions to the principle of participation for certain groups of children than its other UK counterparts, and Tisdall (1997: 122) argues that "Scotland may not only have more fora where children's rights can be ignored, but these fora may also be able to do so in a wider range of circumstances". Cases in point are the sections of the Act relating to the participation of children looked after by the local authority. There are instances within the Act where the views of looked-after children and young people are not given the attention emphasised in both the UN Convention (Articles 3 and 12) and in the principle of "paramouncy" of the child's welfare within the Act itself (ibid.).

Children tend to be taken into local authority care for their own protection, either from neglect, exploitation or abuse, or because they are out of control. However, there has been increasing concern in recent years about the extent and quality of protection given to young people in care[1] (see, for example, Marshall *et al.*, 1999; Barry, 2001a). In Scotland, this concern led to the recent development of care standards which inform and influence the way that children and young people are treated in care, and the protection and dignity afforded them within the care environment (Scottish Executive, 2000).

Young people in or leaving care in Scotland were interviewed as part of a wider research project undertaken by Save the Children with funding from the Joseph Rowntree Foundation, drawing samples of young people from within the four countries of the UK. A total of 108 young people throughout the UK were asked about their experiences and views of growing up, their aspirations for the future and the supports and obstacles they experienced as they approached adulthood. Because of the emphasis on competence and responsibility as a precursor to adulthood (see, for example, Franklin, 1986), Save the Children was keen to elicit the views of young people who had assumed a level of responsibility as children that adults might consider beyond their years and inappropriate in childhood. Four specific groups of young people were identified, namely, those who had been involved as active participants in youth organisations as children (in North East England); young mothers (in Northern Ireland); care leavers (in Scotland) and young people who had worked while still at school (in Wales and South West England). The findings from the four groups were written up separately (Barry, 2001a; Horgan, 2001; Nevison, 2001; Vulliamy, 2001) and a fifth publication explored the transitional experiences of the four groups combined (Barry, 2001b).

The focus of this chapter is on the views of the sub-sample in Scotland, most of whom had been in care since the UK's ratification of the UN Convention and/or the implementation of the Children (Scotland) Act 1995. The Scottish study consisted of thirty-four young people aged 15–25 who were contacted mainly through social work departments in two geographical areas. Fourteen of these young people were still in residential units or foster care, and the remaining twenty had left care. There was an even mix of male and female respondents and the average number of years spent in care was seven while the average age that they entered care was just under 10 years old. The respondents were encouraged to identify and recount key issues which affected them as they grew up and many cited issues such as relationships, family, social work or school. Within these themes, they were asked about the skills they had acquired in the past, what skills they regretted not having had, what helped and hindered them, and what their goals were for the future.

This chapter focuses on their experience of family life prior to being taken into care as well as on their views about growing up in care.[2] It is argued that there is a mismatch between protection and participation for many of these children and young people as a result of moves between family and care, their limited rights as children and their restricted voice. The research described below suggests that family life offered little protection for these children, and in fact, their high level of competence and responsibility within the family implied quite the opposite, that these children more often protected their parents than *vice versa*. Within the care system, on the other hand, protection was certainly evident if the concept of protection is taken to mean a removal or denial of responsibility for children and young people as well as being given a place of safety. However, it is argued that a focus on a form of protection which denies children and young people responsibility in care significantly affects their ability to develop competencies in preparation for adulthood and to practise these through meaningful participation in matters affecting them as children.

Levels of protection prior to entering care

It has been well documented (Fisher *et al.*, 1986; Department of Health, 1999; NCH, 1999) that the vast majority of children in care come from backgrounds of disadvantage, from reconstituted (containing a step-parent to one or more of the children) or single-parent families, with low parental supervision and educational under-achievement. This sample in Scotland seemed on the whole to reflect those statistics. Those who had experienced family life prior to entering care had come from reconstituted family backgrounds. Few gained any formal qualifications at school. Of the total sample of 34 respondents, 26 suggested that they had entered care because their families eventually could not cope with them, either through mental or physical illness of a parent or because as children they were not receiving, or responding appropriately to, parental supervision. The remaining eight respondents suggested that they entered care specifically because of neglect or abuse of either themselves or their siblings.

These statistics on the surface suggest that, because of these young people's vulnerable backgrounds, protection – as in a place of safety – was indeed of paramount importance when taking them into care. However, it seemed that their levels of competence and responsibility within the family were either played down or not acknowledged in the interests of protection once in care and this had major implications for their right to participation.

Caring for others

Receiving protection because of their status as children was not something these young people equated with childhood. On the contrary, as stated above, many suggested that they had been giving protection to others rather than receiving it themselves. A total of 20 of the 34 young people in the sample chose to talk about caring for other family members before being taken into care.[3] Some suggested that one or both of their parents could not cope on their own because of illness or drug/alcohol abuse and that the young people took on a caring role as a result (see chapter 12). These young people not only attended to the specific needs of parents but also to the more general needs of younger siblings:

> I had to do everything for [my mother] as well. I was cooking, change the bairns' nappies and get up and feed them during the night. They said [my younger brother] would never walk cos he was handicapped but we got him walking.
>
> (22-year-old male)

> I've learnt how to take care of myself and how to keep myself ... [from] the age of five really. ... I was still a child trying to do an adult's job. It was just an everyday occurrence to us. I'd get home from school ... and cook the dinner, do whatever, put on the washing ... and I would go down to the pub and sit in the pub until [my mother] was finished in the pub and then go home with her ... at the age of 9, 10 years old, I was going into the supermarket and doing a week's shopping for thirty pounds for a family of three.
>
> (19-year-old male)

Many saw such responsibility as being a normal and expected facet of childhood and family life, whether welcomed or not. There was, however, a somewhat pessimistic air of resignation overall about these young people's role in the family which tended to skew their image of childhood as one of survival in the face of adversity and consequently, they often had low expectations of others, especially "adults". Their experience of early responsibility was equated more with "feeling adult" and considering themselves older than their years: "I always felt I was more of an adult than a kid" (20-year-old male); "I think I've been an adult all my life ... I feel old" (19-year-old female); "I feel really, really old ... cos I've been through more than anybody else, but I just don't like being with people the same age as me" (15-year-old female).

Experience of abuse within the family

Several young people in this research mentioned physical or sexual abuse within the family prior to entering care, irrespective of whether or not this was the reason for their being referred to care. This abuse further undermined their image of the family and of childhood as being protective:

> I've still got all the mental issues in my head about the family. ... I still remember like stuff from before I was five, what my father done to my mother and stuff, the violence and stuff like. I remember seeing him trying to kill her one night and things like that. And like that all haunts me all the time. ... I don't really class myself as having parents or a parent. I class myself as having somebody who cared for me and had problems and couldn't do it properly.
>
> (19-year-old male)

> things weren't really too great with my mum and her boyfriend and he used to hit me. I just wanted to come into care. I just wanted to leave my mum and my sister. I just wanted the social workers to take me away.
>
> (16-year-old male)

> [My mother] was treating me like a slave, even when I was a wee laddie. At five year old I was making the dinner and getting the coal in ... on the odd chance I did get to go out and muck about, they would shout down, can I make them a cup of tea. They'd come to the door, shout ... and I'd make them a cup of tea. [What would have happened if you didn't do it?] I'd get battered.
>
> (20-year-old male)

The apparent lack of support from significant adults following disclosure of physical or sexual abuse was also a major issue for them. Such adults mainly comprised other family members, the police and social workers:

> the way social work handled it. It was all swept under the carpet ... they never got anything done about [the abuse]. They sent a policewoman here and she didn't believe me at all and she made it quite clear from the start that she was interrogating me.
>
> (16-year-old female)

> I was put into a long term foster placement where the foster mother abused me. I had stitches in my head, stitches in my arm. I tried everything to get out the foster home and the police wouldn't believe me. The social worker wouldn't believe me. I was there for six years. ... [What did the social worker say when you said you were being abused?] "Don't tell lies".
>
> (19-year-old male)

Competencies in childhood

With the level of responsibility many were taking on as children, coupled with the risk or presence of abuse and exploitation, many of the respondents had developed skills and strategies for survival both within the family and with other people. Their competencies were gained more by default than design and were self-taught rather than learnt positively from others. The skills they developed as children were, however, more practical than emotional – for example, cooking, parenting and housekeeping skills rather than assertiveness or communication skills. These latter skills seemed to develop more with maturity and experience and, on reflection, many regretted not having had such skills as children – the skills and confidence to voice their concerns in a constructive way about the lack of attention being paid to their own needs and wishes:

> rather than say anything was wrong, I would just sit there and keep my mouth shut and not say a word which – I think I would rather have spoken out when I was younger than to speak out now.
>
> (23-year-old male)

> Yeah, assertiveness and confidence would have been a good one and like at that age I was sort of was like "I'll tell a few fibs here and there and they'll like me better" and all that. I did all that and it made things worse, you know.
>
> (19-year-old male)

> I would have liked to like not be silly and stupid and immature. I'm glad I'm sort of better at handling – like I'm better at handling things. ... I used to get so worked up if [the staff] like sort of keep me in my room and not let me out until I'd had a discussion ... and I used to get so worked up and I used to scream and I would end up [crying] at the end of it cos I wasn't getting my way.
>
> (15-year-old female)

This tendency to blame themselves for not being listened to or heard was prevalent amongst these young people. They viewed their predicament both within the family and within care as being of their own doing, or as being a natural facet of childhood. The competencies they developed to cope with this predicament were perhaps more appropriate to survival on a remote island than to "normal" family life and yet they had remarkable resilience in the face of often incessant adversity:

> you've got to put a brave face on. You've got to be strong because if you don't, everything will come down on top of you, you know ... you've just got to be positive and just keep thinking in your head "just get on

with it, just get on with it". Because if you let it all start ripping into you, well, wallop, it will take you right down.

(19-year-old female)

Protection versus participation in care

As suggested above, looking after other family members as well as themselves gave these young people a level of competence which seemed to be more highly developed than in other people their age and they were used to a certain level of autonomy within the family as a result. Those who entered care following unprecedented responsibilities within the family often found their competencies had become redundant as a consequence of the increased protection they received. Once in care, their level of responsibility and autonomy was often dramatically reduced as social workers, residential workers and foster carers took over the role of ensuring their care and protection.

Protection in care

Much of their diminished responsibility on entering care, and the concurrent feeling of protection and safety, was welcomed by the majority of young people in the sample, as a burden lifted from their shoulders, a safe haven from violence and a chance to relive their lost childhood:

> I went into care, started meeting new people and had a sort of a more stable house, you know. The first people [that] were sober and I had my dinners cooked for me. I didn't have to go in and cook my own dinner. I didn't have to do my washing. ... That was something I hadn't had for years, you know, a stable home, no violence and stuff.
>
> (19-year-old male)

> when I went into care, I had no fear of getting battered when I went to bed or when I came in from school.
>
> (20-year-old male)

This feeling of relief from responsibility or fear was often more acute for those entering residential rather than foster care – possibly because the foster family structure sometimes reminded them of their negative image of their own family. In residential units, however, they often enjoyed the feeling of being in "a large family" with other young people of similar age and experience and many felt extreme relief at being referred into residential care from often hostile and lonely family backgrounds:

this is like my home. ... All the staff in here are like all my parents. Even the kids.. I do have my friends ... we do get a lot of care, we do get a lot of help if we need it and you do get a lot of support.

(15-year-old male)

Being put in care is actually one of the best things that has happened, honestly, because like if I hadn't been put in care, it probably would have been me ... getting hit by my mum's boyfriend.

(16-year-old female)

On the other hand, foster care was slightly different because some of these young people saw it as a poor replica of their own ideal of family, where their own parents should have been taking care of them:

I think foster care is too much for a child to handle for the simple fact there's a female and a male and it's just like your mum and dad and you feel they're ... taking over your mum and dad's role.

(21-year-old female)

Often they were the only child in the foster family with possibly older foster parents looking after them. Often also, they had been removed from a community they knew well to one in which they were an incomer with the resultant potential for bullying at school and a feeling of isolation and discrimination. Some, who went into foster care from violent family backgrounds, mentioned experiencing further violence within their foster families. Often for these young people, such feelings of insecurity went against the ethos of the care system as being one of protection.

Moves between placements, which tended to happen more as a result of breakdown of foster rather than residential placements, and consequent moves between schools, only served to exacerbate these forces of social exclusion and vulnerability. Many talked of having had several moves of placement which affected their friendships, their education, their ability to trust others and their overall feeling of stability and safety:

the moving was confusing. I've been in that many houses, you get lost. ... I don't know. I didn't trust anybody. I think that's just cos anytime I have trusted somebody, they've always turned their back on me. Nobody's been around for us. They've never stayed around long enough.

(16-year-old female)

The moving about [was unhelpful] because like, I'd eventually make a friend in one house and we'd have to move. Then after a couple of [moves] I gave up. I thought I'll not make any friends, I'll just be by myself. [When did you think that?]. The age of 7.

(20-year-old male)

I felt I was different to everybody else basically. ... It's hard. ... I had to go into a brand new school, with brand new people and explain to them why I had just appeared out of the middle of nowhere.

(23-year-old male)

Participation in care

As mentioned earlier, the majority entered care because of a lack of appropriate or adequate parental care or supervision. However, there tended to be little negotiation with, or participation of, these children in the process of decision-making about going into care and for many this was a particularly harrowing time in their lives:

The social worker said to me "we're just taking you away for a couple of nights so your mother can have a rest and have a break and you'll be back in a few days" and that was five years ago, six years ago ... I knew as soon as the social worker said to me, I knew she was lying at the time, I just knew.

(16-year-old male)

I remember wakening up and the two policemen being there and then [the social worker] came in ... and then my mother was brought back from the pub, blazing, screaming and shouting. ... I was always worried cos like I'd looked after my little sister and I'd been told what could happen and I always thought that if that had happened, me and my sister would be split up and I'd never see my sister again. ... That was quite a sort of worry.

(19-year-old male)

Many also resented the loss of autonomy and responsibility that they had previously within the family and saw the care system as treating them more as "incompetent" children than as people with existing responsibilities and competencies:

I just want them to listen to me. I'm at the stage where, you know, I think I'm an adult and ... they should be listening to me. But they still treat me like a child.

(16-year-old female)

We never got to make the decisions. We were always just told what was happening ... it was always [the care staff] made the decision, they said what was right and they said what was wrong, but we never got to say.

(21-year-old female)

Having come from families where often they felt isolated and alone, and caring for relatives with little support, attention or protection, they were suddenly immersed in an environment which emphasised the care and protection of children *as* children. In so doing, adults may have inadvertently played down, undermined or denied existing competencies which the young people saw as giving them the "adult" qualities of self-determination and autonomy. Overall, these young people had a positive image of themselves as being mature and able to cope in difficult circumstances, irrespective of the lack of praise or encouragement from adults in their lives. Those who had experienced responsibility as children saw themselves as more mature than their years and certainly more "adult" than most adults would give them credit for: "I mean, if you're a 16-year-old and you think you're mature and you think you can handle yourself, then you should be given a chance, not to be told every five minutes" (15-year-old male).

Being taken into care was a traumatic experience for some, as they were entering an unknown world with little if any preparation for this change. It seemed that there was little attempt by professional workers to ensure continuity for the young person between the two worlds of family and care. Some suggested that on entering care, no assessment was done of their level of competency and responsibility within the family prior to that time; there was little opportunity to reflect back on the circumstances and experiences that may have triggered their referral into care; and a lack of proactive support in resolving the problems of the past. This resulted in some feeling deskilled, anxious about what or who they had left behind and unable to come to terms with the turn of events which had removed them from the family:

> they should take into consideration what you've been through before you go into the children's home but the children's home is more of an issue of what's going on about you then, but it should be what's going on about you before you've went into the children's home ... then and before that. But they don't ... there should have been a wee bit more communication between a single child and a member of staff. I mean, we had care workers, like a care worker, but ... if I went to them and said "I want to go and see my mum and my dad, I'm really, really missing them", they like "well you can't go home" and that was final. There was no explanation. "You can't go home because. You're not going home". [Did you ever phone your social worker to try and intervene?]. Oh aye. ... You'd get no response. No response whatsoever. I mean, I got more response off the care staff than I did with the social work department.
>
> (21-year-old female)

Intervention versus participation

Within the care system, these young people experienced often their first direct experience of adults other than their immediate family and their first taste of professional intervention in their personal lives. What these young people seemed to want most from adults was a listening ear, someone who they could talk to about problems in their lives, who would genuinely listen and possibly advise them. They would also have benefited from encouragement and support to develop and practice the competencies needed for independence and adulthood (in terms of communication, confidence, assertiveness and practical skills). Some found these qualities in certain workers, but all too often these workers moved to other jobs, or alternatively the young person moved to another placement, and rarely was there consistency and continuity within and between staff teams, in terms of social workers, residential workers and foster carers: "each time I moved I got a brand new social worker ... starting from scratch again with somebody else and ... they've got to get to know you first before they can really help" (23-year-old male).

> [It was difficult] not knowing where I would be ... and not knowing who's going to be in the house the next morning. Not knowing how long you would be there for, and how long you would be at that school for.
>
> (19-year-old male)

Despite the fact that listening skills are seen as fundamental to the ethos of social work, the views and experiences of these young people contrasted strongly with this ideal. The most common fault levelled at social workers was their seeming *inability* to listen and involve young people in planning and decision-making. Social workers were singled out as being particularly unhelpful in this respect, mainly because they were seen as holding the power and the responsibility for children and young people in care:

> Social workers are a pain. That's what I think, just a pain. They haven't got a clue. They come in, they sit down, they even try and make choices for you. ... They try and say "well, foster care is the best for you". How do they know that?
>
> (15-year-old male)

> I think [social workers] should listen to you, listen to who they're dealing with instead of taking everything on themselves. ... Listen to the other point of view instead of listening to their own all the time, cos that's what social workers do, is listen to themselves. They think they know better.
>
> (20-year-old female)

However, children and young people involved in the care system are unlikely to know about the hierarchy of decision-making processes which involve social workers, panel members and parents in often complex negotiations with or for the child in his/her best interests. However, equally, these young people rarely knew or could exercise their right to participate in, or voice their concerns about, decisions relating to their best interests. The lack of participation in decisions about moving placements, for example, was of particular concern to many, resulting in feelings of being either kept in the dark or openly deceived by their social workers: "It was basically pack your bags and go" (16-year-old male); "I didn't know I was moving, Social Work just said we were going on holiday for a wee while" (15-year-old female).

Whilst many regretted not being given more autonomy when in care, they also regretted not having more support on leaving care. This may sound contradictory, but it would seem that although these young people had developed competencies as children which helped them to manage house-keeping and look after relatives when they were younger, they did not feel, on reflection, that these skills were adequate or well enough developed for living independently of professionals or parents in the future. Whilst being in care was seen as comforting for many following earlier traumatic family experiences, often the protection given to them in care divested them of certain competencies or responsibilities and gave them a false sense of security and support which quickly evaporated on leaving care: "you've got eight staff about you every day and every night and then all of a sudden you've got no one" (21-year-old female); "I would have liked to learn a wee bit more with coming out into the big wide world. Knowing it's going to be hard … instead of it all just hitting me in the face at once" (21-year-old female).

> You actually need something between the age of 16 and 18 if you leave care at 16. You need people to come in once a week and have a cup of tea with you, make sure you're budgeting, make sure you're feeding yourself, not spending it on drugs, you know. Doing your washing and all that. … I didn't know about the dole. I didn't know I could go and sign on at sixteen years old. … I didn't know nothing about that. … So I had no money.
>
> (19-year-old male)

Throughcare and aftercare services and training for young people in care are becoming more of a focal point for social services departments, but these young people suggested it was too little too late. They would have wanted more practical skills training for adulthood (such as housekeeping, budgeting, dealing with benefits agencies, etc.) at an earlier age in care rather than six to twelve months prior to leaving care. They would also have preferred greater responsibility within care according to their past experiences of family life and their increasing levels of maturity and self-determination. Only through participating in planning and decision-making and taking on responsibility, with support, could these young people be able to practise and build on the competencies they had learnt in the past.

Balancing rights to protection and participation

As children within their families, the majority of this sample had competencies which went unrecognised by adults but growing up in care left many feeling ill-prepared for the responsibilities of adulthood. There was little continuity of support and few opportunities to exercise rights which would ensure that these young people had as smooth a transition to adulthood as possible. As Tisdall (1997: 150) points out: "Children cannot automatically be expected to take on adult responsibilities when they reach legal majority, if they have been prevented from developing and practising these skills before then."

These young people seemed particularly vulnerable in terms of consistency of care, protection and participation throughout their childhood. They tended to experience, on the one hand, a lack of protection from the family and, on the other hand, protection in care which was inappropriate to their maturity and experience. In so doing, they were often denied the right to participate in planning and decision-making not only during their childhood but also in preparation for adulthood.

The level of responsibility that some of these young people had as children was only apparent to them once they entered the care system and were divested of some of that burden. Some implied that they did not want to go into care because they were concerned about the health or safety of other family members left behind. Others suggested in retrospect that if more support from health or social services had been available, they would not have needed to go into care in the first place, but could have jointly managed the situation at home with the help of outside agencies. These concerns were rarely voiced at the time, given many of these young people's scepticism about their own communication skills when they were younger and the listening skills of those closest to them. However, the majority of the sample knew little about their right to protection and participation, and hence tended to blame themselves for their own predicament. Nevertheless, these findings highlight the importance of professionals and parents having the skills to listen to and hear what young people need and want and the will to work in partnership with them to achieve young people's rights to full protection and participation.

Given the emphasis in both the UN Convention on the Rights of the Child and the Children (Scotland) Act 1995 on protection as well as participation of children and young people, it is important to ensure that these two elements are not mutually exclusive, but interdependent and developed in parallel. In the research study described in this chapter, the mismatch between protection and participation was significant to these young people. Within the family, prior to being taken into care, young people reported that there was virtually no protection and yet a high level of responsibility. However, within the care system, there was seen to be too much protection at the expense of their right to participation. This roller-coaster ride between protection and participation and between family and care may only serve to damage the longer-term social and emotional development of children and young people.

In conclusion, this chapter has suggested that while legislation is in place for the appropriate protection and participation of children and young people, there is still a need for closer and more trusting relationships between professionals and children and young people in order to ensure not only the latter's protection but also to encourage their full participation in matters relating to their welfare and development. Young people can only effectively participate through acquiring communication and assertiveness skills and developing self-confidence, as well as receiving adequate information and an open response from professionals. Whilst they need to feel adequately protected from exploitation, abuse, neglect and discrimination by the people closest to them, children and young people nevertheless have the right and the capacity to contribute to processes of decision-making which affect their welfare. The concept of participation for children and young people must therefore be given equal and parallel attention to the concept of protection.

In order for this to happen, the findings from this research would suggest that the right to protection for all children and young people needs not only to be ensured in practice as well as in legislation, but also to be informed by children and young people's own assessment of their competencies, wishes and needs. Equally, having secured the right to appropriate protection, children and young people should be encouraged to exercise their right to participate in decisions about their welfare based on their own experiences and competencies. However, their rights to protection and participation can only be guaranteed if professionals and parents, with adequate resources and training, meet their legal obligations to work in the best interests of children and to consult with them on matters relating to their welfare. There is an urgent need to acknowledge the rights as well as the needs of children and young people, if the UN Convention and the Children (Scotland) Act 1995 are to become significant watersheds in the history of children's rights in the UK.

Notes

1   Although the official terminology has changed from young people in "care" to young people "looked after", the majority of young people in care themselves feel more comfortable and familiar with the old terminology, which is used throughout this chapter.
2   It has not been possible to include a discussion here of the involvement of these young people with the Children's Hearings system in Scotland as a result of being admitted to care. For this, see Hallett and Murray (1998).
3   Because of the qualitative nature of the research, where the narrative was left very much in the hands of the respondent, it was not possible to obtain more quantitative data on the whole sample systematically, but only for those choosing to mention certain aspects of their lives. Much of the data cannot therefore be easily numerated and it should be borne in mind that numbers given may, as a result, be an under-estimate of the overall incidence of any given finding.

References

Barry, M. (2001a) *A Sense of Purpose: Young care leavers' views and experiences of growing up*, London: Save the Children/Joseph Rowntree Foundation

—— (2001b) *Challenging Transitions: Young people's views and experiences of growing up*, London: Save the Children

Department of Health (1999) *The United Nations Convention on the Rights of the Child*, second report by the United Kingdom, August 1999, London: The Stationery Office

Fisher, M., March, P., Philips, D. and Sainsbury, E. (1986) *In and Out of Care: The Experiences of Children, Parents and Social Workers*, London: BT Batsford

Franklin, B. (1986) *The Rights of Children*, Oxford: Basil Blackwell

Hallett, C. and Murray, C. (1998) *The Evaluation of Children's Hearings in Scotland, Volume 1: Deciding in Children's Interests*, Edinburgh: The Scottish Office Central Research Unit

Horgan, G. (2001) *A Sense of Purpose: Young mothers' views and experiences of growing up*, London: Save the Children

Marshall, K., Jamieson, C. and Finlayson, A. (1999) *Edinburgh's Children: The Report of the Edinburgh Inquiry into Abuse and Protection of Children in Care*, Edinburgh: City of Edinburgh Council

NCH (1999) *Factfile 2000*, London: NCH Action for Children

Nevison, C. (2001) *A Sense of Purpose: Young participators' views and experiences of growing up*, London: Save the Children

Scottish Executive (1999) *Information on Children Looked After as at 31st March, 1999*. Online. *http://www.scotland.gov.uk/library2/kd01/info-01.htm*

Scottish Executive (2001) *Draft National Care Standards: Second Tranche: A Consultation Paper*, April, Edinburgh: The Scottish Executive

Tisdall, E.K.M. (1997) *The Children (Scotland) Act 1995: Developing Policy and Law for Scotland's Children*, Edinburgh: The Stationery Office

Triseliotis, J.P., Borland, M., Hill, M. and Lambert, L. (1995) *Teenagers and the Social Work Services*, London: The Stationery Office

Vulliamy, C. (2001) *A Sense of Purpose: Young workers' views and experiences of growing up*, London: Save the Children

15 Children's Express

A voice for young people in an adult world

Stephanie Williams

The feud between rival loyalist paramilitary groups in Protestant Belfast is putting pressure on children to choose sides. Wrestling has become the latest playground craze. Twelve years old and pregnant: how does it really feel? Mobile phones: should they be banned at school? What is it like to be young and gay and living in Northern Ireland? Who are you going to ask about what is really going on in kids' lives, if not children themselves? Children's Express is charity with a two-fold mission: to give young people a voice, to get their views into arenas where they can actually influence policy-makers and opinion formers, so that adults will begin to believe that children can make a vital contribution to their lives. It operates like a news agency, delivering articles and broadcasts produced by teams of young people aged 8–18 to mainstream national, regional and local media.

In the process Children's Express (CE) is also training young people, helping them to develop skills and levels of confidence which allow them to achieve things – like being taken seriously by a newspaper, magazine or broadcaster – that they never believed might be possible.

Children's Express's mission is to give young people the power and means to express themselves publicly on vital issues that affect them, and in the process to raise their self-esteem and develop their potential. In its work it aims to:

- ensure that children have the skills and support to enable them to express their views on issues that concern them
- bring these concerns to the attention of policy-makers and opinion formers
- encourage children's development as good citizens
- motivate adults to take an interest in children's issues
- provide a supportive and nurturing environment
- work on a national basis
- become a recognised and respected source of objective view on youth issues

Children's Express began operations in New York in 1975. The brain-child of a former Wall Street lawyer and business entrepreneur, Robert Clampitt believed passionately that what children thought and said *did* matter. He wanted to create a forum for children to report on the news, and set up a monthly magazine "by children, for children". It is illustrative of the way children defy adult expectations that when Clampitt took a team of CE reporters to the 1976 Democratic Convention to interview people like the hot-dog vendors and balloon sellers to find out what it is like to prepare for so many people in Madison Square Gardens, the team quickly realised that the real issue facing the press was who was going to be Vice President. No one paid any attention to 12-year-old Gilbert Giles when he got into a lift with a group of Jimmy Carter's senior aides. CE was transformed overnight when kids from the magazine scooped the world's press on Carter's choice of Walter Mondale as his running mate at the convention. From then on, news and comment by Children's Express was delivered into adult media.

The programme was soon breaking new ground in journalism, examining issues of importance to children and young people and bringing them to national attention. In 1982 its columns were nominated for the Pulitzer Prize, and in 1983 UPI began three years of distributing the Children's Express column to newspapers across the US. It won Emmy and Peabody Awards in 1988 for coverage of the Presidential campaign. Children's Express news teams have covered the past seven Presidential elections, trav-elled on assignment across the US, and to a number of countries where children have been caught up in conflict – including, most recently, Bosnia. Currently, Children's Express has bureaux in Washington DC, New York and Marquette, Michigan. An independent programme "Y-Press" operates using Clampitt's principles in Indianapolis. In January 2001, a new bureau opened in Tokyo.

UK developments

Several UK agencies, including Community Service Volunteers and the "Who Cares?" Trust had been impressed by the work of Children's Express in the United States. But they lacked the resources to set up a London bureau. In August 1994, a group of volunteers decided to run a pilot in London to establish the feasibility of setting up a permanent UK operation. Thirty-one children, from the most impoverished areas of Tower Hamlets, Hackney and Islington, were recruited to take part in a six-week training programme. They were identified from over 100 applicants who had responded to posters in schools and youth groups in inner London. The sole basis of selection was enthusiasm.

For the first week, four "teen" editors were flown over from the New York bureau to train the British teams in research, story development, inter-viewing and editing. The stories the children chose to work on were tough: what it is like to be young and in detention, what life is like for a 15-year-old living on the streets, and how a teenager copes with pregnancy. The work resulted in a two-page spread in the *Guardian* (5 October 1994), a half-hour documentary commissioned by Channel Four television and tremendous enthusiasm among both adults and children who had taken part. In December 1994 Children's Express (UK) became registered as a charity.

Before long articles by teams of young people from the London bureau began to be published in the nation's papers with growing regularity. Meanwhile demand to replicate the programme began to build in other parts of the country. CE began expansion outside London in partnership with Save the Children Fund in Newcastle in 1996, and moved onto the creation of small "satellite" operations in a comprehensive school in Birmingham and a youth centre in Sheffield in 1998 funded by the Department of Education and Employment. Thanks to funding from the National Lottery Charities Board, a UK-wide strategy of training and satellite support began the process of implementation in late 1999. Children's Express now operates from six centres in the UK with full-time bureaux in London, Belfast, and Newcastle and part-time satellites in Sheffield, Birmingham and Plymouth. Further expansion is planned for a new satellite in Blackburn with Darwen in 2001, and a bureau in Scotland in 2002.

To date over 500 children have been trained to become young journalists at Children's Express, but hundreds more have been involved by being invited to tell their stories in interviews or say what they think on issues in round-table discussions. Meanwhile, CE has succeeded in publishing and broadcasting more than 350 stories, reaching millions of adults every year. Over the past five years, CE's media strategy has been based on developing a good relationship at the highest levels with national newspapers, radio and television companies, moving on to develop associations with the regional press and radio, and a variety of magazines. The aim was not only to build profile, but to demonstrate the quality of the work that the young people produce. The result has been the growth of an impressive portfolio of cuttings: CE articles have been published with most of the leading national titles (chiefly with *The Times, Guardian, Daily Telegraph, Daily Express* and *Observer*), and with publications such as the *Times Educational Supplement,* and newspapers local to bureaux and satellites: the *Highbury and Islington Express, Sheffield Star, Belfast Telegraph, The Newsletter, Irish Times, Plymouth Evening Herald, Birmingham Post, Newcastle Chronicle* and *Northwest Post.* Children's Express journalists have guest edited the *Architects' Journal* (3 October 1996) and the Local Government Association's millennium supplement of *Voice solo* on the next generation (November 1999) and travelled to Tanzania with Christian Aid and the Co-operative Bank to investigate third world debt (April 1999).

The next stage of development will focus on delivering more work to radio and television. CE journalists have already made numerous appearances on Radio 4's *Woman's Hour*, the *Today* programme and the World Service, as well as on Radio 5 Live and Greater London Radio. But as the technology of producing radio pieces becomes simpler and adult radio producers join the CE staff, this aspect of the work is expected to increase.

In television, Children's Express broke new ground in the UK with *Sex from 8–18*, three one-hour programmes for Channel 4 broadcast in June/July 2000. From late summer 1999, teams from London, Newcastle, Sheffield and Birmingham began the task of seeking out, preparing and interviewing ninety young people for three one-hour programmes on teenage sexuality for Channel 4. The interviews, straight to camera, formed a continuous theme throughout the series. The questions were simple and open; the answers disarmingly honest and frank: "The closest we've got to sex in school is like, don't sleep with other people's husbands and wives. That's really the closest we've got", said David, 10. "That was just the Ten Commandments, though", said Caroline, 10.

For many adults, the candour of the interviews gave them a poignant reminder of their own adolescence. The series was hailed as one of the most informative programmes ever to tackle the issue. It broke new ground by having young people interview one another on television on a serious issue and demonstrated the special insight and power achieved when young people are interviewed by their peers.

The third strand to CE's work in making children's voices heard in arenas where they can be expected to influence adult policy-makers is through the regular participation of teams on the platforms of conferences and seminars – reporting on their own investigations and the views of young people they have collected. These appearances can have a major impact on policy-making. CE teams were the first young people to deliver evidence to the Blair government's newly formed Social Exclusion Unit (SEU) in June 1998 – on children's experience of living on neglected housing estates. CE first became aware of the frightening realities of life for children on many estates through a round-table discussion on kids' relationship to TV and other aspects of their lives. "Room with a viewer" was published in the *Guardian* in the spring of that year. The piece began with the quote from one child: "It's like a horror movie outside, it's terrible. I spend almost the whole time in my bedroom watching TV." CE then launched an investigation into life for children on three of Britain's estates: two in London and one in Luton. The evidence was presented to the SEU and later formed the basis of a piece for the *Observer*. Six months later, CE teams met the SEU again to present evidence on teenage pregnancy.

A major milestone was marked by CE's own first public seminar on how the media stereotype young people ("KIDS THESE DAYS ... ", April 1998). The result of analysing a week's worth of newspaper cuttings containing references to children in September 1997, the seminar illustrated graphically how negatively young people are portrayed in the press. In July 1999, a CE team reported on how easy it was (or rather, was not) for a 15-year-old girl in a wheelchair to visit a variety of venues in Islington, north London to an audience of 450 at the Scottish Arts Council's conference on "Children,

Participation and the Arts". In spring 2000 teams from London and Birmingham presented research on young people's use of the Internet and their awareness of its dangers at "Kids Helping Kids" a conference at the House of Lords. This showed that when children have "got into trouble" on the Internet, their relationship with their parents has been crucial – and that if kids are to be safe using the web, parents have to make time to learn how to use it themselves. Follow-up articles were published in the *Times* and the *Birmingham Post*.

So how do we do it?

Currently Children's Express targets children aged 8 to 18 from areas of limited opportunity, in particular the most impoverished areas of inner cities – but the programme is open to all. Work takes place after school, at weekends and during the holidays. The basis of all the work CE does, whether in producing stories for publication or preparing for a conference presentation, is journalism. The children take responsibility not only for producing their stories, but the way the programme is run. The organisation exists to support the activities of the children to make sure that they have the resources, encouragement and advice they need.

Recruitment

Recruitment takes place through contacts with other voluntary organisations, schools and youth clubs. Generally young people from CE make a presentation about the programme and invite children to fill in an application form which asks why he/she would like to join Children's Express. A waiting list is also kept. Once a training programme has been scheduled those on the waiting list are approached in order of their place on the list – and the ages and genders needed to balance the programme. Optimal membership of CE bureaux has been found to be around 150 children. Satellites can work with up to thirty.

In London the bureau is located in Islington, north London. Two-thirds of children are from racial minorities; about a third come from single parent families. They come mainly from Hackney, Tower Hamlets, Newham and Islington. However, almost all London boroughs are represented, some children coming from as far away as Wandsworth, Walthamstow and Deptford. The mix of young people is exceptionally diverse.

In Newcastle-upon-Tyne, the CE bureau is run by Save the Children Fund on the Cowgate Estate in the northwest of the city. Here CE is helping to motivate those who are at risk of failing at, or already have been excluded from, school. The estate may be taken as a model of urban deprivation: surrounded by major roads three miles from the city centre, 69 per cent of children live in families where no-one is earning; 31 per cent in lone parent households; 84 per cent of families do not have a car. Almost all the children have to struggle to overcome the stigma of poverty and to succeed academically.

Most youth organisations working with young people in Belfast are not located in the city centre. Instead they tend to operate within specific Catholic or Protestant Communities or in areas that fall on the peace-line. Before setting up in Belfast in April 2000, widespread consultation was held with young people from all sectors of the community to determine where a bureau could be located and when it should be open so that children from all over the city could attend on their own, and feel safe doing so. The process identified certain areas they felt were neutral within the city centre and not affiliated to any particular community. CE is exceptional among youth organisations in locating its work within the city centre. Belfast CE members feel safe and not under threat. Key to our success is the fact that the issue of where young people come from, whether the Shankill or the Falls, is outwieghed by their interest in sharing issues that cut across all communities.

In Plymouth, Sheffield and Blackburn with Darwen, CE has worked with the local authorities to draw children from schools in Education Action Zones; in Birmingham, the satellite is currently located within a comprehensive school but there are plans to move it into the city centre when funding has been secured. Each satellite meets on one or two afternoons per week after school.

Peer training

Every child who joins Children's Express is required to go through a two to four day induction and training programme – facilitated by older, more experienced members. This is a key part of the programme: teenaged trainers are seen as role models and mentors and play a crucial role in encouraging young people's ownership of the whole ethos of Children's Express. "The trainers from London were cool, mental. You can look at them and think you want to be like them", reported one young person on feedback forms following a training week in Belfast in April 2000. "I look at myself as a role model for the younger members", said 16-year-old Gemma Burr from Newcastle. "I can show them the right way to go because I have experienced things they have yet to go through."

Subsequent training sessions are held to focus on acquiring specific skills (for example on holding meetings, research techniques, leading round-table discussions, and how to edit). But most is learnt "on the job".

Roles and responsibilities

The programme operates in two tiers. Younger children, aged 8 to 13, are reporters; editors are older and more experienced, aged 14 to 18. The ideal story team is five: three reporters and two editors. The team works together to research the story, develop the angle and questions. Key techniques used are brainstorming, focusing, deciding what they really want to know, determining criteria for questions and then ordering questions.

Reporters are responsible for coming up with story ideas, researching the topic or interviewee, writing questions, conducting the interview and discussing it with the teenage editors after the story is completed. Editors are responsible for making sure this process is delivered, working alongside reporters to suggest and review story ideas, establish angles, set up stories and schedule meetings and interviews, and helping reporters to research. They make sure all the equipment (tape recorders, tape, microphones and camera) is working and that the team gets to the interview on time. During the interview they take notes to discuss with the reporters later, and ask any follow-up questions. Following interviews, they debrief reporters and work with an adult editor to prepare the final story.

Every aspect of the story, from basic interview to impressions afterwards, is tape-recorded. Not only does this mean that the programme is open to all, regardless of academic ability and certain disabilities, but it ensures that CE has an accurate record of interviews and proceedings around the story.

Producing stories

The metaphor used at Children's Express for producing stories is the process of climbing a mountain. To get to the end of your journey – in CE's case a published article – you need to use the right tools and plan your route carefully. Here the processes of adult journalism have been broken down into a series of basic elements. Children's Express members have to go through many stages to get their story into print.

Story ideas

Children's Express members submit story ideas all the time, in response to what is happening in their lives. They meet monthly to brainstorm ideas and recommend stories to pursue. Children's Express also receives ideas from staff, outside organisations and commissions from publishers and broadcasters. All stories must have a legitimate youth angle.

Monthly newsletter

Sent to all Children's Express members, the monthly newsletter gives an overview of what has happened in the previous month, details of stories being set up in the following weeks and encourages members to sign up for stories that interest them.

The briefing

Once a story has been scheduled, members volunteer to create the standard CE news team: three to five reporters and two editors. The team is responsible for gathering background information (newspaper articles, press kits, internet research) on the story in hand. The story team comes together to discuss relevant issues surrounding their chosen story subject. With guidance from adult journalistic staff, members review the most appropriate approaches for a story. Possible interviews are discussed, then appropriate contacts made to set up interview times and locations. Questions are prepared.

Interview

Interviews are conducted by the whole team, either in person or over the phone. Reporters take turns asking the questions they have prepared, while editors address any follow-ups during the interview. All interviews are recorded onto tape. Editors take notes about the setting and manner in which the interviewee responds.

Debriefing

As soon as possible after an interview, the team gets together for a debriefing in a quiet place. Using their notes, the editors interview the team about the content of the interview (recreating the story), the setting, the interviewee's appearance and manner, and their own reactions to what was being said. This step is also recorded onto tape and ensures children's views are conveyed in the finished article.

Round-table discussions

The alternative source of information for a story is the round-table discussion, orchestrated by editors. Other reporters, editors and children from outside CE sit round a tape recorder to discuss a topic about which they have direct experience – for example, bullying, teen suicide, the use of drugs at schools, or being the child of gay parents. Where a range of views are sought, themes or a few open questions are used by editors to stimulate debate between around six young people. A round table is different from a series of mini-interviews because members develop an argument between them. It is also a valuable forum in which young people can explore their experiences and feelings in a supportive environment.

Transcribing

The tapes from the interviews, debriefings and round tables are transcribed by an adult. Electronic and printed copies of the transcript are returned to Children's Express, ready to be edited.

Editing

The final editing process pulls together all the strands that go together to make a Children's Express story. Background research and transcripts of interviews, debriefings and round tables are all scrutinised by members and newsroom staff. The most important points are highlighted in the transcripts and all relevant passages are joined together to make the finished article. The article is tailored to the publication to which it will be sent.

Published story

During the production of the story, adult staff will have been preparing to place the article with an appropriate newspaper or magazine. All members of the team who have worked on the story get a by-line – their names in print.

The journalistic process and its impact on child development

"All you need is interest and willingness to work and follow the rules. The most important keys to a good interview are curiosity, preparation and concentration." Thus the *How to do it guide* (Children's Express Foundation, New York 1992) on the role of reporters within the process. In addition to these qualities, teen editors need to possess team leadership, tact and diplomacy, planning and organisational skills. They have got to be aware of the different abilities and experiences of individual team members and able to communicate and support action on feedback from staff journalists. "Teen editors are the managers of Children's Express. They have broad responsibilities relating to every aspect of CE journalism, including training, research, reporter briefings, news team leadership, debriefings, editing, logistics and planning. They must set the example as role models and mentors to the reporters, while looking for advice and guidance from adult staff" (*How to do it guide,* Children's Express Foundation).

In order to operate the programme in a way that ensures that its young people have acquired the skills needed at each stage of the story process, CE is currently working to identify the developmental steps implicit, but not explicit, in the programme, and prioritise them in the order in which members generally need to gain the skills which support the process. Full progression by members through the programme is expected to improve other areas in which young people take responsibility within CE, notably governance. The distinction between reporters and editors will be retained but enhanced – ceasing to be an automatic progression as it is at present, and treated as a role to be earned.

A sample of some of the basic skills required in the delivery of the story process are given in Table 15.1.

New methods of guidance and training to ensure that all young people will develop these skills are to be developed over the coming year and incorporated into bureau practice.

Table 15.1

Ideas	Jobs	Skills and qualities
Reporters	Generate story ideas based on their own experiences, what they see in the world around them, and what they read, see or hear in the media	Imagination Awareness of environment Willingness to contribute
Editors	Help the story team select the best idea(s) from those available (satellites and smaller bureaux) Select the best ideas from those proposed by the reporters' board for inclusion in the bureau newsletter (larger bureaux)	Recognise the qualities that make a story idea achievable and saleable Respect and accommodate the differing interests of different age groups

Research	Jobs	Skills and qualities
Reporters	Reporters read research – editors help gather it Talk to people they know who might be able to help with the story Look out for useful information in newspapers etc. Study research materials and make notes of what they find out	Understand the importance of research in preparing a story Know what they are looking for Ability to distinguish between fact and comment
Editors	Work with adult editorial staff to find useful briefing material Work with story team to evaluate and make notes on useful material	Have ideas on where to gather research material Understand how to do, and guide, useful Internet research Distinguish between helpful and unhelpful research material Understand the need to make sure research is balanced Recognise when it may be necessary to re-evaluate the chosen angle, based on the research Motivate story team to focus on job

Briefing	Jobs	Skills and qualities
Reporters	Talk about what they've learned from the research Listen to what others have to say Have ideas about people to interview	Presenting and listening
Editors	Present main points of research Support and facilitate discussion of research by story team Make notes of key facts, figures and opinions	Chairing/facilitation of discussion Note taking

Table 15.1 continued

Questions	Jobs	Skills and qualities
Reporters	Turn the things they've learned – and the gaps in their knowledge, into 20 interview questions	Understand how to use research to write interview questions
		Understand the importance of the different kinds of interview questions
Editors	Collate question ideas from reporters, eliminating duplication Identify where question types (e.g. "Devil's Advocate") or subject areas have been missed out Allocate interview questions to team	Organisation and administration

Interviews	Jobs	Skills and qualities
Reporters	Ask questions clearly, and listen to the answers	Confidence in speaking
	Think of and ask follow-up questions	Listening
		Awareness of the team – don't talk over each other
		Politeness to interviewees
Editors	Take responsibility for team getting to the interview (with staff assistance)	Understand good interview technique and help team achieve it
	Take responsibility for having correct equipment, and for conduct of the interview	Understand how to achieve quality tape recordings
	Do not ask written questions – concentrate on answers, and asking any follow up questions that reporters miss	Concentration
	Thank interviewee and write them a thank you letter afterwards	Represent Children's Express positively to the public

Children's Express succeeds because its sources are closer to the ground

There is an inevitable tension between working with mixed teams of often-irresponsible young people and delivering high-quality copy, on deadline, into the nation's top media. But that is where its strength lies. There is a clear awareness among adult journalists that there is a youth agenda out there, and that they are not getting the stories and perspectives they need to attract young readers, viewers and listeners. More and more journalists are living in offices, talking on telephones, away from the realities of everyday living for many young people. For them, CE offers fresh angles, practical investigations which only young people can carry out and in depth interviews with vulnerable young people. CE can obtain the views of very young children – as well as provide rapid responses to breaking news. These approaches, serious, often tough, which draw attention to the realities of life for many of their peers make the best CE stories. Increasingly as the organisation grows bureaux and satellites work together on the same issues, bringing a regional perspective to bear on many investigations – again a valuable resource in the media world.

Over the past five years Children's Express has proved time and again that it can deliver copy that is ready to publish, on time. The key is in careful planning, and a close working relationship between adult staff and young members – who come to know each other very well. CE employs professional journalists who are in charge of any commissions undertaken for the media, discussing angles and the direction of stories in detail with editors beforehand – and then supporting the team to make sure the story is edited and delivered, to length, on time.

To editors, CE offers:

Fresh angles   Images of teenagers swearing at the headteacher and acting up to cameras filled column inches and TV screens throughout the autumn of 1996 as pupils at the Ridings School in Halifax were declared "unteachable". Children's Express felt that there had been much more going on than met the eye. Early in 1998, they spent a day winning the trust of pupils and talking to them about the media attention.

When "Would you put the Ridings on your CV?" was published in the *Times Educational Supplement* in April 1998 it revealed how the pupils felt they had been used and manipulated by the media who sacrificed balance in pursuit of sensation. The news editor was delighted with the originality of the piece and declared this was something she wanted more of on her pages.

In-depth interviews with vulnerable young people   "When Dad's behind Bars" was published in the *South London Press* in December 1999. A team of four reporters from the London bureau spoke to two teenage girls about how their lives had been changed, and were given graphic pictures of the terrible distress and tensions imprisonment of a parent causes a child. As Gemma Fitzpatrick, 16 said: "It was a shock to think your parent is capable of doing something so wrong they end up in prison." Poignantly they described how keeping in touch through brief public visits in prison was no substitute for the close relationships they had had at home, and that increasingly keeping in touch with their fathers was difficult for them.

A year earlier, 12-year-old Jenny Teague discovered she was Britain's youngest mum when journalists from the *Sun* arrived on her doorstep to tell her the news. Within days of her exposure by that paper, a full-scale media circus had developed. Nevertheless, Jenny believed that the one way she could hope to set her story straight was through the media. A CE team got to know her. Jenny trusted them not to misrepresent her. She and her mother were able to look at the copy before it was sent to the press.

Measures such as these mean young people are more prepared to talk to Children's Express and are more truthful about giving their answers. The assistant editor of the *Independent* cited "Prisoner of the press" as an exemplar of serious reporting of children's issues in the *Press Gazette.*

Gathering the views of very young children   Interviewing primary school children and their younger peers requires a great deal of patience and skill from the team. One of the biggest challenges is persuading youngsters that they are not being tested or that there are no right and wrong answers, but that their own opinions and experiences count. Children's Express can invest the time adult journalists don't have to ensure both good copy and a positive experience for interviewees. Testimony to this is the fact that Children's Express teams ran the monthly column "Learning Curves" in the *Times Educational Supplement* in various guises for two years.

Practical investigations   "Shopkeepers are bang out of order" for the *Highbury and Islington Express 1997* was put together by teams of kids working in twos and threes attempting to buy fireworks from shops and market stalls in Islington. Armed with a check list drawn up by the team they observed and recorded shopkeepers' reactions as children who were far too young to be sold fireworks legally proceeded to succeed – or not succeed – to do so. A similar story was published by the Belfast bureau in October 2000.

Only young people can do it

The power of Children's Express for the young people in the programme and those who read their articles, or see them deliver presentations is that every process at CE is based upon *a role for young people which only they can fulfil.* CE's young journalists and interviewers research and report on issues from a perspective *only they can offer.* They do a *real* job, which is recognised in the outside world by the sale of articles about real life in the real world. Training is carried out with real recruits. There is a degree of risk about the process: not everything works every time, interviews may not go well, an article may not be published. All of this supports young people in their transition from school to the workplace.

Monitoring and evaluation processes have found that participation in Children's Express:

* has an impact on developing potential: building confidence, self-esteem, leadership and responsibility;
* increases literacy and general knowledge and delivers basic skills;
* gives young people something to do which they enjoy. In Newcastle, the youth crime rate on the Cowgate Estate has dropped by 50 per cent. More than half of those in the London programme have participated

for more than two years and more than a third have been members for over one year
- involves learning across all age ranges;
- fosters an appreciation of diversity. Young people have the opportunity to meet a range of people of all ages from different cultures, backgrounds and parts of the UK;
- develops a sense of citizenship and community involvement. CE members learn to look at issues from different points of view and appreciate the opinions of others. They learn that their views are valid, that they have a right, and a responsibility to contribute to the community;
- gives children an effective voice, uniquely ensuring that their views find their way to audiences of adult policy-makers.

And, as we have seen, the media like the programme too.

16 Involving young people in research

Perpetua Kirby

Researching children and young people

> No longer can researchers assume that those social science methods that are used to study adults can be used in the same way with children. Instead, researchers need to give some thought to ways in which innovatory methods of social investigation can be developed and used with children so as to gain access to children's perspectives of the worlds in which they live and work ... [children's perspectives] can also be obtained by children working with other children who themselves gain insights into how a research team is developed and works.
>
> (Burgess, 2000: xv)

Until the 1980s children's views were not reflected in research. Subsequently researchers have begun to collect children's and young people's own accounts of their lives. This shift in practice has followed the recognition of children's rights to participate in society, plus a growing concern and focus on the welfare of disadvantaged children (Boyden and Ennew, 1998). The UN Convention on the Rights of the Child has been a primary influence shaping this change of focus. Other legislation in the United Kingdom has also emphasised the importance of consulting children – including the Children Act 1989, the Code of Practice on Special Education Needs (Department for Education, 1994) and the recent Quality Protects programme. There is now a growing expectation and requirement that children and young people be consulted about decisions affecting their lives, and about the services provided for their use. A growing interest in the concepts of empowerment and participation in the political arena has been mirrored by an increasing awareness for the potential of user involvement in research.

While for many decades research has focused on childhood, there has recently been a change in methods. This change reflects the move from a developmental model of childhood, in which children were seen as "becoming adults", to a perception of children as valid social actors in their own right. In the past, research was dominated by psychological explanations of child development; in traditional methods children are observed, measured and tested (James and Prout, 1990; Pettitt, 1996; Greig and Taylor, 1999). For example, traditional ways of researching pre-school children might include interviews and a Pre-School Behaviour questionnaire for parents or teachers, and observation of children (possibly through a two-way mirror) completing a task in order to assess the difference between their actual and presumed potential performance (Greig and Taylor, 1999).

More recently, child-focused research has emphasised a respect for children's and young people's competency to take part in research, a recognition that they have different competencies and interests to adults, and the use of age-appropriate methods (Boyden and Ennew, 1998). A range of qualitative and participatory methods enable children and young people to express their views and experiences using familiar means of communication, such as drawing, role play, mapping and group work (Kane, 2000; Lewis and Lindsay, 2000; Marchant *et al.*, 1999; Johnson *et al.*, 1998; Johnson, 1996). Child-focused research using participatory methods is commonly referred to as Participatory Rural Appraisal (PRA), and it is seen as much as a methodology as a set of research methods or techniques.

> The successful use of participatory techniques lies in the process, rather than simply the techniques used. Thus, the genuine use of participatory techniques requires commitment to an ongoing process of information sharing, dialogue, reflection and action.
>
> (Kane, 2000: 138)

This new approach has been used with children and young people, including very young children. For example, a recent study examined the "voice of children" under 5 years old in evaluating services (Clark, 2000). The study combined observation and interviews with children, with asking them to take photographs, produce drawings and make an audio-tape recording as they directed the researcher on a tour of their environment. These children were also involved in interpreting their own data, by discussing what they were doing, the choices they made, and selecting shots for a photographic display.

As well as involving children and young people more fully as research respondents – as in PRA – there has been a growing movement (albeit slowly growing) to involve those who constitute the focus of the research in designing and conducting research with their peers. Paulo Freire (1972) was one of the earliest proponents of participatory research; he stressed that only when those who are objects of research instead become the subjects, will action be taken and reality transformed. Over the last two decades feminist researchers, black researchers and those with disabilities have challenged the structural hierarchies within the research context and in wider society. In the last five years this type of work has been developed with young people, and sometimes with children, where they are involved in designing and conducting research projects. It is this type of participatory research – which is both inclusive and collaboratory – that is discussed in this chapter: "We define participatory research as the systematic inquiry, with the *collaboration* of those affected by the issue being studied, for purposes of education and taking action or effecting social change" (my italics; Green *et al.*, 1997: 54).

Much of the work involving young researchers has been undertaken by non-governmental organisations – including overseas – and this has primarily been with marginalised and disadvantage young people, such as care leavers (Saunders and Broad, 1997; Hobbiss *et al.*, 1998; West, 1995), those with mental health needs (Laws, 1998; McKeown *et al.*, 1999), young refugees (HAYS, 1998), disabled young people (Educable, 2000; Morris, 1998; Ash *et al.*, 1996), street children (Khan, 1997), working children (Ratna, 2000), ethnic minorities (Howarth, 1997), drug users (Fast Forward Positive Lifestyles Ltd, 1994) and those living in inner-city areas (Children's Rights Commission, forthcoming; Chopyak, 1999). Some studies have focused on schools (Fielding, 2001; Cuninghame, 1999)

Very recently, there has been a debate by academics and other researchers about involving young researchers. Some of the largest funders of social research in the United Kingdom have demonstrated an interest in this methodology. Both the Joseph Rowntree Foundation and the Economic and Social Research Council (ESRC) have funded research involving the participation of young researchers, to a greater or lesser extent (e.g. Triumph and Success Project; The Routes Project; Walker and Kushner, 1999; Candappa, 2000; Webber and Longhurst, forthcoming) and have commissioned reports exploring this methodology (The Routes Project Team, 2001; France, 2000; Kirby, 1999).

The main reasons why young people have been involved as researchers are that this is a way of involving them as citizens, and it enables them to have access to decision-making structures and to take action for themselves. In addition, it aids the young researchers' personal development, by increasing their skills and knowledge. Participatory research has also been considered a good method of collecting quality research data, a more ethical and democratic way of conducting research, and one which "recognises children as social actors in their own right" (Candappa, 2000). This chapter explores these ideas further below. First, three case study examples are presented. Second, the different ways in which young people can be involved as researchers are examined. Third, young people's capacity to conduct research is assessed and, finally, the chapter considers how participatory research attempts to challenge the power imbalances in youth research.

Involving young researchers: case studies

Case study I: young researchers participate in adult-led research

The Dutch government commissioned a university to explore family policy, following citizens' concerns about the moral decay of youth. Young researchers aged 14 and 15 years old, from different ethnic origins, were trained and supported to conduct a total of 247 ten-minute interviews with their classmates. A university researcher wrote a report based on their interviews, and then this report was discussed in three "brainstorming sessions" which were attended by nine young researchers, two representatives of the ministry, and one university researcher, and chaired by two independent facilitators. In the first session they defined and ordered the main problems and causes in the interviews. The second session produced a list of solutions to the identified problems, and in the third session they chose which solutions should be highlighted in the final report to the minister. It was concluded that "not only were the young participants themselves enthusiastic about the outcome of the brainstorm sessions, but the representatives of the Ministry shared their enthusiasm and agreed with the proposals made" (De Winter *et al.*, 1999)

Case study II: young researchers provide advice

Save the Children received funding from the Joseph Rowntree Foundation to conduct a UK-wide research study on young people's experience of transition from childhood to adulthood, involving young people aged 14–27 in all stages of the research process. The project had an adult advisory group which included representatives from young people's organisations, and also set up small "steering groups" of young people in each area where the research was being undertaken. These young advisers were paid for their time and met at regular intervals to advise the research team on the likely issues in transition for young people, the appropriate use of language, the interview methods and the background information sent to the interviewees. They also piloted the interview schedule, although with their permission the data gained from these interviews were used in the final write up. The young advisers were not involved during the fieldwork phase of the project, but they reconvened to discuss the findings and to elaborate the recommendations, to help write up a young people's summary of the research and to plan the presentation and dissemination of the research findings (Barry, 2001; Barry, see chapter 14).

Case study III: young researchers undertake their own research

The National Teen Action Research Centre (NTARC) is an after-school training and employment programme that is youth driven and adult guided, and is comprised of young people aged 14 to 19 years old. They conducted community-based research in New York because high-school students disagreed strenuously with an environmental agency expert about air pollution levels. The agency listened to the young people and provided them with the necessary equipment to undertake their own research. The youth group collected and helped analyse data on diesel exhaust exposure and lung function among a sample of Harlem students, which demonstrated levels of pollution far above those initially proposed. The students co-authored the report published in the peer reviewed *American Journal of Public Health* (July 1999) (Chopyak, 1999).

How to involve young researchers

Young researchers have been involved in researching the views of children, young people and adults. They have been involved to varying degrees in research. For example, some offer only an advisory role to adult-led research – helping them to design young person friendly research tools – whilst some groups of young people conduct their own research project, making decisions about the aims and methods to be used, plus conducting the fieldwork. For a fuller discussion about how to involve young researchers, including numerous case study examples, see Kirby (1999).

Young researchers can be involved in some or all of the many different stages of research, although they are more frequently involved in setting questions and collecting data, than in the analysis and report writing. They are rarely involved in setting the research agenda or objectives, which is an issue that some young researchers have questioned.

The degree to which young people are involved in making research decisions varies across projects. They may simply *express their views* about the research topic as research respondents, and be *informed* about decisions made by others. Alternatively, they may *influence decisions* by giving their opinions about what and how things should be done. They can have more power by being partners with the adults and making *joint decisions* or else be supported to be the *main deciders* about what to do. They can also have varying amounts of decision-making power at each of the different stages of the research, from setting the aims, through designing the research to the analysis and write up. When young people help make decisions they do not have to undertake all the research tasks, for example, they may help choose which topics should be included in an interview schedule but not refine the wording of the questions or undertake the fieldwork. Young people do not always possess the time, interest, skills or confidence to undertake all tasks. They may exercise power and decide they do not want to carry out certain tasks, or else adults may make that decision; alternatively these decisions can be negotiated.

Research projects have tended to be either youth projects supported by adults or adult projects with input from young people. There is a marked absence of research where both adults and young people establish a dialogue and work together as partners; in which the skills and knowledge of both are valued and incorporated. By democratising the research process, responsibilities can be shared and this helps to reduce a "them and us" mentality (Sinclair Taylor, 1999). The level of decision-making power given to young people and workers will vary depending on the context, subject and reason for the research. Participation will also vary according to the young people's capacities, which is in part determined by their age and experience. This choice, however, should always be considered seriously and openly discussed. If not, there is a danger that young people will be excluded unnecessarily, included when it is inappropriate, or manipulated to appear to be participating when in fact adults make key decisions:

> I think you could say it's a project engineered by a group of adults that have wanted young people to be involved in it. And that's what it is. But I don't think I personally would agree with it being a young person's project ...

> You see it differently to me. You see the university using us and I see it as us using university. Because they're using our research and I think it was us that picked that up. Maybe not picked the questions but we'd a great deal of input on those questions and where they went.
>
> (young researchers; quoted in France, 2000)

Adults have an important role in supporting young people, and working *with* them, which means they also have to be involved in making decisions. France's (2000) evaluation of a peer research project concluded that "having research consultants not as equal partners is problematic: they need to have considerable influence at certain times in the design and analysis stage". Rajani agrees:

> Adolescent participation ... does not mean that whatever young people say be wholeheartedly and uncritically endorsed, or that they be left alone to do whatever they want to do. While there is a role for autonomy, in most cases adolescents act in connection with adults.
>
> (Rajani, 1999: 12)

Many young people will not want to get involved in research, which presents a major problem for participatory researchers. Robson (2001) concluded that disadvantaged or disaffected young researchers "may be unreliable", they can "become easily bored" and are "often uninterested in social issues – even those that have an impact on them". Young people will need a lot of convincing that their involvement is going to have a positive impact for them and their community, and this may takes years rather than months to achieve with some groups. To help encourage involvement it is important to consider how participants will personally benefit from taking part. With the right support, young people can develop personal skills (such as computing, public-speaking and inter-personal communication), knowledge about research, and find out more about relevant policy issues, their rights and available services. For some, one of the major incentives for taking part is the opportunity to help their community. The participants often welcome the opportunity to meet people, make friends in the group and make local contacts with adult agencies. Confidence and self-esteem can be improved, and they may gain increased future employment opportunities. Young people are often paid for their time and/or reimbursed by residentials and social activities. It is also important formally to recognise their contribution, for example, by producing a certificate of achievement, offering to write job references, and having their name on the final report. As one young researcher recalled:

> I got involved in Educable [research project] because I wanted to find out how to do research but also to know more about different attitudes and how to end discrimination against disabled people.
>
> (quoted in Educable, 2000)

No small group of young researchers can ever be truly representative of a heterogeneous target population, although the assumption is that they will be closer than outsider adult researchers. It is important, of course, to ensure that young researchers reflect the gender, ethnicity, class, relevant interests or experiences of the target population of young people, as well as – or sometimes instead of – their age.

Young researchers: capacities and impact

Supporting young researchers

Involving young people in research takes a lot of time and requires a great deal of worker support. The emphasis is on workers who can ensure the rather dry topic of research is made engaging and fun for young people. Both youth work and research support are needed, frequently requiring different specialist workers. Young people also need a lot of training to be able meaningfully to participate, combined with plenty of role-play practice if they are to carry out fieldwork, particularly in the areas listed below (Worrall, 2000; Kirby, 1999; Broad and Saunders, 1998):

- negotiating with organisations to help access young people for the research
- approaching a young person to ask if they will take part in the research
- explaining the research
- explaining confidentiality
- asking questions, including probing
- using recording equipment and writing notes
- dealing with disclosure or an interviewee being upset
- ending the interview

Research validity

Waldman and Hague (1996) found that young people who had previously been trained as peer educators made good young researchers. Not all young people (or children) will be able to participate in research to the same extent, as Dyson and Meagher (2001) concluded in a review of several case studies of research involving young people:

> Research is ... a highly technical process which many professionals spend an entire lifetime perfecting. Perhaps unsurprisingly, the experience of our case studies is that some young people lack the skills, expertise and attitudes, to become involved in anything other than a periphery role.
>
> (Dyson and Meagher, 2001)

They argued that, for this reason, it is problematic to involve young researchers to generate adequate research:

> Insofar as young people have problems with the technicalities and practicalities of research, they inevitably compromise the trustworthiness of that research. Badly designed studies, poorly-conducted field work, weak analysis and mis-interpretation of data cannot be expected to generate "safe" knowledge.
>
> (Dyson and Meagher, 2001)

The validity of the research will vary from project to project and it is important to separate criticism of bad practice from criticism of methods per se; participation should never be an excuse for poor research. For participatory research to be meaningful, and influential, there needs to be an emphasis on rigorous research standards. If young people are simply judged by the standards that researchers set themselves however, then they are bound to fail.

Participatory research is a challenge to the positivist tradition that asserts a researcher can be an impartial bystander and objectively record the external world. Instead, participatory researchers acknowledge that they are active agents in the research process and the world they are researching. This is highlighted by the following extract from an investigation of gender identity involving peer researchers in a primary school:

> Like participant observation, the children's involvement in the survey, required them to be both insider and outsider, to be simultaneously passionately engaged in the precarious business of securing a gender identity, and yet somehow disengage themselves from that process in order to be observers and cataloguers of that gendered world. The

research activity cannot itself be disengaged from the children's own projects of "self-making".

(Warren, 2000: 130)

The participatory approach introduces the need for additional ways of measuring the validity of research – rather than simply using traditional measures of objectivity – such as egalitarianism, shared ownership and equal opportunities to participate (Hobbiss *et al.*, 1998).

It is difficult to train a group of young people so that each member is able to undertake every research task (given the usually limited available time). Instead, division of labour within the young research team, and with the adults, can help to ensure that each young person undertakes the tasks they are most capable and willing to do. Rather than expecting young people to become "professional" researchers overnight, the emphasis should be on recognising and incorporating their existing capacities – which will often be different to adult capacities – and secondly by helping them to develop the skills necessary to participate more fully. Sometimes this will mean only involving young people as advisers and at other times they can participate more fully. It is important to ensure that either young people are recruited who can be supported to acquire the required skills and knowledge, or the research design is tailored to meet the existing capacities and interests of the participating young people. An evaluation of peer research showed how a group of young people competently developed a conceptual understanding of research issues:

> Debates about power, gender and agenda setting are endemic tensions embedded within debates about research methodology and relationships between funders and researchers. It is clear from the previous discussions that these young people recognised these tensions in their own work showing how issues of confidentiality, bias, identity and power are factors that need considering in tackling research methodology. Such knowledge amongst a group of 15 to 19 year olds, shows how effective this method has been in developing peer researchers capable of thinking and implementing research.
>
> (France, 2000)

An underlying assumption of participatory research is that the data will be more meaningful if those being researched are involved in its collection. Firstly, it is often assumed that young people will be better able to access hard-to-reach young people in the community, although this often does not prove to be the case; some young respondents will not want to participate whoever conducts the research. Young people can successfully help design appropriate and innovative research tools, which help to engage young respondents in research. Involving young researchers can also help to reduce the social power imbalance between the researcher and the researched, enabling the respondent to feel more relaxed, use a common language and open up. This is not to say they establish *the truth*, but possibly a *different* perspective from an adult professional interviewer. Saunders and Broad (1997) found that "the range and quality of the data, specifically its relevance and reliability, was enhanced by peer research", and the young researchers in their study felt some young people had been more honest than if they had been interviewed by "professional researchers". Muddle (1993; cited in De Winter *et al.*, 1999) found that young people appreciated being interviewed by others their own age: "'It gives you more confidence', 'It's easier to talk', and 'Great, better than some old phoney' were some of the [young respondents'] reactions" (Muddle in De Winter *et al.*, 1993: 906).

More research is needed on the impact of young interviewers on respondents, including asking respondents whom they would prefer to be interviewed by, and certainly someone's age alone is not enough to elicit good interview responses (Robson, 2001). The young person's new role also changes their status from being a "peer" to a "researcher" and this can affect the extent to which other young people will open up to them. Young people may not always want to talk to their peers, particularly when it is about a personally sensitive topic (such as mental health) (Laws *et al.*, 1999), and there are times when an independent "professional" would be more appropriate. Young researchers can also face many of the same problems that adults researchers have, such as a lack of respondent interest, biased replies, and low response rates.

There is a need for more triangulation – in which adult researchers use different or the same methods as young researchers – which could help throw different perspectives on the same topic. Young researchers should also be encouraged to use child-focused approaches to researching other young people's views, which enable respondents to participate more fully, rather than replicating traditional research. There is scope to use and develop more age appropriate methods (such as PRA methods) with their peers, such as video and arts, rather than always expecting them to use interviews and questionnaires.

Ethical practice

There have been a few times when young researchers have been found not to be empathetic with those they are researching (Kirby, 1999). If there is concern, for example, that unskilled young researchers will impact negatively on respondents, then they may have to be prevented from conducting fieldwork. Research must ensure the rights of all young participants, not just the researchers. Even young children have been found to be able to understand the importance of ethical practice. In a Child to Child health project exploring safety with medicines, a group of children decided against asking other young children to try opening medicine bottles in case they did this at home, and instead the group decided to carry out the tests themselves (Occleston and King, 1998).

The need for adequate ethical practice is as true for adult researchers as it for young ones. There are few ethical guidelines for those researching children and young people (Morrow and Richards, 1996; Alderson, 1995; Stanley and Siber, 1992), and a need for far more debate and discussion about how to ensure the rights of those being researched; including issues such as informed consent, child protection and considering appropriate follow-on support for research participants.

> Continuing professional development for researchers with children should include increasing sensitivity to identification and resolving ethical issues, and in ensuring that practitioners' research is not only valid and useful, but also ethical.
>
> (Lindsay, 2000: 20)

Analysis and dissemination

Involving young people in the analysis of research data is one of the hardest stages of participatory research. In many projects an adult researcher undertakes this role, or sometimes young people participate in some of the analysis tasks – such as helping to interpret respondents' comments and explaining the findings (Worral, 2000; Kirby, 1999). Young people often do not want to be involved as they see this stage as difficult and boring. Their lack of involvement presents a sticking point in participatory research, as analysis is arguably one of the most powerful stages of the whole process. Inevitably workers will usually have to undertake more of the analysis and theory building, but attempts need to be made to involve young people where possible, which requires skilled workers who are able to translate complicated ideas and jargon. Also, the young community being researched needs to be informed of the research results using an accessible language and format – such as posters, leaflets and video – rather than long and dry reports. This feedback is important for ensuring the young people maintain some ownership of the project outcomes.

Challenging power in research

Morrow and Richards (1996: 98) noted that "ultimately, the biggest ethical challenge for researchers working with children is the disparities in power and status between adults and children". Child-focused approaches help to redress this imbalance. Ultimately, however, funders – dictated by political agendas – hold the reins of power by deciding what research is commissioned. There is potential and unresolved conflict between the political push for increased local democracy (participation and user-involvement), whilst UK government departments demand evidenced-based practice using traditional evaluation methodology. Another influence on research is professional researchers' own interests and the need for career rewards, such as status.

Perhaps worse is when research is shelved, rather than used to implement change. Kurt Lewin's assertion that "research that produces nothing but books will not suffice" (1946; cited in Denscombe, 1998: 58) is one with which many young people can sympathise.

> Understandably, young people are sceptical about the real significance of surveys, reports and recommendations. They do not need or want a survey that effectively describes their lives and aspirations, but sits on a shelf without making any difference.
>
> (Shaw *et al.*, 1998: 20)

The result of disadvantaged communities being over-researched, with little change for those people, is one reason why young people are frequently unwilling to participate as respondents. The extract below, from an evaluation study of a crime prevention programme, highlights their lack of engagement in research. The author concluded that his attempts to be empowering were not enough and, instead, it is important to engage the powerless from the beginning and "allow them to decide what gains they desire from the research process" (France, 1996).

> Participation in the [evaluation] research meant little to them, as it was unlikely to improve their lives in the immediate future. The national evaluation and its purpose were unknown and young people had no stake in its success. Why should they make an effort? "Messing about" or lack of interest may have therefore been a method of rejecting the processes and structures imposed upon them by the research, suggesting that instead of being empowering it was in danger of exploiting young people's good nature.
>
> (France, 1996: 177)

This supports Paulo Freire's (1972) argument that research must be done with people who are objects of research, rather than for them; this demands that research responds more to needs at the bottom, instead of being initiated from the top. Participatory research aims to increase young people's ownership of the process by enabling them to make decisions about what and/or how their lives are researched, to ensure they learn, take action and effect social change. The process is partly about the social education of young people – informing them about research methods, policy and related issues, and developing their critical awareness ready for future action (Hart, 1992). A young researcher commented: "Because of the research I understood how I was treated and how young people are still being treated by society" (quoted in Kirby *et al.*, 2001)

The majority of young researchers are empathetic with their peers; they tend to be particularly concerned about the welfare of the respondents, and want to do something more to help than just report their experiences.

Sometimes young researchers discuss their own related experiences with the young respondents, either during the interview or more frequently after it has finished.

> [Young] interviewers felt responsible for interviewees who became upset, and wanted to ring them later to see how they are. They felt frustrated at not being able to help people with their problems or situations, and did not know what to say to some people to support them.
>
> (Saunders and Broad, 1997: 7)

This empathy possibly reflects the closer links between the peers, and raises questions about the role of the researcher to intervene and assist those whom they research. Too little consideration has been given to the impact that a research interview may have on a young person, particularly when discussing sensitive topics, and the most researchers tend to offer young interviewees is a list of relevant services to access themselves. Ann Oakley (1981) cautioned professional researchers that "in the "feminist interview", the closeness and intersubjectivity remain artificial and temporary". But where local people research within their own community, this relationship is more stable and ongoing. Peer research helps to encourage dialogue and may help initiate future collaboration: "The research project gave me some focus in how I can continue to help my community" (young researcher; quoted in Kirby *et al.*, 2001).

Several groups of researchers have indeed gone on to conduct further research and campaign work to address issues facing themselves and other young people. This illustrates the way in which participatory research attempts to break down the distinction between research and its use (i.e. practice); instead it makes research integral to development work and recognises that research is a form of social intervention, not just an application of research methods (Hedges, 1997).

Participatory research tackles the oppressions that more traditional research approaches have perpetuated, by offering an alternative method of inquiry. But the educational aspect of this methodology must be a dialogue, and not just about the social education of young people. Whilst the adults have knowledge of research methods, policy, etc., participatory research also values the young researchers' own knowledge about the actual lived experience of young people and their competency to contribute to the research process (Hedges, 1997).

Involving young researchers is egalitarian and improves young people's access to decision-making. It tackles the oppressions of adultism by challenging the wider structural inequalities that young people face in society, and demonstrates their ability to participate. For young people to be empowered, however, adults need to relinquish power. Chambers argued that to ensure we "put people first and poor people first of all" a new professionalism is needed in which "those who are powerful have to step down, sit, listen, and learn from and empower those who are weak and last" (Chambers, 1997: 2). Letting go of power is one of the hardest challenges for professionals, including researchers (France, 2000), and establishing a dialogue demands humility:

> How can I dialogue if I always project ignorance onto others and never perceive my own? ... How can I dialogue if I start from the premise that naming the world is the task of an elite ... at the point of encounter there are neither utter ignoramuses nor perfect sages; there are only people who are attempting, together, to learn more than they now know.
>
> (Freire, 1972: 71)

The debate about when, how and why to involve young researchers is in its infancy. Some "cannot resolve the argument as to whether it is right or wrong to engage children within the process of research" (Greig and Taylor, 1999: 160), whilst others are exploring how best to undertake this type of work. Young people do not have to be involved in all or even many stages of research – unless they want to be – but it is important for researchers to value young people's own knowledge, to learn from it, and to build it into the research process. Ultimately, their involvement in the production of data affects the uses of research; it helps make us accountable to those we research, and ensures we consider their interests, as well as our own.

References

Alderson, P. (1995) *Listening to Children: children, ethics and social research*, London: Barnados

Ash, A., Bellew, J., Davies, M., Newman, T. and Richardson, L. (1996) *Everybody In? The experience of disabled students in colleges of further education*, Ilford: Barnados

Barry, M. (2001) *Challenging Transitions: The views and experiences of young people growing up in the UK*, London: Save the Children/Joseph Rowntree Foundation

Boyden, J. and Ennew, J. (1998) *Children in Focus – a manual for participatory research with children*, Stockholm: Rädda Barnen

Broad, B. and Saunders, L. (1998) "Involving young people leaving care as peer researchers in a health research project: a learning experience", *Journal of the Social Services Research Group*, Vol. 16, no. 1, pp. 1–19

Burgess, R.G. (2000) "Foreword", in Ann Lewis and Geoff Lindsay (2000) *Research Children's Perspectives*, Buckingham: Open University Press

Candappa, M. (2000) *Extraordinary Childhoods: the social lives of refugee children*, ESRC Children 5–16 Research Briefing, January 2000, No. 5

Chambers, R. (1997) *Whose Reality Counts? Putting the first last*, London: Intermediate Technology Publications

Children's Rights Commission (forthcoming) *Consultation with Children and Young People in London (preliminary title)*, London: Children's Rights Commission

Chopyak, J. (1999) "Communty-Based Research: research for action", *The Evaluation Exchange*, Vol. 5, No. 2/3, pp: 14–15

Clark, A. (2000) "Listening to young children: perspectives, possibilities and problems", paper presented at the 10th European Conference on Quality in Early Childhood Education. EECERA Conference, Institute of Education, London, 29 August–1 September

Cuninghame, C. (1999) *Research School,* in Aslam, F., Kirby, P., Oldham, J. and Newton, S. (1999) Report on the Whitley Abbey Community School Project 1998–1999. Smethwick: Save the Children

De Winter, M., Kroneman, M. and Baerveldt, C. (1999) "The social education gap report of a Dutch peer-consultation project on family policy", *British Journal of Social Work*, Vol. 29, pp. 903–914

Denscombe, M. (1998) *The Good Research Guide*, Buckingham: Open University Press

Department for Education (1994) *Code of Practice on the Identification and Assessment of Special Education Needs*, London, HMSO

Dyson, A. and Meagher (2001) "Reflections on the case studies", in The Routes Project Team (2001)

Educable (2000) *No Choice. No Chance*, Belfast: Save the Children

Fast Forward Positive Lifestyles Ltd (1994) *Drugs Information for Young People: peer research project findings*, Edinburgh: Fast Forward Positive Lifestyles Ltd

Fielding, M. (2001) "Students as radical agents of change: a minute correction to the essential is more important then a hundred accessories", *Journal of Educational Change*, Vol. 2, No. 3

France, A. (1996) "Exploitation or empowerment? Gaining access to young people's reflections on crime prevention strategies", *Groupwork*, Vol. 9, No. 2, pp. 169–185

—— (2000) *Youth Researching Youth: the triumph and success peer research project*, Leicester: National Youth Agency

Freire, P. (1972) *Pedagogy of the Oppressed*, London: Penguin

Green, L.W., George, M.A., Daniel, M., Frankish, C.J., Herbert, C.P., Bowie, W.R. and O'Neil, M. (1997) "Background on participatory research", in D. Murphy, D. Scammell and R. Sclove (eds) *Doing Community-Based Research: a reader*, Amherst, MA: The Loka Institute

Greig, A. and Taylor, J. (1999) *Doing Research with Children*, London: Sage

Hart, R.A. (1992) "Children's participation; from tokenism to citizenship", *Innocenti Essays*, Vol. 4, pp. 19–22, UNICEF

HAYS and Kirby, P. (1998) *Let's Spell it Out: peer research on the educational support needs of young refugees and asylum seekers in Kensington and Chelsea*, London: Save the Children

Hedges, C. (1997) *Research and Participation: methodology and methods*, Newcastle: Save the Children (internal paper)

Hobbiss, A., Cakvert, C. and Collins, L. (1998) "Participative research: a way of creating research partnerships with young people", conference presentation and abstract for *Collaboration in Health Research*, Bradford: Bradford Institute for Health Research, University of Bradford

Howarth, R. (1997) *If We Don't Play Now, When Can We? Report of the research into the play and leisure needs of Bangladeshi children in Camden*, London: Hopscotch Asian Women's Centre

James, A. and Prout, A. (1990) (eds) *Constructing and Reconstructing Childhood*, London: Falmer Press

Johnson, V. (1996) "Starting a dialogue on children's participation", *PLA Notes: Notes on participatory Learning and Action*, No. 25, February, Special Issue on Children's Participation, London: IIED

Johnson, V., Ivan-Smith, E., Gordon, G., Pridmore, P. and Scott, P. (eds) (1998) *Stepping Forward: children and young people's participation in the development process*

Kane, C. (2000) "The development of participatory techniques: facilitating children's views about decisions which affect them", in P. Christensen and A. James (eds) *Research with Children: perspectives and practices*, London: Falmer Press

Khan, S. (1997) *Street Children's Research*, Dhaka: Save the Children

Kirby, P. (1999) *Involving Young Researchers: how to enable young people to design and conduct research*, York: York Publishing Services Ltd

Kirby, P., HAYS, Wubner, K. and Lewis, M. (2001) "The HAYS project", in The Routes Project Team (2001)

Laws, S. (1998) *Hear Me! Consulting with young people on mental health services*, London: Mental Health Foundation

Laws, S., Armitt, D., Metzendor, W., Percival, P. and Reisel, J. (1999) *Time to Listen: young people's experiences of mental health services*, London: Save the Children

Lewis, A. and Lindsay, G. (eds) (2000) *Researching Children's Perspectives*, Buckingham: Open University Press

Lindsay, G. (2000) "Researching children's perspectives: ethical issues", in A. Lewis and G. Lindsay (eds) *Researching Children's Perspectives*, Buckingham: Open University Press

Longhurst, K. (2001) "Youth perceptions of security: promises and pitfalls", in The Routes Project Team (2001)

Marchant, R., Jones, M., Julyan, A. and Giles, A. (1999) *"Listening on all channels" – consulting disabled children and young people*, Brighton: Triangle

McKeown, C., McAllister, J., Rose, J. and Berry, D. (1999) *Unacceptably Low: care leavers and mental health*, Newcastle: Save the Children

Morris, J. (1998) *Don't Leave Us Out: involving disabled children and young people with communication impairments*, York: York Publishing Services Ltd

Morrow, V. and Richards, M. (1996) "The ethics of social research with children: an overview", *Children and Society*, Vol. 10, pp. 90–105

Oakley, A. (1981) "Interviewing women", in H. Roberts *Doing Feminist Research*, London: Routledge

Occleston, S. and King, P. (1998) *Shared Learning in Action: working towards empowerment through education*, Bolton: D2

Pettit, B. (1996) *New Perspectives on Children and Childhood: the implications for Save the Children*, London: Save the Children

Rajani, R. (1999) *Adolescent Participation: a strategic approach*, New York: UNICEF

Ratna, K. (2000) "The impact of collective organisation and action on resiliency and coping – the case of Bhima Sangha", conference paper *Children in Adversity: ways to reinforce the coping ability and resilience of children in situations of hardship*, Oxford, September 10–12, www.childreninadversity.org

Robson, E. (2001) "The Routes Project", in The Routes Project Team (2001)

Saunders, L. and Broad, R. (1997) *The Health Needs of Young People Leaving Care*, Leicester: Centre for Social Action, De Montfort University

Shaw, S., Edward, E., Desbonnes, M., Pacquette, D., Lawrence, S., Newby, J., James, L. and Allen, H. (1998) *Youth Research Project: report and recommendations*, London: Paddington Arts

Sinclair Taylor, A. (1999) "The UN Convention on the Rights of the Child: giving children a voice", in Ann Lewis and Geoff Lindsay (eds) (1999) *Researching Children's Perspectives*, Buckingham: Open University Press

Stanley, B. and Siber, J.E. (eds) (1992) *Social Research on Children and Adolescents: ethical issues*, Newbury Park, CA: Sage

The Routes Project Team (2001) (Clark, J., Dyson, A., Meagher, N., Robson, E. and Wooten, M.) (eds) *Young People as Researchers: possibilities, problems and politics*, Leicester: Youth Work Press

Waldman, J. and Hague, F. (1996) "Modelling", *Young People Now*, September 1996, pp. 28–29

Walker, B.M. and Kushner, S. (1999) "The building site. An educational approach to masculine identity", *Journal of Youth Studies*, Vol. 2(1), pp. 45–58

—— (forthcoming) *Boys' Sexual Health Education: implications for attitude change*, York: Joseph Rowntree Foundation

Warren, S. (2000) "Let's do it properly: inviting children to be researchers", in A. Lewis and G. Lindsay (eds) *Researching Children's Perspectives*, Buckingham: Open University Press

Webber, S. and Longhurst, K. (forthcoming) "Youth participation of citizenship and security in Russia, Germany and the UK" (research project name), School of Social Studies Centre for Russian and East Eastern European Studies, University of Birmingham, <http://www.bham.ac.uk/cmil/>

West, A. (1995) *You're on Your Own: young people's research on leaving care*, London: Save the Children

Worrall, S. (2000) "Young people as researchers: a learning resource pack", London: Save the Children

17 Children's Rights Commissioners for the UK

Gerison Lansdown

Introduction

During the last decade of the twentieth century the human rights of children finally became visible. Following its adoption by the UN General Assembly in 1989, the Convention on the Rights of the Child has achieved near universal ratification. The 1990 World Summit for Children witnessed 71 heads of state making a commitment to give a high priority to the rights of children and the 1993 World Conference on Human Rights reiterated the principle of "First call for Children" declaring that the rights of children must be a priority within the UN.[1] This widespread formal endorsement of the human rights of children, however, is rarely matched by a corresponding translation of rights into law, policy and practice. The gulf between the rights rhetoric and the realities of children's lives remains considerable in most countries in the world.

It has become increasingly clear that independent institutions dedicated to the promotion and monitoring of children's rights are essential to the creation of cultures which take those rights seriously. The Committee on the Rights of the Child, the international body established to monitor states' progress in implementing Convention rights, has consistently pressed governments to introduce such bodies as a necessary measure for the realisation of children's rights (Hodgkin and Newell, 1997). These concerns are replicated in the broader field of human rights where there has been growing pressure over recent decades throughout the UN system to create national human rights institutions to promote recognition of human rights. In 1993 the World Conference on Human Rights affirmed the importance of institutions to protect human rights, advise governments, remedy rights violations and educate about human rights. In the same year, the UN General Assembly endorsed a set of principles setting out the essential responsibilities of institutions dedicated to promoting and protecting human rights.[2]

In response both to these international developments and to demands from human rights organisations at national level, there are now a significant number of countries which have established human rights institutions, some of which include children under an umbrella responsibility for the protection of rights and others, children's ombudsmen or commissioners, which are dedicated exclusively to children (Lansdown, 2001a). In Europe, for example, ombudsmen or Children's Rights Commissioners exist in Austria, Belgium, Denmark, France, Hungary, Iceland, Norway, Portugal, Russian Federation, Spain and Sweden, while proposals are currently being developed in Germany, Ireland, Latvia, Poland and Switzerland. Outside Europe, bodies exist in Australia, Canada, Costa Rica, Guatemala, New Zealand, the Philippines and South Africa. There is wide variation in the legislative base underpinning these institutions. Some operate within government as an agent of that government, some have been established with a child welfare rather than children rights emphasis, whilst others have a direct mandate to promote and monitor implementation of the Convention on the Rights of the Child. What they all have in common is a commitment to promoting the rights and interests of children. And their introduction has derived from an acknowledgement that existing structures were inadequate to undertake that task effectively.

The UK context: support for a Children's Rights Commissioner

The UK government, when examined in 1995 by the Committee on the Rights of the Child, was questioned on whether it had given consideration to the proposal for establishing a body to monitor implementation of the Convention rights. The government delegation argued that there were already a wide variety of mechanisms in place to protect the interests of children, that the Convention did not require them to establish such a body and that the creation of an additional body would merely serve to confuse.[3] This argument would appear to misunderstand the proposal which is to establish a body with a clear and defined remit to monitor and promote implementation of the Convention on the Rights of the Child, a remit not shared by any other statutory body. The Committee was not convinced by the government's arguments and recommended, as it has to many other governments, that it consider establishing an independent body to monitor and promote implementation of the Convention.

Since then, there has been a change of government, but disappointingly, to date, there has been little change in policy on this issue. Although the Labour Party under John Smith's leadership had an explicit commitment to introducing a Children's Rights Commissioner in its 1992 manifesto, this was dropped by Tony Blair and has not been reinstituted. Paul Boateng, when Parliamentary Under Secretary of State, did inform the Health Select Committee, during its investigation into looked-after children in 1998, that whilst the previous government had opposed the idea of a Children's Rights Commissioner, the government was now reopening consideration of the proposal. He went on to say that he found aspects of the envisaged role "very attractive" (Select Committee on Health, 1998). He commissioned, within the department, a review of Children's Rights Commissioners in a number of other countries. However, in response to the recommendation of the Select Committee that a Children's Rights Commissioner should be established, the government commented that, having looked at the information from those countries, it was not persuaded that it "would be desirable to create such a national mechanism additional to the role of the courts, the police, and the prosecuting authorities, the various commissions (Parliamentary, Health and Local government) which already exist, the responsibilities of local and health authorities, to deal with complaints and the various inspection and regulatory arrangements for ensuring that safeguards for children are properly implemented and that their voices are heard" (Cm 4175, 1997–98).

More recently, in the Care Standards Act 2000, the government introduced a provision to appoint a Children's Rights Director for England whose responsibilities are defined as "such functions as shall be prescribed". It has argued that this appointment provides an alternative to the creation of a Children's Rights Commissioner. However, whilst this post, with its recognition of the importance of protecting the rights of children living away from home, represents a significant and welcome advance, the proposal does not in any way substitute for an independent, statutory institution to protect the rights of all children. The functions of the Children's Rights Director will be limited to the inspection and regulation of residential provision for children living away from home. In other words, it will have a remit for protecting a very limited aspect of the lives of around 200,000 children. It is a valuable initiative but goes nowhere near the proposal for a Commissioner charged with responsibility for promoting all the human rights of all children.

The All Party Parliamentary Group for Children supports the case for a Children's Rights Commissioner. Three debates on the issue have been tabled by backbenchers in the past year. The Health Select Committee, in its report of 1998 on looked-after children recommended that "there should be a Children's Rights Commissioner within the UK. ... We urge the government to introduce the necessary legislation to create the office of Commissioner as soon as possible, preferably in the next session of Parliament" (Select Committee on Health, 1998). An Early Day Motion calling for a Commissioner has attracted 87 signatures in 2000. The proposal has the support of the Liberal Democrats and in the Second Reading of the Care Standards Bill, the Conservatives stated that they now supported the need for a Children's Commissioner for England. In other words, there is a growing body of support at Westminster calling on the government to act.

Some progress in heightening the political focus on children has been made. In the late summer of 2000, the government established a new Cabinet Committee on "Children and Young People's Services", chaired by the Chancellor of the Exchequer, as well as a new cross-cutting Children and Young People's Unit, located in the DfEE (now DfES). The brief of the Unit is to develop a cross-departmental strategy for children and young people and to administer the Children's Fund, a fund worth £450 million established by the Comprehensive Spending Review in 2000 to tackle child poverty and social exclusion. However, these measures, whilst representing a considerable advance for children, do not substitute for an independent body to monitor and promote children's rights. And although the newly elected government has stated in June 2001 that it will give serious and open consideration to the proposal for a children's rights commissioner, no commitment is yet forthcoming. Markedly more movement is evident in the rest of the UK. In Scotland, in 1999, Sam Galbraith, the Scottish Minister for Children instructed the Education, Culture and Sport Committee in the Scottish Parliament to "undertake an inquiry into how children's rights, needs and views should be taken into account in developing and implementing policy and delivery of services. In particular, the Minister would be interested in views the Committee might form on whether or not it would be desirable to appoint a Children's Commissioner and if so, with what remit". In Wales, the Children's Commissioner for Wales Act 2001 has now established a Children's Commissioner whose remit is to promote the rights and welfare of all children "ordinarily resident" in Wales. In addition, the Commissioner can act to protect the rights of young people who are over the age of 18 and who have been in the care of the local authority.

In Northern Ireland, a Human Rights Commission was established in March 1999 under the terms of the Good Friday agreement. Its remit extends to promoting the human rights of children and one of its initial activities is to investigate the rights of young people caught up in the criminal justice system. The children's non-governmental organisations (NGOs) welcomed its establishment and are actively working with it although they are also pressing for the creation of a separate body specifically to promote the rights of children.

There is significant support outside government. A poll commissioned in 1996 for the Gulbenkian Foundation by the NSPCC found that 85 per cent of respondents thought the UK should have an independent office able to investigate problems like child abuse and put pressure on the government for change (Hodgkin and Newell, 1996). Furthermore, over 100 statutory, professional and voluntary bodies from the fields of health, child protection, play, education, community development, childcare, adoption, early years, poverty, disability and youth justice are actively committed to the establishment of a body to promote the human rights of children (Children's Rights Alliance for England, 2001). This broad alliance indicates that in whatever field people are working with children, they identify the need for an independent body with powers to act on behalf of children to give higher priority to their rights and interests. In April 2000, an office of Children's Rights Commissioner for London was established as a three-year project of the Children's Rights Alliance for England with a remit to promote a children's perspective and respect for the views of children in all aspects of London government. It will also serve as a demonstration project highlighting the benefits of a body dedicated to promoting the rights of children. The previous year, a Children's Rights Commissioner was set up in Oxfordshire as a joint initiative between Save the Children and Oxfordshire social services. The Commissioner is intended to encourage local services to develop their policy and practice in accordance with children's rights and to enhance children's own participation in local government.

The need for bodies to protect the rights of children

The human rights of all people are important and justify specialised institutions to monitor and protect their realisation. However, there are groups within society for whom the realisation of those rights is more difficult: children are one such group. In the same way that it is recognised that it is not only acceptable but necessary to exercise positive discrimination in favour of certain groups to challenge inherent disadvantage, so it is necessary to provide additional help to children if their rights are to be adequately protected (Lansdown, 2001a). Five considerations support the claim for additional help to secure children's rights.

First, children's healthy development and active participation are crucial to the healthy future of any society. It is in the interests not only of children but the whole of society that their rights and interests are fully respected. The costs of failing children are high. Messages from research confirm that what happens to children in the early years and even before birth significantly determines their future growth and development. This, in turn, determines their life chances and their cost or contribution to society over the rest of their lives.

Second, children have fared badly from public policy over the past twenty years. The most recent figures indicate that nearly one third of children are living in relative poverty in the UK – 4.4 million people – placing us near the bottom of the league tables of child poverty in rich nations.[4] Child deaths from accidents are the second highest in Europe. The UK has one of the highest rates of children held in custody, with numbers currently increasing, and the conditions under which many of them are held have been described by the Chief Inspector of Prisons as "unacceptable in a civilised society".[5] Social security benefits, housing benefits and youth services to young people have been cut. And during the 1990s, truancy and school exclusions grew, as did the incidence of mental ill health and homelessness amongst young people. There is virtually no entitlement to social housing for young single people.

Third, children are more affected by the actions – or inactions – of government than any other group. They are extremely heavy users of public services – education, health, childcare, child protection, play, public health. Almost every area of government policy affects children to some degree, either directly, or indirectly. And children's dependence and developmental state make them disproportionately vulnerable to the conditions under which they live – poverty, poor housing, environmental pollution, traffic congestion. Yet it has become increasingly apparent that children suffer from fragmentation of public services, with all the consequent inconsistencies of philosophy and practice, duplication of provision, poor communication, and inadequate solutions to complex problems (Hodgkin and Newell, 1996).

Fourth, children have no vote, nor access to the powerful lobbies that influence government agendas. They have little, if any, access to the media. While there is now the beginning of a debate on the need to encourage the involvement of children in decision-making, little concrete action has developed at national level. In reality, the views of children do not inform the actions of central government. Furthermore, there are particular difficulties for children in using the legal system and courts to protect their rights. Responding to children's concerns and complaints and remedying their rights requires special arrangements. In other words, the mechanisms that are employed by adults to exercise their rights are largely unavailable to children.

Finally, children are still too often viewed as recipients of adult protection rather than as subjects of rights. Children's rights continue to provoke considerable hostility and suspicion. The government has obligations under international law to recognise the human rights of children as individual citizens. It is not sufficient to assume that those rights will be adequately protected by parents, nor that there is no role for the state in protecting the rights of children within the context of the family (Lansdown, 2001). While parents are normally the most significant advocates for their children's rights, children's economic, social and emotional dependency renders them particularly vulnerable to abuses or neglect of their rights by those responsible for their care. In seeking to safeguard the human rights of children, governments not only have responsibilities in the public arena but must also adopt a pro-active commitment to intervening to protect children from the actions and inactions of parents, families and other carers.

In summary, a powerful case can be made for the development of dedicated institutions with a brief to monitor and promote children's rights and ensure that children are given consistent and high priority within government.

The role of Children's Rights Commissioners

Over the past ten years, detailed proposals for independent, statutory Children's Rights Commissioners throughout the UK have been developed and there is a broad consensus amongst NGOs as well as professional bodies and the local authority associations on the nature of the institution required to provide effective protection and promotion of children's rights (Newell, 2000 and Rosenbaum and Newell, 1991).

The aim of a Children's Rights Commissioner would be to protect and promote the human rights of children in a number of ways. First, the Commissioner should influence policy-makers and practitioners to take greater account of the human rights of children and promote compliance with the principles and standards embodied in the UN Convention on

Children's Rights and other relevant treaties. Second, the Commissioner should promote respect for the views of the child and help develop mechanisms through which those views can be heard. Third, the Commissioner must promote awareness of the human rights of children to both children and adults and finally, seek to ensure that children have effective means of redress when their rights are violated.

Influencing policy-makers and practitioners to take greater account of the human rights of children

The Commissioner would have responsibility for promoting implementation of the UN Convention on the Rights of the Child, but would also have regard to other relevant treaties including the International Covenant on Civil and Political Rights, the International Covenant on Economic, Social and Cultural Rights and the European Social Charter as well as rights embodied in domestic law.

The Commissioner would fulfil the responsibility of promoting respect for these rights through:

- the production of reports on any aspect of policy or practice affecting children – this would include reacting to the proposals of others as well as initiating new ideas;
- commenting at the earliest possible stage on proposed new legislation likely to impact on children's lives;
- requiring the government to issue a child-impact assessment on any proposed policy or legislation likely to impact on children's lives;
- undertaking formal investigations where concern has been expressed either by children themselves or by interested adults that the rights and interests of children are being abused or neglected.

Promoting respect for the views of children

Article 12 of the Convention on the Rights of the Child states that children have the right to express their views and have them taken seriously in all matters affecting them. This right is fundamental to the exercise of all substantive rights. It applies both to decisions that affect individual children as well as matters which affect them as a body. However, although it is perhaps the most well known of all the principles in the Convention, it is far from adequately implemented in respect of children in the UK. In education, for example, (except in Scotland) children have no right to any democratic structures in schools through which to contribute their views and concerns: they are excluded from governing bodies, they have no right of appeal against a permanent exclusion, there are no formal complaints mechanisms, and no national networks, such as unions of school students, through which to advise or inform government. There is no statutory provision of advocacy for looked-after children nor any obligation on parents to take account of their children's views when making major decisions that affect them.

A Commissioner would have a central function in promoting implementation of Article 12. Work would need to be directly informed by the views of children themselves in order that it reflected their priorities and perspectives. So doing would ensure that proposals being presented to government, reports, responses to government initiatives, research priorities and strategies for dissemination incorporated the views of children and young people. The Commissioner could also monitor compliance with Article 12, promote and disseminate models of good practice and provide a source of expertise and support to the government on developing more effective mechanisms for promoting children's active participation in government at both local and national level.

Promoting awareness of the human rights of children to both children and adults

Any real commitment to cultural change must start with children. Article 42 of the Convention on the Rights of the Child places an obligation on governments to make its provisions known to adults and children alike by appropriate and active means. Rights have little relevance if they are not known or understood: promoting awareness is an integral part of the process of enhancing respect for human rights. To date, little has been done by the government to fulfil this obligation, and the citizenship curriculum, due to be introduced in schools in September 2001, fails to include any obligation to teach children about the Convention on the Rights of the Child (see chapter 18). Far from understanding their rights, very few children currently even have any knowledge that the Convention exists (Alderson, 2000). A Children's Rights Commissioner could play an important role in monitoring how far the government is complying with the obligation, encourage it to take further action and help with proposals on how to do so more effectively.

The Commissioner would also play a part in analysing the availability of government statistics on children, identifying gaps or the need for disaggregated data. It could also usefully undertake or commission research as part of the process of acquiring the necessary information on children's lives to assess compliance.

Seeking to ensure that children have effective means of redress when their rights are violated

It is not proposed that Children's Rights Commissioners should have the role of investigating individual complaints from children. In England, in particular, given the numbers of children, such a function would undoubtedly swamp all other work. Evidence from many of the Human Rights

Commissions abroad that do have a duty to investigate and resolve complaints often find that it eats up their resources and deflects the Commission from work which would have had a more strategic, long-term impact.

Not only would it detract attention from other key tasks, but it is arguably not the most effective structure for providing complaints procedures for children. There is already a range of systems in operation for making complaints which might be duplicated if the Commissioner took on this function. Furthermore, it is preferable, where possible, that complaints procedures should be available and accessible in the locality of the child and that systems should exist which are service related. Where the Commissioner would have a key role would be in:

- Monitoring the availability, effectiveness and usage of complaints procedures that already exist, for example, under the Children Act 1989, the NHS complaints procedure, Commissioners for local administration. The Commissioner would need to identify whether children were using these procedures and, if not, find out why and how they could be improved. She or he would also need to press for effective models for complaints procedures, adequate resourcing, provision of information and publicity about the procedures, better training for staff;
- Identifying gaps in the provision of complaint procedures – for example, in many European countries, children in school have a statutory entitlement to make complaints and have them heard within a defined period. No comparable system applies in England and the Commissioner could take an active role in pressing for extending the availability of complaints mechanisms;
- Analysing the findings from children's complaints to identify patterns of concern, and feeding these patterns into policy proposals and recommendations for change.

It is proposed, however, that the Commissioner would have powers, in exceptional circumstances, to assist with or initiate legal cases where it is the best or the only way to help a child realise his or her rights.

Essential characteristics of national human rights institution for children

In order to fulfil the role of promoting and protecting children's rights effectively, there are a number of essential features which must characterise the institution.

First, it would need to be independent from any government body and free to determine its own policies and programme of work consistent with the powers and duties incorporated in its legal framework. It would, of course, be funded from public funds but the government would not be empowered to direct, control or otherwise interfere with its work.

Second, the institution would need to be informed by a commitment to implementation of Article 12, the right of children to express their views on all matters of concern to them. It would need to ensure both that its work was directly informed directly by the views of children and young people but also that it gave priority to establishing structures through which their views could be directly and effectively represented to other bodies.

Third, the institution would need to work collaboratively and closely with the wide range of organisations working with and for children and young people in the voluntary, statutory and private sectors which encompass a great deal of expertise, experience and provision.

Fourth, it would need to establish a comprehensive overview on children's rights. Children are users of a wide range of services. There is too often a lack of integration or collaboration in the development of policy that impacts on their lives. The institution would have a remit across all areas of children's rights and policy which would facilitate a more effective overview on the overall impact of government policy on children. It would encourage greater co-ordination between government departments, local authority departments, between agencies working at local level and voluntary organisations.

Fifth, the institution would need to be established with statutory powers. The ultimate authority of the institution would rest on its ability to act independently, produce well-researched information, exhibit a credible and respected public presence and respond effectively to important issues affecting children. However, it would need certain statutory powers and duties if it is to serve as an effective body in monitoring and promoting the human rights of children. First and foremost, the statutory base should be linked to a commitment to promote full implementation of the Convention on the Rights of the Child, alongside any other relevant international human rights treaties and instruments.

Sixth, the institution must be visible and accessible to children if it is to be used by them. It needs therefore to be high profile and promote itself directly to children. It needs to be non-bureaucratic in its procedures and will require the development of information and materials which are targeted at different age groups and disseminated through the media which children use.

Finally, it must establish an exclusive focus on children. Children have not traditionally been viewed as subjects of rights and insofar as they are considered at all in the human rights field, they take a fairly low priority. While many of the rights of children are those shared by adults, children have additional rights by virtue of their youth and vulnerability – the right to be listened to and taken seriously, the right to protection from sexual abuse, the right to alternative care if unable to live with their family, protection in the process of adoption. Without an exclusive focus on children, not only is there a danger that their priorities will not be given adequate consideration, but that their specific rights are likely to be disregarded.

Moving forward

Now is a highly opportune moment for the government to take action. At the international level, the Committee on the Rights of the Child is pressing governments, including the UK, to introduce a body to monitor implementation of the human rights of children. The government is due to report to the Committee on the Rights of the Child in 2002 when it will be asked how it has responded to the Committee's earlier recommendation that consideration be given to setting up an independent body to monitor, promote and protect children's rights. Increasing numbers of European governments have already acted on these recommendations. In Ireland, the President of the Irish Republic signed the Irish Human Rights Commission Bill into law in June and the new body is expected to be up and running early in 2001. The government has also made a commitment to introducing a statutory Children's Rights Commissioner and is currently (November 2000) drafting the necessary legislation. In Northern Ireland, a Human Rights Commission already exists and in Scotland, action is in progress to explore the case for both a Human Rights Commission and a Children's Rights Commissioner. A statutory Children's Rights Commissioner has been established in Wales. In Westminster there is growing support amongst MPs for the creation of such a body.

Of additional significance is the entry into force of the Human Rights Act 1998 in October 2000 with its profound implications for enhancing protection of human rights for all citizens, including children, through incorporation of the European Convention on Human Rights. However, there is evidence that a significant majority of public authorities are ill prepared and ignorant about the responsibilities it imposes on them. A survey undertaken for IPPR early in 2000 found that many organisations fulfilling vital public functions are unaware of the Act and have received no information advising them on their obligations. The government itself needs advice and guidance if it is to develop its objective of a preventive rather than litigious passage for the Act. The government has repeatedly stated that it intended that the legislation should herald a culture of respect for human rights in this country. If this is to happen, there is a pressing need for a Human Rights Commission, and a Children's Rights Commissioner, either as a dedicated post within such a Commission or established as a separate but closely linked body to facilitate that process (Spencer and Bynoe, 1998).

Conclusion

The UK government voluntarily incorporated the European Convention on Human Rights into domestic law. It voluntarily ratified the UN Convention on the Rights of the Child in 1991. In so doing, it has undertaken a number of obligations to children. The government is correct in stating that the Convention on the Rights of the Child does not require it to introduce a statutory body to monitor and promote the rights of children. However, it does impose obligations to "undertake all appropriate legislative, administrative and other measures for the implementation of the rights ... in the ... Convention" (Article 4). It does impose an obligation to ensure that both children and adults know about the Convention rights and their implications (Article 42). Evidence from the ten years since ratification reveals that these duties are not being complied with satisfactorily. The creation of a Children's Rights Commissioner would serve to enhance the process of promoting a culture of respect for human rights in this country. It would provide a resource to government in developing training, public awareness and the development of structures for meaningful children's participation. It would help identify the changes needed to law, policy and practice necessary for implementation of the Convention. It would promote the creation of structures for challenging violations of rights. Importantly, it would serve to demonstrate not only the government's commitment to respect for the human rights of children, but also a willingness to be held to account on that commitment.

Children have rights as children which must be respected. However, investment in those rights will not only have significant beneficial consequences to them as individual children throughout their lives, but also to society as a whole. Establishing human rights institutions which will contribute towards the realisation of children's human rights represents a small investment with significant long-term outcomes. It makes economic, social as well as moral sense. The government must be persuaded to see the argument.

Notes

1   Vienna Declaration and Programme of Action adopted by the World Conference on Human Rights, Vienna, 25 June 1993, UN Doc. A/CONF.157/24.
2   Principles relating to the status of national institutions, UN General Assembly resolution 48/134. 20 December 1993, annex.
3   Committee on the Rights of the Child, Consideration of States Parties reports: UK, CRC/C/SR.204, 27 June 1995.
4   *Child Poverty in Rich Nations*, Innocenti report Card, issue No 1, Florence, Innocenti Research Centre June 2000.
5   Unannounced Inspection report of HM Chief Inspector of Prisons, Feltham Young Offender Institutions and Remand Centre, December 1998.

References

Alderson, P. (2000) *Civil Rights In Schools Project Report*, Social Science Research Unit, Institute of Education London
Children's Rights Alliance For England (2001) *Campaign For A Children's Rights Commissioner*, London, CRAE
Hodgkin, R and Newell, P. (1996) *Effective Government Structures for Children*, London, Gulbenkian Foundation
—— (1997) *Implementation Handbook For the Convention on the Rights of the Child*, New York, UNICEF

Lansdown, G. (2001a) *Independent Human Rights Institutions for Children*, Florence, Innocenti Research Centre
—— (2001b) "Children's Welfare and Children's Rights" in P. Foley, J. Roche and S. Tuckers (eds) *Children in Society: Contemporary theory, policy and practice*, Basingstoke, Palgrave, pp. 87–97
Newell, P. (2000) *Taking Children Seriously*, London: Gulbenkian Foundation
Rosenbaum, M. and Newell, P. (1991) *Taking Children's Rights Seriously*, London, Gulbenkian Foundation
Select Committee on Health (1998) *Children Looked After By Local Authorities*, Select Committee on Health Second Report, London, The Stationary Office, July
Spencer, S. and Bynoe, I. (1998) *A Human Rights Commission: The Options For Britain and Northern Ireland*, London, IPPR

18 Citizenship education
Who pays the piper?

Carole Scott

Introduction

At the turn of the century discourses about young people, including those
which dominate the academy, focus on the "problematic" rather than the
"normal" and construct a youth "collective" as undisciplined and rebellious (Humphries, 1981), as muggers and weapon-carrying hooligans
(Cotterell, 1996), and as being "out of control" (Coffield *et al.*, 1986;
Griffin, 1993). Young urbanites appear as "potential criminals", arousing
large-scale suspicion among adults (Scott, 2000). Such discourses, however,
have helped to shape policies which have had a considerable impact on
young people's lives. Prefacing other, nationally-expressed concerns about
youth apathy, low educational achievement, declining post-16 educational
and vocational participation, they have contributed to the rhetoric of
"raising standards" and "long-term social exclusion" (Pearce and Hillman,
1998). In turn, this has prompted a UK national social inclusion policy
agenda for young people which has deployed the Social Exclusion Unit,
the Excellence in Cities Education Initiative 11–16, Gifted and Talented
and Learning Mentor Strands, Excellence Challenge Fresh Start, the New
Deal Initiatives 16–24, and the Criminal Justice service. This policy agenda,
accepted with great alacrity but little public debate, has been centrist and
authoritarian in its approach (Dale *et al.*, 1990; Jeffs, 1995).

Specific concerns have been voiced about young people's alleged lack of
interest in civic involvement (Crace, 2000), while European disquiet has been
expressed (European Commission, 1998) concerning an alleged disappearing
sense of belonging. However, "inclusion" seems to be little more than a
political expedient, reflecting successive governments' concerns that they are
losing their national audience. The decline of ideologically based politics, in
tandem with the decreasing party political involvement of adults (Willis,
2000), and falling voter turnout, threatens to undermine the legitimacy of
local government (Brown and Elrick, 1999), and is worrying parties and
national governments. Perhaps, unsurprisingly, there has been a growing
rejection of traditional party politics among young people, who lack enthusiasm for the formal political process, experience central government as

remote and may be poorly informed about the traditional political sphere (Bruce *et al.*, 2000; Hall and Williamson, 1999).

Young people's "apathy"?

The well-rehearsed themes of youthful innocence, ignorance, cynicism and distrust are being blended discursively to produce a new myth – that of "politically apathetic youth". It is unwise however to speculate about "young people's" political behaviour without identifying the different meanings of "democratic" politics as they understand them. The political climate in which young voters have been nurtured across the last twenty-five years has changed greatly as the industrial base of Britain has collapsed and dissolved traditional voting patterns. The ideological base of major political parties has changed with traditional "voter identity" becoming confused. Working-class adults (especially unemployed people) vote less, or not at all, while many do not register to vote. For others, politicians and the day-to-day protocols of politics seem broadly irrelevant and apathy is perhaps a predictable response. A significant number of children, like their parents, no longer live within or experience a culture of clear party allegiance or voting.

Many youngsters, however, are affected directly and indirectly by unemployment and changes in the labour market, which can affect their political decision-making. "Long-term" unemployment may mean an entire childhood of hardship, producing experiences which generate scepticism, if not cynicism, about politicians' ability to effect change. The material circumstances of unemployment differ among individuals, but for children one important outcome is their inability to participate in mass cultural forms: a major resource in the construction of the contemporary self (Scott, 2000). Such day-to-day material circumstances contribute greatly to the grounding of the logic upon which young people eventually exercise their franchise.

Children, it seems, like their parents, are knowledgeable about single-issue politics from the global to the personal, and value being consulted (Forna, 2000; Jeffs, 1995). Many show early interest in political affairs (Franklin, 1986), are concerned about equal opportunities and the environment, with almost half 16–21-year-olds undertaking voluntary work (Forna, 2000). Many do vote. But evidence concerning young people's political interest reveals marked differences, with increased participation among more wealthy (Berry *et al.*, 1991), and employed young people (Galbraith, 1992).

Recent policy decisions by both Conservative and Labour governments, moreover, have curtailed opportunities for young people to participate in certain spheres. The introduction of contributions towards tuition fees for higher education, for example, has diminished – if not removed – young people's right to equal educational opportunity and risks involving them in financial debt. Further, UK employment policy has excluded many young workers from minimum wage legislation, reinforcing their social standing as "of lesser status".

Such "blanket" policies operate to different effect, of course, across different socio-economic groups: youngsters dependent on limited family income to support them have seen their autonomy, capacity for participation, and real choice radically diminished. At first glance, this hardly seems to be a policy agenda designed to engage young people and encourage their political involvement. Growing poverty has exacerbated the situation for many of them who now find themselves seriously disadvantaged and unable to articulate their concerns and exercise their rights within the political sphere. Many risk permanent marginalisation as they mature (Geddes, 2000). So, providing a grounding in "civics" embodying democratic ideals, imbued with local and regional inflection, seems entirely sensible and morally sound – but not to reduce apathy. Rather, this would better be to develop young people's understanding of contemporary democratic process and practice for establishing rights claims. A citizenship education strategy must aim to emancipate.

The government response – National Curriculum citizenship education

In Britain, the concern about what constituted citizenship and how it might be transmitted to young people can be traced to the period following the World War II (Hall and Williamson, 1999). Dominant discourses (Marshall, 1950) emerging against the backdrop of achievement of political and civil rights were shaped by the "building and development culture" of that time and focused, euphorically, on national integration. But the subsequent post-industrial collapse in the 1980s, with its particular effects on young people, found discourses about citizenship focused more on problems of social exclusion, and loss or denial of rights for many of them.

Closer to the millennium, the debate concerning young people's civic "participation" shifted again to stress not only their "rights" but also their "responsibilities" and highlighted the role of formal education as the key provider. The Educational Reform Act (1988) aimed to promote the spiritual, moral, cultural, mental and physical development of pupils at school and as citizens of society, and to prepare them for the opportunities, responsibilities and experiences of adult life. In 1990, the government established the importance of positive, participative citizenship intended to provide motivation for pupils to become engaged (National Curriculum Council, 1990). Further notions of citizenship education as a part of a national strategy (School Curriculum and Assessment Authority, 1996) were designed to "improve" but lagged behind many other countries (Voiels, 1998).

Second-wave feminist thinking contributed to citizenship debates, by highlighting diversity, and raising awareness of status relationships being grounded not only in class, but mediated by ethnicity, region, age and gender (Lister, 1997). The newly elected Labour government continued the debate but argued for tackling inequality and social exclusion by promoting opportunity and participation (Cm 5805, 1998). Given the abstention of 43 per cent of 18–24-year-olds from voting, the Secretary of State for Education devised a strategy for increasing political participation – the 5–16 National Curriculum for Citizenship Education (Department for Education and Employment, 1999a), which aimed to inform and engage young people politically. This Curriculum for Citizenship fuelled a popular myth, for there has never been a "golden age of citizenship" (Patrick and Schuller, 1999)

Positioning citizenship education in the 5–16 National Curriculum defines, and arguably prescribes, British citizenship through four "Key Stages" (age-stages), with each having Statutory Attainment Targets, which define the type and range of performance that the majority of pupils should characteristically demonstrate. Furthermore, the National Curriculum model subscribes most appropriately to a didactic belief system, for standardised, graded programmes, target setting and attainment recording, which all make this the least risk-laden and most efficient pedagogy for the teacher-administrator to monitor and record progress and attainment.

Citizenship education is to become compulsory for pupils to learn and teachers to teach (Crace, 2000) in state-maintained schools by September 2002, however coercive or unjust. Here, it should be noted that, arguably, it could be introduced into schools with the minimum disruption by timetabling it formally and discretely in dedicated "Citizenship" lessons. To date, however, decisions about the style of delivery rest with each school, there being no close guidance. Assessment guidance is to follow (Department for Education and Employment, 1999a).

Education for citizenship: problems of method

There are number of problems with education for citizenship formulated in this way. First, because the idea of learner participation is enshrined within the philosophy of citizenship education, active involvement in democratic politics is essential. Citizenship cannot be "taught" didactically, nor assessed by test scores. Children "live" citizenship (Dewey, 1916) through experiences within their own society. In school, therefore, the young citizen comes to understand active citizenship, not only formally, but by witnessing and experiencing political relationships and processes in practice through the informal curriculum. Children's citizenship education grows through their engagement as practice rather than rhetoric.

Active citizenship education in school must signal the end of "safe" role-play and simulation both in citizenship lessons and other realms of school life. It is a cross-curricular ideal, for democratic practice must permeate the learner's lived world. "Engagement" and "participation" emerge through a methodology of partnership between teacher and learner, where the latter is valued and enabled to research, listen, speak, analyse, evaluate – to have a "voice" in the learning process. The child must possess rights in lessons, which presumes that the rights-holder is able to make and exercise choices

(Archard, 1993: 65). So, the child learns to participate in "real" settings which provide increasing scope for responsible action and with a growing experience of taking responsibility.

Central, therefore, to the integrity of citizenship education is its mode of delivery – ideally through a skills-based curriculum in which the teacher is facilitator and the learner has rights of incorporation. To eschew this pedagogy for a didactic model is to teach the learner informally that contradictions and double standards are intrinsic to a citizen's *modus operandi*. This would risk civic rights and responsibilities being understood as "out there", for some adults only and of increasing irrelevance to young people. So, citizenship education is a necessary "journey of risk" as the participating child must be invested with power as increasing trust is placed in their capacity to direct their own progress.

Citizenship education must also incorporate the right of the learner and the teacher to choose to abstain. Participation must be by agreement, for securing participation by coercion would represent a threat to liberty (Forna, 2000). One strong characteristic of adolescence, however, is to challenge, and democratic ideals must incorporate affirmation and respect for the wishes of those young citizens who wish to construct themselves as "out of it". And here, surely, is the place for listening to young people – the need for more sensitive research into young people's political attitudes, grounded in a philosophy of inclusion, an ontology of engagement-as-empowerment, and designed to stimulate active citizenship through programmes which have relevance for youngsters, as they see it. Ultimately, however, choosing not to be affiliated must remain a citizen's right.

Educating future citizens

There is a second problem. The Department for Education and Employment (DfEE) has been "centralist" and "dictatorial" (Blunkett cited in Willis, 2000) in implementing its educational philosophy. Consequently, to construct a democratic model of delivery for active citizenship – a training in philosophical awakening and the investing of power in children – would represent a significant ideological shift. Anyone committed to defending and promoting the rights of children would want to scrutinise such a development closely.

It is clear that in England and Wales educational philosophy has been infected by free market economic principles. Its executive force, the DfEE and its militia, OFSTED, appear to view the education of children as preparation for work. So far as a rights and responsibilities programme of citizenship education is concerned, this necessarily places the right-holding of the child in the future tense – not as "being" but as "to be" – a relationship which permeates rhetorically through citizenship programmes. Citizenship education is clearly aimed to generate worker-citizens: and of the future not the present.

The content of citizenship education for schools is also problematic if a rights claims curriculum is to flourish. Highly prescriptive, its emphasis is on de-contextualised factual knowledge rather than on socially placed learning. Learners have no scope to explore democracy democratically. Educational discourses reflect the dominant idea of "youth as emergent" and the citizenship programme shares and reflects this view. Children are not invested with the rights and responsibilities of citizens of "today". Evidence in their communities abounds as to their "potential", yet "potential" in school is rhetorically positioned as being in the long term. Tragically for their rights claims, schools have missed the opportunity to guide youngsters' energy and intellectual and organisational capacities into civic participation. But most importantly, they have failed to acknowledge children and young people as valued members of the democracy about which they are learning.

School culture and the prospects for citizenship

There is a third problem here. There is no tradition of listening to children in the shaping of British education policy. Legislation has always cast young people in the mould of "powerless subjects" (Jeffs, 1995), and the resulting pedagogy for classroom delivery has been largely didactic, an ideology and epistemology intrinsically flawed in teaching citizenship, as it privileges the educator and offers little territory for exercising responsible, independent, action by the learner. Schools are undemocratic institutions for staff and children in which to learn to be a citizen (Scott, 2000). Schools are characterised by anachronistic Fordist features, including "mass production" through a standardised curriculum and mass examining, a standardised production line in academic year-groups, an inspectorate, surveillance and monitoring, performance targeting, accountability, and publication of results tables (Best, 1993 and Ball, 1987). There is no scope for children to speak or to be listened to.

For their part, school heads and governors have little genuine autonomy given the general shift of power from the local to central government. The reality of "financial decision-making" is financial "administration", which leaves little scope for autonomy or flexibility. Failure to meet targets involves financial implications, which inhibit the development of a risk culture. As Jeffs (1995) notes, schools must police a system they can barely influence. The way citizenship education is being delivered reflects this impasse – National Curriculum citizenship rhetoric is long on worthy statements (Crace, 2000) but offers little detail, with concerns being raised about contradictions in interpretation (Hall and Williamson, 1999), tokenism (Hart, 1992) and atavism (Crace, 2000) in its pilot applications. In truth, educators themselves are subjugated and schools have never displayed a culture of consultation which is vital if citizenship education is to flourish.

Teachers' knowledge and beliefs are significant for the way they structure children's learning and consequently for the outcomes of young people's educational experience of citizenship (Richardson *et al.*, 1991, and Bennett *et al.*, 1997). Teachers are highly resistant to change and the need to provide opportunities for children to reflect and examine critically will create discomfort for teachers who are ill at ease and untrained in debating democracy (Voiels, 1998). "Participation" also carries risks for the child in the classroom, for it presumes respect for diversity of view: a value perhaps not shared by the teaching cohort in their practice. So there is a strong possibility that teaching citizenship inappropriately, within a climate of double standards in which the child's subordination is revealed clearly to them, will prompt many more young people to "disengage" from democratic processes before they reach statutory leaving age.

To deliver active citizenship effectively requires radical change. At present, the child will learn in school that "governance" it is a top-down model, designed obsessively to administer budgets within the rhetoric of "resources" and "results" which confuses "leadership" with administration, and "vision" with targeting, where teachers are delivery personnel and the curriculum is nationally enforced. "Listening" and "contributing" are then played out exclusively through interactions about money and standards. This model would seem not only to militate against learning of true democratic processes but negate their value within the logic of the learner. Having children emerging in this climate, increasingly politically aware, increasingly "engaged" and seeking participation would be to expose their governors', managers', and their teachers' own impotence and could signal a move to place this on the agenda of the next school council for debate! Indeed, active citizenship does not sit comfortably on the school curriculum in England and Wales.

It would be unwise here to underestimate the intellectual capacities of children: nor their resilience, which might prove costly to them later. In an undemocratic climate of learning, children seem destined to live citizenship "passively". However, they will respond actively and individually. Some will "buy" it. Among the more astute, some will realise the hypocrisy and dishonesty of the "citizenship package" and respond with disaffection, or cynicism; others may engage as "active learners" in their discontent – as disruptive. How will this outcome be graded, when it falls to the teacher to assess? Assessment of "achievement" and "results" in citizenship education is inherently elusive, for "learning outcomes" are surely life-long? However, "level of disaffection" is one which could emerge. Undoubtedly more worrying and perhaps more injurious to the child, National Curriculum citizenship education holds the potential for a new construction, a new myth – enter the "failed" citizen. How will it be interpreted by careers personnel or prospective employers, reading a child's National Record of Achievement?

Educating "citizens of the firm"

A fourth problem arises from the process whereby the individual, family and social needs have become increasingly subordinated to the market (Willis,

1990; Robertson, 1992). Arguably, third millennial citizenship risks becoming grounded in the market and popular consumption. Educational philosophy's sublimation to the market economy is pervasive. Cash-conscious schools, looking for ways to deliver an active curriculum involving the community, are encouraged by the partnering philosophies of contemporary political parties to look for financial support from the local business community rather than central government. The result is that children become "citizens of the firm" rather than "citizens of the community".

Cohen (1999) argues that in the context of citizenship education this reciprocity constitutes a violation of children's rights. For children's civic "engagement" and "participation" are being re-produced by the market – as consumption and the upholding of capitalist principles. "Participation" in citizenship education seems rooted in "enterprise" with strong messages about "entrepreneurial-skill" development and "work-related learning". "Thinking skills" are mediated through financial capability. Also, exemplars used in consideration of "justice" are worrying. For example, "deviance" is presented within narrow parameters, refracted as young deviants and street crime, theft as shop-lifting, stealing cars, thus eclipsing white-collar and corporate crime. Enshrined in "community", in citizenship education, is "business community" where "values", "morals", and "ethics" are hijacked by capitalism. "Participation" means "buying a ticket". It is clear "whose values" are being promoted, and "whose rights".

The National Curriculum citizenship programme reflects this widespread victimisation of children in the classroom which is endorsed by politicians through their "partnering" with the business community whose stated aims are to make profit for its owners. Firms are offering consultation, writing materials, promoting themselves and manipulating behaviour overtly and covertly at all levels of educational delivery (DfEE, 1999a). Unsurprisingly, business ideology permeates citizenship education literature fostering a new and insidious symbiosis; and at a time when other governments are proposing banning commercials aimed at children (Cohen, 1999). Britain, allegedly the most consumerist country in Europe, has dismissed even mild regulation and is opening its school doors to such commercial interests (DfEE, 1999b).

Competition is an act of aggression, having no educative place in a progressive, peaceful, society other than within some fantasy realm of "informed" and "free" choice. While this generalising view may be variously contested, competition ideology should surely not play any part in the education of the young citizen. Classrooms have become battlefields for hearts and minds. For the policy of "partnering" means businesses offering money and resources in return for "presence" in the child's habitus (Bourdieu, 1981). Such a policy of exposure to and indoctrination by mass marketeers, using teachers – whom infants are told to trust – as promoters, must be seen as highly irresponsible behaviour, if not a system of psychological abuse.

This is a strong, not hysterical, claim. Cohen (1999) argues that children with their "empty memory banks" are highly retentive and particularly vulnerable to mass marketing messages designed to inculcate brand worship. This is no new claim about education. But when the adult community endorses the large-scale enticement of children into the business world as "education-for-citizenship" as quasi-citizens, it is not only "packaging" them for their role as consumers – but also telling them "it's OK citizenship" (Cohen, 2000). Such a partnering philosophy driving notions of citizenship risks spawning values of "inclusion" by exclusion.

Children in community – education for "second class citizens"

There is a fifth and final problem with this conception of civic education. Citizenship is not only "lived" in school but in the community where the child as young citizen gains increasing understanding of what constitutes justice through her/his own experience. For the British child these "lessons" may take place on the street – at the bus stop, in shops and shopping malls, in car parks and bus station concourses – in social interaction with the adult world. Shopkeepers, bus drivers, security guards, the uniformed police, and their own parents thus become informal educators of citizenship. But how can young people be motivated about their communities when nothing out there reflects the young person? It is remarkable that children are able to select from this the positive experiences that they do from community involvement and volunteering.

Knowing how to work with local people is integral to social inclusion and citizenship (Brown and Elrick, 1999). So experience centred in the child's own community is the key provider which is then contextualised more widely. Sadly, "the community consciousness" has a long way to go in fulfilling this role. Young urbanites form a marginalised age class. Their movement is restricted, out of fear and distrust, within aims to protect, monitored by city surveillance methods within the security-obsessed fabric (Merrifield and Swyngedouw, 1995) of urban society. On these landscapes of power and simulated places of consumption (Turner, 1996), they are subjected to a new authoritarianism within youth policy (Jeffs and Smith, 1996). Entering the adult domain, the child experiences such difference and inequality first-hand, and learns that rights are contractual, that the child is not a citizen, a rights-holder, but a citizen-to-be, with role-models all around him/her, and that civic "participation" depends on consent by adults.

Further the contemporary child develops within the hegemony of resignation (Miliband, 1994) in a climate of privatised domestic activity and decreasing human contact and interaction (Patrick and Schuller, 1999), thereby lacking active contexts in which to be a citizen. So, "active", in the legal sense of freedom to act, and the normative sense of having responsibility to act (Hall and Williamson, 1999) disappears from the child's lived experience of "community". Children's understanding is that "civics" is defined by power-holding elite groups through *invested* rather than *divested* power in the adult realm of behaviour. It has little to do with children.

Conclusion – lost to the child-snatcher

Education and community policy-makers must research more sensitively, to explode mythical generalisations concerning young people's apathy. Children must be awarded the right to participate within their communities while adults must work to rebalance their present relationship with young people.

Politicians must listen more carefully to children who demonstrate significant political "engagement". Children and young people's distrust and disdain of conventional politics may represent a sensible appraisal and a logical response to contemporary political structures: young people have seen their "Emperors" and are under-impressed. Strategies for engagement must not insult young people's intellectual capacities, and must educate for politics-as-empowerment rather than introducing publicity initiatives destined to reveal politics-as-circus and politicians-as-clowns.

Research, moreover, is necessary to explore the ways in which young people are represented in texts. Worse, some scholarly writing practices have contributed to the marginalisation of politically and often economically disenfranchised groups (Hammersley, 1995; Scott, 2000). Particularly significant is the need to focus on citizenship literature in schools, to understand more about how it is actively appropriated by young people. Society constructs the children it needs. This is worrying, because contemporary citizenship education, given its link with business, represents a genuine threat to rights claims. Mass producers must maintain mass sales, achieved through marketing and persuasion, which constructs "individuality" through association with brand names. The key behaviour required is repeat buying, and the key characteristics needing to be germinated and cultivated for this are rebelliousness and dissatisfaction. For "voting" read "consuming".

There are more serious threats to the body politic. British policy-makers must acknowledge the dangers of subliminal advertising and join the growing opposition to commercialisation in schools. Here, again, the research community must contribute. Contemporary marketing aims to develop a desire for "individuality" – but of the "right type" – so as to be included in the group. But this represents a sublimation of the will. Gathering children within a business-laden citizenship curriculum, at an age when the construction of identity and self is critical, cultivates a civic rationale embodying materialism, competitiveness and self-centredness, and contextualised within a strong "gang" inflection.

Privileging partnering with business ethics as a *modus operandi* for teaching democratic politics, without questioning the morality of competitiveness, is a high risk strategy. The risk is getting the young "citizens" we deserve, coerced through pro-market dogma to be consumerist, acquisitive, rebellious, irresponsible and hypocritical – "citizens of capitalism" – their

rights claims stolen by a contemporary "Pied Piper" – National Curriculum
citizenship education.

References

Archard, D. (1993) *Children: Rights and Childhood*, London: Routledge
Ball, C. (1987) *The Micro-Politics of the School*, London: Methuen
Bennett, N., Wood, L. and Rogers, S. (1997) *Teaching Through Play: Teachers'
  Thinking and Classroom Practice*, Buckingham: Open University Press
Berry, J.M, Portney, K.E. and Thomson, K. (1999) "The Political Behaviour of the
  Poor" in Jencks, C., and Peterson, P.E., *The Urban Underclass*, Washington:
  Brookings Institute
Best, J.H. (1993) "Perspectives on De-regulation of Schooling in America", *British
  Journal of Educational Studies*, pp. 122–133
Bourdieu, P. (1981) *Situating Social Theory*, Oxford: Oxford University Press
Brown, M. and Elrick, D. (1999) "Best Value From Local Government? A Commu-
  nity Development Perspective", in *Scottish Journal of Community Work and
  Development*, Spring 1999, pp. 39–53
Bruce, S., Ritchie, J. and White, C. (2000) *Young People's Politics: Political Interest
  and Engagement Amongst 14–24 Year Olds*, YPS for National Centre for Social
  Research, York: York Publishing Services Ltd
Cm 5805 (1998) *New Ambitions For Our Country: A New Contract for Welfare*,
  London: The Stationery Office
Coffield, F. *et al.* (1986) *Growing Up At The Margins*, Milton Keynes: Open Univer-
  sity Press
Cohen, N. (1999) "The Childhood Snatchers", *New Statesman*, 1 November, pp.
  8–11
—— (2000) "Behind Closed Doors", *New Statesman*, 12 June 2000, pp. 9–12
Cotterell, J. (1996) *Social Networks and Social Influences in Adolescence*, London:
  Routledge
Council Of Europe (1985) *Recommendation No. (85)7 of the Committee of Ministers
  to Member States on Teaching and Learning about Human Rights in Schools*,
  Strasbourg: Council of Europe
—— (1996) *History Teaching and the Promotion of Democratic Values and Tolerance:
  A Handbook for Teachers*, Strasbourg: Council of Europe
Crace, J. (2000) "The New Citizens", *Guardian Education*, 15 February, p. 2
Dale, R. *et al.* (1990) *The TVEI Story*, Buckingham: Open University Press
Department for Education And Employment (1999a) *Citizenship, 5–16*, Qualifica-
  tions and Curriculum Authority
—— (1999b) Educational Action Zone Advisory Service, and "Meet The Chal-
  lenge", HMSO, in *Education Business Partnership NewsLetter*, No. 43, March,
  Published by Business in the Community, sponsored by Unilever
Dewey, J. (1916) *Democracy and Education*, New York: Macmillan
Education Reform Act (1988) London: HMSO
European Commission (1998) *Treaty of Amsterdam, Education and Active Citizen-
  ship in the European Union*, Luxembourg: Office for Official Publications of the
  European Communities
Feinberg, W. (1983) *Understanding Education*, Cambridge: Cambridge University
  Press

Forna, A. (2000) "Broken Engagement" in *Search*, 33, Spring, pp. 14–15

Fornas, J. and Bolin, G. (1995) *Youth Culture in Late Modernity*, London: Sage

Franklin, B. (1986) *The Right of the Child*, Oxford: Blackwell

—— (ed.) (1995) *The Handbook of Children's Rights: comparative policy and practice*, London: Routledge

Frost, R. (2000) "A New Future, 2000", *Guardian*, 16 May, p. 17

Galbraith, J.K. (1992) *The Culture of Contentment*, London: Penguin

Geddes, M. (2000) *Partnership Against Poverty and Exclusion – Local Regeneration Strategies and Excluded Communities in the UK*, Bristol: The Policy Press

Gmelch, G. and Zenner, W.P. (1996) *Urban Life*, Illinois: Waveland Press

Griffin, C. (1993) *Representations of Youth*, Oxford: Polity Press

Gutmann, A. (1990) "Democracy and Democratic Education", paper presented at the International Network of Philosophy of Education Conference, London, in Griffith, R. (ed.) (1998) *Educational Citizenship and Independent Learning*, Gateshead: Athanaeum Press, p. 31

Hall, T. and Williamson, H. (1999) *Citizenship and Community*, National Youth Agency, Leicester: Youth Work Press

Hammersley, M. (1995) *The Politics of Social Research*, London: Sage

Hart, R. (1992) *Children's Participation: From Tokenism to Citizenship,* Innocenti Essays No. 4, Florence: UNICEF International Child Development Centre

Holden, C. and Clough, N. (1998) *Children as Citizens: Education for Participation*, London and Philadelphia: Jessica Kingsley

Humphries, S. (1981) *Hooligans and Rebels: An Oral History of Working Class Childhood and Youth 1889–1939*, Oxford: Basil Blackwell

Jeffs, T. (1995) "Educational Rights in a New Era", in Franklin, B. (ed.) *The Handbook of Children's Rights: comparative policy and practice*, London: Routledge, pp. 25–39

Jeffs, T. and Smith, M.K. (1994) "Young People, Youth Work and a New Authoritarianism", *Youth and Policy*, 46, pp. 17–32

—— (1996) "Getting the Dirtbags off the Streets: Curfews and Other Solutions to Juvenile Crime", *Youth and Policy*, 53, pp. 1–14

Lister, R. (1997) *Citizenship: Feminist Perspectives*, London: MacMillan

Marshall, T.H. (1950) *Citizenship and Social Class and Other Essays*, Cambridge: Cambridge University Press

Merrifield A. and Swyngedouw, E. (eds) (1995) *The Urbanisation of Injustice*, London: Lawrence & Wishart

Miliband, R. (1994) *Socialism for a Sceptical Age*, London: Polity

National Curriculum Council (1990) *Curriculum Guidance 8: Education for Citizenship*, York: National Curriculum Council

Osler, A. (1998) "Conflicts, Controversy and Caring: Young People's Attitudes Towards Children's Rights" in Holden and Clough

Patrick, F. and Schuller, T. (1999) "Towards an Active Citizenship Curriculum", in *The Scottish Journal of Community Work and Development*, Spring 1999. pp. 83–88

Pearce, N. and Hillman, J. (1998) *Wasted Youth: Raising Achievement and Tackling Social Exclusion*, London: Institute of Public Policy Research

Plato (1935) *The Republic, Book One*, Irwin, T. (ed.), London: Everyman

Richardson, V. *et al.* (1991) "The Relationship Between Teachers' Beliefs and Practices in Reading, Comprehension and Instruction", *American Educational Research Journal*, 29 (3), pp. 559–586

Robertson, R. (1992) *Globalisation, Social Theory and Global Culture*, London: Sage

School Curriculum and Assessment Authority (SCAA) (1996) "Education For Adult Life: Social, Moral and Spiritual Education", Discussion paper, No. 6, London

Scott, C.A. (2000) "Going Home With the Chaps: Concerning the Degradation of Young Urbanites, and their Social Space and Time", *Youth and Policy*, 69, August, pp. 17–41

Turner, B. (ed.) (1996) *The Blackwell Companion to Social Theory*, Oxford: Blackwell

Voiels, V. (1998) "New Teachers Talking Citizenship" in Holden and Clough, pp. 196–205

Willis, P. (with Jones, S., Canaan, J. and Hind, G.) (1990) *Common Culture: Symbolic Work at Play in the Everyday Cultures of the Young*, Milton Keynes: Open University Press

Willis, P. (2000) "New Bill is a Fog of Confusion", *Guardian*, 18 January

19 Making it happen: young children's rights in action

The work of Save the Children's Centre for Young Children's Rights

Tina Hyder

Introduction

"Babies consulted about council policy"

This local newspaper headline provocatively caricatured a recent Centre for Young Children's Rights (CYCR) project, working with an Early Years Development and Childcare Partnership (EYDCP) on listening to children. The article attacked the council for what it described as "an extreme example of [a] pro-listening policy", where under fives had "been asked their views on their food, toys and environment" (*Highbury and Islington Express*, 26 May 2000). Its predictable target was the perceived waste of money by the local council (although technically the EYDCP is an independent agency). More interestingly, the hostile tone of the article reflects the commonly held belief that children are not worth listening to. It is the opposite belief – that even the youngest children have a right to be heard – that is at the heart of CYCR's work. The newspaper article illustrates well the context within which CYCR operates; a context where the ridiculing of children's rights is seen as common sense, and the attempt to consult children seen as money wasted.

CYCR aims to promote the rights of young children and to act as a bridge between the theory and practice of the realisation of rights for young children. This is achieved by developing, testing and advocating the use of approaches that will enable adults and organisations to listen to even the youngest children – encouraging adults to make that conceptual shift towards the recognition of the rights of all children. The goal of the Centre is to ensure that all young children have the opportunity to express their views on the matters that affect them and to participate in the places where they spend much of their time. At the same time, we support those children who are socially excluded, through discrimination or poverty, to have their say about their lives.

While much of our work is with children themselves, we also aim to inform and work in partnership with those adults who work daily with children in early years, play settings and schools, so that the principles of listening to children and young children's participation are embedded in everyday practice. This chapter has three broad sections. The first places the work of the CYCR in the context of Save the Children's (SC-UK) global commitment to the realisation of children's rights. The second looks closely at some recent and current development projects conducted by the CYCR. The third explores some of the issues that arise when promoting young children's rights.

Children's rights and Save the Children

The founder of Save the Children, Eglantyne Jebb, was responsible for drafting the first Charter of the Rights of the Child in 1923. She argued that Save the Children's practical work needed to be complemented by the much wider support which would be achieved by a heightened awareness of adult's obligations towards children. In order to bestow international status on this work, she approached the League of Nations which in 1924 adopted the charter as the Declaration of the Rights of the Child. This was the very first human rights declaration adopted by any inter-governmental body and significantly predates the adoption of any other international standards codifying universally recognised human rights.

Since the adoption of the Convention by the United Nations (UNCRC) in 1989, Save the Children organisations in other countries have been active in promoting awareness of the Convention and its deployment around the world. In everyday practice children's rights are central to the work of Save the Children internationally. This entails:

* Working towards a progressive realisation of children's rights through programmes of practical action, research and advocacy;
* Playing an active role in building alliances world-wide to promote, support and implement children's rights;
* Developing and promoting training on children's rights for staff, partners, children and others;
* Analysing the potential to contribute to the promotion, implementation and reporting of the UN Convention in every country in which we work;
* Supporting organisations run by children and young people to enable them to defend their own rights.

(Penrose and Bell in Cuninghame, 1999: 58)

Save the Children's programme in England is delivered by six development teams based in the main centres of population. Each of these bases is a focus for work to advance children's rights. Article 12 of the UNCRC refers to the child's right to express an opinion on issues that affect them. In England this is now the central thrust of Save the Children's programme of work (Cuninghame, 1999). The work is conducted with children and not for them, focusing on realising their right of access to all of the benefits and safeguards of citizenship. Save the Children does not believe that children should only have partial rights or be viewed as 'not yet' people. Children are a group of people with developing competencies and are as capable of participating in decisions that affect them as are adults. In some areas of rapid change, or on issues of particular relevance to them, they are likely to be more so.

Set against this is the reality of a tradition of excluding children and young people from decision-making in the United Kingdom. Children are the silent quarter of the population that cannot exercise the basic democratic principle of participation in the law-making process that binds them. They are also the last substantial group in society to have to entrust their rights to others to exercise (Cuninghame, 1999).

The Centre for Young Children's Rights

The Centre for Young Children's Rights is part of the London Development Team, one of the six England development teams: it was launched at the Young Children Can! Conference in 1999. The Centre was a development from SC's Equality Learning Centre (ELC), an influential early years resource, information and training centre that aimed to build a bridge between the theory and practice of equality in the early years. The work of the CYCR builds upon the experience of the ELC by ensuring that all work is underpinned by a commitment to tackling discrimination. CYCR aims to increase understanding of the ways young children's rights can be realised and to provide a platform for young children to express their views. By young we mean children up to the age of 11, but with particular focus on children under the age of 8.

The team of four development workers supported by the team leader carries out a range of short-term and long-term projects that aim to:

- increase opportunities for young children to have a say about the services they use and the issues that affect them;
- raise awareness of the underpinning principles of children's rights;
- develop effective consultation methods;
- ensure that those children who are disadvantaged or marginalised have an opportunity to be heard by policy-makers and others.

To achieve maximum impact for the Centre's work, projects are often developed in partnership with other national and local agencies, for instance, local authorities, school or early years development and childcare partnerships. The development work is supported by an information worker who runs a reference and resource library and provides an information service on all aspects of children's rights, especially equality and ways to support young children's participation.

The team undertakes consultancy, offers training, produces publications and develops community-based initiatives on a range of issues related to the realisation of young children's rights. We have a significant resources collection of materials on young children's participation, ranging from information on methods to ethical and practical considerations when seeking children's views. The service can be used by anyone working with children. Recent and current work can be grouped on a continuum from one-off consultation about a specific issue to projects that aim to embed the ethos and practice of listening to children within a service or institution long-term. The next section aims to give a flavour of CYCR's project work

Listening to children

Consulting children about specific issues

Members of the CYCR have worked on a series of consultation projects focusing on specific issues with groups of young children. Examples include gathering the views of young children on the state of children's rights in the UK (Pandrich, 1999). Their views as well as those of older children from around the country were presented as part of the UK government's report to the Committee on the Rights of the Child which monitors the UK's progress towards implementing the rights of the child. Another example of work initiated by the team is a project with children in the East End of London on how to involve children on an ongoing basis in the development of a new children's museum in Stratford (Miller, 1999). The Children's Discovery Centre, an interactive under-8s space focusing on all aspects of language, is about to be launched and will work in partnership with local children. Three further projects are described in some detail below. Although they differ greatly, they have in common the belief, backed by some practical methods, that young children have something to say about the issues affecting their lives.

Children's views of smacking

> It feels like someone banged you with a hammer (5-year-old girl)

> And sometimes if you smack, if it was an adult like my daddy, he can smack very hard. ... He can smack you like a stone ... and you'll cry (7-year-old boy)

> (Willow and Hyder, 1998: 46 and 60)

In 1997 the European Commission on Human Rights found that the UK government was in breach of Article 3 of the European Convention on Human Rights, which states that no one shall be subjected to inhuman or degrading treatment. The finding related to a case where a young English boy had been repeatedly beaten with a garden cane by his stepfather (this is permitted under UK law following a case in 1860 that allows parents to use 'reasonable chastisement' when disciplining children). The judgement of the European Commission was later reaffirmed by the European Court on Human Rights, which means that British law must now be changed (see chapter 23 by Newell).

At the time the government indicated that it would issue a public consultation on physical punishment – although it has said that a reconsideration of smacking will not be part of the process as "smacking" is not the same as "beating". However it appeared that the views of the people most affected by physical punishment, that is children themselves, were not to be sought. Therefore Save the Children (a member of staff from CYCR) and the National Children's Bureau aimed to consult with children aged between 4 and 7 to ensure that their views could also be represented to government.

Seventy-six children from across the country took part in the consultation exercise in the form of group interviews with a specially designed storyboard featuring an alien called Splodge who asked children questions such as "Who knows what a smack is?" The results were published in a report entitled *It Hurts You Inside: Children Talking About Smacking* (Willow and Hyder, 1998).

The message from children was powerful. Smacking does not work, it hurts and it's confusing. Smacking sends a dangerous message to children that it is acceptable to use violence if you don't agree with someone, or if someone annoys you. *It Hurts You Inside* has been submitted to the government as part of the response from Save the Children to their consultation document *Protecting Children, Supporting Parents: A Consultation Document on the Physical Punishment of Children* (2000). Nevertheless, the voices of children who contributed to *It Hurts You Inside* have already reached decision-makers. The report generated a good deal of publicity when it was launched and children's views and voices were heard on television and radio. The government is now well aware that children have views on smacking, and that some children are optimistic about the impact on policy of airing their views. As one 7-year-old girl said: "If there is a lot of people, like I don't know 70 or something, then I think he [Tony Blair] would definitely change the law" (Willow and Hyder, 1998: 86).

This project was unusual and significant in ensuring that the voices of such young children had been heard by government on a matter of such key concern to them.

Children's views on health services in London

> There's lots of information but children do not see it or pay attention because it is not fun or big enough for them to see. To change this I would make the information more interesting.

> Doctors should tell (you) more about what is going to happen.
>
> (Save the Children, 2000)

CYCR has been commissioned by the NHS Executive for London to find out what children think about health and health services in London. Children from a number of primary schools, a play centre and a refugee support project were given opportunities to comment on their experiences of using GPs, hospitals, dental and other health services. Over 100 children took part in the process. All the schools or centres involved had worked with Save the Children before. Ways of working with children were fun and interactive and included art and drawing, group games, puppetry and so on. The youngest children taking part were aged 5.

When asked how health services could be improved, a few comments were "if they [doctors] sat down in their spare time and talk[ed] to the children" and "you wouldn't have to book an appointment, just go straight in". Dentists could be better if "they didn't have all those frightening tools around – they could put them in drawers" and going to hospital could be better if "they had more fun things to do because you have to wait so long (I had to wait 2 hours)". Many children had very positive experiences of dentists and doctors: "It's fun it's got toys" and "when I'm brave I get a sticker" were two views. Meanwhile, someone still felt that "It doesn't matter whether you are good or not, you still have to go". There were various views about hospitals: "Sometimes there's a lot of blood and dead people and the food is nasty"; on the other hand – "they help people get better and save lives and they smell nice and the nurses are friendly".

These views enabled the report's authors to draw up recommendations included in a report that was used to influence the development of health services in London. The report *A Child's View* was submitted in autumn 2000 and is published by the NHS Executive, London.

This project demonstrates that public services such as the health service are interested in seeking the views of all users, including young children, in order to make more effective the services that are on offer.

"In safe hands"

> It's kind of scary ... one day the government can say go back and suddenly we have to get packed and leave to another country.
>
> (10-year-old refugee, cited in the video accompanying Hyder and Rutter, 2001)

In association with the Refugee Council, CYCR has worked with young asylum seeking children and their families to produce a video with supporting information about how schools and early years settings can support refugee families. The video outlines the circumstances from which many refugees have fled and what families face on their arrival in the UK. It suggests guidelines for good practice and hopefully will enable staff teams around the country to really focus on the best ways to support a group of children who have already shown remarkable resilience.

The Immigration and Asylum Act 1999 has resulted in the creation of a group of "second class" citizens who are seeking asylum and refuge in this country. The impact of the Act on children and families is that families making applications for asylum can now be sent anywhere in the country, perhaps to areas with little history of positive community relations. In addition all welfare entitlements have been withdrawn and this means that families will be expected to live on vouchers (to be exchanged at a few shops) and a small amount of cash. Save the Children is campaigning to ensure that the asylum-seeking and refugee children are recognised as children first and foremost and therefore are entitled to the same support and treatment by the state as any other child. The "In Safe Hands" project is a good example of working directly with children who talk about their lives which at the same time spotlights examples of good early years and primary practice that may help practitioners around the country improve provision for asylum-seekers and refugees.

Embedding the process

One of the aims of the CYCR has been to work with organisations that wish to embed the process of consulting children and increasing their participation within their services. Three examples are given below. As a general observation, what is noticeable about these projects is not any changes in the day-to-day activities with children, but marked changes in the attitudes of staff, practitioners and planners towards children's involvement.

Children as partners in planning

> As adults, we tend to underestimate how much children know and understand. ... We learnt that it is important to find out what children already know and build on their knowledge by expanding it. We can only find out what children know by listening. Listening to what children are actually saying is empowering to the child.
>
> (Nursery Officer, north London)

CYCR worked with early years and play staff in two north London boroughs on a "Listening to Children" project. The aim was to work closely with staff to raise awareness of children's rights and the ways that children could participate more actively in their settings, and also contribute to the planning and the evaluation of services. Both councils were keen to consult with children, as recommended in government guidance for early years development plans. Since the EYDCPs have responsibility for children up to the age of 14, in reality the views of much younger children are not always sought.

Rather than view this opportunity as way of finding out what children think on a one-off basis the aim of the partnerships has been to embed the philosophy and practice of listening to young children within everyday childcare in each authority. Staff developed 'listening to children' projects in their own settings after training by CYCR staff. Experience was disseminated around each authority through conferences and additional in-service training and practice development. Projects varied from situations where children were actively involved in choosing menus to selecting toys and reorganising play space. One early years setting established a project where children aged from 3 upwards participated in setting their own learning goals, sharing their learning with others and contributing to their own record keeping. An important principle has been that work is ongoing.

Rather than noting significant changes in practice the impact of the project has been most noticeable in the way early years and other staff talk about their attitudes towards children. Recognising children's capacities and really engaging in joint decision-making has been challenging for staff but appears to bring enormous benefits in relation to children's developing sense of self-esteem. A manual, *Children As Partners In Planning: A Training Resource to Support Consultation with Children*, containing the children's rights training exercises was launched in autumn 2000.

Citizenship

> If you are brown or black or something you have a right to play with everyone.
>
> (5-year-old boy in reception class; Project notes)

A partnership project between Save the Children and Camden Local Education Authority focused on citizenship from a children's rights perspective. The aim of the project was to develop a framework within which primary-age school children could examine the notion of citizenship, building upon a foundation of the practical experience of being a citizen with rights. Linking children's rights and citizenship proved to be highly successful, for children, teachers and schools.

Members of the CYCR team worked with four classes in four different primary schools in a north London education authority. Each team member paired up with a class teacher, supported by advisory teachers. Adults worked together with children from reception class to year 6 to produce activities for a term's project on citizenship and children's rights. With the youngest children the concept of rights was approached through the use of a story about relationships and feelings, developing ideas about expressing opinions and taking the views of others into account and moving eventually to activities and discussions about rules, ending with a focus on rights. Children in all cases were involved in evaluation of the sessions and this aspect of the project was one of the most powerful from the perspective of the teachers involved: "Now I feel how it is going and have a feel for the mood of the class. I adapt and change things as needed ... there is not a rigid structure. They have been telling me what they want to do and how they want to do it and so there is a more enjoyable lesson" (teacher; Project notes).

One of the long-term aims of this project was an assessment of its impact on each school. Once children find out about their rights – but more importantly have the opportunity to give their views about aspects of the school day - this can impact on the whole school community. The project has been written up and will be published as *Citizens By Right* (Trentham Books, 2001).

The Charter Mark

A very recent project that is aiming to embed the notion of consultation with children and young people into public services and other organisations has been initiated by a member of the CYCR team. The Charter Mark scheme is a government award to agencies that provide a service to the public. The award demonstrates that the agency has met ten criteria of a quality service. At its heart is the idea of users being consulted on the services they receive. SC-UK is working in partnership with the Cabinet Office to make the Charter Mark assessment process take account of the views of children and young people.

In 1999 1,200 agencies applied for the Charter Mark: 800 were successful. As the new evidence requirements are introduced, the Charter Mark has the potential to give thousands of children and young people the opportunity to make their views known and influence the services they receive (see Chartermark web-site details below).

At a court in London, for example, parents of young children regularly visit to make inquiries and to be with relatives. The Court has few facilities for young children. If applying for the Charter Mark, the court will have to take into account the needs of young children and so consult them about the type of facilities they feel to be appropriate and consider necessary.

These projects described above indicate the range of work that the team is and has been involved with. They also demonstrate the model of work adopted to date: namely, developing pilot projects that are then disseminated to a wider audience via the writing and publication of articles, the organisation and provision of seminars and the convening of conferences.

"In their best interests": issues arising

> Adults are used to making decisions for children "in their best interests" because children – especially young children – are assumed to be incapable of rational thought, to have little self-control and to be unable to consider the views of others. Yet when children are given the opportunity to express their opinions, the results often confound these assumptions.
>
> (Miller, 1997: 6)

We have learned that children do have something to say. There are increasing examples of young children making informed decisions in areas of their lives that were previously closed to them, for instance consent for surgery (see chapter 8 by Alderson). As Alderson explains, "children become competent by first being treated as if they are competent" (Alderson, 1993). The main challenge is not just to find a range of ways of communicating with children to enable them to express their views and opinions, but to change the way that young children are perceived. As Lansdown (1995: 38) suggests "we do not have a culture of listening to children".

There is undoubtedly still a good deal to learn about how to involve young children in a meaningful way. Some of the practical questions which have arisen from our practice over the past two years include:

- What is the relationship between listening to children and consulting them?
- Is consultation about what adults want rather than what children want?
- What methods are appropriate for consulting with/listening to young children? How do we approach consulting children on sensitive matters such as racism and physical punishment?
- What sort of practical issues arise? How do we gain access to children and ensure that informed consent is given? How representative are the views of a group of children?
- Can only those adults who have an established relationship with children effectively consult them?
- How do we ensure that children receive feedback? How do adults adequately represent the range of views expressed by children?
- What is the impact of children's views on decision-makers? How do we assess impact?
- How do we involve children in an ongoing and meaningful way in evaluation of the services they receive?

Lansdown outlines a framework for listening to children that provides an excellent starting point which can be summarised as follows:

- Ensure that children have adequate information appropriate to their age with which to form opinions;

- Provide them with real opportunities to express their views;
- Listen to children's views and consider them with respect and seriousness;
- Tell children how their views will be considered;
- Let them know the outcome of any decision.

(Lansdown, 1995: 38)

From our work we would extend that base with the following points. First, if children are not used to being consulted or expressing an opinion it may take some time for them to participate fully, if at all. Do not to expect children to be certain about their feelings and thoughts if they haven't had many opportunities to be heard before. Second, it is important that children feel safe so that they have the confidence to make decisions and take risks. It is helpful, if possible, that adults working on consultation with children already know children or can build good trusting relationships. If issues are raised that need to be followed up, then an adult who knows that child and family is better equipped to do this if they have been with the child as they have been talking. Third, part of feeling safe is about feeling heard and noticed – a child needs to know that her/his opinion is of value in itself. Fourth, working in small groups is sometimes more effective than consulting a child alone or in a larger group. Fifth, ensure that children are given opportunities to express opinions and take decisions as often as possible and not just on matters that are of interest to adults. In an early years setting this might mean that children could help themselves to food at mealtimes or decide on menus. Sixth, it's very important that adults create times when they feed back what has happened as a result of children expressing their views. Children need to see that what they say makes a difference. And, finally, consulting children can be built into the everyday practice of a setting so that children regularly express their views, are heard and take decisions. Children can effectively be involved in planning how and about what they wish to be consulted and in many cases can consult each other about specific issues. Where consultation is to be built into the everyday practice of a setting, parents should be informed that this is the case.

Access to children and informed consent

It is important that all participants (children and parents/carers) have sufficient information about a consultation exercise. Parents should be approached for written consent and should be able to withdraw their children. Schools and play settings can act as gatekeepers and may feel that some issues are too sensitive to be discussed with younger children. The smacking consultation proved to be one such instance. However, whenever teachers allowed the workers running the consultation exercise to approach parents, in every setting some parents gave permission for their children to take part. Children, of course, should always be given the option to not take part in a consultation exercise if they do not wish to. Alternatively, children can on many occasions run consultation exercises for themselves. Young children regularly gather information through interviews, perhaps using tape recorders or video recorders with responses represented by using graphs or pictures (see also chapter 15).

As far as ways of working with children are concerned, there are many techniques or specific strategies to discover what children think about particular issues: most of them arise from or are extensions of existing good practice. The most important point is that these methods or techniques should be fun, interactive, promote self-expression for the children and should not rely simply on the use of language, but deploy art and drama too. It is crucial that methods for establishing children's views are inclusive and guaranteed to articulate the voices of all children including those who are disabled, very young children or children with English as an additional language and those from black and minority ethnic groups. Some of the ways in which CYCR has been working with children are set out below:

- *Persona dolls*, for example, are child-sized dolls with a personality of their own who can be introduced to a group of children who may develop a relationship with the doll. They have been used in America as well as the United Kingdom to introduce issues of diversity to young children. Using a combination of story and questions and answers, groups of children can engage with a doll who may have a problem to solve or may be asking children questions about how they feel (Brown, 1999). Puppets also enable younger children to engage with a story and to talk about how they feel.
- *Speech bubbles* can be drawn on large pieces of paper and a group of children can fill in their thoughts using words or pictures. Older children can use speech bubbles on A4 and fill in their own speech bubbles.
- *Agree/disagree* is also effective and involves children moving to a point on a line in response to their agreement or disagreement with a number of statements: children are asked to "take a position" (quite literally). The children are then asked why they have chosen to stand where they have. This can be adapted and incorporated into games such as "port and starboard".
- *Stories and story boards* offer further scope for exploring children's viewpoints. Well-known children's stories can be used to initiate discussion about particular issues. In one recent project the team used fairy tales and fables to initiate discussions and other activities about feelings and emotions. In the case of the smacking consultation a storyboard was commissioned featuring a character, an alien, who had some questions about life on earth, including smacking.

- *Pictures and drawings, art:* young children usually enjoy drawing. They will often draw a picture in preference to talking when asked what they think. If children are emergent writers, it is often helpful if an adult or more competent writer is able to write down what a child says about a drawing. Children can use collages to describe their favourite foods and activities. Children can identify their favourite activities, foods, people, and areas by using photographs and video. Polaroid cameras are particularly effective.
- *Making choices:* post boxes can be set up to enable children to vote and express an opinion. For instance, if children are making decisions about the new equipment they want to buy for a setting, very young children can cast a vote in the box with pictures of lego, bricks or animals. Children can also use stickers to express a preference.
- *Music, poetry and drama:* music and music-based activities are all about self-expression. For instance children can bang, clap, stamp, sing, loudly or softly to indicate agreement or disagreement.
- *Drama and make believe* both enable children to explore their feelings and to put themselves in someone else's shoes. Asking children to be Queen or King for the day is just one way of finding out what is important to them and what they notice about the world. This is particularly effective with younger children.
- *Circle time* offers children the chance to talk about issues that are important. If children don't want to speak there are lots of interesting and fun ways to find out what children think.
- *Happy masks/sad masks:* Children make masks by drawing, painting or sticking pictures from magazines onto circles of card – one showing a happy face and the other a sad face. Children can then be asked about how a rule/activity/action makes them feel. For younger children of 2 upwards a similar activity is 'Thumbs up/thumbs down" or "Happy trains/sad trains" – where children can express their feelings physically (Miller, 1997).
- *Talking to teddy:* The Daycare Trust gave children the chance to say what they liked about childcare and what they thought was important. In *Listening to Children: Young Children's Views On Childcare: A Guide For Parents* small groups of children were invited to join a discussion about their nursery. Children were asked about how they would ensure that 'teddy' would enjoy going to nursery.

Thinking about making a nursery that the teddy would enjoy was fun for the children. Children drew upon their own experiences to tell us how to make sure the teddy had fun at nursery. ... These insights can help us to see how children would like to be treated when they start at nursery.

(Daycare Trust, 1998)

Children said about teddy's arrival "He would be a bit shy but staff would come and say: 'Come on, do you want to come and play?' Children would say 'come on teddy'. It would be good if all his friends said 'come and play with us' ". Children could also draw pictures and a Polaroid camera was available. Children's conversations were recorded on the topics of friends; food; fun outside; finding out; and feeling safe and loved. The results have been published in an attractive leaflet that can help parents talk to their own children about what is important to them about nursery.

The future

In the 1995 edition of *The Handbook of Children's Rights*, Gillian Alexander said of children's rights in the early years:

> Developing skills in listening to children and enabling them to participate in decision-making, is an area of considerable difficulty for practitioners. A major challenge for early years services is to develop the skills, mechanisms and commitment to ensure that children have a voice.

With some justification CYCR can claim to have made a significant contribution to meeting the challenge of developing the practice of listening to young children. The further challenge lies in two areas. First, to influence those who plan and run services for children to use the framework of the UN Convention as an essential starting point when thinking about the rights of the youngest children. The second, but more pressing and challenging issue, is the need to evaluate the impact of increasing children's participation. What are the implications and consequences of listening to children? Assessing these outcomes will be crucial to the agenda of the Centre in the future.

References

Alderson, P. (1993) *Consent to Surgery*. Open University Press
Brown, B. (1999) *All our Children: A guide for those who care*. Early Years Trainers Anti Racist Network
Chartermark@cabinet-office.gov.uk
Cuninghame, C. (ed.) (1999) *Realising Children's Rights: Policy, practice and Save the Children's work in England*. Save the Children
Daycare Trust (1998) *Listening to Children: Young children's views of childcare: a guide for parents*. Daycare Trust (leaflet)
Fajerman, L. and Treseder, P. (2001) *Children Are Service Users Too! A toolkit for consulting children and young people*. Save the Children partnership with 2001 Chartermark
Fajerman, L., Jarrett, M. and Sutton, M. (2000) *Children as Partners in Planning: A training resource to support consultation with children*. Save the Children

Hyder, T. and Rutter, J. (forthcoming) *In Safe Hands: A resource and training pack to support work with young refugee children.* Save the Children and the Refugee Council

Klein, R. (2001) *Citizens by Right,* Stoke on Trent: Trentham Books.

Lansdown, G. (1995) *Taking Part, Children's Participation in Decision Making.* Institute for Public Policy Research

Miller, J. (1997) *Never too Young: How children can take responsibility and make decisions.* National Early Years Network and Save the Children

—— (1999) *A Journey of Discovery: Children's creative participation in planning.* Save the Children

Pandrich, C. (ed.) (1999) *We Have Rights OK* (wishfish). Save the Children

Save the Children (2000) *A Child's View,* available from the NHS executive in London

Willow, C. and Hyder, T. (1998) *It Hurts You Inside: Children talking about smacking.* National Children's Bureau and Save the Children

For more information visit www.savethechildren.org.uk

Part V

Children's rights

Comparative perspectives

20 Childhood and children's rights in China

Andy West

China is big. Diversity and differences are almost defining characteristics. So it is necessary to begin by outlining the social and historical context within which children, childhood and children's rights are set in China. This size and variety, means that only a brief, and to some extent arbitrary, survey of China, children and rights issues can be presented here.[1]

The setting

China's large land mass is outmatched by the fact that it possesses the world's largest population: one fifth, over 1,218,000,000 people.[2] There are officially fifty-six nationalities: one majority (Han) with fifty-five minority groups. Many minority groups each have a population greater than most European countries. The climate ranges from sub-tropical in the southern Yunnan province, to ice and snow in the north-east Heilongjiang. There is a national (Beijing) time zone but the north-west unofficially operates a two-hour difference (for daylight), and many local people set their watches two hours earlier. The east of China has well-irrigated agricultural plains, the west has huge desert spaces and mountains. There is a single language with a standard spoken form (Mandarin or Putonghua) but over eight major dialects, almost mutually unintelligible, for example, Cantonese, Shanghaiese.

The international context includes contested boundaries and regions, notably Tibet (Xizang Autonomous Region), the Spratley Islands in the South China Seas, Taiwan (province of the People's Republic of China, or the Republic of China), borders with India and Pakistan. A huge overseas Chinese population is long settled in South-east Asia and more recent migrants of one or two generations in Europe and the United States.

Throughout the twentieth century, China experienced massive transformations in society, ideology and politics, yet retained a sense of continuity with a 4–5,000 year civilisation,[3] interrupted by Western incursion in the nineteenth century. This civilisation was characterised by dynastic cycles (rebellion–stability–greatness, then corruption–oppression–problems, leading to rebellion, and renewal). More recent historical paradigms describe changing social/state relationships in a scheme drawn from Marxist-Leninist-Maoist thought (slave, feudal, pre-capitalist etc. societies). The long dynastic sequence was followed by the troubled period leading up to 1949, and the "new society" of the second half of the twentieth century is itself now undergoing change.

Loss of power in the nineteenth century was heralded by the British government enforcing the sale of hard drugs in China for trade, creating widespread addiction. The Opium Wars brought land and trade concessions for European powers. Losses continued in the twentieth century, when, despite Chinese support for the Allied European forces, German concessions were awarded to Japan in 1919, and during the later Japanese invasion and atrocities in Nanjing. War with Japan continued alongside a civil war until the revolution succeeded. Global political and economic isolation followed because of an espoused and initially immensely popular political ideology. Circumstances changed towards the end of the twentieth century: American-Chinese rapprochement in 1974; transfer of the Taiwan seat on the United Nations Security Council to the Beijing government; economic reform and opening of the country to the outside world; return of European colonies, Hong Kong (1997) and Macau (1999). Economic reform begun in 1978 has had the greatest impact across the country, while highlighting and increasing the rural–urban divide and income inequality, and dominate social and political life today.

Children

What of children in this population mass, with all its ethnic differences, and environmental and geographical variety? What of children's rights at a time of social, legal, economic, and political change? Given the range of diversity, the sheer quantities involved, is it really possible to provide a brief and realistic assessment of the state of children's rights? To look at China is to look at issues for children across a world region: there are difficulties because of local differences in culture, society, environment etc., but there are also benefits, in obvious cross-locality issues, and in a macro-perspective on economic and other policies. A uniformity of policy in China is part of a process of maintaining stability, keeping the huge country together against internal tensions. Economic change and the potential market size raises the question of globalisation, the impact of international businesses, trade, policy, and the appropriation and use of cultural icons and themes to promote ideas and profits. Such issues await a careful analysis if the details of children's lives, views, circumstances, and issues of difference between children, are not lost in the changes.

Since this discussion is intended primarily for a Western audience, the question of Western representations of China and Chinese children is raised before exploring some themes in the condition of childhood, some issues for children and children's rights. There is not space to discuss differences and local concepts of childhood. The life of a Muslim Uyghur child in Xinjiang, a Buddhist Dai child in Yunnan, a prosperous child in Shanghai, girls and boys, indicate just some childhood variations, united by Chinese nationhood and, given the external interference over the past two centuries, generally a proud nationalism.[4]

Western imagery

Images of China have been circulating in the West for centuries.[5] Aspects of Chinese life alien to Western perceptions have been emphasised in the production and consumption of such images. The closure of China to most outsiders in recent history has meant that these images have been sustained.[6] Contemporary Western visitors are often surprised at the degree of urbanisation, modern high rise buildings, and the little remaining of old compounds clustered around small alleyways. Tourists rarely enter rural areas, where older, poorer dwellings also lie juxtaposed with modern housing. Older Western perceptions have synthesised with a modern characterisation of Chinese bureaucratic uniformity and insensibility that has often used children as a vehicle to reinforce images condemnatory of the Chinese state.

> Because China is a so-called Communist country, there is a tendency by the mainstream media in the West to perceive China as an undifferentiated block in which everyone everywhere has to be the same. The fact that there is a world of difference between urban and rural China and that local governments can and do respond to and implement central policies differently tends to be ignored. Because of their eagerness to condemn Communist ideas and practice there is a tendency by mainstream Western media not to take into consideration how local conditions and traditional influences have interacted on rural development since 1949.
>
> (Gao 1999: 256)

Something similar could be written about images of children and their rights in China. Sensational stories, usually of abandoned babies,[7] suggest the benefits of Western/capitalist/market systems as opposed to Eastern, Chinese, communism. Individual charity is contrasted with a supposedly uncaring state that has intervened in family life and imposed a ration of one child. Chinese struggles against son preference and discrimination against disabled children (common in many countries) are usually not discussed, nor are the problems of lack of appropriate social services (also globally widespread) and the difficulties of economic transition. The point is not to diminish problems in China affecting children and issues about their rights; but the portrayal of a country of uncaring people and an uninterested state is inaccurate.[8]

One child?

The population boom in the 1950s and 1960s posed a problem for the government after Mao Zedong. The ideal of a large family with many sons became realisable through improved health care and reductions in infant mortality rates, and was encouraged by Mao as a move toward national self-sufficiency (see Gao, 1999: 33–34; Croll, 1994: 181–197). In the 1970s, projections of population size, and resources required, caused alarm especially for economic transition (see Croll, 1994). In 1979–80 the one-child policy was formally adopted:

> In explaining the need for the policy the government has tried to convince the public not only that China has too many people; moreover its "population quality" badly needs improvement through "prevention eugenics" meaning that marriages of mentally retarded people, close relatives and patients with hereditary diseases must be prevented to avoid births of children with severe medical problems.
>
> (Jing, 2000b: 143)

Enforcement of the policy has involved the use of localised birth quotas and permits, and medical checks on marriage (ibid.). The policy has been seen as a children's rights issue, but the problems raised are often not the policy per se but attitudes around gender and disability (which *are* important rights issues), or discussions revolve around right to life/anti-abortion beliefs, or parents' reproductive rights, or a child's right to have a brother or sister.

The policy has affected families in numerous ways. Traditions emphasising filial duty, especially through the male line, have not completely disappeared. Cultural preference for a son does not fit with the one-child policy, and ways are sought to avoid the limit. Related concerns include the psychological effects of most children being only children, and their peer relationships. The policy was introduced at the same time as economic reform, and the implementation of the one-child family has occurred while a set of structural dualities have emerged to delineate changing modern social life. The rural–urban divide has magnified, income inequality has increased, regional inequalities have become evident. The life of a well-off child in the urban east coast will be massively different to a child in a poor family in the rural west. Some families attempt to improve their circumstances, and avoid the birth quota by moving. Migration is becoming an important social issue, affecting children in various ways.

But the one-child policy is not as simple it seems. It is effectively limited to the urban, majority Han population in registered employment. Minority groups may have more than one child, and in rural areas the policy is apparently formally ignored. In practice, in rural areas, parents who have a first child who is female, or a disabled boy may try again for a non-disabled male. There are a number of dimensions to Chinese childhoods and only some can be considered here.

Gender

Historically the importance of male children was linked to patrilineal inheritance and patrilocal residence: girls married into the husband's family, coming under the rule of their mothers-in-law. Continuation of the male line was important for security in old age. Ancestors were venerated and for the line to expire brought great shame. In the early nineteenth century the prevalence of female infanticide caused a profound imbalance in sex ratios. "As many as 20% of the men [were] unable to find wives and start families making them a rootless and volatile group capable of swinging into action with a raiding party at any time" (Spence, 1999b: 183, from Perry, 1980). Yet preference for sons continued, highlighting the importance of gender equality moves instigated early in the Communist republic, with new laws on marriage and divorce. These changes were seen as groundbreaking, but their importance is now contested. Some commentators suggest that changes to gender relationships have been overestimated (Stockman, 2000: 9). Others recognise the difficulties still faced by women (especially in rural areas) but "on the whole, the Communist regime has taken a giant step towards the emancipation of women in rural areas" (Gao, 1999: 235–8). One impact has been on child marriage, for example, "there has not been a child bride in Gao Village since the 1950s" (ibid.: 235).

Discrimination against girls, especially in rural areas, is in turn linked to patterns of excess female mortality, deriving from less attention paid to their nutrition and health care needs in poorer areas. Such discrimination is reported as selective, affecting mostly girls with older brothers or sisters (Li and Zhu, 1999). Any detailed evidence for abandonment and infanticide is lacking (or not public), and the practices may be understood locally as a form of abortion for unnamed children (ibid.). Unwanted girls are often adopted locally (Gao, 1999), sometimes by being "abandoned" on the doorstep of a childless couple. On the other hand, adherence to the one-child policy has in many places meant love, value and future hopes placed on a single daughter, and brought some shift in perceptions of female children. This issue is a good example of the difficulties of generalising in China, where the majority of children are clearly valued.

Little Emperors and family life

Jia is said to cover the meaning of the English words family and home, "so basic in Chinese tradition is the idea of a family's physical togetherness" (Terrill, 1999: 16). Relationships within the family were traditionally well ordered, and members still do support each other in and against the outside world.

> You are not encouraged to defend your privacy and autonomy within the family – your letters are for any member of the family who can read, and you will be thought selfish and unnatural if you try to keep your

acquisitions to yourself. The boundary you have to defend is not the one around your private self but the one around the family unit.

(Jenner, 1994: 115)

These relationships of sharing and cooperation have implications for children's lives and expectations.

Parents have absolute rights to enter their children's private space and the children can use their parents' personal belongings as they wish. There is no privacy and everyone learns to handle the complicated human relations that follow from this. The Chinese attitude towards life takes shape in this environment and it has the family at its core.

(Yang Dingping in Dutton, 1998: 210)

The coincidence of the one-child policy and economic reform contributed enormously to changes in the nature of childhood in China in the last decades of the twentieth century. Two contrasting views of childhood were suggested in the 1980s: pressures and strains through regimented lives and the rigid controlling influence of parents, or parents' indulgence of a happy, carefree, single child (Baker 1987 quoted in Chee, 2000). Families place all their hopes on their one child: boys and girls experience both the devotion and generosity of parents, and pressure to do well. Concerns over the single-child family emerged in public and private: first, children receiving too much love and attention, becoming "Little Emperors" within the family; second, children experiencing loneliness and difficulties in peer relationships; and third, pressures to do well, carrying the burden of the family's expectations.

The term "Little Emperors" appeared in the early 1980s through a series of press articles. "They are often described as insufferably spoiled, showered with attention, toys and treats by anxiously overindulgent adults, because their parents and grand-parents have tried hard to focus their energies on catering to the whims of their one little link to the future" (Jing, 2000a: 1). One reason for popular attention is concern over the psychological states of children without siblings: "widely differing, even contradictory theories about their psychological characteristics are advanced year after year in bewildering succession" (ibid.: 2).

Outcomes include an increase in obesity among urban children, and apparently an increase in children's decision-making and voice within the family. The rise in obesity has been linked to the economic and social transition and a change in diet to more Western proportions of higher fat and lower carbohydrates (Guldan, 2000). Also, Western multinational fast food chains (Watson, 1997), and their local imitators throughout urban China, are much liked by children. Children's preference for this type of food and setting, and their success in persuading parents to take them there, is one example of their greater role in family decisions. Watson observed children ordering food for the family in a Hong Kong restaurant, which would have been shocking twenty years ago (1997: 100). A 1995 survey found that children in Beijing influenced their parents on food purchases twice as much as children in America, and determined nearly 70 per cent of the family's overall spending: "in short we are witnessing the emergence of a child specific culture of consumption in China" (Jing, 2000a: 7).

A child with no brothers or sisters with to play with needs friends. "While a lack of siblings can be a problem for children anywhere in the world there is a greater impact for children in the urban areas of China where the majority of children are only children" (Chee, 2000: 58). Competition for peer friendships may arise because of loneliness (ibid.). Children compare with peers "possibly because it serves the process of self-understanding"; the peer group "helps the child develop a concept of himself [sic] through the way peers react and treat children" (ibid.). Chee cited "harsh peer pressure" which strongly influenced children's consumption of snacks – "pressure to consume certain foods" (ibid.: 53). Chinese children are seen as a huge potential market, especially for Western firms anxious to bring new products to China (ibid.: 68).

Children experience parental pressure, particularly on education. "One child said 'my friends and I all feel that our parents don't care enough about us. They are only concerned about how well we do in school' " (Chee, 2000: 64). Some children find school pressures intolerable, run away or harm themselves: recently the government announced measures aimed at relieving overload and ensuring mental well-being (*China Daily*, 17 February 2000).

One further aspect of many Chinese children's lives is the increasing number of single-parent families and reconstituted families, through divorce (see Au, 1996). The latter is also reported as a reason for children running away from home. In Hong Kong an increasing number of extramarital affairs (especially workers crossing to mainland China and maintaining two families) was seen as part of a growing trend in Asia, including China, and this raises more questions about the future nature of family life (see Family Service, 1995).

Migration

An important element in Chinese economic reform has been the phenomenon of some places and people getting rich first (to paraphrase Deng Xiaoping, who said it was acceptable). The severe poverty experienced in parts of (mainly rural) China coupled with the opportunities perceived to exist elsewhere in the country (often in urban areas) has brought a massive increase in migration. Large numbers of a "floating population" – families, couples, individuals – have moved to seek new chances, and now live on the margins of cities. Some register in their new location, others live there unofficially.[9]

There are particular issues for children in migration. An official household registration is important for residence and for access to a variety of services (see Dutton, 1998). Children in the floating population may be unable to attend school (special schools have recently been established). Movement in the floating population is a means of circumventing the one-child policy, through avoiding registration and birth controls, in order to have a son or even a small family (ibid.: 144–7 for an interview with one father). In some cases parents migrate and leave children to be raised by grandparents.

The question of migration, and especially the driving forces of poverty, incorporates problems such as trafficking and street children. Some older children and young women have reported using migration to new economic zones in Guangdong as a means of escaping quasi-arranged marriages or parental control, asserting an independence, although they send money home to their family (see Lee, 1998). Others are less fortunate. The promise of a better, richer life has meant for some girls and young women being trafficked in the commercial sex trade (see, for example, Mahatdhanobol, 1998), but there is much trafficking within China of both boys and girls. Boys and young men may also be lured into leaving home and then controlled in criminal activities by adults: some escape and take up a life on the street until being found by the local authorities. During a 1999 government campaign against trafficking thousands of children were reported rescued (various local press).

A large number of street children is another phenomenon much associated with economic "marketisation" reform around the world (see also chapter 24). Mongolia is a stark example of such new policies leading to family and child homelessness. In China numbers of street children have increased and the government, aware of the social impact of economic reform elsewhere in the world, has invested in work in this area. But since the phenomenon of "street children" always raises questions of definition and other issues (such as child labour) we should now move on to consider some issues for children that raise questions of rights, law and government responses.

Issues and problems

A few issues and problems related to children's rights are outlined here. Many current circumstances and concerns arise from the parallel paths of economic change and the need to develop a new social welfare infrastructure. The work unit systems and ideology of the "new society" were intended to wipe out social ills and, officially at least, problems did not exist. The emergence of phenomena such as street children, the increasing realisation of other elements of "dark society" such as child abuse, coupled with the changes of responsive mechanisms, are all sensitive topics. While recognition of need is increasingly spoken about openly, children's rights are not served by often inappropriate or insensitive interventions ("interference").[10] Hong Kong has a different, charity/NGO based social service system, but the concerns below exist, in different circumstances.

Separated children

One important issue (the focus of much Western media) is the question of children separated from or with no parents in China. As with many social institutions and structures in China, it cannot be considered without reference to historical context and government provision. The institutions and departments responsible for these children are the equivalent of a "care" system for children without parents, which has a long history in China. Mendes Pinto in the mid sixteenth century noted various forms of social protection provided by the Chinese state – something first noticed by Marco Polo almost three centuries earlier:

> Orphans abandoned by their parents, fed by wet nurses, and placed in special city schools where they are taught to read and write, and to practice one of the "mechanical trades". Then come the blind children, employed by the owners of hand-operated flour mills to work the machines for which no sight it needed. Those who are too crippled to work the mill equipment are employed by the rope- or basket makers in hoisting the cordage and weaving the rushes.
>
> (Spence, 1999a: 30)

To some extent, current institutions, known as "welfare homes" or "orphanages" in translation, reflect these earlier city schools.

Welfare homes are often large. In some areas, homes principally serve girls and disabled children, and are medically oriented, emphasising clinical resources (and are sources for increasing Western adoption, yet another issue). In other areas, particularly minority regions, orphanages may have equal numbers of (non-disabled) boys and girls, for example, 150 children in an orphan school in Yili, Xinjiang. But overall, numbers of children in welfare homes are comparatively small, less than 18,000 in 1993. Standards and levels of care vary according to resources available. Modern buildings are constructed where possible and new practices developed, often making use of external learning. For example, rehabilitation training; reconstruction of large institutions to operate as small group family-style homes (Wright, 1999); development of new and existing foster care practice. The Ministry of Civil Affairs, charged with overall responsibility for policy, is developing further standards of care practice. Low development of residential practice is a global issue, raised in British services in the 1990s.

Disability

Most children with disabilities are cared for in family homes: in the past they were not seen much in public, and these attitudes still remain. Some children with severe impairments are abandoned and subsequently cared for in welfare homes, or are placed in homes by parents unable to cope and who visit. In 1982 Fraser wrote:

a deformed or mentally handicapped child represents a tragedy anywhere in the world but in China such unfortunate children bear a special burden. There are institutions for the severely mentally and physically handicapped, but it is safe to assume they are primitive in the extreme. Foreigners are never taken to such places, even when requests are made by special interest groups. Only a few Chinese I met could confirm that institutions for the handicapped even existed.

(1982: 416)

The language and sentiments here would now be contested, especially by disabled groups who do not see themselves as tragic. But welfare homes have opened, both to foreign visits and to the development of practice. Community support for parents and children has been introduced in places.

Changes in disability status have been seen: "the last ten years have seen great advances for deaf children in China" (Calloway, 1998: 28). Prejudice against deafness in the early twentieth century was severe; Calloway suggests that deaf children are still seen as a "burden on their families and on society" (ibid.: 31). In the 1950s new policies for deaf children's education were initiated, and by 1998 there were over 700 deaf schools. The main policy has been speech training, but there is currently interest in the development of sign bi-language education.

Children born with hare-lip and cleft-palate have another disability with particular social stigma. In some areas and among some minority groups, belief systems incorporate severe retribution against these children. Although remedial operations are now commonplace, in some rural areas an awareness of such possibilities is unknown, and coupled with poverty and discrimination, many children have grown up in isolation, experiencing problems in local society. Awareness campaigns and sponsored operations have been initiated by local charity federations (quasi-NGOs).

Street children

This phenomenon attracted attention in the late 1980s and the government has responded with the development of Street Children Protection Centres. Recent newspaper publicity in China (Ma Guihua, 2000) has contributed to an opening up of the issue, recognising that parents do contribute to the numbers, citing "improper behaviour on the part of the parents, such as gambling, drug-addiction and child beating" as reasons for children's departure to the street.

The complexities of definition are evident in that not all "street children" are homeless and alone: some are under the control and direction of parents or other adults, selling flowers, begging or engaging in criminal activities. Official figures cited in 2000 (and in previous years) were 150,000–200,000 street children in China, regarded by some as an underestimate deriving from a limited count. Policy and practice on street children is developing and broadening to include a range of children in difficult circumstances: it is associated with other issues, such as children who are separated from their parents, trafficking, education (dropping out of school), health, HIV/AIDS (through sexual exploitation and drugs). It is in this area that the lack of an existing social services structure is evident, and new practice development is uneven but changing.

Child labour

There are examples of exploitative child labour reported in the media in China, and many of these cases involve children who have been trafficked or kidnapped. For example, in a private goldmine in Qingdao (*China Youth News*, 12 September 2000), or assembling Christmas tree lights in Zhejiang (Macleod and Macleod, 2000: 26). The scale of the problem is difficult to assess: the Hong Kong *China Labour Bulletin* in 1995 produced a figure partially based on school drop-outs, which indicates difficulties of definition (ibid.). Many families need or prefer to have their children working in rural areas, and the problem may not be exploitation, but missing education. One Hong Kong commentator suggested most child labour is in small rural and township enterprises (ibid.: 25). There is a debate in China about whether school students who willingly work should be classified as child labour: children, for example, who work in restaurants have been permitted to do so by authorities in Jiangxi and Nanchang but not in Beijing (*China Youth News*). In urban areas, work undertaken by "street children" may be highly visible, often exploitative, involving long hours, such as for many flower sellers, or may involve more hidden sex work.

Abuse

As child sexual abuse becomes more acknowledged, there is some public recognition that perpetrators may be people known to the child, but there is considerable resistance to the notion that family might be involved (see Morarjee, 2000). More openly discussed is the question of physical abuse, in particular the beating of children (Hesketh *et al.*, 2000). Local newspapers are now regularly carrying stories about physical abuse, especially punishments by teachers, in a condemnatory fashion. At the end of 1999 what was billed as the first seminar in China on child abuse was held in Shaanxi province, and a conference on child abuse was held in Hong Kong. This area is likely to become of significant national concern in the near future.

Education

Issues in this arena are varied and include the complexities of minority languages as well as both the shortfall and quality of teachers, the proximity of local schools and access to education. Tuition is free and enrolment rates are high, but drop-out rates, because of administrative and other fees, particularly affect poor families. Discrimination impacts on opportunities for girls and disabled children, and pressures from parents and teachers cause some children to run away. Language is important, because many ethnic minority children grow up in families knowing only a minority language, such as Uyghur or Tibetan, and schools need to respond to this. Government is concerned with developing "quality" education, through improved methodologies and other provision, and the sector is changing, yet still encompasses a range of issues for children.

Health

As with education, health incorporates a number of issues. Access to good quality water is not yet universal and availability of health practitioners is limited in some areas. Chinese health epistemology is different to Western, but access to both systems through doctors trained in Chinese and Western medicine exists in urban areas. The commercialisation of health services has introduced new barriers to access for many. Another increasing concern arising from economic reform is the intrusion of Western companies promoting milk substitutes as baby food.

HIV/AIDS was officially recognised as a major problem in China in 1998: before this it was seen as a Western disease. It is primarily associated with intravenous drug use, especially in border areas such as Yunnan and Xinjiang provinces, and with commercial sex activities. For children and young people there are clearly issues around drug use, but for very young children instances of HIV orphans have been reported (where both parents have died, or one has died and the other has left to form a new relationship).

Children's rights and the law

Government promulgations since early 1996 of "using laws to run the country" (Lam, 1999: 75) have been seen as reinforcing the rebuilding of legal institutions begun in the 1980s (Jenner, 1994: 143). Basically, the shift is from a form of governance through rules and regulations devised by government toward laws that can be tested in courts. The change has a number of implications for children: their rights can now be incorporated in law, but much of the existing system depends upon regulations which guide the work of relevant government departments such as the 1991 Regulations Forbidding Child Labour (in addition to any local practice and procedure which may have developed).

China ratified the United Nations Convention on the Rights of the Child (UNCRC) in 1991, and that same year signed the Declaration of the Plan of Action at the World Summit for Children. A National Plan of Action for children in China was created following on from the Summit, and was the focus of attention in the 1990s. Relevant laws include Protection of Minors Act 1992, Adoption Act 1999, Prevention of Juvenile Delinquency Act 1999. Implementation of legislation depends upon new knowledge and a basis for practice in local governments. The Juvenile Justice Act emphasises protection and education, in a move away from social control perspectives (Wong, 1996: 176).

In the latter part of the 1990s, interest in the UNCRC as a framework for implementing policy on children became evident. Creating an awareness, understanding and knowledge of the UNCRC has been a strategy pursued by government-led agencies such as the Women's Federation, and taken up by Civil Affairs Bureaux which are responsible for welfare homes and care of street children.

Children's participation

One particular test of children's rights is the more contested question of children's participation. On the one side are traditional childhoods in China emphasising obedience, respect and duty towards parents, and on the other a governance system of local committees down to village and neighbourhood levels with significant participation potential. Social changes have included children becoming involved more in family decision-making, but pressures to perform at school, and for marriage, can be directive and coercive. Participation in the form of peer education has become recognised as a type of quality education, and promoted. Child participation in government structures and local decision-making, or in institutional management (for example schools), has been raised and recognised as a practice to promote in some places, but much remains to be done in promoting the idea and methods.

Conclusion

Attempting to look at children's rights in this one country is immensely difficult simply because China contains one fifth of the world's population. The processes of "transition" of economic and social reform at the end of the twentieth century have had considerable impact on Chinese childhood, and provided both opportunities and problems for many children that are enormously different to the experiences of their parents. A series of binary divides, especially rural–urban and income inequality, on top of the severe poverty of some areas, create vastly different childhood experiences and chances.

Children in China face a unique situation through the one-child policy, parental indulgence, educational pressure, and the increased importance of peer relationships. Many children also face difficulties which will need to be addressed using the concept of rights as a basis, such as the right to identity, to education, and to protection. The government in China faces an enormous task in its responsibility for 20 per cent of the world's children: the shifting of attention from the Atlantic to the Pacific Rim will increase the need to look closely at children's issues and rights.

Notes

1 This chapter is based on personal experience with officials and children, and English language sources. It focuses on mainland China. More could be written even without primary material, and this chapter is merely an introduction to some issues.
2 The initial results of the November 2000 census will be available in mid 2001 or later.
3 See Gilley, 2000 for a short account of the contested but politically important length of Chinese history.
4 See Lipman, 1997 and Saffran, 1998 for discussions of the construction of ethnic difference. Given the minorities population, little has been specifically included here about minority children.
5 See Spence, 1999a. The most famous early Western image producer, Marco Polo, may not have visited China.
6 Saïd's discussion of Orientalism is apposite (1978).
7 See *Sunday Times*, 27 August 2000, "China keeps killing 'surplus' babies"; *Sunday Telegraph*, 30 July 2000, "Dumped to die on a festering rubbish tip".
8 Such a portrayal developed in the 1990s after a film and book alleged children were killed/deliberately left to die in orphanages. These accounts caused outrage in China and increased sensitivity to foreign aid. The issues, practice and political contexts, substantiation etc., are too lengthy to pursue here. Children's rights issues are often emotive and any writing can be seen on a continuum from an apologia for appalling practice or, at the other end, a caricatured insult
9 There is a burgeoning literature on the topic of migration. See for example, references in a general text such as Stockman, 2000.
10 Given the under-development of social services many new initiatives are undertaken in partnership with international agencies, too many to be referenced here. Caution is required, because the need for resources and the dogma of some foreign agencies/individuals can lead to the introduction ('imposition") of inappropriate Western models, which have question-marks over their sustainability.

References

Au, E. (1996) "Divorce and Single-Parenting in China: Challenges to Family Restructuring" in Lo, T.W. and Cheung, J.Y.S. (eds) *Social Welfare Development in China: constraints and challenges* Chicago: Imprint Publications, pp. 121–134

Baker, R. (1987) "Little Emperors Born of a One Child Policy" *Far Eastern Economic Review* 137 (28) 16 July, pp. 43–44

Calloway, A. (1998) "Deaf Children in China" *China Review* 9, pp. 28–32

Chee, B.W.L. (2000) "Eating Snacks, Biting Pressure: only children in Beijing" in Jing (2000)

Croll, E. (1994) *From Heaven to Earth: images and experiences of development in China* London: Routledge

Dutton, M. (ed.) (1998) *Streetlife China* Cambridge: Cambridge University Press

Family Service (1995) *Study on Marriages Affected by Extramarital Affairs* Hong Kong: Caritas-HK

Fraser, J. (1982) *The Chinese* Glasgow: Fontana

Gao, Mobo C.F. (1999) *Gao Village: A Portrait of Rural Life in Modern China* Hong Kong: Hong Kong University Press

Gilley, B. (2000) "Digging Into the Future" *Far Eastern Economic Review*, 20 July

Guldan, G.S. (2000) "Paradoxes of Plenty: China's Infant- and Child-Feeding Transition" in Jing (2000)

Hesketh, T., Zhang, S.H. and Lynch, M.A. (2000) "Child Abuse in China: the views and experiences of child health professionals" *Child Abuse and Neglect* 24(6), pp. 867–872

Jenner, W.J.F. (1994) (second edition) *The Tyranny of History* London: Allen Lane

Jing, J. (ed.) (2000) *Feeding China's Little Emperors: Food, Children and Social Change* Stanford, CA: Stanford University Press

—— (2000a) "Introduction" in Jing (2000)

—— (2000b) "Food Nutrition and Cultural Activity in a Gansu Village" in Jing (2000)

Lam, W.W.-L. (1999) *The Era of Jiang Zemin* Singapore: Prentice Hall

Lee, C.K. (1998) *Gender and the South China Miracle* Berkeley: University of California

Li, S. and Zhu, C. (1999) "Gender Differences in Child Survival in Rural China: a county study" Xi'an: Population Research Institute

Lipman, J. (1997) (1998 edition) *Familiar Strangers: a history of Muslims in Northwest China* Hong Kong: Hong Kong University Press

Ma Guihua (2000) "Helping the Street Children" *China Daily* 23 October 2000

Macleod, C. and Macleod, L. (2000) "China's Hidden Army" *China Review* 17: 25–29

Mahatdhanobol, V. (1998) *Chinese Women in the Thai Sex Trade* Bangkok: Chulanlongkorn University

Morarjee, R. (2000) "Sexually Abused Children Locked in a Silent World" *South China Morning Post* 23 October

Ngai, N.-P. (1996) "Youth Policy in China: a legal perspective" in Lo, T.W. and Cheung, J.Y.S. (eds) *Social Welfare Development in China: constraints and challenges* Chicago: Imprint Publications

Perry, E.J. (1980) *Rebels and Revolutionaries in North China, 1845–1945* Stanford, CA: Stanford University Press

Saffran, W. (ed.) (1998) *Nationalism and Ethnogregional Identities in China* London: Frank Cass Publishers

Saïd, E. (1978) *Orientalism: Western Conceptions of the Orient* London: Penguin Books

Spence, J. (1999a) *The Chan's Great Continent: China in Western Minds* London: Penguin Books

Spence, J. (1999b) (second edition) *The Search For Modern China* New York: WW Norton & Company

Stockman, N. (2000) *Understanding Chinese Society* London: Polity Press

Terrill, R. (1999) (second edition) *Madame Mao: The White Boned Demon: A Biography of Madame Mao Zedong* Stanford, CA: Stanford University Press

Watson, J. (ed.) (1997) *Golden Arches East: McDonald's in East Asia* Stanford, CA: Stanford University Press

Wong, D.S.W. (1996) "The Changing Conceptions of Juvenile Delinquency in China" in Lo, T.W. and Cheung, J.Y.S. (eds) *Social Welfare Development in China: constraints and challenges* Chicago: Imprint Publications

Wright, J. (1999) *A New Model of Caring for Children in Guangde: residential child care resource manual* Anhui, Hefei: Anhui Provincial Civil Affairs, Guangde County Civil Affairs, Save the Children UK

21 The state of children's rights in Australia

Moira Rayner

The lucky country

What is it like to be a child in Australia? About 4.8 million children live on an enormous island continent, mostly in coastal settlements and within striking distance of a beach or a swimming pool, playing grounds and school. Their drinking water is mostly clean, basic health care is free and they are likely to have their own bedroom, in a reasonably sized and affordable house. Australia is a "lucky country" – unless the child is Aboriginal or a Torres Strait Islander; or has arrived in the country without proper travel documentation, or has a disability, or needs the care of the state: then the luck changes.

About a fifth of Australia's children and young people live in poverty, the fifth highest rate in the industrialized world.[1] Demographically children are much more likely to be poor if they come from indigenous and some ethnic or national backgrounds, or if they have a disability, or just one parent in the household. Australia has the sixth highest unemployment rate for children and young people in the OECD and suicide is the second most common cause of death for young males aged between 15 and 24, behind traffic accidents.

One of Australia' s prime ministers in the 1980s, Bob Hawke, announced that by the year 1990, no Australian child will be living in poverty. That year, Australia ratified the UN Convention on the Rights of the Child (UNCRC), and child poverty had grown. It then missed the timetable for lodging its first report to the UN Children's Rights Committee in 1993. Since then it has faced significant and justified criticism from within and without on how it treats its own children, particularly Aboriginal and Torres Strait Islander children. Real human rights abuses have been revealed, and left without redress.

Indigenous child health and welfare is a national disgrace. Indigenous infant mortality rates are more than three times higher than the rate for other Australian infants. The detention rate of indigenous children is up to 18 times higher than for other children: the welfare interventions in Aboriginal lives are treble the national average.[2]

In the late 1980s the rate and circumstances of deaths in police or prison custody of Aboriginal people led to a Royal Commission. This exhaustively documented the wretched position of indigenous children after decades of the enforced removal (on doctrinal grounds) of Aboriginal and Torres Strait Islander children from their families and how that affected their health, happiness and adult life (or death) choices.[3]

What is not fully appreciated is that the practice continued right until the late 1960s, leaving what the Human Rights and Equal Opportunity Commission's (HREOC) later investigation described as a "stolen generation".[4] The federal government has resolutely refused even to acknowledge that these horrors occurred.

Australia has not welcomed refugee children either. They are either deported or detained on arrival if they do not have proper travel documents. A HREOC inquiry into the treatment of asylum-seekers published in 1998 found instances of children being detained for years in punitive and inappropriate conditions.[5] In 2000 Amnesty International reported one instance of a 3-year-old being put in leg restraints and detained with his father in a suicide-proof cell without windows, toilet or shower for thirteen days, and being denied food and medical attention.[6]

Children are detained with adults in reception centres. These tend to be in isolated, desert-like areas with poor facilities for education (if any) or recreation, and no support for victims of trauma and torture. Private contractors, whose major experience is in running jails, run some detention centres. On 22 June 2000 *The Australian* revealed that a complaint of sexual abuse by a 12-year-old boy against his father and other men had been concealed by the private operators and not reported to South Australian authorities as the law in that state required. The facility itself has been described as a "hell hole" by the eminent Australian, Malcolm Fraser.

There is no advocate for refugee or asylum-seeking children in those centres, and the law was changed, after a court win by HREOC, to limit access to the Human Rights Commissioner or the Ombudsman for all "illegal immigrants". The government continues to defend the practice of detaining child refugees in detention centres.[7]

Australia's record on child abuse and prevention is also not good. The 1980s and 1990s were regularly beset with child abuse scandals. A Queensland government sex abuse help line was overwhelmed with stories of sexual assaults on children in the 1980s. In New South Wales (NSW) a Royal Commission into suspicions of corruption in the NSW police force unexpectedly found evidence of police involvement in paedophile activity and cover-ups and failure to protect children by the state's welfare authorities. A separate inquiry into child sexual exploitation had to be convened.[8] In Queensland the report of a 1999 inquiry found abuse of every kind in residential care and detention centres together with inadequate resources to support families and (as everywhere else) gross overrepresentation of Aboriginal and Torres Strait Islander children in the system.[9]

Child abuse notifications have continued to rise. It is hard to get an accurate picture since each state has different criteria, mandatory reporting provisions and methods of analysing the data and evaluating their own effectiveness in responding. Overall, notifications that required investigation nearly doubled between 1988/89 and 1994/95. Abuse allegations affecting indigenous children are nearly six times more likely to be substantiated than for other children, in some states.[10] The governments of the Northern Territory and Western Australia spend much more on imprisoning and punishing Aboriginal children than on early intervention, specialist support or diversionary programmes.

It is also clear that the message of mandatory reporting laws – "Just tell the experts and we'll deal with it", and its underlying optimism that if the reports reveal vast suffering governments will respond – is fundamentally flawed.

At the same time as the reports are mounting, the states are cutting back in children's services. In Victoria, when mandatory reporting was introduced after the slow torture and death of a 2-year-old, Daniel Valerio, by his step-father in 1994, the budget for early intervention and family support services was slashed weeks after the legislation was passed. The reporting rate skyrocketed anyway. An independent report on the effect of mandatory reporting six years later found that the mandatory reporting regime had failed to improve Victoria's child protection system. It had produced too many false reports, subjecting families to groundless investigations, and had led experts to discount and prioritise according to an informal set of priorities, undermining faith in the system. It had also flooded the services. In the year before its introduction, 15,182 notifications were made. By the end of 1994 this had risen to 26,585. In 1999–2000 36,762 suspected cases were reported to authorities. Less than a third of notifications came from mandated professions (and were much less reliable) and there had been little effect on the number of cases substantiated.[11] In NSW the first independent review of child abuse reporting by the ombudsman found that 55 per cent of all reports had been "mishandled".

Are the resources invested in such systems worth it, in terms of outcomes for children's rights? Australia has been criticized by UN committees for its treatment of vulnerable children. The most susceptible are Aboriginals (land rights, deaths in custody, overrepresentation in the criminal justice system), refugees and ethnic minorities (detention and denied citizenship). By the year 2000 the Australian government headed by a new Prime Minister, John Howard, had become so irritated by these criticisms that it announced plans to withdraw from active cooperation with the human rights committees.[12]

Australia has no national policy or agenda for children. With the economic difficulties of the 1990s and a rapid retreat into politically cautious decision-making, many promising developments were stillborn, thanks to reduction in government activity and the privatisation or corporatisation of many services. Children's services were among the first public services to feel the pinch. The consequences were predictable and have been realised: increases in reported rates of child maltreatment and neglect, avoidable illness and disability. A family that lacks support cannot provide what the UNCRC posits as the foundation of children's rights in its Preamble, "an atmosphere of love and understanding".

Children's rights did not figure in fiscal planning or pruning. Yet there is still a public yearning for some golden age of the family, coupled with widespread intolerance of the adolescent or difficult child.

The division of responsibilities for children

Why did the ratification of the UNCRC not make children's rights part of a national agenda? Australia has not implemented the Convention obligation to raise levels of awareness of human rights generally. That has been largely left to its Human Rights and Equal Opportunity Commission, which has not had the funds to do it.

Australia is a federation, and its states have distinct powers and responsibilities from the national government. It was settled as a collection of military colonies though contrary to myth only two, New South Wales and Tasmania, were originally convict settlements. The land mass was neither settled after a war and conceded in a treaty nor purchased. It was simply taken over for wealth creation and to deal with an excess of population because, according to English notions of the time, it was "empty" – its Aboriginal occupiers had such different concepts of possession and trade that their rights were ignored.[13] Its isolation encouraged small-scale political preoccupations. It was not until the twentieth century, an age of global wars and migration waves, that an Australian perspective began to grow, from self-regard to concern for neighbours. The consequence is that in Australian political and philosophical thought human rights are not familiar concepts. The founding fathers even considered and decided not to have a bill of rights in their new Constitution. Constitutional reform seems blocked for time to come.[14]

Australian laws, institutions and policies about children are divided among the original six Australian colonies, now states[15] and two self-governing mainland territories.[16] Each vigorously guards its sovereignty and possesses its own Governor, written Constitution, legislature, executive and judiciary. The Australian Constitution establishes a "Commonwealth" of states and territories, and a system of federal courts dealing with the laws made by the federal parliament and federal public servants. It is largely silent on rights, and preoccupied with the balance of state/federal power.

With a population of fewer than 20 million people Australians are blessed with nine sets of governmental arrangements; hundreds of "local" government bodies peculiar to each state, and legal and administrative responsibilities for children are divided among them all.

The federal government has exclusive power to make laws in some areas – divorce, corporations and social security, for example – but the states possess the balance. Where the federal government does have exclusive powers, a state law which conflicts with it is, by virtue of Section 104 of the Constitution, invalid to the extent of the inconsistency. The federal parliament does not have the authority to make laws binding the states about education, child protection, how offending children should be treated by the criminal justice system or, simply, children's civil and political rights, with one exception, the power to make (and make laws to implement) international treaties. It has financial power – social security benefits are federally planned and delivered – but relies on others to deliver social services such as housing, education, childcare, child protection and family support services.

The laws, policies and institutions that affect children most closely – welfare and child protection, health, education, and crime – are the states' responsibility, yet most of the funds needed to provide services for children, education and families derive from taxation, which is controlled by the federal government.[17]

The states and territories are competitive and find it inconvenient to agree and collaborate. The result is inconsistencies, overlaps and gaps in laws, services and programmes for children, and little more than acknowledgements of the need for cooperation, collaboration and harmony. How well Australian children's rights are protected and the necessities of a decent life provided and how much they participate in important decisions and the lives of their communities depend on where children happen to live.

The federal government could, in principle, implement the UNCRC under its power to make laws to implement treaties and its international obligations. It has done this in Tasmania twice: once to prevent a dam from being built, and more recently to overturn on "sexual privacy" grounds laws criminalising homosexual behaviour in private between consenting adults.[18] But it has not so acted to protect children's human rights, even under provocation, such as the mandatory sentencing laws of Western Australia and Northern Territory that target some vulnerable children (of which more below).

There are pragmatic reasons for its reluctance. Australia's public infrastructure is managed at state or local level. State courts and government agencies administer most of the relevant law and policy, especially in the case of children. State and territory governments are notoriously sensitive to "anti-child-rights" political manoeuvring. States' cooperation in implementing UNCRC obligations would be necessary. The states are closely involved in the preparation of reports to international bodies on the implementation of treaties.[19] Electorate support for the federal government is organised on a state and territory basis. Local issues matter federally.

Treaties do not become part of Australian law unless they are incorporated into it by statute[20] or when courts use them in interpreting common or statute law. Australia has a human rights watchdog – the HREOC[21] – which can provide only conciliation of complaints. In the case of sex, race and disability discrimination, an unresolved complaint may proceed to be heard in the Federal Court if the complainant has access to legal advice and the means to meet legal costs awarded if the action fails.

Each state and territory has also developed its own equal opportunity or anti-discrimination regime, all slightly different, but with local dispute resolution and adjudication structures. In those states that outlaw "age" discrimination there are usually exemptions for discrimination against children.

The division of legislative and bureaucratic authority over children has affected the development of children's law, policy and practice, even in terms of parental rights and responsibilities (unless the parties were married and the Federal Family Law Act 1975 applied). Each state and territory has its own laws and policies with respect to ex-nuptial children, offending children and children in need of care and protection. The laws that prohibit child abuse or expose children to the criminal law change at the borders.

There is no national children's policy or federal solutions to the kind of problems that have left Australia's government so vulnerable to legitimate criticism. Without a coherent, consistent and permanent voice for children at both national and state level, UNCRC implementation cannot be achieved. Australia has a "Stronger Families and Communities Strategy"[22] in which children are barely mentioned except as the subjects of research (a longitudinal study of Australian children), referrals for places in childcare, and the focus of volunteers and local strategies for families at risk. There is no reference whatever to children's rights in that policy. Federal governments have not created even a portfolio affecting children's policy: it is generally subsumed under "family" or women's or "welfare" portfolios. The voice of the child is not heard in Cabinet.

The voice of the child

Article 12 of the UNCRC requires that children's views be taken seriously in the decisions that affect them. To be heard, adults must expect children to participate: they cannot simply assume the decisions they make about children are proper and in their best interests. Traditionally, in the courts children were treated as either forensic objects or persons under a legal disability. This began to change in 1975 when dramatic changes to Australian divorce laws for the first time gave children the right and the new Family Court the power to order that they be separately legally represented. The new legislation even, for a time, required the Family Court to give effect to the wishes (as to custody and access) of children of 14 or more, though this was too threatening to survive for long (now judges may give discretionary weight to the wishes of any child who chooses to express them).

Though the federal Family Court can direct that children be represented it cannot require the (state) legal aid bodies to provide assistance, though the separate representative must now be appropriately trained, after recommendations from the Family Law Council in 1996.[23] Only Victoria requires that offending children must be legally represented. Children in institutional care have no advocates. Failing to provide legal representation as a matter of right was recognised in the 1999 report of the Queensland review of institutional child abuse as contributing to the damage done.[24] No government has made proper provision for appropriately trained legal advocates for children or adequately funded children's specialist legal services.[25]

The imposition of adult sentences on children under "three strikes and you're in" legislation, discussed below and increasingly popular in some states, takes a deadly aspect if children are also denied competent legal representation. Specially trained lawyers are thin on the ground – almost as thin as the budgeted provision of services for them. Here again the federal/state division comes into play. The federal government funds legal services for "Commonwealth matters" which includes separate legal representation in the Family Court of Australia, but not for day-to-day advocacy in criminal or care jurisdictions which are a matter for the states. The states choose whether and what to fund for children whose advocacy is, as a result, ad hoc and reactive or simply not available. Recommendations for a national scheme for child advocacy have been made by the NSW's Standing Committee on Social Issues of the Legislative Council of New South Wales;[26] the federal Family Law Council[27] and the Australian Law Reform Commission, whose outstanding report documented the parlous state of children's representation throughout the country, and recommended a national overview through a specialist powerful advisory unit close to the heart of executive government – in the office of Prime Minister and Cabinet.[28] None of these have been acted upon. There seems little point in recognising a child's right to participate in decisions that affect them, then denying the means of expressing those or any views.

Children's Rights Commissioners?

Australia does not have a federal Children's Rights Commissioner. It does have commissioners for sex, race, disability and Aboriginal and Torres Strait Islander social justice, privacy and "human rights". Some HREOC commissioners have been active on behalf of children's human rights – the 1988 national inquiry into child homelessness shamed governments into developing national programmes to tackle the problem.[29] But fearless advocacy for children has a price. Over the last two years the role, resources, powers and status of HREOC have been severely cut back by government. Commissioners who have displeased the government with their children's advocacy have not been reappointed.

Recommendations continue to be made and ignored, including the latest call for a specialist commissioner within HREOC or a "Children's Ombudsman" made by the Joint Standing Committee on Foreign Affairs, Defence and Trade.[30] In all the debate on how best to protect children's rights,[31] all endorse the principle of a dedicated Office for Children attached to the office of the Prime Minister and a national government agenda or strategy for children[32] and many have added a call for a national Children's Rights Commissioner.[33]

Three states, Queensland, Tasmania and New South Wales, have established Commissioners for Children (in NSW, the Commissioner for Children and Young People).[34] These are disappointing. None of the enabling statutes are predicated on the UNCRC. None provides advocacy for individual children. Each focuses on child protection because they were triggered by child abuse concerns. The very office was seriously damaged by controversy surrounding the departure of the first Queensland Commissioner and his replacement, in early 1999, without a merit selection process. Weaknesses in its powers and functions were addressed after a recent governmental review,[35] but the Commissioner is now also required to vet would-be workers with children for their possible paedophile interests. This built upon the NSW model.

The New South Wales Commissioner for Children and Young People enjoys a broader range of functions; a clearer and more accountable reporting relationship; and has a qualified power to conduct special inquiries into issues affecting children. But s/he must also screen adults for child-related employment[36] and develop and administer a voluntary accreditation scheme for persons working with people who have committed sexual offences – police and professional functions best performed elsewhere than in a children's rights office.

The Commission is part of a raft of NSW child-protection (not children's rights) measures: a Community Services Commission which has investigatory functions for all persons in institutional care including children; a special office within the NSW Ombudsman's office to investigate complaints about public service employees on children's issues, and a "children's guardian" for children in state care. Significantly, the budget for children's services in NSW continues to be pared away.

At least the NSW and Queensland Commissioners for Children can act with a degree of independence even if this falls short of the ideal. The Tasmanian Commissioner for Children[37] lacks autonomy, power and security of tenure. However, in all such cases the quality of the office holder often enables them to outperform the limitations of the office. The first Tasmanian Children's Commissioner, a barrister with a remarkable track record in children's rights advocacy, was appointed in 2000.

Two other major areas of concern should also be noted.

Intellectually disabled girls

In Australia there has long been a practice of "sterilising" intellectually disabled girls without either the child's or a court's permission. In Marion's Case[38] the High Court held that children who have the maturity and intelligence to fully understand what is proposed can give or withhold effective and valid consent to medical treatment even if they are intellectually disabled. If they cannot only a court has authority to consent to sterilisation procedures carried out for non-therapeutic purposes, citing the "fundamental right to personal inviolability existing in the law" and the "invasion of the right to personal integrity".

Justice Brennan, in a minority opinion, expressly declined to determine such applications on the basis of a child's "best interests", pointing out that "the best interests approach depends upon the value system of the decision-maker. Absent any rule or guideline, that approach simply creates an un-examinable discretion in the repository of the power" and adopted instead an explicit human rights measure: the degree by which the impairment of human dignity would be affected by the decision.

In spite of this very clear statement about rights, the practice of sterilising young women without either their or a court's consent has continued, according to the report published in November 1998 by HREOC.[39] Two years later concern that the practice was still so widespread was such that the Senate requested a review of the practice.[40]

Aboriginal children's rights

The courts are not, of course, an adequate way to protect children's rights. Earlier reference was made to the documented evidence of a "stolen generation" of Aboriginal and Torres Strait Islander children, and the devastating effect this had on Australia's indigenous population. In 2000, two middle-aged Aboriginal survivors of the child removal era failed in their claim for damages for the removal, abuse and neglect that had followed their being placed in "care" because it was simply impossible to prove that the then Director of Native Affairs had misused his power, according to the standards required in the Federal Court.[41]

The courts having failed – and giving a damaged adult a remedy is never a satisfactory remedy for a child's wrongs – it is a matter for the representatives of government to make reparations but the federal government has resolutely refused even to apologise, in face of demands, requests, massive public demonstrations and the recommendations for a Reparations Tribunal made by a Senate Inquiry in 2000, continuing even to claim that "no more than 10 per cent of children were taken" and that the removals were benevolently intended as well as lawful.[42]

The disruption to family life caused by separation of indigenous children from their families had a deleterious effect on the survivors – parenting skills, sense of self and purpose as well as a legacy of mental health and social problems, and educational difficulties. Education is a means of breaking that cycle. In this, too, they are at a disadvantage. Those schools that have allowed indigenous children to succeed must operate differently. One such school was closed down in Victoria in December 1992. The battle for the reopening of Northland Secondary College was to establish an important precedent for the education rights of disadvantaged children.

The then government's justifications were purely financial: closure would save the expense of repairing the building and help reduce expenditure on education generally for the state. The school had been uniquely successful in encouraging not only Aboriginal but also other deprived and marginalised students to complete their secondary education and undertake other training through an inclusive curriculum linking the school to parents, families and the wider community. Two Aboriginal children complained that they could not meet "mainstream" high school criteria of educational achievement, curriculum and teaching methods if the College closed. Removing it was indirectly discriminatory on the grounds of their race.

The Equal Opportunity Board found that Aboriginal students could not effectively access an education system that was designed for a majority culture insensitive to their cultural heritage and needs. It ordered that the school should be reopened forthwith. The government appealed. There then ensued two years of litigation, the Premier, at one point, announcing that "beating them" (the two children) was a "crucial test of his right to govern". In late 1996 it ended in success for the students who had, by this stage, been out of education for two years.[43] The Supreme Court of Victoria said that it could be unreasonable to discount the appalling effects on a particular child of exclusion from education by virtue of their Aboriginality, in favour of economic considerations. It was the first time, in an Australian court, that an indigenous child's right to an education was weighed in the balance and found at least as important as a state government's "big picture" financial objectives.

Mandatory sentencing

There have not, as yet, been any such successes for children subjected to mandatory sentencing regimes. In 1992, Western Australia (WA) introduced the first such juvenile sentencing legislation, in deliberate and direct breach of the UNCRC. An Aboriginal child is 18.6 times more likely to be in custody than non-indigenous children, in Australia. In Western Australia, the rate is 32 times.

The legislation of that year was a political response by a government heading towards defeat in the polls to a perceived crime wave involving stolen vehicles and the deadly pursuit of very young joy riders by very young police officers. After a dreadful accident on Christmas night 1991 when a young pregnant mother and her toddler were killed in a high-speed car chase involving a 14-year-old Aboriginal boy in a stolen car, hotly pursued by police, the government introduced Australia's first mandatory sentencing laws.

The Act provided for automatic jail terms based on categories of prescribed offences. It overturned the fundamental principle that detention should be a sentence of last resort for the shortest appropriate time on its head. It excluded all judicial review. It removed judicial discretion. Worse, most offenders in the prescribed categories were Aboriginal boys, with appalling histories of abuse, exploitation and neglect.

The federal government criticised the legislation, but did nothing to override it, as it had the power to do. The Act was later broadened to cover adults and despite clear research evidence that it was a failure,[44] retained and "improved" several times. There was a 25 per cent increase in the number of indigenous peoples in WA prisons. The legislation proved so popular in its home state that other states took it as a model.

The Northern Territory (NT) government improved upon it in 1997. Its legislation provided that adults (defined as people aged 17 or older) found guilty of certain property offences were subject to graduated mandatory minimum terms of imprisonment from the very first offence. The offences included the pettiest of property crime and unlawful entry to buildings or use of vehicles. The result was an increase in the prisoner population in the Territory by 42 per cent in one year.[45] The majority of these were young Aboriginal males.

In 1997 the UN Committee on the Rights of the Child expressed concern at this legislation and its effects on Aboriginal juvenile detention.[46] The federal government ignored the Committee: the WA and NT governments expressed disdain. Attempts were made to introduce legislation to prohibit mandatory sentencing of juvenile offenders into the federal parliament – the federal government had acted to override the NT's "euthanasia" laws the previous year – which did not win the support of the federal government. Then, on 10 February 2000 a 15-year-old orphaned Aboriginal boy from Groote Eylandt, a remote indigenous community, hanged himself at a juvenile detention centre, where he was serving a mandatory 28-day term. He had been jailed for thieving a petty collection of pencils, paints and pens from his old school.

Again, there was universal condemnation of the laws and their lethal effect on vulnerable children, from HREOC to judges, magistrates and major churches. In the Northern Territory the proportion of indigenous prisoners jumped to 67 per cent of the total prison population.[47]

The federal government had to act because of pressure within its ranks. Rather than override the legislation, it negotiated. The NT government agreed to raise the "adult responsibility" age to 18 and promised to introduce diversionary programmes for children. The federal government gave the NT $20M to do so. The NT promptly assigned the first tranche towards additional police to meet their "increased workload". The UN High Commissioner for Human Rights was requested by the UN Secretary General to examine whether the mandatory sentencing laws were in breach of the UNCRC and ICCPR. The Senate Legal and Constitutional References Committee reported in March 2000 that the laws were inappropriate to a society that values human rights. The UN Committee on the Elimination of Racial Discrimination called on the federal government to consider overriding those laws, on the ground of the rise in the incarceration rate and mandatory sentencing laws which appeared to target offences committed disproportionately by indigenous Australians, particularly children;[48] was then accused of "bias" by the federal Attorney General. The UN Working Group on Arbitrary Detention was to visit from 21 April, and the Human Rights Committee and Committee Against Torture were to arrive later that year. On 30 March 2000 the federal government (under pressure) had announced a review of its participation in the UN treaty system. On 28 August it announced that it would cease to cooperate, except in extraordinary circumstances, with UN committee visits.

In September 2000, all domestic remedies having been exhausted, Aboriginal groups lodged a complaint with the UN Human Rights Committee under the Optional Protocol to the ICCPR over the mandatory sentencing laws, based on removal of judicial discretion, the discriminatory effect of the laws on Aboriginal people, and denial of a fair trial.[49] Meanwhile the WA Labor party announced that it was still in favour of mandatory sentencing at its 2000 annual conference!

Natural justice and the UNCRC

There is little point in advocating for children's rights from the high moral ground. It is important to do whatever it takes to create government institutions that are sensitive to human rights and accountable for their breach. This very nearly happened, when in 1995 Ah Hin Teoh fought a decision to deport him without considering his dependent Australian children's rights under the UNCRC, not to be parted from their parent without their consent. The High Court decided that the UNCRC ratification in 1990 had changed the content of the rules of natural justice.[50] It had set up a "legitimate expectation" that government officials would act fairly when making decisions that would affect children. It had created an enforceable procedural requirement that the Commonwealth's immigration officials at least consider Australian-born children's rights when they were deciding to deport their custodial parent.

Legally, it gave international human rights instruments as much effect as published, considered statements of government policy. According to earlier cases citizens are entitled to expect that these will guide administrative discretion and should be warned if they will not – no more than that. Administratively, of course, it was deeply inconvenient. More than 900 international instruments – nobody was entirely certain – had been adopted over the years! It led to one of the most shameful acts of government.

Children's rights have to be more effectively monitored and enforced than any other human rights, because children cannot claim them for themselves. They have to be respected while they are children. And it was precisely this that the Commonwealth government moved to prevent, under both ALP and Coalition governments. The Immigration Department demanded and got legislative action. The ALP Attorney General proposed a law that would nullify the domestic effect of Australia's international obligations. It had not passed before that administration went out of office. The next Attorney General conceded that the Teoh decision had not led to a flood of, or any, legal claims. There was no need for an Act. Then, on 25 February 1997, he and the Minister for Foreign Affairs none the less jointly announced that the Commonwealth did not intend to be bound by its international covenants when they signed them. Legislation was drafted to make this an unarguable principle of Australian statute law. It was reintroduced in 2001.

Civil society and children's rights advocacy

What is it like to be a child in Australia? A happy life, if s/he has chosen her parents wisely. But children's rights are not high on the political agenda. It will take the concerted efforts of parents, children and children's groups to change this. If they could make some key demands with one voice, it would make a political difference. The demands should be primarily upon the federal government, which has the primary responsibility for the well-being of Australian children because it undertook the international obligations of the UNCRC (with the states' consent), acquired the capacity to make laws to implement those rights, and has the resources to set up programmes and policies to achieve it.

The federal government should have a national policy about and a strategy for children, and a responsibility to effect the co-ordination of the programmes and services that promote children's well-being scattered among portfolios and departments, each acting as though each of its programmes and policies can be quarantined, and that Australia's children are someone else's responsibility.

It should be asked to establish a cross-portfolio children's policy unit in the office of the Prime Minister; with the power to establish, co-ordinate and monitor a whole-of-government children's policy, backed with the authority of this office and reporting to Parliament. Ministers should be obliged to report upon the implications of their portfolio decisions on children's well-being before policy proposals go to Cabinet. Public servants should be instructed to consider UNCRC rights when making their decisions affecting children, and indeed the public service ethos would change dramatically if the PM did so.

The federal government should also take responsibility for researching, planning and ensuring that adequate funds are spent on a national children's services programme, delivered by the states but funded by the tax system. We cannot leave children's services to market forces.

A Children's Commissioner may be only a symbolic appointment but it would send a powerful message if it were accompanied by administrative change and was a powerful, independent voice for children. In the interim, the third sector could establish a non-government "Commissioner", or children's ombudsman, as a public voice for children outside the institutions of government.

Such a Commissioner should use the law. Test cases, using existing law, to protect and promote children's rights tend to be taken seriously. The success of the Northland Secondary College complaint discouraged education bureaucrats from seeing Aboriginal schools as soft targets for cost savings. There has subsequently been another win. In January 1997, 28 final-year students whose pictures in front of their struggling high school were published by a newspaper under the banner "The Year We Failed" persuaded a New South Wales jury that they had been libelled three years later. The case was settled with a public apology and undisclosed damages. Newspapers will think twice before they stick the boot into disadvantaged students.

Adult institutions must take the rights of Australian children as seriously as they do the country's overseas reputation. It is bizarre that the federal government was willing to protect children's rights overseas – from "sex tourists" in developing countries, for example[51] – but remains unwilling to give leadership in providing services for children that will keep Australian-based children well, happy, and help them achieve their potential as adult citizens. Since 1990 Australians have, "in principle", accepted that children have human rights but, in practice, not implemented them. The UNCRC is a sign of selfhood, visibility and inclusion: a citizen's charter. It is time Australia grew up, and made it work.

Notes

1 *Child Poverty Across Industrialised Nations.* UNICEF (1999).
2 *Child Abuse and Neglect.* Australian Bureau of Statistics and Australian Institute of Health and Welfare (1997).
3 *Report of the Royal Commission into Aboriginal Deaths in Custody.* Australian Government Publisher, Canberra, ACT (1990).
4 *Bringing Them Home. Report of the National Inquiry into the Separation of Aboriginal and Torres Strait Islander Children From Their Families.* Human Rights and Equal Opportunity Commission, Sydney, NSW (1997)
5 *Those Who Come Across The Seas: Detention of Unauthorised Arrivals*, Human Rights and Equal Opportunity Commission, Sydney, NSW (12 May 1998). Copies of HREOC publications are available from www.hreoc.gov.au.
6 *Sydney Morning Herald*, 7 December 2000.
7 In May 2000 there were more than 510 children in Australia's detention centres, 28 unaccompanied. Six months later there were said to be 231 children in detention. The Minister for Justice could not say how long they had been held – 651 had already been released – but claimed that it must be in their "best interests" to stay with their parents (*Sydney Morning Herald*, 28 November 2000).
8 *Paedophile Inquiry Report of the Royal Commission into the NSW Police Service.* Government Printer, NSW (26 August 1997).
9 *Commission of Inquiry into Abuse of Children in Queensland Institutions.* Queensland Government Printer, Queensland (May 1999).
10 Western Australia and South Australia. See Australian Institute of Health and Welfare, *Child Abuse and Neglect*, Australia (1999). www.aihw.gov.au.
11 *The Age*, "Abuse Report Law Flawed", 20 October 2000
12 Media release from Attorney General, *Improving the Effectiveness of UN Committees* (29 August 2000). www.law.gov.au/aghome.

13 The legal position was not rectified until the High Court's decision in *Mabo* v *Queensland* (1992) 107 ALR 1 which overturned the terra nullius principle.

14 A Constitutional Convention called in 1998 (the author was an elected delegate) declined to discuss the development of constitutional rights, in favour of devising the terms of a referendum on becoming a republic. The referendum failed in 1999.

15 New South Wales, Victoria, Queensland, Western Australia, South Australia and Tasmania (in order of population).

16 The Australian Capital Territory (where Australia's capital, Canberra, is located) and the Northern Territory (a tiny, relatively recently, self-governing body with a very high proportion of Aboriginal and Torres Strait Islander residents).

17 The introduction of a federal Goods and Services Tax in July 2000 will loosen the federal grasp over allocation of tax revenue by putting GST revenue under state control.

18 Using its obligations under the International Covenant on Civil and Political Rights.

19 This helps to explain why Australia's first report to the UN Committee on the Rights of the Child, due in January 1993, was years late.

20 For example, the federal Racial Discrimination Act 1975 expressly implemented Australia's obligations under the Convention on the Elimination of all Forms of Racial Discrimination and explicitly provided that racially discriminatory laws were invalid by virtue of that legislation. The Sex Discrimination Act, implementing the Convention on the Elimination of all forms of Discrimination Against Women, did not have such a provision, though Catholic bishops urged in 2000/2001 in the high court that it should be subject to the UNCRC (to limit single women's access to reproductive technology "in the interests of the child"). Many other international treaties are referred to the Schedule to the federal Human Rights and Equal Opportunity Commission Act 1986. This does not incorporate them in Australian law, but may raise "legitimate expectations" that they will be taken into consideration by administrative decision-makers (see the High Court's decision in *Minister of State for Immigration and Ethnic Affairs* v *Ah Hin Teoh* (1995) 128 ALR 153).

21 Human Rights and Equal Opportunity Commission Act 1986. In 1999 an attempt to call it the "Human Rights and Responsibilities Commission" – the name gives a flavour of the federal government's view of "rights" generally – fortunately failed to pass.

22 The policy can be viewed on www.facs.gov.au.

23 *Involving and Representing Children in Family Law*, Report (August 1996). Family Law Council. http://law.gov.au/flc.

24 *Commission of Inquiry into Abuse of Children in Queensland Institutions.* Queensland Government Printer, Queensland (May 1999).

25 *Seen and Heard. Priority for Children in the Legal Process.* Report No. 84, Australian Law Reform Commission and Human Rights and Equal Opportunity Commission, Sydney, NSW (1997).

26 *Inquiry into Children's Advocacy.* Report No. 10 (September 1996). The recommendations included funding of institutional advocacy for individual children and the establishment of a children's commissioner in the federal Human Rights and Equal Opportunity Commission.

27 *Involving and Representing Children in Family Law.* A Report to the Attorney-General prepared by the Family Law Council, Canberra, ACT (August 1996). This recommended national training and segregated legal aid funding for children's separate legal representatives.

28 *Seen and Heard* (see note 25).

360 *Moira Rayner*

29 *Our Homeless Children. Report of the National Inquiry into Homeless Children.* Human Rights and Equal Opportunity Commission, Sydney, NSW (1989). The author was a consultant to the review and wrote a report on Australia's compliance with the UN Declaration on the Rights of the Child.

30 *A Review of Australia's Efforts to Promote and Protect Human Rights.* Joint Standing Committee on Foreign Affairs Defence and Trade, Australian Government Printing Service, Canberra, ACT (1994), rec. 9.8.2 and *Report on Public Seminars* (20 and 25 September 1996), Joint Standing Committee on Foreign Affairs Defence and Trade, AGPS, Canberra, 1997, recs. 1–2. Cited in *Seen and Heard* (note 25).

31 See also *Seen and Heard* (note 25); *United Nations Convention on the Rights of the Child.* 17th Report, Joint Standing Committee on Treaties, Parliament of the Commonwealth of Australia, 1998, Chapter 5, pp. 165–192; Inquiry into Children's Advocacy, Parliament of New South Wales Legislative Council Standing Committee on Social Issues, Report No. 10 (September 1996), Chapter 2, pp. 33–49 and Chapter 8, pp. 195–208.

32 Ibid. at pp. 133–150.

33 Ibid. at n. 8. Joint Standing Committee or Treaties, recs. 23–26, pp. 195–197; *Seen and Heard*, rec. 3, p. 140 (see note 25). See also Moira Rayner, *The Role of the Commonwealth in Preventing Child Abuse*, Australian Institute of Family Studies, Melbourne (1995).

34 The Children's Commissioner and Children's Services Appeals Tribunals Act 1996 (Queensland) came into force in November 1996; The Commissioner for Children and Young People Act 1998 (NSW) came into force in December 1998; The Children and Young Persons and their Families Act 1997 (Tasmania) received royal assent on 5 November 1997, and it was proclaimed in 2000. Part 9 of the latter Act establishes the Commissioner for Children.

35 *Review of the Queensland Children's Commissioner and Children's Services Appeals Tribunals Act 1996.* An Issues Paper, Queensland Government Printer (1998).

36 In December 2000 she announced that over 86,000 persons had been vetted and just 12 blocked from employment.

37 Established under the Children, Young Persons and Their Families Act (1997) (Tasmania).

38 *Secretary, Dept of Community Services and Health* v *JWB and SMB* (1992) CLR 218.

39 *The Sterilisation of Girls and Young Women in Australia – A legal, medical and social context,* by Susan M Brady and Dr Sonia Grover. This can be read wwwda.org.au or downloaded from HREOC at www.hreoc.gov.au.

40 On 11 March 2000.

41 *Cubillo & Gunner* v *Commonwealth* (2000) FCA 1084.

42 *Sydney Morning Herald*, 30 March 2000.

43 *Sinnapan et anor* v *State of Victoria* (1994) EOC 92–567; 92–654; 92–611. *State of Victoria* v *Sinnapan et ors* (1995) EOC 92–663; 92–698; 92–699.

44 *Repeat Juvenile Offenders: The Failure of Selective Incapacitation in Western Australia.* Research Report No. 10. November 1993. Richard W. Harding (ed.) Crime Research Centre, University of Western Australia.

45 *Year Book Australia 1998.* National Figures on Crime and Punishment. Australian Bureau of Statistics, Australian Government Printing Service, Canberra, ACT (1998).

46 *Committee on the Rights of the Child, Concluding Observations on Australia's first report under the Convention on the Rights of the Child*, adopted 10 October 1997.

47 *Canberra Times*, 30 March 2000.

48 *Concluding Observations, Committee on the Elimination of Racial Discrimination* (24 March 2000).
49 *Lateline* Channel 9, 13 July 2001. *The Times* London, 13 July.
50 *Minister of State for Immigration and Ethnic Affairs* v *Ah Hin Teoh* (1995) 128 ALR 153 (see note 20).
51 Crimes (Sex Tourism) Amendment Act 1994. However the special prosecution unit was closed down by the government in 2000.

22 A Commissioner for Children's Rights in the Flemish community in Belgium

Ankie Vandekerckhove

Introduction[1]

Inspired by the UN Convention on the Rights of the Child,[2] other relevant international guidelines[3] and examples from other countries, the Flemish[4] Parliament on 15 July 1997 voted to enact a law[5] establishing a Children's Rights Commissioner and the Children's Rights Commissioner's Office. After a public selection process, conducted outside parliamentary influence, the first Commissioner was selected and officially appointed by the Flemish Parliament on 13 May 1998. After an initial period of setting up the office and recruiting a multidisciplinary staff, the Commissioner's Office really began work in January 1999.

The law sets out the main principles and tasks of the new Office. It is, in its broadest sense, intended to provide an independent voice for children at the parliamentary level: a "megaphone" for children in a political forum where they are not represented. Children may not have their own place in political life, but they are part of society, here and now. Children are certainly not formally citizens (because they lack the adult political rights which bestow citizenship), but they are citizens in as much as they experience – along with everyone else – the consequences and effects of policy decisions in their daily life. The Children's Rights Commissioner's Office is there to protect and promote their rights and interests.

The link with the parliamentary level, as opposed to the executive level, is very important for the democratic and independent status of the Commissioner's Office: all political actors (parties) can be addressed and we do not depend on the Cabinet or the policies of any single minister. But before discussing the work of the Children's Rights Commissioner, it is important to make some brief observations about the position of children in Flemish society.

The ambiguous position of children

Over the past years a good deal has been written about the changing position of children within societies which are themselves experiencing considerable change.[6] But currently children seem to be at an ideological crossroads.

First, the status of children might be described as being simultaneously "not yet" on the one hand but being "already" on the other. The distinction between these two states is drawn by adults, who designate children as competent or not at different ages and in different spheres. We can illustrate this tendency by the following example from Belgium.

In the area of penal law, minors have been, for a long time, protected in the sense that they were considered to be legally incapable of committing criminal acts. Separate legislation and distinctive social services were considered necessary to deal with problems of juvenile delinquency: children were not punished but "helped" and re-educated. Such legislation was not primarily aimed at repression but more at social control. In recent years, however, a public debate has introduced the search for more appropriate (more repressive?) answers to the apparently increasing delinquency by minors.[7] More and more people believe that juveniles should be held responsible for their criminal acts and should be punished accordingly. The debate about their responsibilities under penal law is being conducted in the justice and welfare departments, with age-limits as low as 12 being advocated.

At the same time, there is a debate about the age at which young people can freely consent to and engage in sexual acts. One proposal, which triggered heated debate, was the suggestion that the age of consent be lowered from 16 to 14. The proposal was never enacted since the majority of adults consider young people unable to handle their own sexuality under the age of 16. (Needless to say not a single young person took part in the debate.)

So, at the same time, within the same society and political climate, different notions of competence and responsibility coexist. Children are considered to be able to commit crimes at 14 years of age but are judged incapable of developing, exploring and experimenting with their own sexuality. There are other examples of children's competence decided by adult definitions. Thus we find children acknowledged to be competent as consumers or semi-professional sportsmen, while they remain incompetent and unable to start legal procedures or to take part in political life.

Second, there is a contradiction between children having rights but being unable to exercise them. We have just celebrated the tenth anniversary of the CRC, but this does not mean the work is done. Actually, we received some questions from children asking us whether there was anything for them to celebrate. They now learn, slowly but still, that they have rights but they also learn that they can't enforce them when their rights are violated. Isn't this a strange and ambiguous message to send to children? Stating that minors are people too and that they therefore should enjoy all human rights is an incomplete statement as long as they have to rely on the goodwill of adults to ensure that their rights are genuinely and effectively respected. Although new legislation (on e.g. student councils and the possibility of being heard

by a judge) has been enacted during the past years, an overall right to participate is still far from reality.

Third, there is a difference in the way we view children as individuals and
children as a group or a social category: an issue addressed by academic Jens
Qvortrup (1998: 111–25). Policy-makers don't tend to view minors as a
permanent social category within society. They see them mostly as adults in
the making. When children do receive some attention as a social group, it is
mostly in a negative way. The way that media report children and young
people offers an obvious example (see chapter 1). While most people like
(their) children, sometimes even adore them, society as a whole is much
more equivocal in its expressed attitudes. Even the word "youth" has a negative connotation and is often linked with problems arising from
unacceptable youth subcultures, truancy, drug (ab)use, delinquency etc.
Space for children and young people has become scarce with hardly any
specific attention to the needs of this group of citizens in policy and
budgetary allocations. It seems that people who do not vote are largely
missing from the political agenda.

Functions of the Commissioner's Office

The law of July 1997 formulated different tasks for the Children's Rights
Commissioner and her team. In general terms the Children's Rights
Commissioner's Office has to monitor the implementation of the
Convention on the Rights of the Child. This includes checking whether
legislation is consistent with the principles of the Convention on the Rights
of the Child, giving advice on how the Convention can be put into practice
and, finally, stimulating child-friendly policies in which the social position of
children can be strengthened. The greatest effort is expended on the issue of
participation for children, since this is the most debated element of the
Convention on Children's Rights. The Commissioner's office has made
several recommendations to the Flemish Parliament and other authorities
on a wide range of topics including family mediation, youth care, youth
work, advertisements on TV, sports, education, discrimination etc.

The Commissioner's Office also *informs* the general public, children as
well as adults, about the contents and the importance of the Convention on
the Rights of the Child and raises public awareness about children's issues.
This involves the Office in a number of activities. Every year, for example,
we establish and promote a specific campaign[8] which involves activities for
children and targets messages at adults and policy-makers. In 2000,
prompted by the local elections, a referendum for children was held with the
results being sent to the newly elected community councils. The annual
Children's Rights festival will be set up as an ideal city for children. A
booklet is planned for publication containing practical tips and information
and strategies for children to claim their rights in their own communities.
The rights-related themes and topics for the booklet were gathered from

questions and suggestions received from children throughout the preceding year. In addition to these campaigning activities, the Children's Rights Commissioner's Office also publishes a range of leaflets for different age groups containing information about children's rights and an interactive website was launched in November 2000 (www.kinderrechtencommissariaat.be).

The 1997 law also requires that the Commissioner's Office undertake studies exploring the circumstances and living conditions of children. This is an important but difficult commitment to meet. An effective child policy requires knowledge about children but this information is to date too sparse and fragmentary. What, for example, are children's attitudes towards school? How do they relate to their parents? How important are media to them? These are questions that we have been answering from an adult perspective for a long time, while the perceptions of children themselves are undoubtedly very different. Only when we begin to address issues from the child's perspective, will we be able to find the correct answers to their concerns and needs. Throughout 2000, a substantial social research inquiry has been planned and conducted with data gathered about the different ways in which children view their daily life at home, in school and in their neighbourhood. On completion, the study has provided essential insights into children's perspectives on the world around them. Access to such child perceptions is vital to performing the task of being a "megaphone" for children to the policy-makers.

The Children's Rights Commissioner's Office also receives and investigates complaints on possible violations of children's rights. This task is fundamentally different from that of any social service. We do not handle cases in the sense of solving a problem, but we investigate whether the relevant service providers have administered their commitments correctly. Or, on those occasions when such services are not available, we advise the authorities of the need to set up appropriate helplines. This difference is sometimes difficult to explain to the general public. Many cases, for example, involve complaints from children about not being heard in court proceedings. The Children's Rights Commissioner's Office cannot intervene in such individual cases – not only because the judicial power is independent (a "sacred" and central democratic principle), but also because we do not have the resources that a judge has at her/his disposal to investigate the claims of both parties in order to respect the rights of both sides. What we *can* do on these occasions is argue the general point that a system of legal aid is necessary for minors and that Article 12 of the UN Convention is legally binding on our judges.

In addition to all these other commitments, the Commissioner's Office needs to stimulate and facilitate the participation of children in our society. This is achieved by setting up our own activities with and for children but also by explaining to them how they can set up or ask for participative structures themselves.

The Commissioner's Office also has to report annually to the Flemish

Parliament about all its activities and achievements. The date set for each report is 20 November every year and we take advantage of the situation to put children's rights on the political and media agenda. The annual report is also an instrument with which to apply pressure on policy-makers. If certain recommendations have not been implemented we can report that omission and stimulate public discussion, public opinion and possibly change. Every year the official report is also redrafted into a more popular, accessible and "younger" version and distributed through schools, libraries, youth services etc. because we feel that, in the end, we need to be responsible and answer for what we do for children and young people in the first place. A final note on the annual report. The Children's Rights Commissioner's Office has no brief nor capacity to decide or interfere in individual cases: we can only give general policy recommendations. Since we are not elected politicians, these recommendations are not binding, only advisory. While handling complaints we exercise broad investigatory powers: we have access to relevant documents, visit institutions, demand explanations.

Working principles

It is obvious that the Convention on the Rights of the Child is our most important instrument: both as a checklist and an agenda. The first refers to the Office's more reactive work, checking laws and practices for their compliance with the Convention and looking into violations of rights. The second (the rights agenda) signals the more pro-active work of the Commissioner's Office which involves stimulating child-friendly measures and decisions and working on the promotion of rights.

We try to work on the basis of a mandate from children. Ultimately, it is children who should draw up our agenda and decide the focus for our activities. To be able to do so however, we need to invest in making ourselves known to children, as well as publicising the potential benefits which the Children's Rights Commissioner's Office can achieve for them. Translated into the particular focus of the Office, this means that we will only investigate a case when we are sure that the child itself wants us to. Many complaints are still filed by adults,[9] and we check, where possible, if the child shares the adult's view of the case. If not, we will refer the adult to other, more appropriate services.

In our work it is important to bring out the *emancipatory* powers of the Convention on the Rights of the Child, in a way which means that adults should no longer serve as advocates for children, but should help to organise ways which empower children to engage in self-advocacy. We need to focus on children's own capacities, instead of patronising them. In this context we work mostly on participation rights, not least because that "P" of the Convention is generally less known by adults than the other two "P's" representing protection and provision. But resistance to children's rights is still all too evident especially regarding participation rights.

Within the Children's Rights Commissioner's Office we also took the option of working to raise awareness of the more *basic* provisions – school, play, youthwork, media, and space for children in general – rather than focusing on the potentially more contentious areas. This is not to suggest that matters like child abuse and youth care are not important, but to emphasise that children have the right to be seen, heard and taken into account when they do not have problems or are judged to be causing problems for society. It is to emphasise that children are part of society, here and now, and as such they deserve the relevant attention on all matters of public policy. This in many ways represents an attempt to change attitudes towards children rather than an emphasis solely on immediate results.

Finally, the Children's Rights Commissioner's Office works as a team, which is conceived in a multidisciplinary way which uses, draws upon and contributes to the development of the various perspectives of law and criminology, sociology, pedagogy, social work and media studies in the conduct of its work: all disciplines are represented currently in the Office.

Target groups

Children are, of course, our most important target group. We either reach them directly through our informative flyers, stickers and other material or through events like the annual Children's Rights Festival. Indirectly they are the target group in the sense that we try to influence policies for their benefit and to strengthen their position in society.

We realise however that making a reality of children's rights will never be possible without targeting the *adult society* as well. In the beginning it is adult society that will have to make the shift towards more child-friendly practices: parents, teachers, social workers, politicians, doctors and all other adults who are related to children (that means everyone!). Through conferences, debates, representations and the media we take the message of the Convention on the Rights of the Child to the broader public and clarify and translate it and illustrate its applicability to daily life in Flemish society. We also offer children's rights education to relevant professional groups.

Quality requirements

Having described the Flemish Children's Rights Commissioner's Office, it may be useful to compare this office against the general quality requirements[10] described in research findings from studies conducted at the Ghent Centre of Children's Rights based in the University of Ghent.[11] Many of these criteria relate to the service itself, but the basis issue is that there has to be a degree of political will and a supportive public attitude to foster the development of a body to monitor children's rights of the kind which the Commissioner's Office represents. When such political will and public support is absent, the Convention on the Rights of the Child can be used as a powerful strategic tool: pointing out the binding character of this legal document can firmly support the work of children's ombudswork.

Official status

Any ombudsservice should be established by law in which the competences and independence guarantees are clearly formulated with no room for interpretation. By "law" we mean a rule made by the legislative power rather than the executive. The law itself as well as the control on the outcome of the recommendations is then more democratic. The Children's Rights Commissioner's Office was set up by law which gives the office an official and legal basis. By doing so the Flemish Parliament has made it clear it wanted to give ample opportunities for an independent monitoring body and has given a strong symbolic sign for the importance given to children's rights.

Permanent

Although one could say that the ultimate goal would be to become obsolete and unnecessary, one has to remain realistic. Focusing on children's rights (human rights in general) is a never-ending task. While the appointed Children's Rights Commissioner is limited to a maximum of two terms of five years, the Office as such is a permanent body.

Authority

A high degree of moral authority is needed for recommendations of the Office to have any effect. This requirement is partially met by the official status of the Office, but real authority has to be earned by and reflect the intrinsic quality of the work itself.

It is therefore important that the statements of the Children's Rights Commissioner's Office are based on sound factual information and scientific research, rather than on unfounded opinions or ideas. It is, for example, not our aim to achieve media coverage as often as possible but only when we really have relevant things to say or issues to raise. Moreover, the people who staff the Office need to be credible and professional, with knowledge and experience in the field.

Objective and independent[12]

The only obligatory directives for the Commissioner's Office come from the Convention on the Rights of the Child and the interests of children. The

Children's Rights Commissioner's Office does not serve any other interest(s). The agenda and priorities are not established by any political or hidden agenda. The Children's Rights Commissioner's Office has to resist pressures which may arise from any lobbying group, political party, ministers or others. It is vital to focus on the children's agenda to the exclusion of other groups seeking to use the Office for their benefit. Many adults undoubtedly use the service to find answers to their own questions, thinly disguised as children's issues, but at times the line between the interests of children and those of their parents can become very blurred.

Responsible

The Children's Rights Commissioner's Office is accountable to the public and public authorities for what it does and how it works. It needs, therefore, to report annually on its activities and its spending, since it is a public office funded by taxpayer's money. In our reports we explain why some issues are fundamental and why we prioritise some issues above others. This will automatically increase the understanding of the Convention on the Rights of the Child and its legally binding status. Our annual report is also redrafted for young people since this is the constituency to whom the Office owes the greatest responsibility.

Comprehensive

The work of the Children's Rights Commissioner's Office needs to cover all policy domains – including education, health, social work, environment – since the Convention on the Rights of the Child is similarly comprehensive. It needs to broaden and inform the minds of policy-makers in ways which make it clear that there are not that many specifically child-focused areas but that all policy areas and decisions typically influence children's and adults' lives equally. An integral policy for children is advocated as well as an equal focus on the three P's.

Accessible

An open attitude towards children and being easy to contact is very important. Children can contact us every day through mail, website, email and telephone or they can visit the Office. Cases are dealt with in a non-bureaucratic way. We try to keep an open line of communication. It is impossible to stress the importance of participation rights, of course, without creating participative ways of working with children and young people in the organisation of the Office's own work regimes. There is still much to address and achieve in this area, partly because as adults we are not used to children's participation and partly because the target group, children, still need to learn about their rights to participate.

Aims

The Children's Rights Commissioner's Office has to set attainable goals and results. Looking at the comprehensive nature of the Convention on the Rights of the Child it is practically impossible to work on all aspects of the Convention's prescriptions. Agenda setting and annual planning are important, as is the need not to spread the organisation's resources too thinly by focusing on too many subjects or projects at the same time. In 1999 the focus was on the tenth anniversary of the Convention on the Rights of the Child. In 2000 we focused on the rights of the child in his/her daily living environment: family, school, community.

Broad powers

The necessary legal competences are the power of investigation, of initiation, of refusal, of deciding how the budget will be spent and of setting priorities, without being influenced by third parties. But having these broad powers does not include assuming the powers of other institutions like the court or the schoolboard etc. Services like the Children's Rights Commissioner's Office cannot, and should not, be able to overrule decisions made by other authorities; it can however criticise them and try to convince them to decide otherwise by informing them about the Convention on the Rights of the Child, its legally binding nature and its consequences.

Discretion

As in all ombudswork, discretion towards the "client" must be guaranteed. Anonymity must be guaranteed when requested and we need to be able to keep our sources secret, if necessary. A set of deontological rules has been written down and regulates our daily work.

Media

The Children's Rights Commissioner's Office needs the media, both the adult and the children's media. Children also need media to be able to enjoy their right to information. If those media aren't accessible the Children's Rights Commissioner's Office has to work on that and stimulate that access. At the same time there is always the risk of being exploited by the media. The issues need to be presented carefully and in the right context: this means representing children's competences rather than negative news about young people which too frequently forms the focus of media reporting.

Realism

The aims of the Commissioner's Office need to be realistic if the ambition is to create change. In this sense we need to keep a close eye on the political agenda to identify politicians' priorities. We are not obliged to be driven by their agenda, but it is helpful to know politicians' priorities, as well as what does not interest them, in order to define our own strategies.

International context

It is useful to keep close contact with other ombudsservices for children, both to learn from each other's experiences and to strengthen our actions towards policy-makers (see also chapter 25). Also, international fora (the UN and the Committee on the Rights of the Child) are important on questions of interpretation and implementation of the Convention on the Rights of the Child. In Europe the existing ombudsservices have organised themselves into the European Network of Ombudspersons for Children (ENOC). ENOC supports countries who want to establish monitoring agencies on children's rights, offers a forum for thematic discussions among members and is working on relations with international institutions, such as the Committee on the Rights of the Child, the Council of Europe and the European Union.

Resources

Any service like the Children's Rights Commissioner's Office needs sufficient financial support and trained personnel to complete its tasks effectively. It has to be more than just "window dressing": it needs to be powerful enough. Too often it is considered a luxury service, that can only be funded when there are "leftovers" (if any). Initially, the authority seemed reluctant to offer financial means to an independent service, over which they have no control. Working seriously, in a positive, supportive and explanatory way can create changing organisational cultures and remove these early suspicions, lack of trust or fear of the unknown.

Pitfalls

During the first working years, it became clear that it was necessary to watch out for different forms of improper use of the Children's Rights Commissioner's Office. We are established to stimulate the implementation of the Convention on the Rights of the Child, to advise on child-friendly policies and to be there for children themselves. Sometimes, adults contact us with questions or topics which are in fact their own, not the children's. This is not what we should be working on, especially since there are many services for adults already. It is also not for us to decide issues in political manifestos: to each his own responsibilities! The Children's Rights Commissioner's Office should not be used to take decisions in the political realm, when politicians themselves fail to do so. We may be working towards politics, but we are never part of it!

Another difficulty is the balance we need to maintain between reactive and proactive work. It is reasonable (realistic?) to expect that the Children's Rights Commissioner's Office will work mostly in a reactive manner during its early years, reflecting the need to work diplomatically and slowly to achieve results in the longer term.

The fact that we work for such a varied target group can also raise problems. Children range from 0 to 18 years of age and constitute a very diverse group. The work with them has to be adapted for these various age groups, which involves a good deal of time and effort. We also need to reach adults and policy-makers. Public messages aimed at one group can cause misunderstandings with the other. Diplomacy is needed here too, without giving in over the essential children's rights message.

Some people have the wrong idea about what we actually do. Many believe we can solve every problem like a *deus ex machina*: they don't always understand that we cannot overrule decisions of judges, schoolboards and other competent bodies. Some also think we are yet another social service where they can find help for their concrete problems, while we are more of a referral service, working on a structural level.

Conclusions

Promoting children's rights is a never-ending story: travelling the same road again and again, at first having to create a "market" in the sense of getting people interested and convinced about the importance of human rights in general and children's rights in particular. On occasions it is certainly a bumpy road, but it is never boring.

Notes

1 This text discusses the general framework of the Flemish Commissioner for Children's Rights. For more specific information on activities, projects, campaigns etc., please contact us on kinderrechten@vlaamsparlement.be.

2 The UN Convention on the Rights of the Child, approved by the General Assembly on 20 November 1989.

3 For example, the so-called Riyadh guidelines, para. 57.

4 Belgium is a federal state, divided into several authority levels, of which the Flemish Community is one.

5 In the Belgian legislature the word "law" is specifically reserved for national legislation, whereas the legislation of Communities and the Regions is called a "decree". For the sake of clarity I will use the word "law", since a decree has a similar power, but the terminology can cause confusion.

6 Verhellen, E. (1999) *Understanding Children's Rights.* Ghent University, Centre for Childrens' Rights (with contributions from M. De Paepe, F. Mortier, M. Flekkøy, B. Franklin, P. Jaffé, J. Qvortrup, M. de Winter).

7 It remains to be confirmed whether there is an actual increase in crime by youth, or whether it is more an increase in public attention to crime committed by young people.

8 1999: the tenth anniversary of the Convention on Children's Rights 2000; local elections in October 2000.

9 In the first year, 38 per cent of the complaints were from children.
10 These criteria were also discussed at the Commemorative meeting on the Tenth Anniversary of the Convention on the Rights of the Child in Geneva, 1999.
11 Spiesschaert, F. en, Verhellen, E.: *Synthesenota. Kwaliteitsvereisten inzake de opvolging van de levensomstandigheden van kinderen en inzake het toezicht op de implementatie van de UNO-Conventie betreffende de Rechten van het Kind*, KBS Initiatiefgroep "Kind in de Samenleving", Gent, 28 juni 1991.
12 The decree of 15 July 1997 states the following in art. 8, §3: "within the boundaries of his competence, the Children's Rights Commissioner does not get instructions from any authority. The commissioner fulfills his function in complete independence".

References

Qvortrup, J. (1998) "Sociological Perspectives On Childhood" in Verhellen, E. (ed.) *Understanding Children's Rights* Ghent: University of Ghent Press, pp. 111–125
Verhellen, E. (1999) *Understanding Children's Rights* Ghent: University of Ghent Press

23 Global progress towards giving up the habit of hitting children

Peter Newell

> In the judicial, social and educational circumstances in which we live, we must not make compromises that can endanger the welfare and physical well-being of minors. ... If we allow "light" violence, it might deteriorate into very serious violence. We must not endanger the physical and mental well being of a minor with any type of corporal punishment. A truth which is worthy must be clear and unequivocal and the message is that corporal punishment is not allowed.
>
> (Israel Supreme Court, 2000: 145)

This was a fine message for children at the dawn of the year 2000 from a Supreme Court judge in Israel. The Court's judgement, later confirmed by legislative change in the Knesset, made Israel the tenth state in the world to ban all corporal punishment.

Meanwhile, in the Department of Health in London, officials were putting the last touches to a consultation document entitled *Protecting Children, Supporting Parents* which took a very different approach to hitting children. A hopefully last-ditch attempt to defend the archaic concept of "reasonable chastisement", it posed some chilling questions. For example:

> Are there any forms of physical punishment which should never be capable of being defended as "reasonable". For example – physical punishment which causes or is likely to cause injuries to the head (including injuries to the brain, eyes and ears)?
>
> (Department of Health, 2000: 15)

Remember, this is a government Department of *Health* asking the question.

Since *The New Handbook of Children's Rights* was published six years ago (1995), there has been significant progress towards ending social and legal acceptance of the common practice across the world of hitting children. It is shaming that adults should have deliberately excluded children from the rights they take for granted to be protected by legislation from deliberate assault by others. It is shaming that the smallest and most vulnerable of people should be the last to be protected by the law.

The UN Convention and hitting children

The Universal Declaration of Human Rights and the two International Covenants on Civil and Political Rights and Economic, Social and Cultural Rights assert *everyone's* right to respect for their human dignity and physical integrity, and to equal protection under the law. Given the universality of human rights, this should have led fifty years ago to states taking action to ensure equal protection of children's human dignity and physical integrity and to discard these disreputable justifications for hitting children – "reasonable chastisement", "lawful correction" and so on.

But it has taken the United Nations Convention on the Rights of the Child (UNCRC) to confirm that children, too, are holders of human rights. The adoption in 1989 and almost universal ratification of the UNCRC has forced states to re-examine their laws, policies and above all their attitudes to children. The Committee on the Rights of the Child, Treaty Body for the Convention, has perceived challenging corporal punishment as a central strategy for improving the status of the child. Article 19 of the Convention requires states to take "all appropriate legislative, administrative, social and educational measures to protect the child from all forms of physical or mental violence, injury or abuse, neglect or negligent treatment, maltreatment or exploitation including sexual abuse, while in the care of parent(s), legal guardian(s) or any other person who has the care of the child".

In a concluding statement to the Committee's General Discussion on Children's Rights in the Family, organised as its contribution to International Year of the Family in October 1994, the Vice-Chair stated:

> As for corporal punishment, few countries have clear laws on this question. Certain States have tried to distinguish between the correction of children and excessive violence. In reality the dividing line between the two is artificial. It is very easy to pass from one stage to the other. It is also a question of principle. If it is not permissible to beat an adult, why should it be permissible to do so to a child? One of the contributions of the Convention is to call attention to the contradictions in our attitudes and cultures.
>
> (Committee on the Rights of the Child, 1994, para. 46)

As it examines reports from states in all continents, the Committee on the Rights of the Child has raised the issue, and recommended that all corporal punishment – however light – should be prohibited and the legal reform accompanied by comprehensive public education campaigns to promote positive, non-violent discipline.

In 1995, it was the turn of the UK to have its first report examined. There was a long discussion between government officials and the Committee, summed up in the official report which quotes the Deputy Chair of the Committee as saying:

It was the Committee's experience that difficulties arose whenever a "reasonable" level of corporal punishment was permitted under a State's internal law. To draw an analogy, no one would argue that a "reasonable" level of wife-beating should be permitted. His conclusion was that the United Kingdom position represented a vestige of the outdated view that children were in a sense their parents' chattels. In the Scandinavian countries and Austria, stricter legislation had resulted in fewer cases going to court than in the United Kingdom, rather than the reverse. ... The notion of a permissible level of corporal punishment was thus best avoided.

(Committee on the Rights of the Child, 1995a, para. 63)

The Committee's concluding observations on the UK report stated:

The Committee is disturbed about the reports it has received on the physical and sexual abuse of children. In this connection, the Committee is worried about the national legal provisions dealing with reasonable chastisement within the family. The imprecise nature of the expression of reasonable chastisement as contained in these legal provisions may pave the way for it to be interpreted in a subjective and arbitrary manner. Thus, the Committee is concerned that legislative and other measures relating to the physical integrity of children do not appear to be compatible with the provisions and principles of the Convention, including those of its articles 3, 19 and 37. The Committee is equally concerned that privately funded and managed schools are still permitted to administer corporal punishment to children in attendance there which does not appear compatible with the provisions of the Convention, including those of its article 28, paragraph 2.

(Committee on the Rights of the Child, 1995b, para. 16)

The Committee went on to recommend:

The Committee is also of the opinion that additional efforts are required to overcome the problem of violence in society. The Committee recommends that physical punishment of children in families be prohibited in the light of the provisions set out in articles 3 and 19 of the Convention. In connection with the child's right to physical integrity, as recognised by the Convention, namely in its articles 19, 28, 29 and 37, and in the light of the best interests of the child, the Committee suggests that the State party consider the possibility of undertaking additional educational campaigns. Such measures would help to change societal attitudes towards the use of physical punishment in the family and foster the acceptance of the legal prohibition of the physical punishment of children.

(Committee on the Rights of the Child, 1995b, para. 31)

Asked in Parliament what action it proposed to take in response to this recommendation from the Committee, the then Conservative government in the UK responded: "None" (*Hansard*, col. 370, 9 February 1995).

Just as the Committee on the Elimination of Discrimination Against Women (another human rights Treaty Body) has been preoccupied with domestic violence to women, so the Committee on the Rights of the Child is now leading the challenge to violence to children. Representatives of the two Treaty Bodies met in 1998 in Geneva to discuss action against family violence. They agreed that "zero tolerance" is the only possible target. As with violence to women, the problem for children is traditional attitudes, culture and some interpretations of religious texts. But a practice which violates basic human rights cannot be said to be owned by any culture, nor dictated by any religion.

The "Guidelines" of the Committee on the Rights of the Child on the information it wants from states preparing their second and subsequent reports under the CRC ask:

> whether legislation (criminal and/or family law) includes a prohibition of all forms of physical and mental violence, including corporal punishment, deliberate humiliation, injury, abuse, neglect or exploitation, inter alia within the family, in foster and other forms of care, and in public or private institutions, such as penal institutions and schools.
>
> (Committee on the Rights of the Child, 1996, para. 88)

The UK will be examined on its second report in 2002; if the government has still failed to respond fully to the Committee's recommendation, we can be confident that the Committee will express even deeper concern. The CRC is not enforceable through a court; it relies on states taking their obligations to children seriously, and ultimately on the power of international embarrassment – not enough, it appears, to shift our government's unconstructive and punitive attitudes to children.

New Labour, the European Court and "Children Are Unbeatable!"

Three years after the unequivocal recommendation of the Committee on the Rights of the Child, in September 1998, the "New Labour" government was faced with a judgment of the European Human Rights Court which it could not ignore (European Court of Human Rights, 1998). A young English boy, known as "A" to protect his anonymity, had made an application to the European human rights machinery in Strasbourg (the European Commission and Court of Human Rights – since amalgamated into a single institution, the Court). The boy had been beaten repeatedly by his stepfather with a garden cane. The stepfather was prosecuted, but used the defence of "reasonable chastisement" and was found not guilty by the jury. During the trial the judge directed the jury:

> If a man deliberately and unjustifiably hits another and causes some bodily injury, bruising or swelling, he is guilty of actual bodily harm. What does unjustifiably mean in the context of this case? It is a perfectly good defence that the alleged assault was merely the correcting of a child by its parent, in this case the stepfather, provided that the correction be moderate in the manner, the instrument and the quantity of it. Or, put another way, reasonable. It is not for the defendant to prove it was lawful correction. It is for the prosecution to prove it was not.
>
> This case is not about whether you should punish a very difficult boy. It is about whether what was done here was reasonable or not and you must judge that.
>
> (European Court, 1998: 4)

The judge was demonstrating with real clarity how the existence of this defence discriminates against children.

The process in Strasbourg was then in two stages. In 1997 the European Commission on Human Rights found unanimously that A's rights had been breached. The government issued a press release which quoted Paul Boateng, then a Junior Minister for Health. He described the beating of the boy as "cruel, inexcusable … has no place in a civilised society". Mr Boateng went on:

> But it has nothing to do with parents who exert discipline by smacking their children when they misbehave. We respect that right. The overwhelming majority of parents know the difference between smacking and beating.
>
> (Department of Health, 1997)

The minister stated that the law would be changed to give children "better protection", and promised a consultation. It was the combination of the opportunity provided by the requirement that the law must be changed and the promised consultation on how to change it, together with the defence of smacking by ministers, which led to the formation of a new Alliance. "Children Are Unbeatable!" was launched at a meeting of children's and professional organisations hosted by the National Society for the Prevention of Cruelty to Children (NSPCC) in March 1998.

The Alliance has two inter-linked aims: that children should have the same protection as adults under the law on assault, by removing the defence of "reasonable chastisement" altogether, and the promotion through public education of positive, non-violent forms of discipline. The statement of aims explains:

The traditional defence of "reasonable chastisement" works against the aims which we and the government of a modern Britain share: the encouragement of positive parental discipline in all families, and assurance of effective child protection in the few cases where it is needed.

We believe it is both wrong and impracticable to seek to define acceptable forms of corporal punishment of children. Such an exercise is unjust. Hitting children is a lesson in bad behaviour.

Removing the defence of "reasonable chastisement" and thus giving children in their homes and in all other settings equal protection under the law on assault is the only just, moral and safe way to clarify the law. While technically this would criminalise any assault of a child, trivial assaults, like trivial assaults between adults, would not be prosecuted. There already exist adequate means to prevent unwarranted or unhelpful prosecutions. It would on the other hand ease prosecution in serious cases. It would eliminate the current dangerous confusion over what is acceptable and provide a clear basis for child protection.

There is ample evidence from other countries to show that full legal reform, coupled with the promotion of effective means of positive discipline, works rapidly to reduce reliance on corporal punishment and reduces the need for prosecutions and other formal interventions in families. Using positive forms of discipline reduces stress and improves relationships between children, their parents and other carers.

(Children Are Unbeatable!, 1998)

By the end of 2000 the Alliance included more than 300 organisations and many prominent individuals. The collective concerns of Alliance supporters range very widely. They cover, for example, the fields of health and mental health, crime and violence prevention including domestic violence; disability; churches and faith groups; mediation, counselling and the promotion of positive relationships; human rights and the law; early years care and education; children and young people in care and youth work. In particular, the Alliance includes many organisations working directly with families and promoting positive parenting. The membership demonstrates that protecting children from all corporal punishment is regarded from many different perspectives as a key and necessary strategy for achieving fundamental social goals, for building a better society.

In September 1998 the European Court of Human Rights released its judgment, echoing the Commission and unanimously finding that the boy's right to protection from "inhuman or degrading treatment or punishment" (Article 3 of the European Human Rights Convention) had been breached and that UK law had failed to provide adequate protection. There must be "effective deterrence" to protect children and other vulnerable individuals. The Court quoted Article 19 of the UN Convention. It ordered the government to pay the boy £10,000 damages and his legal costs. Having found a breach of Article 3, the European Court, following its usual practice, did not go on to consider the boy's claim that the beating had also breached his right to physical integrity (Article 8) and to protection without discrimination (Article 14). This enabled ministers again to greet the judgment with a condemnation of "beating" but condoning of "smacking".

When the consultation paper eventually appeared in January 2000, it rejected in strong terms the idea of banning all physical punishment.

> The government's view is that it would be quite unacceptable to outlaw all physical punishment of a child by a parent. Nor, we believe, would a majority of parents support such a measure. It would be intrusive and incompatible with our aim of helping and encouraging parents in their role.
>
> (Department of Health, 2000: 6)

Instead, the paper asked very limited questions about what sorts of punishment should and should not be considered "reasonable" (as quoted above, p. 374). It seems inevitable that in quite a short time this consultation document will be a source of real embarrassment to this country. Encouraging a debate on how hard parents should be allowed to hit children, with what implements, on what parts of the body and at what age is hardly a dignified occupation for a serious department of government. Can you imagine a similar discussion being posed about treatment of women, or dogs and cats? But we have to remember, of course, that the first law to protect children from cruelty was introduced in the UK sixty years after the first legislation to prevent cruelty to animals.

In 1999 the UK became the last country in Europe to end corporal punishment in all its schools. The continuing legality of corporal punishment in UK private schools had been condemned by three international human rights Treaty Bodies, including – as quoted above – the Committee on the Rights of the Child. The Independent Schools Joint Council, representing the overwhelming majority of private schools, backed prohibition. Yet the New Labour government declined to take a position on the issue; it did allow parliamentarians a free "conscience" vote, and both MPs and peers overwhelmingly backed the ban, which also applies to nursery education.

But – moving backwards again – in August 2000 the government, this time the Department for Education and Employment, produced another consultation document. This one, on draft National Standards for Day Care, proposes that childminders should be permitted to smack children (but not shake them) with parental permission (Department for Education and Employment, 2000). All organisations concerned with day care and with children's policy had been emphasising their support for an absolute ban on smacking in all forms of day care for more than a decade. The National Child Minding Association has run a particularly vociferous campaign. But the government ignored this strong consensus: "This is a very small exception which enables us to justify publicly that we are protecting children without becoming a nanny state" (Letter from Margaret Hodge, Parliamentary Under Secretary of State for Employment and Equal Opportunities, Department for Education and Employment, 12 October 2000).

People from most other European countries find these persisting politicians' attitudes to children very bewildering and upsetting. Is it the product of violent upbringing? Or is it simply a terror of being regarded as a "nanny state" government? Either way, it is deeply disrespectful of children. More than three centuries ago, in 1669, a "Children's Petition" was delivered to Parliament by a "lively boy", protesting on behalf of the nation's children at the violence of school corporal punishment (Freeman, 1966: 216). It took more than three centuries for Parliament to respond fully to that petition. In April 2000, Article 12, an organisation of children and young people dedicated to promoting their rights under the UN Convention, held a "Stop Smacking Us" march to 10 Downing Street, to deliver a petition and various messages to Tony Blair, the Prime Minister (Article 12, 2000). The march received very sympathetic national and international media coverage.

This is a new dimension of the campaign to end all corporal punishment: children's voices are at last being heard on an issue which concerns and hurts them deeply. Can you imagine a government holding a consultation on how to change the law to protect women from violence which only consulted men? Yet when the Department of Health consulted on how to reform the law allowing "reasonable chastisement", they made no arrangements to consult with children. In the other countries making up the UK – Wales, Scotland and Northern Ireland – the officials organising devolved consultations were at least sensitive enough to commission surveys of children's views.

To fill the gap in England, the National Children's Bureau and Save the Children commissioned research in 1998 into the views of 76 five- to seven-year-old children on smacking (see Hyder, chapter 19, pp. 314–15). Among the questions, the children were asked was: "What does it feel like to be smacked?" These children defined smacking as hitting; most of them described a smack as a hard or very hard hit. Smacking hurts. They said children responded negatively to being smacked, and that smacking was "wrong". Only one of the 76 said that a smack was "a tap", and she added "only harder". Other descriptions included: "It feels like someone banged you with a hammer"; "It's like breaking your bones"; "It really hurts"; "It's like someone punched you or kicked you or something" (Save the Children and National Children's Bureau, 1998).

Giving up the habit: developments outside the UK

Outside the UK, in the context of implementation of the Convention on the Rights of the Child, there has been accelerating progress to respect children's fundamental rights through legal reform. At least ten states have prohibited all corporal punishment: Austria (1989), Croatia (1999), Cyprus (1994), Denmark (1997), Finland (1983), Germany (2000), Israel (2000), Latvia (1998), Norway (1987) and Sweden (1979). In addition, in 1996 Italy's Supreme Court in Rome declared all corporal punishment to be unlawful, but this has not yet been confirmed in legislation. The judgment stated:

> the use of violence for educational purposes can no longer be considered lawful ... the very expression "correction of children", which expresses a view of child-rearing that is both culturally anachronistic and historically outdated, should in fact be re-defined, abolishing any connotation of hierarchy or authoritarianism and introducing the ideas of social and responsible commitment which should characterise the position of the educator *vis-à-vis* the learner.
>
> (Italy Supreme Court, 1996: 407)

In Belgium early in 2000 a new clause was added to the constitution to confirm that children have an absolute right to moral, physical, psychological and sexual integrity. The legal effect of the change is not yet clear. It follows a recommendation from the Belgian National Commission against Sexual Exploitation of Children, which also proposed ways of supporting adults in using non-violent child-rearing. The Commission concluded:

> The absence of violence in relations with children cannot be limited to a self-imposed obligation nor to a personal style of child rearing practised by certain people. The absence of violence should be a norm respected by the whole of society, not only because even today too many children are the victims of acts of violence, but because children and their integrity as persons should be always and everywhere respected. ... Respect for children and violence against them can never go together. If one of the characteristics of a society which thinks of itself as civilised is the absence of violence, there can be no justification for violence against children.
>
> (Cappelaere, 1997: 11)

In states in every continent there have been moves to end corporal punishment outside the family home (for example, recently in Korea, South Africa, Ethiopia, Thailand, Trinidad and Tobago, Zambia and Zimbabwe). Nevertheless, in 2000 there still remain at least eighty states where school corporal punishment remains legal and common and at least 60 in which corporal punishment is still used as a sentence of the courts for juvenile offenders and/or as a punishment within penal institutions for juveniles (EPOCH-WORLDWIDE, 2000).

It was in 1979, International Year of the Child, that Sweden became the first country to prohibit all physical punishment and humiliating treatment of children. Traditional rights of parents to hit their children existed unchallenged in Sweden until 1949. In that year, when a new Parenthood and Guardianship Code was introduced, there was discussion about limiting severe physical punishment. Parents' right to "punish" was amended to a right to "reprimand". Abolition of school corporal punishment came into effect in 1958, and in all other Swedish childcare institutions in 1960. In 1967 the criminal law on assault was changed to remove the provision which excused parents who caused minor injuries through physical punishment. In 1977 the Swedish Parliament set up a Children's Rights Commission. Its first proposal was that an explicit ban on subjecting children to physical punishment or other degrading treatment should be added to the Parenthood and Guardianship Code. Consultation found little opposition, and early in 1979 a Bill was passed by a majority of 259 to 6. The law now reads:

> Children are entitled to care, security and a good upbringing. Children are to be treated with respect for their person and individuality and may not be subjected to physical punishment or any other humiliating treatment.
>
> (Parenthood and Guardianship Code,
> Amended 1983, Chapter 6, Section 1)

Implementation of the new law in Sweden was accompanied by a substantial education campaign. Milk cartons arriving on Swedish breakfast tables carried a cartoon of a girl saying "I'll never ever hit my own children", and an explanation of the law. Swedish children were a major target for the education campaign: the Bill was used to teach pupils the process of law-making in Parliament, so that they learnt its content too, and it was built into other parts of the curriculum including child development. The Ministry of Justice circulated 600,000 copies of a pamphlet entitled *Can you bring up children successfully without smacking and spanking?* which was translated into ten minority languages including (probably most importantly) English. The pamphlet emphasises:

> while the purpose of the new legislation is indeed to make it quite clear that spanking and beating are no longer allowed, it does not aim at having more parents punished than hitherto. ... The law ... now forbids all forms of physical punishment of children, including smacking etc, although it goes without saying that you can still snatch a child away from a hot stove or open window if there is risk of its injuring itself. Should physical chastisement meted out to a child cause bodily injury or pain which is more than of very temporary duration, it is classified as assault and is an offence punishable under the Criminal Code. In theory at least, this was still true before the new Bill came into force, although it was not generally known. However the advent of the new law has swept all doubt aside, although as before trivial offences will remain

unpunished, either because they cannot be classified as assault or because an action is not brought.

(Swedish Ministry of Justice, 1979: 1)

One of the many "red herring" arguments produced by adults to ridicule the idea of legal reform against physical punishment is that it seeks to "criminalise little smacks". But this predictably misses the point. The proposal is not for a new law but simply to extend existing laws on assault, which theoretically protect adults from all assaults however trivial, to protect children too. Trivial assaults of adults by adults do not get to court, and, for exactly the same reasons, trivial assaults of children would not either. At the moment our law defends not just trivial assaults of children, but gross invasions of their physical integrity, including beatings with sticks, belts, and slippers.

Gunnel Linde, a well-known Swedish author, writing in the Ministry of Justice pamphlet, saw the reform as a natural historical development:

We have already done away with the right to beat one's wife and servants. We have done away with the right to strike children at school. ... bringing up a child is much easier if you do not resort to beating. Children want to like you so very much it is a pity to destroy a feeling of kinship and mutual understanding by beating. You don't go round hitting your friends, do you? Why should you hit your children then?

(Swedish Ministry of Justice, 1979: 4)

It is more than twenty years since Sweden implemented its ban on all corporal punishment. This has enabled a detailed research review of the effects, revealing entirely positive trends. The goals of the ban were to alter public attitudes towards corporal punishment, establish a clear framework for parent education and support, and facilitate earlier and less intrusive intervention in child protection cases. Public support for corporal punishment has declined markedly. Whereas in 1965 a majority of Swedes were supportive of corporal punishment, the most recent survey found only 6 per cent of under 35-year-olds supporting the use of even the mildest forms. Practice as well as attitudes have changed; of those whose childhood occurred shortly after the ban, only 3 per cent report harsh slaps from their parents, and only 1 per cent report being hit with an implement (contrast the position in the UK and other countries where a quarter or more of young children are hit with implements). Child abuse mortality rates are extremely low in Sweden; for 14 years from 1976 to 1990 no child died as a result of abuse.

Increased sensitivity to violence to children has led to an increase in reporting of assaults, but there has been a declining trend in prosecutions of parents, and a substantial reduction in compulsory social work interventions and in numbers of children taken into care. Remarkably, in comparison with the position in many other industrialised countries, overall rates of youth crime have remained steady since the 1980s. The proportions of young people who consume alcohol, experiment with drugs and commit suicide have also all declined. The review concludes:

> While drawing a direct causal link between the corporal punishment ban and any of these social trends would be too simplistic, the evidence presented here indicates that the ban has not had negative effects. In terms of its original goals of modifying public attitudes toward corporal punishment and facilitating early identification and supportive intervention, it has certainly been successful.
>
> (Durrant, 2000: 6)

In stark contrast to the situation in Sweden, in any state where corporal punishment has not been challenged through legal reform and public education, one can with confidence predict a very high frequency of violent punishment. To take just one example, a large-scale interview study of children and young people aged between 10 and 20 in Alexandria, Egypt, published in the September 1998 edition of the international journal *Child Abuse and Neglect*, found that more than a third of the children (37 per cent) were disciplined by beating with hands, belts, sticks and shoes and that a quarter of these children reported that harsh discipline led to physical injuries of variable severity which included fractures, loss of consciousness and permanent disability. Most of the children believed their punishment was deserved; only 29 per cent felt it was cruel – a common finding of research into corporal punishment, demonstrating how the habit is passed on from one generation to another.

A related study involving more than 2,000 school students found very high rates of corporal punishment in Alexandrian schools – despite the fact that corporal punishment in schools was banned by ministerial decree in 1971. Figures show 79 per cent of boys and 61 per cent of girls reported corporal punishment using hands, sticks, straps, shoes and kicks; more than a quarter of boys and 18 per cent of girls reported that beatings caused injuries (Youssef and Youssef, 1998: 959–985).

The imperative for ending all corporal punishment of children is that of human rights. But there are other compelling arguments. First, hitting children, far from being a useful form of discipline, is a lesson in bad behaviour. We do not want our children to learn that using violence is a valid or constructive way to sort out conflicts. Research into the harmful physical and psychological effects of corporal punishment, into the relative significance of links with other forms of violence, in childhood and later life, add further compelling arguments for condemning and ending the practice (see, for example, Leach, 1999 and Straus, 1994).

But there is a serious danger that in becoming too preoccupied with this absorbing research people forget the human rights imperative for action now: we do not look into the effects of physical discipline on women, or on animals. It is enough that it breaches fundamental rights.

This is, above all, a very personal issue. Most people, in the UK and other states, were hit as children. Most parents in most countries have hit their own growing children. We do not like to think badly of our parents or of ourselves. Thus, people's experiences as children and as parents get in the way of just and logical thoughts and action. If it were simply an intellectual matter, we would have given up hitting and humiliating children decades if not centuries ago. If we can quickly build on the progress made in the last few years, and leave behind the sickly adult hypocrisy that still talks of hitting children "for their own good", of "loving smacks", we could indeed transform our world.

References

Cappelaere, G. (1997) *Les Enfants Nous Interpellent/Kinderen Stellen Ons Vragen*, Brussels: Service federal d'Information
Committee on the Rights of the Child (1994) CRC/C/SR176, 10 October 1994, para. 46 (NB: all reports of the Committee on the Rights of the Child are available on the web-site of the United Nations High Commissioner for Human Rights <www.unhchr.ch>)
—— (1995a) CRC/C/SR.205, 30 January 1995
—— (1995b) CRC/C/15/Add.34, 15 February 1995
—— (1996) *General Guidelines Regarding the Form and Contents of Periodic Reports to be Submitted by States Parties under Article 44, paragraph 1(b) of the Convention*, CRC/C/58
Department for Education and Employment (2000) Consultation Pack: *National Standards for the Regulation of Day Care*, 28 July, London: Department for Education and Employment
Department of Health (1997) Press Release "Government to clarify the law on parental discipline", 7 November, London: Department of Health
—— (2000) *Protecting Children, Supporting Parents. A Consultation Document on the Physical Punishment of Children*, London: Department of Health
Durrant, J. (2000) *A Generation Without Smacking – The impact of Sweden's ban on physical punishment*, London: Save the Children UK
European Court of Human Rights (1998) Judgment of the Court in the case of *A v UK*, 23 September 1998 (all judgments of the Court are available on the web-site <www.dhcour.coe.fr/hudoc>)
Freeman, C.B. (1966) "The children's petition of 1669 and its sequel", *British Journal of Educational Studies*, vol. 14, pp. 210–225
Hyder, T and Willow, C. (1998) *It Hurts You Inside – Children Talking About Smacking*, London: Save the Children and National Children's Bureau
Israel Supreme Court (2000) Criminal Appeal 4596/98 *Plonit v A. G.* 54(1) P. D.
Italy Supreme Court (1996) Supreme Court of Cassation, 6th Penal Section, 18 March 1996, Rome (Foro It. II 1996, 407: Cambria, Cass, sez VI, 18 Marzo 1996, 407
Leach, P. (1999) *The Physical Punishment of Children – some input from recent research*, NSPCC Policy and Practice Research Series, London: NSPCC

Straus, M. (1994), *Beating the Devil Out of Them: corporal punishment in American families*, New York: Lexington Books

Swedish Ministry of Justice (1979) *Can You Bring up Children Successfully Without Smacking and Spanking?*, Stockholm: Ministry of Justice

Youssef, A. and Youssef, K. (1998) "Children experiencing violence I: Parental use of corporal punishment"; "Children experiencing violence II: Prevalence and determinants of corporal punishment in schools", *Child Abuse and Neglect*, Vol. 22, No. 10, September 1998, pp. 959–985

Contact organisations

Article 12 (2000): Article 12 is an organisation of children under 18, advocating their rights under the Convention on the Rights of the Child. It can be contacted c/o 8 Wakley Street, London EC1V 7QE

Children Are Unbeatable! (1998): details of the Children Are Unbeatable! Alliance, including lists of supporters, can be obtained from the Secretariat, c/o 77 Holloway Road, London N7 8JZ (020 7700 0627). www.childrenareunbeatable.org.uk

EPOCH-WORLDWIDE, 2000: EPOCH-WORLDWIDE (EWW) is a network of 79 non-governmental organisations in over 40 states which share the aim of ending all corporal punishment of children through education and legal reform. EWW researches the status of corporal punishment in all states and monitors progress towards ending it. For information contact EPOCH-WORLDWIDE, 77 Holloway Road, London N7 8JZ (020 7700 0627)

Global Initiative To End All Corporal Punishment of Children, launched 2001, aims to speed up abolition of all corporal punishment of children. See www.end corporalpunishment.org; for further information contact info@endcorporalpunishment.org

24 Outside childhood

Street children's rights

Judith Ennew

In February 1993 UNICEF hosted 34 experts from 20 countries at the *Spedale degli Innocenti* in Florence to take part in the fourth Global Seminar of the International Child Development Centre (ICDC) usually referred to as the "Innocenti Centre".[1] The building was designed by Brunelleschi, constructed between 1419 and 1424 in order to care for the orphaned and abandoned children of the city state. It is extraordinarily beautiful. Above the loggia runs a series of medallions by Della Robbia, each depicting a baby, described by E.M. Forster in *A Room with a View* as "those divine babies whom no cheap reproduction can ever stale ... with their shining limbs bursting from the garments of charity, and their strong white arms extended against circlets of heaven" (Forster, 1978: 39). Patricia Light, formerly the Information Officer at ICDC, who used to pass through the archways of the loggia every day on her way to work, believes that these babies gave Eglantyne Jebb the idea for the emblem of the first five-point Declaration on the Rights of the Child and the original logo of agencies in the Save the Children Alliance. The experts who met in February 1993 may have paid these divine babies only a passing glance. Their discussions concerned children with a different kind of visibility, who have also come to be a kind of modern icon – street children.

Later that same year, I stood at the opposite side of the Piazza to the loggia of the Innocenti in the early morning before another meeting about working children, taking a few moments to watch the developing November light bring the dull terracotta to life. Under the archways a heap of rugs and blankets began to stir. A girl emerged from a sleeping bag and methodically began to pack her belongings into a bundle. Within moments she was ready and had left the Piazza. I estimated that she was about 14 years old. The Florentines crossing the square to work or to bring their well-wrapped toddlers to the nursery school that now operates in the Innocenti did not seem to see her.

Children inside buildings and inside families are often contrasted with those who are outside both. Unlike Brunelleschi's building, this tendency is a modern phenomenon. Until the beginning of the eighteenth century, family life was lived far more in the public domain. The streets were the location for commerce, social life and socialisation. Children were less separated from adults, and private life was not confined to a special domestic sphere, inside houses and nuclear families (Aries, 1979). As Patricia Holland points out, the defining characteristics of modern, Western childhood are dependency and powerlessness; the idea of the unhappy child completes the concept. Unhappy children do not have adults to depend on, who will be powerful on their behalf or, if they need to be rescued, to put them back into childhood which stands, in ideological terms, for happiness, play, innocence and some kind of essential goodness in human nature. Child victims, of which street children are the most visible in visual reproductions, have also come to stand for the dependency and powerlessness of the developing world: "In the act of looking at these presentations, viewers recognise themselves as both adult and Western, as individuals with the ability to change a child's life for the better without changing their own for the worse" (Holland, 1992: 150). In contrast, children who work "have rarely found a place in available imagery". But street children have a particular image problem, "it needs only slight shift of perspective to see the child on the streets as an undesirable vagrant" (ibid.: 161) or, as in the case of the girl I observed sleeping outside the Innocenti, for passing pedestrians not to see her at all.

It is no coincidence, I would claim, that the Convention on the Rights of the Child was drafted during the same decade as an unprecedented increase in interest in groups of children called "street children". Both the Convention and a number of initiatives for these children sprang from the same source, in activities connected with the United Nations International Year of the Child in 1979. In the juxtaposition of the Convention and the image of the street child the entire discourse of children's rights stands revealed. The Convention, in drafting process, the resulting text and in its implementation, takes as its starting point Western, modern childhood, which has been "globalised" first through colonialism and then through the imperialism of international aid (Detrick, 1992; Fyfe, 1989: 163; Boyden, 1990).

One of the most crucial aspects of this nation of childhood is domesticity. The place for childhood to be played out is inside – inside society, inside a family, inside a private dwelling. This means that street children are society's ultimate outlaws. As children are increasingly conceptualised as vulnerable and in danger from influences outside the private world of the family, so they are increasingly banished from the streets. In the Western world they have lost the freedom to explore the world of peer group relationships and the geography of their community. Modern streets are for the circulation of traffic and pedestrians, they are no longer the locus of social life and socialisation (see also chapter 9). Modern streets, particularly at night, have come to be thought of, particularly in North America and northern Europe, as morally dangerous, especially for children (Boyden, 1990: 189). Children who join police, prostitutes and adult vagrants on this arena at night are not only outside society, they are also outside childhood.

Street children and the Convention on the Rights of the Child

A number of Articles of the UN Convention on the Rights of the Child affect street and working children jointly and severally most days of their lives.

Article 2

Protection against discrimination is denied to street children who are stigmatised by the street children image, which causes the public and state agents such as the police to view them as asocial and amoral. In Brazil, for example, they are blamed for the majority of street crime despite statistical evidence to the contrary (Ennew and Milne, 1989: 152). In extreme cases this leads to their violent deaths at the hands of police and vigilantes (Dimenstein, 1991).

Article 3

With very few exceptions, state provision for street children is taken less in their best interests and more in the interest of cleansing the streets of their presence. Far from being placed in situations of care under the supervision of competent staff with adequate standards of safety and health, many are placed in adult prisons, in violent and overcrowded reformatories, or in orphanages staffed by unqualified and often abusive personnel, where pitifully inadequate resources make a mockery of any attempts to provide reasonable care.

Article 4

Article 4 of the Convention states that countries must provide for children "to the maximum extent of their available resources". In the words of Thomas Hammarberg, one of the members of the Committee on the Rights of the Child, this means that "it is not sufficient to give children what remains when the needs of other groups have been satisfied" (in Ennew and Milne, 1989: 5). Hammarberg's comment applies to an even greater extent to children outside childhood, already marginalised by society and not in receipt of any welfare provision, either from families or from the state.

Article 6

The child's "inherent right to life" and to "survival and development" is denied to those street children who are gunned down in Brazil, Guatemala and South Africa, as well as to children who die or are permanently disabled as the result of working in hazardous conditions, like the explosion in a fireworks factory in Meenapatti, Sivakasi, on 12 July 1991, in which over forty children died (Bhima Sangha, 1991).

Articles 7 and 8

The rights to name, nationality and identity that are enshrined in these articles are denied to many street children. Like so many disadvantaged children in developing countries they are born to families so marginalised that their births are never registered. In essence they have no existence, which means they cannot later register for school, work or welfare. This underscores their outlaw status. As the Executive Director of UNICEF, Carole Bellamy, has remarked, "A birth certificate is a ticket to citizenship. Without one, an individual does not officially exist and therefore lacks legal access to privileges and protections of a nation" (UNICEF, 1998: 5).

Articles 9, 10, 18, 20, 21 and 27

All the provisions of articles dealing with separation from parents, family reunification and adoption apply with particular force to street children. Moreover, as a visible group of children needing to be rescued from the street, they are an especially handy target for middle-class concern. This means that they are frequently in danger of being taken off the streets and either placed in institutions or for adoption, without attempts being made to trace their natal families and perhaps support a reunification process. Their lack of documents reinforces this process. There is often an assumption that the family is "a structure they have never known", despite the evidence that they not only have experienced family life but also often have some contact with parents or other kin (see, for example, Aptekar, 1988; Swart, 1990; Tyler *et al.*, 1992).

The principle in Article 18 that parents have "the primary responsibility for the upbringing and development of the child" is accompanied by the state's responsibility to "render appropriate assistance" to them in this task, which is also implied in Article 27. The lack or inadequacy of welfare provision, childcare facilities and other appropriate supports to parents fosters the conditions in which children are obliged to work to ensure family survival and may leave home because of intolerable conditions. What is amazing is that so many marginalised families manage to hold together and care for their dependent children in situations of dire poverty. If they did not perform this superhuman task so well there would be many more children on the street.

Article 20

Street children are frequently the product of abusive or neglectful parenting. Society has already failed to protect them from that. What is more, they are also both abused and neglected on the street. Programmes to rehabilitate them are almost always under-resourced and there have been few attempts to systematise or evaluate the work that is carried out, mostly by non-governmental organisations (NGOs). Reports of sexual, physical and emotional abuse by expatriate workers in street children projects began to emerge in the late 1990s. This reflects failures in recruitment and professional supervision, which are also violations of Article 3. It also shows the need for applying to this special kind of aid worker the kind of extraterritorial legislation sometimes used to combat the better publicised exploitations of child sex tourism (Ennew, 2001).

Article 22

Refugee children, especially when they are unaccompanied by adults, often become street children whose legal status is particularly insecure. This can be compounded by other disadvantaging factors, as in the case of the Portuguese-speaking children from Mozambique who were reported to be scraping a living on the streets of Anglophone Harare, the capital of Zimbabwe. Some would have had a Shona-speaking heritage, which they would share with some Zimbabwean citizens. All would have been coping with memories of violent experiences in conflict zones.

Article 23

Some children find themselves on the streets because they have an impairment or disability. In the absence of adequate social support, families may find it impossible to cope with severe physical, mental or behavioural problems experienced by their children. It may seem that there is no future for disabled family members apart from a lifetime of begging. In other cases children become disabled as a result of life on the streets. Traffic accidents, violence and drug use all have greater capacity for damaging the young and entail more peril for children than they do for adults.

Article 24

Life on the streets can be particularly unhealthy and unhygienic, as can be seen from the following catalogue of the health problems suffered by a 15-year-old during seven years of living on the streets: scabies, lice, fleas, conjunctivitis, impetigo, amoebic dysentery, giardiasis, ascaris and gonorrhoea. More recently, he was infected with HIV (Connolly, 1990: 1). A further problem for street children is accessing medical care. Because of their appearance and the stigma surrounding their existence they are often chased away from hospitals and clinics.

Article 26

The inadequacy of social security and social assistance systems for marginalised populations as a whole has adverse affects on unnumbered millions of the world's children. The fact that children have to seek a living on the streets and that their families are unable to provide sufficient overall support to keep them from living on the streets is an extreme symptom of this widespread social neglect of the most vulnerable groups. A further irony is that the type of work that children do on the street, in the informal sector, is not subject to the social insurance schemes that could provide a measure of protection. Likewise, children who work in the formal sector tend to do so illegally, below the minimum age for work. That is one of the reasons why they are employed. It keeps down the wage bill for employers. This amounts to a double disadvantage for street and working children. Because they are outside the family they cannot receive the benefits of social security. Because they are outside the formal sphere of work, despite the fact that they are workers, they are ineligible for social insurance.

Articles 28, 29, 31 and 32

As all street children work for survival it is axiomatic that they are not protected from economic exploitation. Moreover, child labour laws are seldom implemented and may even work to the detriment of child workers by expelling them from the formal labour market and obliging them to seek an income in casual, poorly paid, exploitative and hazardous activities. In June 1999 the International Labour Conference adopted a new Convention (182), designed to combat the "most hazardous forms" of child labour. Although street children are not named as such in this instrument, they are almost always included in the groups of children targeted for interventions by the International Programme for the Elimination of Child Labour, which has been operating as part of the International Labour Organisation since 1993.

There are those who claim that the provision of compulsory education is all that is required to eliminate child labour (see for example Weiner, 1991). But education alone cannot do this unless children are freed from the necessity to work for survival. More children, moreover, would attend schools if the education was relevant to their lives, experiences and aspirations in content and more interactive and respectful in its methods. The Jomtien Declaration of 1990 has strengthened international commitment to basic education, but so little investment is made in secondary education that only 54 per cent of girls and 61 per cent of boys worldwide are enrolled in school beyond primary level and are able to develop the skills required to participate in the formal labour market (UNICEF, 1999). For the rest, a lifetime of work in the informal sector may start in their early teens. For urban boys this is likely to be in the street.

Article 33

Not all street children are drug addicts, although some of the more lurid literature implies this and is thus connected to the stigmatisation of and discrimination against these children. However, drugs (particularly solvents) are easy and cheap to acquire and many children resort to regular use. Although there are some rehabilitation intervention programmes there is no consistent policy either at national or international levels that aims specifically to protect children from drug abuse.

Articles 34, 35 and 36

Sensational accounts of street children often state or imply that they are all involved in prostitution. The truth is less exciting and more sordid. Many children, both male and female, sell sex at some time during their lives on the streets, but they are not all prostitutes; many who are, would rather not be and sell sex only as a last resort. Many others do not sell sex at all. However, street children are increasingly suffering from a further discrimination because of the spread of HIV infection amongst them. Sexually transmitted diseases are a common health hazard, not only because of prostitution, but also because of the sexual relationships many have with each other, which some experience as warm and caring.

Far from being lucrative, child sex is cheap. That is one of the most insufferable features of its essential tragedy. Children have no power to ask for a high fee from adult customers.

The highest profits in child sexual exploitation are not made from the sexual transaction itself but from the secondary exploitation of those who deal in prurient stories about it. This is not confined to the media. It is quite clear that some NGO activity has a voyeuristic element, not only in advocacy about child sexual exploitation but also in the glamorisation of street children as a group. Street children themselves often feel this acutely. Some do not wish to be given the label at all (see for example Oliveira, 1989). Others complain about the failure of media exposures to produce tangible improvements in their situation (Reddy, 1992: 14).

In May 2000 an Optional Protocol to the Convention, on sexual exploitation, was adopted by the UN General Assembly. This was largely the result of considerable international cooperation engendered by the Congress Against the Commercial Sexual Exploitation of Children in Stockholm in 1996, and promises to strengthen the provisions of Article 34.

Articles 37 and 40

All too often street children are deprived of their liberty, which may reflect the common assumption of their criminality. Even if they are not incarcerated in jails or reformatories they are institutionalised in orphanages and children's homes where the regime may be harsh or abusive and experienced as a form of imprisonment (Reddy, 1992: 98). In many cases, after summary justice, they are confined in adult prisons, where they suffer ill treatment at the hands of both staff and other prisoners. The effects can be traumatic: "Giovanni had been beaten and abused while in prison. He was crudely tattooed all over his body, leaving names scrawled in blue ink, carved into his skin. The wounds were infected. ... The emotional scars were even deeper" (in Rocky 1990: 5).

Street children and participatory rights

In 1992, Roger Hart used the metaphor of a "ladder of participation" to list the steps in so-called child participation. These range from the false rungs of manipulation, decoration and tokenism to what he suggests is the ideal of activities that are initiated by children in which decisions are shared with adults (Hart, 1992: 9). Nearly a decade later child participation has become a little understood and poorly defined fashion. Since the early 1980s, some street children projects have claimed to involve children as participants in planning and implementing projects, and also in political action and campaigning on their own and society's behalf. If they are outside society then they bring a new force to bear on changing society – or so the story goes. One of the political participation models most frequently cited was also examined by Hart in 1992, the Brazilian Movement of Street Children (or "for" Street Children, translations interestingly cannot agree!). More than ten years since it was first described, the Movement is still an icon for popular understanding of what children's participation can mean.

The Brazilian Movement was established in 1985, with its roots in UNICEF's Alternatives for Street Children project work within popular political movements. Anthony Swift's account of its history tells us that "The emerging leaders were securely linked with grass-roots communities and eager to build up an ability to represent their interests at national level. *With its greater experience of power structures and processes*, UNICEF provided valuable counselling" (Swift, 1991: 17, my emphasis). The popular programmes established first local, and then state commissions. In 1985 the state commissions organised and elected the first National Commission of the National Movement for Street Boys and Girls.

Between 26 and 28 May 1986, the first national meeting for street children was held in Brasilia, bringing together 432 street children aged 8 to 16 years from different parts of Brazil selected by ballot from among their peers. Only a few adults were invited to the conference, which discussed the themes of work, education, violence, family, political organisation and health, chosen by the children themselves in a series of preparatory meetings throughout the country. Their conclusions were presented through drama at the closing ceremony. The conference was well covered by the media "with over 15 pages in newspapers and magazines, an hour on TV and innumerable radio items and wire service stories that found their way to Europe" (Fyfe, 1989: 112). The meeting had been a public success, but political effects were less clear. Childhope, the contemporary Bulletin of the street children NGO, states that

> When the movement first met ... almost no government officials came to hear the children. However, some press did come ... and noted the absence of government officials. Consequently, the President of Brazil met with an official delegation of street children following the meeting to assure them that his government was concerned and interested.
>
> (Rocky, 1990: 1)

Subsequently, the Movement was included among NGO members of the National Commission of the Child and the Constitution, which led to legislative changes, including the Statute on the Child (Swift, 1991: 18). Later work includes centres for training street educators and campaigns against violence towards street children (which, nevertheless, continues unabated) (ibid.: 39).

Of the 1986 meeting, Hart says

> The original goal of the event was simply to develop solidarity between the many separate groups of street children, although the choice of Brasilia as a location was designed to sensitise the authorities. However, because the children were so organised and articulate during the debates, the press responded with enormous enthusiasm and congress became a landmark event in creating public awareness about the lives of street children.
>
> (Hart, 1992: 31)

Hart suggests that this happened at that time because of a coincidence between the return to democracy and the role of street educators in the popular movement. He describes the way in which street educators work with street children: "the children raise the themes, develop the activities, and construct the rules for their own functioning, with the street educator working only as a facilitator. The children elect those educators to work with them with whom they feel most comfortable" (ibid.: 32). By implication, Hart feels that this is high on his 'ladder of participation", far from the "manipulation", "decoration" and "tokenism" that usually characterise the physical presence of children in "political" events in the name of participation (ibid.: 8–10). The most common forms of child participation in adult political activities is limited to window dressing, in which children wear appropriate T-shirts, march in adult-regulated processions, sing a sentimental song or present prepared testimony for which they are enthusiastically (even ecstatically) applauded.

The Brazilian Movement has notched up some victories. The discussion of the 1986 Meeting

> as reported in extensive press coverage, was both painful and liberating. Since the conference, exposure of the conditions of street children has become widely disseminated [the Movement] has brought international

attention to the problems of street children and thereby jolted the authorities into action.

(Hewitt, 1992: 57)

Since 1986, in addition to the Statute of the Child, there have been both enquiries and legislative changes in Brazil. These are good signs, but one wonders about the extent to which the activities are actually child-initiated, given that all the prominent co-ordinators and spokespersons nationally are adults (see for example Dimenstein, 1991). For negotiating with police it is arguable that this may be necessary. Moreover, there is no doubt that the Brazilian activities have led to some child involvement at levels previously unexplored. For example,

> Local committees for street and working children, which are found throughout Brazil, offer opportunities for dialogue between the children, government agencies, and non-government organisations [in which] there has been a steadily growing participation by children ... as they become more confident in speaking.
>
> (Hart, 1992: 32)

At national level, however, a tendency towards tokenism and decoration remained. The second meeting in Brasilia in September 1989 showed a Movement that had increased in size. No fewer than 750 street children gathered from 26 states, sponsored by Movement and by the Brazilian Institute of Social and Economic Analysis. Forty organisations were represented, both international and national, with street children and adults from other Latin American countries. The event is described in various Childhope publications: The children "played the guitar and danced. They smoked and discussed politics without fear of being shoved into a cell or prodded toward yet another shelter" (*Our Child Our Hope*, Vol. 1, No. 4, Nov. 1989: 5). The Meeting "featured many activities such as games, singing, puppet-making, and cultural presentations, in addition to children's testimonies, and talks on contraception and sexually transmitted diseases" (ibid.), thus providing a fairly typical mix of adult-supervised recreation, recitation and learning. There was an element of spectacle. One 11-year-old boy is mentioned by name as "one of the great attractions" of the Meeting; there was a march in the streets to the National Congress, which was felt by some observers to be "a political initiative to gain public support for certain candidates running for president in the November 15 election" (ibid.). Certainly there was more political interest than before, the politicians "jockeyed for position next to the children when the press was taking pictures and filming the event!" (*Esperanza*, 1990: 1). Most of these descriptions read like fairly accurate accounts of decoration and tokenism.

Throughout the 1990s, organised child participation in meetings of experts discussing child affairs took three forms: parallel conference, performance and testimony. All three occurred in 1992 at the Second International Conference on Street Children (Health Rights and Actions) in Rio de Janeiro, which was part-sponsored by the Movement. The parallel conference was exactly that – it reported back on the last day. Apart from this, the two lines never met. There was no dialogue. Performance occurred at several points but principally during lunchtime on the second day, when delegates were treated to a display of street dancing. The street child performers wore conference badges and many photographs were taken. The security guard round the university conference hall where sessions took place visibly doubled. Testimony was rather more dramatic than usual. In most street child conference testimony children are given the microphone and asked to talk about their lives on the street. Many are highly articulate and often give moving accounts. On this occasion in Rio the main street child testimony occurred during the opening session. Delegates were first welcomed by Benedito Dos Santos. The street children, six teenage girls, made a theatrical entrance from the rear of the hall, with their heads swathed in cloths that hid their features so that they could not be identified but which gave them the stigmatising image of terrorists. Seated on the platform surrounded by press flashguns and the smaller flares of participants' automatic cameras, they gave testimony about the harsh treatment they had received the previous night in a park called Praca Saenz Pena. With their voices sometimes raised to a shout, often angry, sometimes edged with hysteria, they told how the police had thrown them to the ground, kicked and punched them and threatened to kill them. One 14-year-old, very pregnant, broke down and sobbed into the microphone. As they left to take part in newspaper interviews and more photographs the audience applauded and cheered.

What was the point of this, when all the participants were already fully aware of violence against street children in Brazil and many other countries? In a country in which shame is an important cultural motivator, a small political advantage was gained by the fact that the newspapers reported the majority of the audience to be foreigners (*O Globo*, 4 September 1992). The girls received no direct benefit, and even the political point does not justify exploiting them in this kind of theatre. This was not participation, it was spectacle. Once they had left, the waters of the Conference closed over them. As David Woollcombe noted in a publication six years later, visibility does not equal participation (Woollcombe, 1998).

At the 1993 meeting of the Movement for Street Children there was some lasting controversy about the fact that children from Recife had been taken over and were being used by the adult popular organisation. With this and other indications in mind, it seems true to say that children have little release from adult supervision, even when they are outside childhood and the name of the game is participation. In the words of a sceptical observer of the children's rights movement, "Post-modern paternalism no longer says 'Shut up kids, I know what is good for you' but prefers to say 'Speak up kids, I am your voice'" (Théry, 1991: 105, my translation).

The unwritten rights of street children

As this review of articles of the Convention on the Rights of the Child reveals, street children do not enjoy rights of protection and provision. Indeed, this very non-enjoyment makes them appear to be unnatural children. As far as participatory rights are concerned, their status remains ambiguous. But what about the people that they are, these young people who work for themselves, care for each other and do not, in fact, ask society to rescue them? Do they have any specific rights that challenge the hegemony of Northern childhood? I would suggest that children living in exceptionally difficult conditions, such as street children, may need special rights, or special consideration within the rights as written in the UN Convention. These might include some of the following.

The right not to be labelled

This not only implies that the stigmatising category "street child" leads to unfair and sometimes abusive discrimination, but also that many of the characteristics typically ascribed to children who live and work on the streets are incorrect. They are not abandoned, they usually do have families, not all are drug addicts, prostitutes or criminals. Many such children reject the label "street child" because of its negative connotations.

The right to be correctly described, researched and counted

It follows from the right not to be labelled that children on the street have a right to expect correct information to be collected from and disseminated about them. This means a commitment on the part of the research community to ensure that scientific and ethical methods of data collection are used. It means not using hasty, badly constructed questionnaires, for which most street children are adept at providing equivocal information. It entails careful observation, the use of triangulation, control groups and participatory data-collection techniques in which children are informed about the purpose of the research and to which they give their consent. It is particularly important to avoid exaggerating numbers through guesstimates, and the use of anecdotal case-study material to illustrate (and therefore "prove") the hypotheses of well-meaning service providers (Regional Working Group on Child Labour, 2000).

The right to work, and to do so in fair conditions and for fair wages

Until such time as welfare provision reaches a level at which children do not have to work to provide for themselves and their families, they have a right to be active in the labour market. It is crucial that they should be protected from hazardous conditions, given security of employment and equal wages when they perform the same or similar tasks to adults. Special considerations for childhood are necessary to make sure that children have particular protection from hazards that have a greater or more harmful effect on developing bodies, minds and emotions than they do on those who have grown to adulthood. This means that they have a right to expect the medical and public health communities to know about harmful impacts at different ages and stages of growth, which information is currently not available. It also becomes a duty of health professionals and employers to ensure that the effects of working are monitored. Unfortunately even the baseline information required to carry out such monitoring is absent – in itself a violation of children's rights and a worldwide failure of the scientific community.

In addition children who work must not be denied access to education. This means flexibility of both working and schooling schedules as well as appropriate methods and materials in the education process.

The right to have their own support systems respected

Emphasis in the Convention on the Rights of the Child on the importance of families is based on the modern conception of families as private arenas for the correct performance of childhood. There is no provision in the Convention for respect and support to be paid to children's own friendships and support networks. Given the privileged position of the peer group in the psychology of both pre-pubertal and adolescent children, this is curious. In the case of street children, who usually belong to and contribute to a supportive group of children, this gives a potentially harmful edge to rehabilitation programmes. The friendships and close relationships in these groups are important for the emotional and physical well-being of members. These are strengths to be built on, rather than ties to be broken (Ennew, 1992).

The right to appropriate and relevant services

Many service provision projects for street children are inappropriate. Middle-class adults do not necessarily know what is in the best interest of street children. They arrive with food for children who are well-fed, and bundles of clothes for children who have nowhere to keep spare garments. Research comparing different groups of children in Nepal shows that street children have a better nutritional status than children living in slums, or children in impoverished rural areas (Baker, 1993). Inappropriate service provision not only fails to address the children's most pressing needs, it is also a waste of valuable resources and often serves only to provide the donor with a "feel good" factor. Many street children do not take up the services provided for them because they are inappropriate. In Nairobi, for example, despite suffering from the types of diseases mentioned for the boy discussed above under Article 24, children did not attend a free health clinic. One reason was that it offered curative rather than preventative treatment. The other was that the opening hours were inconvenient. They might have been convenient for the health workers but they clashed with the children's work opportunities (Dallape, 1988: 66).

The right to control their own sexuality

Street children often have sex for money or with each other. But sexual activity is forbidden within the current globalised definition of childhood. This means that children who are taken off the street for rehabilitation are assumed to be rescued from sexual activity until they become adults. In the rehabilitation process they may be taught that their sexual experiences were bad and should be forgotten and rejected. But their sexual experiences were real and are a part of their developing identity. The close relationship with another street child may have been meaningful and powerful, more important than any other relationship thus far. They have a right to expect that this will be addressed with respect by adults.

The right to be protected from secondary exploitation

In Latin America people refer to the "Pornography of Misery". Media, human rights activists, and fundraising departments of development NGOs are all guilty of exploiting the histories of children in stories that emphasise children's vulnerability, exaggerate their weaknesses and turn them into victims. Their own comments show that this is unacceptable to children. Street children are not just handy targets for any passing photographers or journalists who want to make a quick buck from selling an image or an anecdote. Children have a right to their privacy and to respect for their individuality.

The right to be protected from harm inflicted by "caring" social agencies

Unfortunately, street children not only suffer from inadequate provision from society, and inappropriate provision from well-meaning intervention projects. As stated earlier, they are also frequently subject to physical, sexual and emotional abuse within projects from staff and volunteers whom society empowers to care for them. This is inexcusable harm. They have a right to expect that the staff of all projects and programmes set up for their benefit are properly recruited, trained, managed and supported. This means a duty on the part of society to set standards for work with this particular group of children to ensure the accountability of all programmes working on their behalf. Too often the attitude is that anything that cleans the children off the streets must be good. If no one asks questions about the appropriateness of the staff and methods being used, this puts the children even further outside the law than they were on the streets.

Conclusion

The Convention on the Rights of the Child was drafted with a particular type of childhood in mind and treats children outside this model as marginal. This means that children's rights as a concept within the human rights field does not fully engage with the whole range of human beings who are defined as children. A number of articles target children such as street children for particular attention, with respect to child labour and sexual exploitation for example, but this in itself can be seen as a marginalising process. These and other articles may be ambiguous or contradictory in the face of the real experiences of these children. They may suffer from discrimination because they are labelled and targeted. This may have lifelong effects. If they are to have special consideration this should take account of their individuality and not concentrate on the problem category to which they have been assigned.

Notes

1   In 2000 the name was changed to "UNICEF Innocenti Research Centre".

References

Aptekar, L. (1988) *Street Children of Cali*, Durham and London: Duke University Press

Aries, P. (1979) *Centuries of Childhood*, London, translation Jonathan Cape Ltd, Harmondsworth: Penguin

Baker, R. (1993) "Street Children: what do we assume?", unpublished BA dissertation, Department of Anthropology, University of Durham

Bhima Sangha (1991) "A Bhima Sangha Enquiry Committee Report on Blast in Fireworks Factory, Meenampatti, July–October 1991", mimeo, Bangalore: The Concerned for Working Children

Boyden, J. (1990) "Childhood and the Policy Makers: a comparative perspective on the globalisation of childhood", in James, A. and Prout, A. (eds) *Constructing and Deconstructing Childhood: Contemporary Issues in the Sociological Study of Childhood*, London, New York, Philadelphia: The Falmer Press

Connolly, M. (1990) 'Surviving the Streets", *AIDS Action*, August 1990, Issue 11, London: AHRTAG: 1–2

Dallape, F. (1988) *An Experience with Street Children*, Nairobi: Undugu Society of Kenya

Detrick, S. (1992), *The United Nations Convention on the Rights of the Child: A Guide to the Travaux Préparatoires*, Dordrecht, Boston, London: Martinus Nijhoff Publishers

Dimenstein, G. (1991) *Brazil: War on Children*, London: Latin America Bureau

Ennew, J. (1992) "Parentless Friends: a cross-cultural examination of networks among street children and street youth", paper presented at the Symposium of the Sonderforschungbereich 227 Praevention und Intervention im Kindes und Jugendalter, University of Bielfeld, "Social Networks and Social Support in Childhood and Adolescence", 7 October, 1992

—— (2001, forthcoming), "Why the Convention is not about Street Children", in, Fottrell, D. (ed.) *Children's Rights for the Twenty-first Century*, Dordrecht: Kluwer

Ennew, J. and Milne, B. (1989) *The Next Generation: Lives of Third World Children*, London: Zed Press

Forster, E.M. (1978) *A Room with a View*, Harmondsworth: Penguin

Fyfe, A. (1989) *Child Labour*, Cambridge: Polity Press

Hart, R. (1992) *Children's Participation: From Tokenism to Citizenship*, Innocenti Essays No. 4, Florence: UNICEF

Hewitt, T. (1992) "Children, Abandonment and Public Action", in Wuyts, M. Mackintosh, M. and Hewitt, T. (eds) *Development Policy and Public Action*, Milton Keynes: Open University Press

Holland, P. (1992) *What is a Child? Popular Images of Childhood*, London: Virago Press

Oliveira, W.F. de (1989) "Street Kids in Brazil: an exploratory study of medical status, health knowledge and the self", MPH dissertation, University of Minnesota

Reddy, N. (1992) *Street Children of Bangalore*, New Delhi: UNICEF

Regional Working Group on Child Labour (2000) *Improving Action-oriented Research on the Worst Forms of Child Labour: Proceedings of Asian Regional Workshop, 8–10 December 1999, Bangkok Thailand, and Resource Materials*, Bangkok: RWG-CL

Rocky, M. (1990) "Whose Child is This?", *Esperanza*, New York: Childhope USA

Swart, J. (1990) *Malunde: The Street Children of Hillbrow*, Johannesburg: Witwatersrand University Press

Swift, A. (1991) *Brazil: The Fight for Childhood in the City*, Innocenti Studies, Florence: UNICEF

Théry, I. (1991) "La Convenzione Onu sui diritti del bambino: nascita di una nuova ideologia", *Politiche Sociali per L'Infanzia e L'Adolescenza*, Milan: Edizioni Unicopli

Tyler, F.B., Tyler, S.L., Tomasello, A. and Connolly, M.R. (1992) "Huckleberry Finn and Street Youth Everywhere: an approach to primary prevention", in Albee, G.W., Bond, L.A. and Cook Munsey, T.V. *Global Perspectives on Prevention: Primary Prevention of Psychopathology*, Vol. 45, Sage Publications: 200–212

UNICEF (1998) *The Progress of Nations*, New York: UNICEF

—— (1999) *The State of the World's Children 2000*, Oxford: Oxford University Press

Weiner, M. (1991) *The Child and the State in India: Child Labour and Education Policy in Comparative Perspective*, Princeton: Princeton University Press

Woollcombe, D. (1998) "Children's Conferences and Councils", in Johnson, V., Ivan-Smith, E., Gordon, G., Pridmore, P. and Scott, P. (eds), *Stepping Forward: Children and Young People's Participation in the Development Process*, London: Intermediate Technology Publications: 236–240

25 The Ombudsman for children

Conception and developments

Malfrid Grude Flekkøy

What is an Ombudsman?

"Ombudsman" is a Scandinavian term which has been adopted into English, possibly because there really is no adequate translation into English or any other language. The official translation from Norwegian is "Commissioner",[1] but this does not cover the exact content. Institutions which are more or less similar to the Ombudsman have been called "ombudsman-like", "ombuds-type", "Commissions" (as in English translation from Norwegian) or "Bureaux" (in French). Ombud originally meant "ambassador" or "delegate", and was used especially to denote a messenger from the king to the people. In contemporary usage, the opposite is more nearly the case: it has become the word for a person or an office which deals with complaints from a defined, circumscribed group of people or individual members and which speaks on behalf of that group to improve conditions for individuals within the group as well as for the group as a whole. The group may be small (the workers within a small business) or large (all the members of a population in their roles as consumers).

An Ombudsman, often in a position of confrontation with authorities, serves as an independent, non-partisan agent, spokesperson, arbitrator or referee, ensuring that government ministries and others fulfil legislative purpose by suggesting measures for improvement. An Ombudsman has the power to investigate, criticise and publicise, but not to reverse administrative action or revoke administrative decisions. The effectiveness of an Ombudsman, who has to be "a strong figure ... able to secure the attention of the authorities by sheer force of personality" (Melton, 1993) may depend on the person having "sufficient charisma, skill, and political stature and independence to carry out the office's mission" (ibid.). A public Ombudsman, especially one established by Parliament, has particular responsibility in relation to the Parliament, the ministries, and other levels of political and administrative authority, to suggest improvements and to pressure these authorities to fulfil their legislative purpose. Confrontations with public authorities may be necessary from time to time, but typically action takes place quietly, "behind the scenes".

In Norway the Ombudsman for Public Administration was established in 1962, for Consumer Affairs in 1972, the Ombudsperson for the Equal Status of Men and Women in 1979, following the International Year of Women, and the Ombudsman for Children in 1981. The other types of Ombudsmen existed in Sweden and Denmark, but the Ombudsman for Children was the first of its kind. There was some discussion of whether or not the term "Ombudsman" was appropriate, because of the difference between the proposed Ombudsman for Children and the existing Offices which were linked to limited, clearly defined legislation.

Legislation which in some way or other concerns children is often not clearly defined.[2] The legislation providing the purpose of the Ombudsman for Children stated that the Ombudsman was to "promote the interests of children *vis-à-vis* public and private authorities and follow up the development of conditions under which children grow up", the only prohibitions being individual conflicts within the family and cases which had been brought to court. The Ombudsman must therefore keep an eye on all areas of society, give warning of developments harmful for children and propose changes to improve their conditions. He (or she) must be alert to the consequences and implications for children in all parts of the Norwegian legislation, regulations and authorities. The Norwegian Parliament, with a very slim majority, voted to establish the Ombudsman for Children in 1981, taking effect on 1 September 1981. By accepting this mandate, the Parliament gave official recognition to the fact that advocacy for children was necessary and that even Parliament itself needed a watchdog to keep an eye on it and criticise (positively as well as negatively), when necessary.

The Norwegian welfare system for children and parents: a safety-net with holes

The principles of the Norwegian welfare system are simple:

- Necessary services should be available to all regardless of individual income. The cost should be covered mainly by public funding, through a personal income-tax and property-tax system which both diminishes financial differences caused by different income levels and "spreads the expenses" over wage-earners' working years.
- The greatest help should be provided to those who need it most
- The state should act with preventative measures to resolve problems created by the social changes which the welfare state precipitates, or at least intervene with post hoc solutions to problems which emerge.

The system does not always work according to its own principles. Particularly when local and national economic resources are diminishing, while public social expenditures increase, new means of funding are discussed, e.g. in the health sector, by partial payments for some health services, or by establishing private clinics (although supported through public funds) for patients able to pay. Nevertheless services in Norway for children and families, although "patchy", in many community areas do have a level unknown in many other countries.

But one reason for the establishment of an Ombudsman for Children in Norway rather than one of the other Nordic countries, may be that the social welfare system in Norway did not have the emphasis on children seen in Sweden and Denmark. These countries also had recent histories of social democratic government, reflected, for example, in the child welfare systems and the schools. But in Norway there were significant gaps at the "cradle" end of the "cradle-to-grave" system, as noted by non-Norwegian observers: for example, the "lack of a maternal and child health division and other 'standard' offices focused on children's interests, an isolation of schools from other services and a lack of a comprehensive family social support system; with poor standing of Norwegian children on many variables relative to other Scandinavian countries. There is also a tradition of individualism and local control (unlike Sweden) that negates the strong-state, social welfare tradition to some extent" (Melton, 1989, personal communication).

The tradition of local control is reflected in or caused by the combination of a sparsely populated country and the high number of small, semi-independent municipalities. The country has 20 counties and 438 municipalities. Only 97 municipalities have 10,000 or more inhabitants, 252 have fewer than 5,000, including approximately 1,500 children. Sweden, with twice the national population, has only 270 municipalities.

The child in a changing society

As in many industrialised countries, family patterns are changing: few families have more than one or two children, both parents work outside the home, the number of single-parent families is increasing. Familial support systems are lost. An increasing number of families are living in poverty as a consequence of unemployment. How these factors affect children depends on the willingness of society to compensate for these losses and to offset any detrimental effects of these changes.

The proportion of older people in the population is also increasing. Children constitute 20 per cent of the current Norwegian population, but this percentage will decrease to 15 per cent in 20 years. In political institutions, adults who have the closest contact with the needs of children (e.g. parents, especially of young children) are poorly represented. Even in Norway, where women constitute 45 per cent of the Cabinet and over 34 per cent of politicians in the Parliament, mothers of young children are poorly represented. Older people can vote and stand for election, so there is reason to believe that the average age of politicians will increase and support for issues concerning the elderly will do likewise.[3] I do not say this to minimise the needs of older people, but to illustrate the need for strong voices for children.

The Ombudsman for children: "pros" and "cons"

Children as a group have their own particular needs, which must be respected, and may require special measures. In addition, children in a democracy possess three unique characteristics:

1   Children have no influence on the choice of persons or composition of bodies responsible for decisions concerning or influencing conditions under which children grow up. Children have no way of ensuring that the "right" political party or a particular candidate or special issue is on the slate or elected to serve on municipal, county, state or national governing bodies.
2   By contrast, adults have access to additional means beyond the vote, to sway public opinion. Mass media, for example, provide channels through which adults can make their views known and provoke public debate.
3   Legislation concerning the rights of children is still weak compared to legislation governing the rights of adults. The main weaknesses are that the rights of children are: often *indirect* (i.e. the right is given to an adult [often the parents] on behalf of the child); or *conditional* (in the sense that the right is only valid under certain conditions, e.g. when funds are available or when parents are willing to cooperate to ensure the right of the child); or *non-existent* – even in contexts where adults under similar conditions have clearly stated rights and where there is really no reason why similar legislation should not apply to the younger generation.

These considerations provided the rationale informing the establishment of the Ombudsman for Children. There was such strong opposition to the proposal that it was uncertain initially whether the legislation would be enacted. Objections can be summarised under four main headings:

*   The Ombudsman might undermine the authority of parents.
*   Other authorities might renege on their own responsibilities in relation to children.
*   The Ombudsman would be too expensive.
*   The Office could be bureaucratic.

These arguments are rarely heard in Norway today, but they are frequently articulated elsewhere, particularly in connection with implementation of the UN Convention on the Rights of the Child.

The first proposal for an Ombudsman for Children was published in

1968, but gained momentum following the International Year of the Child in 1979. The Act creating the Ombudsman Office for Children was passed by the Storting (Parliament) in March 1981, with a very narrow five-vote majority. In creating the Office, Parliament gave official recognition to the necessity and legitimacy of child advocacy. The interests of children include so many areas, so many other issues, that existing Offices could not cover the whole field nor provide an overview of conditions for children.

Unlike the Ombudsman Offices for Equal Status of Women and Consumer Affairs, the Ombudsman for Children is not responsible for any single law or sets of laws. As noted above, the purpose is to "promote the interests of children *vis-à-vis* public and private authorities, and to follow up the development of conditions under which children grow up" (Act of the Commissioner for Children §3).

The Office wields no decision-making power, nor does it have the right to revoke the decisions of other authorities. Advocacy via the spread of information and documented case presentations is therefore its principal weapon. The Office seeks to increase public knowledge and change the opinions and attitudes of others in such a way as to improve the situation of children.

When first established, the Office had a total staff of four people, an annual budget of approx. $US300,000 (for 1988), one staff member per million Norwegians or one for every 250,000 children at an annual cost of 25 cents per child. One important lesson was, therefore, that results can be achieved even on a low budget. The staff was increased to 5.5 in 1990 and now has eight members. The budget was increased by 25 per cent in 1989 and again by another 25 per cent in 1990 and in 1991–92. The expansions indicate the increasing recognition of the usefulness, the professional status and the popular standing of the Office. The Office handled approximately 2,500 complaints annually, during the first 8 years. The number increased to 20,000 in 1999.

The Norwegian Ombudsman for children: assessments

The first Ombudsman took office two weeks before a general election in which the parties opposing the Office won the majority of the seats in the new Parliament: having promised to abolish the Office, it was abundantly clear that neutrality in terms of party political views was essential. The Ombudsman for Children was evaluated by the Ministry (then the Ministry of Family and Consumer Affairs, now the Ministry for Children and Families), by an American scholar (Gary Melton), by myself in 1989–91 and by a ministry-appointed committee in 1995. A public opinion institute conducted opinion research in 1989 and surveys amongst children were carried out in 1989 and in 1995.

The results of these evaluations can be summarised as follows:

- The Ombudsman was a voice for children, passing on complaints and messages from the younger generation as well as speaking on their behalf.
- Since children and parents cannot be seen separately, the Ombudsman was also a support for parents.
- The Office was effective on a small budget and with few staff. This was important because it shows that an Office of this kind need not be expensive to have some effect. Steadily increased staffing and budget indicate the increasing recognition of the usefulness, the professional status and the popular standing of the Office.
- A number of proposals from the Ombudsman had been quickly accepted in many municipalities as well as by Parliament, particularly those that did not have serious economic consequences, and yet improved conditions for groups of children.
- The Ombudsman was successful in keeping children on the political agenda.
- Only 2 per cent of the sampled population, across all partisan commitment, wanted the Office abolished.
- 75 per cent of Norwegian 7-year-olds knew about the Ombudsman and by age 14 this percentage increased to over 90 per cent.

International developments

Following the establishment of the Norwegian Office, national Ombudsmen for Children were established in Costa Rica and New Zealand, on the state level in South Australia, and city-level in Vienna and Jerusalem by 1989. By 1997 national Ombudsmen had been established in Sweden and Iceland. In Austria each state within the federation (nine in all) has an Ombudsman and efforts are underway to create one at the federal level. In Israel the National Institute for Children has an Ombudsman for all Israel, with a special representative for Palestinian children. In Spain, legislation (January 1996) made provision for each regional Defensor del Pueblo is to have a Deputy Defensor responsible for children. This model is similar to those in Guatemala, San Salvador, Nicaragua and Honduras. In some countries an Ombudsman for Children has been established within an existing organisation, often the Human Rights Commission. This is natural and logical, particularly since the Convention on the Rights of the Child is obviously a human rights instrument. It is, however, as yet too early to say whether or not this solution is good enough, as good or better than establishing an Ombudsman for Children as an independent institution. Much would depend on the mandate of the Child Rights Commissioner and the administrative organisation within the Human Rights Commission.

In Norway the third Ombudsman was appointed in 1996: in New Zealand the third incumbent has held office for about two years while in South Australia the Children's Interest Bureau has been incorporated in the

Ministry (see also chapter 21). In Costa Rica a system of Ombudsmen for various groups still includes one for children, while Belgium has an Office for the Flemish population and another for the French (see chapter 22). Efforts to establish similar offices are under way in other countries: for example in the UK. Interestingly, the most recent Ombudsman for Children has been established in Sarajevo in June 1997, where a combination of three Ombudsmen, under the Public Services Ombudsman, represent the three main ethnic groups of Bosnia-Hercegovina. Portugal and the Russian Federation are also members of the European Network (up-dated information can be found on the internet at www.ombudsnet.org).

These developments illustrate the worldwide interest in the Ombudsman concept. They also show that while the first Offices were established in small, industrialised countries, modifications of this initial model now exist in other countries, including developing countries. In some of these countries political instability is high, with the Cabinet changing every few months. This is, of course, a problem, but perhaps also a compelling reason to establish some kind of permanent watchdog for children.

A variety of models are available for scrutiny by governments and communities contemplating such an Office to identify one which might "fit" the political and cultural traditions of the country. In Switzerland, for instance, it might be interesting to study the Sarajevo and the Austrian model, based on cantons or regions, or accommodating different ethnic, language or religious groups.

An Ombudsman for children on an international level?

Two proposals have recently been made for Ombudsmen for Children on the international level: the first for children in war zones; the second for an Ombudsman for Children within the UN. Let me address some issues about an Ombudsman within the UN which I believe have not been adequately considered. First, it is necessary to clarify what is not – or cannot be – done by other bodies within the UN system, including the Expert Committee on the Rights of the Child and the existing UN agencies and organisations. If there are issues that still fall between the "cracks" it is important to establish whether or not changes in the existing system would adequately "fill these cracks". If an Ombudsman seems to be a good solution, clarification of collaboration models, responsibilities and mandates between the Ombudsman and other bodies is necessary. Another key issue is the degree of independence of the Ombudsman. Should the Office, for example, be established by – but then become independent of – the UN General Assembly, in much the same way that the Norwegian Ombudsman relates to the Norwegian Parliament? If so, it would still be vulnerable to changes of the mandate or the provision of only a small budget as again is the case with the Norwegian Ombudsman. Or perhaps an Ombudsman should be incorporated in an existing body, like the Central American Ombudsman Offices are? Or perhaps an entirely different way of strengthening the rights of children, such as an international Court of Children Rights, would be preferable? In any of these cases the power of the institution, be it an Ombudsman or a Court, to intervene on the national level must be clarified. So there is obviously a long way to go before we are ready to accept – or reject – the idea of an Ombudsman in the UN. But I believe the experiences at the national level will be useful in forthcoming discussions.

A children's Ombudsman: essential features

Although the models examined vary structurally, they are remarkably similar in their roles. In general terms, each is a more or less *independent* body, created to defend children's rights, informed by the following guiding principles:

- The Ombudsman should be a voice for children.
- The Ombudsman should be politically independent.
- The Office should be financially independent.
- The Ombudsman must be accessible to the population, especially children themselves.
- The Ombudsman should be close to decision-making bodies that impact on children.
- The Office must work for, and within, networks at state and local levels, as well as at the non-governmental level.
- The Ombudsman should be legally established or in some other way given authority to carry out its functions (see chapter 17).

The Office must be "a voice for children" and nothing else

This principle has several aspects. First, the Ombudsman should serve as a "voice" or channel of communications between children and the health, welfare and education systems, the judiciary, the local planning boards and, in general, any area of government where decisions are being made which affect children. By transmitting information from children, and by speaking on their behalf, the Ombudsman can make the needs and rights of children publicly known. At the same time, it can impart to children information they need to know. Making sure that children are aware of the Convention and its relevance to their daily lives should now be one of its important functions.

Moreover, the Ombudsman can and should ensure that the literal voices of children are being heard – that is, that the concerns and opinions which children themselves have actually expressed are taken into consideration. Actually hearing the voices of children has been regarded as the most difficult task of an Ombudsman. In many societies, children are still under full adult control. Devising ways for children and youth to exercise their right to participate actively in society could, under these circumstances, be especially complex, but can now be promoted on the basis of the participation rights of the UN Convention. From the point of view of implementing the Convention, the involvement of young people is very important both in the short and long term because (a) it is often easier to change their attitudes than those of adults, (b) they are potential parents, voters and politicians, but (c) most importantly: participation is necessary for the democratic development of the individual and therefore for the development of a democratic world.

The Ombudsman must be *for* children and readily accessible to them. Only children can tell the rest of the population how they perceive the world, which problems and concerns they feel are important and why. Adults can speak on behalf of children, but must surmise, often – but not always – correctly, what is important for children. Adults need the input of children and children need an opportunity to voice their opinions and have an impact on the community in which they grow up.[4] When children are given the opportunity of access to the Ombudsman, the experience is that even preschool children use the office.[5] Children, moreover, present a wider range of problems than adults and are also capable – when given information and support – of improving conditions particularly at the local level. In Norway some proposals first raised by children prompted legislative change. The most important aspect is that adults must recognise and accept that only children themselves can tell us how they perceive their world and that they have innovative and creative ideas about how to improve it.

Being a "voice for children" also means that there must not be any suspicion of a hidden agenda. Some advocacy groups claim to speak on behalf of children, but might actually be using children for other political ends. All child advocates have, apart from their concern about children's interests, their own ideological baggage. Many would be in favour of what they are advocating even if children's issues were not involved. Therefore *all* persons responsible for representing children need to examine their motivation constantly to make sure that their voice is, in fact, a clear voice for children. One way of securing this goal is through professional credibility. This means that the basis for any opinion or statement must be the needs and interests of children, preferably based on solid knowledge and/or research.

The Office must be independent

The Ombudsman must be independent of political parties, but also of all other authorities, organisations and groups: the Office must also be financially independent. This leaves the Ombudsman free to intervene without consideration of bureaucratic rules and hierarchies or other interests and pressures.[6]

Even with an administrative connection to a governmental branch, a precise mandate limiting the scope of his or her activities and a budget within which to work, the Ombudsman can, none the less, be "independent" if the following principles are observed:

- The Ombudsman should be protected from arbitrary dismissal by the government.
- The Ombudsman should, preferably, have constitutional support.
- The Ombudsman should represent a state policy and not the policy of a specific party or government.

The need for party-political neutrality has been demonstrated time and again, not only in Norway, where this need was particularly evident. Experiences in other countries have demonstrated that when the Ombudsman is perceived as a spokesperson for a political party, the efficiency of his or her work as an advocate is markedly reduced. This may be one consequence of a more general principle, namely the personal necessity for role clarity. By this I mean that there should be no doubt at any time that the Ombudsman himself/herself is aware of when he or she is speaking in an official capacity, when he or she is acting in a different role, a different capacity and when he or she is acting publicly, but as a private citizen (which it may well be wise to refrain from doing while in office). In Norway there was some confusion when a well-known TV entertainer became Ombudsman. Was the Ombudsman now perceived as an entertainer? Many children knew more about him as the TV actor than about what he after a few years had done as their Ombudsman. The effectiveness of an Ombudsman may depend on the person having "sufficient charisma, skill, and political stature and independence to carry out the office's mission" (Melton in Flekkøy, 1991b). Such charisma and ability to secure attention can have different roots, e.g. be based on professional acceptability or on the persona of an actor, which again can lead to different Ombudsman styles.[7]

> The source of authority can be derived from (a) *the power of ideas*, the information flow which assumes the facts gathered will result in policies consistent with the way we would like children to be treated, and they would like themselves to be treated (b) *the power of personality*. One of the features of the Ombudsman model, in particular, is that it is a strong-person model directed by charismatic individuals who are listened to because of who they are. (c) *"loot and clout"*, i.e. it is not so much who I am, or what I am saying, but who or what it is that I represent. I have authority by virtue of pure raw power. All may be variably effective in different contexts.
>
> (Melton in Flekkøy, 1991b)

Ombudsmen and other public children's advocates may be in an uncomfortable position, being both party and judge. One example of this position was given by the Spanish Defensor whose questioning of the constitutionality of laws, approved by the Parliament which had appointed him, had created tensions in his relations with the legislative branch of government. However, tensions of this sort may ferment social change and can be fundamental to a monitoring process. Naturally, there is always a risk that an Ombudsman can be too "independent" and not be reappointed for another term of office or have his or her wings clipped by Parliament in other ways, e.g. by amending the legislation of the Office.

The Office should be established close to decision-making

This means that it is reasonable for federations of states to establish state-level offices. In my opinion these nations then also need an Office at the federal level, because it is at this level where the autonomy and decision-making power of the states is established. In some cases the municipal level may be preferable, or – as has been tried in some instances – an ombudsman might be established for a certain sector, e.g. the child welfare system. In such cases there is a danger that the system will be seen in isolation, while cross-sectional responsibility enables the Ombudsman to consider the inter-relationships and dynamics of the total situation for children.

The Office should be legally established

It seems clear that an Ombudsman should preferably be established under statute and should be given specific authority to carry out surveillance functions in well-defined areas of the government. In the first years of the Jerusalem experience, the disadvantages deriving from a lack of legal status were enumerated: cooperation was voluntary, there was resistance to intervention in the educational and child welfare systems, prior permission had to be obtained to read the children's files of public or private agencies. As Melton (1993) pointed out:

> An advocate without a portfolio (e.g., one who does not have explicit statutory authority or has statutory authority that is so broad that it is essentially vacuous) who is, in other words, watching almost anything relating to children, has an inherently suspect legitimacy. More particularly in the early years, and no matter what the specific structure, if it has no specific jurisdiction it will be forever politically 'under the gun' for questions of overstepping boundaries. Where the jurisdiction is ambiguous, advocates have to take on a 'missionary character' and be willing to take chances in terms of the range of issues they examine." It is abundantly clear that any monitoring body, whether inside or outside the government, can carry weight only if it establishes credibility and is "legitimised" by the communities and by the families it serves. To do so, it is essential that the Ombudsman or other similar structure, as mentioned above, clearly serves only the interests of children, i.e., it

should never be suspected of having a hidden agenda. It should avoid "the impossible", selecting issues which could actually be influenced by the work done, with the resources available. The persons involved should be professional, non-bureaucratic and able to make things happen. They should, above all, base their statements and opinions on facts, as far as this was possible. Speaking with facts in hand depends on the availability of valid statistics and data analysis on conditions for children – information which was often missing. One of the practical issues addressed by several of the existing Offices is how to compile and collect facts about children and the conditions under which they grow up. One special aspect of this is getting information from the children themselves, another is interpreting existing statistics with the child as the subject.[8]

The types of facts and information that are needed may also depend in part on the style of work adopted as best suited in the culture of the Ombudsman. Two main trends seem to be current:

1 The legal approach which is based on the case-law approach, looking at the situation of children on a *case by case basis* and
2 The social sciences approach – a systematic, pro-active examination of broad segments of the population.

Each methodology has its role in the larger context of describing national conditions, and it seems important that one does not exclude the other. Conditions affecting children must be expected to change, national and local conditions will also change. Therefore, specific indicators of quality and of change should be flexible. In any case the collection and analysis of appropriate official data is a fundamental issue. For independent advocates, as well as official agencies, the cost implications should not be a major restriction to effective monitoring.

Monitoring and implementation of the UN Convention on the Rights of the Child

The Norwegian Ombudsman Office was established over eight years before the adoption of the UN Convention on the Rights of the Child. This is probably why the Norwegian Act does not institute any responsibility for protecting the *rights* of the child. Ombudsman Offices established later do have an obligation in this respect. However, in 1989, a suggestion was made that the Norwegian Ombudsman should be responsible for the Norwegian States Party Report to the UN Expert Committee on the Rights of the Child (Melton, 1989, personal communication). Also, following the ministry evaluation of the Office in 1995, an amendment to the Ombudsman for Children Act was proposed for Article 3b: " In particular the Commissioner shall: ...

b) ensure that legislation relating to the protection of children's interests"
should include monitoring compliance in legislation and in practical terms
with the responsibilities Norway has in connection with the UN Convention
on the Rights of the Child (my translation, NOU, 1995: 26, 155).

The idea that the Ombudsman could or should have some responsibility
for following up the Convention is therefore evident, in spite of the fact that
none of the other Ombudsman Offices are responsible for implementation
or monitoring of international conventions. This, I believe, reflects the
difference between the Ombudsman Office as described above (p. 405), but
also the comprehensive nature of the UN Convention on the Rights of the
Child. This Convention includes civil and political, social and cultural
rights. It describes the obligations of the state in relation to the child and
indicates responsibilities of parents and other adults. This Convention therefore touches on all aspects of conditions for children, and therefore falls
neatly in with the mandate of the Ombudsmen for Children. However, some
issues need to be addressed:

1   Should the Ombudsman be responsible for the States Party Report?
2   Can an Ombudsman be responsible for the *implementation* of a
    Convention?
3   How can an Ombudsman for Children monitor implementation of the
    Convention and the rights of the Child as described in the Convention?
4   Is an Ombudsman for Children the best or the only possible institution
    for taking on this responsibility?

The first question is simple: If the Ombudsman is to protect and uphold
party political neutrality, the office cannot be responsible for the States
Party Report. These Reports are the responsibility of the government of the
country, and will always present the views of that government. The States
Party Report is therefore always based on party political values and views,
however objective the government seeks to be. However, very many governments are finding it useful to collect information from other sources, of
which the Ombudsman might be one. Also, in many countries non-governmental organisations and other bodies contribute to the evaluation process
by presenting additional or alternative reports to the Expert Committee. The
Expert Committee recognises the importance of this and will often invite
representatives of the organisations to a meeting before the Expert
Committee meets the official representatives of the government.

In monitoring conditions for and implementation of the rights of the
child, the Ombudsman has some unique features. One is the contact with the
children themselves. The other is the wide view the Ombudsman must have,
not only of the variety of situations and problems confronting children and
families, but also of the interaction between different views, problems and
sectors of society. Many non-governmental organisations work for children
by concentrating on a few – or even only one – specific problem areas, e.g.

the organisations promoting breast-feeding. Others work with a wider variety of problems, but focus on a more limited group of the child population, e.g. organisations for children with learning difficulties or organisations for children in care. Other organisations have children as a part – but only a part – of their field of interest, e.g. the organisations for housewives or the political parties. An Ombudsman for Children may – and should be – concerned with the issues promoted by the organisations, but cannot limit perspective or goals in any of the ways indicated. This difference between organisations and an Ombudsman also illustrates the significance of the Ombudsman's collaboration with organisations in order to obtain relevant information and experience, but also to avoid excessive overlapping and guarantee that the interests (or the rights) of children are served in a positive way by both the Ombudsman and the organisations. This is the basis for the more formalised collaboration established between the Norwegian Ombudsman for Children and the National Coalition for the Rights of the Child, which consists of representatives from the non-governmental organisations working in some way or other for children. The Ombudsman Office serves as the secretariat for the coalition, convening meetings, discussing issues of common interest and preparing information for the alternative report to the Expert Committee.

One conclusion is, then, that the Ombudsman may be instrumental and useful in the national work of monitoring implementation of the convention. The implementation itself may be a different matter. Since the Ombudsman has the power to investigate, criticise and publicise, but not to reverse administrative action or revoke administrative decisions, the Ombudsman cannot in general enforce implementation of the Convention. The child's rights to survival, protection and development cannot be provided by the Ombudsman, who, however, does have a responsibility for proposing measures that would secure or improve the conditions necessary to provide for these rights. The participation rights of the child may be somewhat different. These include the child's rights to adequate information (including information about the Convention and about the child's own rights), to voice opinions on and to take part in the decision-making process on issues that concern him/her. An Ombudsman can certainly be instrumental in helping to provide information, but through the unique contact the Ombudsman may have with children, the office may also provide a communications channel between children and the decision-making authorities, serving as a voice for as well as on behalf of the younger population. In this way the Ombudsman may provide children with the possibility of making their views known and therefore perhaps have an influence on the final decision. A different aspect of this is the special (and strong) position the Ombudsman has, based on the experience of and with children, to promote the importance of child participation, tailored to suit the evolving capacities of the child, in a democratic process in the families, in nursery schools as well as in elementary and high schools, within their own organisations (e.g. Scouts or the local brass band), as well as in community planning of their neighbourhoods.

In conclusion, there is still a great deal of work to be done in many countries as well as on the international level, but I believe that a national Ombudsman for Children or a modification designed to fit the traditions, political systems and cultures prevalent in different countries can be very valuable. The existing offices have one thing in common: they have given a voice to children that children did not have before.

Notes

1   To me Ombuds*man* does not have gender connotations. The "Family of Man" includes males and females. But when the English Department of the University of Oslo did not want to accept "Ombud" for use in English, the Ombudsperson for Equal Status for Men and Women objected to "Ombuds*man*" and "Commissioner" was chosen for the common English translation.

2   At one point I started on page 1 of the collection of Norwegian law, to see if I could find legislation which clearly had nothing to do with conditions for children. Except for legislation on elections, property settlements after childless divorce and some similar issues, legislation without some consequences at least for some children was hard to find.

3   In September 2000, this situation was recognised by the Norwegian Minister of Municipal Affairs, who encouraged local politicians to canvas the views of children and youth before making political decisions.

4   The first Norwegian Ombudsman emphasised this very strongly. The success of this message was indicated when adults pretended to be children, believing that *only* children could contact the Office.

5   During the first eight years of the Norwegian Office, the youngest serious complaint came from a 4-year-old. The majority of complaints from children came from 8–14-year-olds, but preschool children were not uncommon.

6   One example of this was the Norwegian "anti-spanking" act, which in spite of political opposition was kept alive in public debate through several years of Conservative government, to be adopted in record time, being well prepared, when the Cabinet changed.

7   I want to emphasise that one style is not necessarily better than the other. Not only will this vary from culture to culture, but also from time to time. There is for instance no doubt that Ombudsman no. 2 in Norway was selected for the job precisely because his strengths (particularly in relation to the media) were exactly the ones most lacking in Ombudsman no. 1. This can be one of the advantages of legally determining a maximum term of office, because it is then possible to pick the person best suited for the job at that particular time or at that particular stage of development of the functions of the Office.

8   One example of how wrong an interpretation can be if the child's viewpoint is overlooked was the conclusion drawn in a Scandinavian report: Swedish children have a better standard of living than Norwegian children, because the Norwegian children more often than the Swedes must share a room with somebody. Had the children been asked, I am sure babies, preschool children and teenagers would have widely different opinions about the consequences of sharing a room.

    Interpreting statistics from the child's point of view can also mean instead of pointing to the fact that the most common family with children has, for example, 1.6 children, we ask: What is the effect on children of having no more than one sibling? (Only approximately 11 per cent of all Norwegian children have an older *and* a younger sibling.)

References

Barneombudet: *Annual Reports 1981–1988* (in Norwegian only) Oslo 1982, 1983, 1984, 1985, 1986, 1987, 1988, 1989, 1999
—— (1991) *Facts about Children in Norway*. Oslo: Barneombudet
Davidson, H.A., Cohen, C.P. and Girdner, L.K. (1993) *Establishing Ombudsman Programs for Children and Youth*. ABA Center on Children and the Law
Flekkøy, M.G. (1990) *Working for the Rights of Children*. UNICEF/Firenze English, French, Spanish
—— (1991a) *A Voice for Children. Speaking out as their Ombudsman*. London: Jessica Kingsley
—— (1991b) *Models for Monitoring the Protection of the Rights of the Child* (mimeo report), UNICEF/Firenze
—— (1993a) *Children's Rights. Reflections on and consequences of the use of developmental psychology in working for the interests of children. The Norwegian Ombudsman for Children: A practical experience*. Belgium: Ghent University Press
—— (1993b) "Children as holders of Rights and Obligations" in Gomien, D. (ed.) *Broadening the Frontiers of Human Rights. Essays in Honour of Asbjørn Eide*. Oslo: Scandinavian University Press
—— (1996) *An Ombudsman for Children: Quality requirements* (seminar paper, University of Ghent)
—— (1997) *The Participation Rights of the Child. Rights and Responsibilities in Family and Society*. London: Jessica Kingsley
—— (1999) *A Framework for Children's Participation*. Belgium: University of Ghent Press
Leira, A. (1985): *Regelmessig barnetilsyn*. Oslo: Institutt for samfunnsforskning, arbeidsnotat 4/85.
—— (1989) *Models of Motherhood. Welfare State Policies and Everyday Practices: The Scandinavian Experience*. Oslo, Rapport 89:7, Institutt for samfunnsforskning
Melton, G. (1993) "Lessons from Norway: The Children's Ombudsman as a Voice for Children", *Case Western Reserve Journal of International Law* 23(3)
NOU (1995) *Barneombud og barndom i Norge* Oslo, p. 26

Index